The Ultimate

500 INSTANT POT RECIPES

Ashley Cook

Warning-Disclaimer

The purpose of this book is to educate and entertain. The author or publisher does not guarantee that anyone following the techniques, suggestions, tips, ideas, or strategies will become successful. The author and publisher shall have neither liability or responsibility to anyone with respect to any loss or damage caused, or alleged to be caused, directly or indirectly by the information contained in this book.

Content

INTRODUCTION

If you think that pressure cookers were robust pots that belongs to the past and a strange part of a grandma's cookware, you're missing out! Moreover, nothing could be further from the truth! Nowadays, this good old kitchen gear is returning in a very big way. Whether you're a newbie or a skilled cook, you'll soon find yourself whipping up grandma's recipes in your Instant Pot. In reality, an electric pressure cooker is a "fusion" of an old-fashioned cookware and advanced technology. You will be pleasantly suppressed what your Instant Pot can do for you. If you want a new, well-balanced and improved life, you should adopt healthy eating habits and embrace a new, super-sophisticated technology. Food is, actually, an integral part of our lives; thus, we should care about where our food comes from. The Instant Pot and this recipe collection will improve your cooking, your health, and your entire life!

Getting to Know Your Instant Pot

Nowadays, we don't have hours to spend in the kitchen; on the other hand, we agree that a well-balanced diet and healthy, homemade meals are the key factors that contribute to a productive lifestyle. Therefore, people, especially busy moms and older people, want kitchen devices that make everyday cooking enjoyable, funny and easy. Inspired by a grandma's way of cooking and the cooking style of the world's greatest chefs, manufacturers develop the third generation cookware where technology and sophisticated design go hand in hand.

The Instant Pot is a programmable multicooker that utilizes high pressure and high temperatures to cook your food as much as 60 to 70 percent faster than regular cooking methods. The Instant Pot is an electric device for automated cooking using a timer. Your time is priceless, isn't it?

- **Should I Buy an Instant Pot Electric Pressure Cooker?**

The short answer is: Yes. If you are passionate about cooking, you deserve an outstanding electric pressure cooker with high performance. The Instant Pot is the seven-in-one cooker, capable of multiple cooking methods, all in one device. Sautéing, steaming, baking, boiling, and slow cooking are just a few of the cooking techniques that your Instant Pot is capable to perform.

In addition to significantly reducing cooking time, the Instant Pot will help you cook amazing one-pot meals. Simply toss your ingredients into the Instant Pot and turn it on. As simple as that! You will be able to cook the whole bird for Thanksgiving dinner, old-fashioned soups, the best meatloaf ever, breads, snacks, and even desserts. The perfect kitchen tool for holidays, potlucks, and family gatherings.

Furthermore, your food retains its nutrients and natural aromas because it is cooked in a sealed environment. This is an easy way to meet your nutritional requirements. For those who are not convinced yet, here is one more argument – the Instant Pot saves your hard-earned money by cooking cheap cuts, beans, and grains in bulk.

This multifunctional cooker offers a number of cooking functions. It does the job of a pressure cooker, slow cooker, rice maker, steamer, sauté pan, and yogurt maker. Here are eight pressure cooking rules to achieve the best results with your Instant Pot:

1. Carefully and thoroughly read the manual that comes with the appliance. Make sure to consult it periodically. Just like when you learned any other new skill, it takes time and patience to get to know your new device.

2. Keep in mind that the Instant Pot takes about 15 to 20 minutes to release the pressure completely; then and only then, you can remove the lid.

3. This is an intelligent kitchen gadget; you can set up your Instant Pot to 24 hours in advance and go about your business; it allows you to plan every meal.

4. Although your Instant Pot has many buttons that may confuse you, they are incredibly simple to use. They all work using the same principles but they utilize different cooking times that are designed for different types of food. In addition, you can always use the "Manual" button and "+" and "-" buttons to adjust the cooking time.

5. When it comes to the minimum liquid requirement, it is about 1 cup of water (broth, milk, tomato sauce) for the Instant Pot. However, if you cook food that absorbs water, you should follow the recipe directions.

6. Most recipes can be adapted to the Instant pot as long as you keep some general rules in mind. The Instant Pot operates at 11.5 PSI so always consult the chart for the proper cooking times. Since the Instant Pot doesn't allow evaporation, you will need less liquid. Further, if you want to thicken the cooking liquid, do it at the end, using the "Sauté" function. And last but not least, do not overfill your cooker; it requires enough room to create the steam.

7. High pressure is default setting on the Instant Pot and it is used in most recipes. Delicate foods such as seafood, eggs and some vegetables should be cooked under a Low pressure.

8. You cannot fry your food in the Instant Pot.

With all of that in mind, pressure cooking may sound complicated. Nevertheless, once you understand the basics, it will open up new possibilities! Thus, with a good cooker and willingness to learn, anyone can become a great cook!

- **How Smart Cooking Programs Work?**

With all of this information, it's time to use that Instant Pot. The cooking programs use four parameters: pressure, temperature, heating intensity, and cooking duration. You need to choose one of these programs and press the right button, but which one.

MANUAL – this is the button you're likely to use the most; you can adjust the pressure levels, time, and temperature according to your recipe. This is an "all-purpose" button.

SOUP – this high-pressure mode creates clear stocks, vegetable and meaty soups, as well as chunky chowders. It allows your soup to simmer without boiling too heavily.

MEAT/STEW – this fully automated function is perfect for cooking inexpensive cuts, achieving great results under High pressure. It results in tender and juicy meat with great texture. Cooking times can vary depending on the thickness of the meat.

BEAN/CHILI – with this program, you can cook dry, soaked and canned beans. Beans turn out great every time; the Instant Pot coos beans much faster and tastier than conventional cookware.

RICE – you can use this setting for cooking different types of rice. White rice takes 8 minutes to cook but you should cook brown rice for 22 minutes. Wild rice requires 30 minutes.

MULTIGRAIN – use this setting for cooking a risotto as well as cereal, pseudocereal (e.g. buckwheat and quinoa) and tougher whole grains.

POULTRY – this program is best for poultry in small portions (12 minutes on high pressure) and larger pieces (25 minutes to reach an internal temperature of 165 degrees F).

PORRIDGE – if you want to make a porridge or congee (a rice porridge with a softer texture), this is the perfect solution for you.

STEAM – you can prepare fish, selfish, and vegetables; you can reheat leftovers as well. Just make sure to use utensils such as a metal trivet or steamer basket.

SLOW COOK – use this program for cooking beans, grains, root vegetables and cheaper cuts. Four-hour slow cook time is a default time. Simply press the "+/-" button to adjust the cook time.

YOGURT – try this two-step program designed for fermenting milk and making yogurt.

SAUTÉ – this function is a true game changer. It redefines one-pot meals with its possibilities for simmering, searing, browning and thickening. You can pre-prepare food or finish them just as you would in a regular pan.

KEEP WARM / CANCEL – Once cooking is completed, press the "Cancel" button; otherwise, this program will keep your food warm until ready to serve.

NATURAL RELEASE and *QUICK RELEASE*

Once your Instant Pot completes its cooking cycle, you can use two ways to release the pressure. Press the "Cancel" button or unplug your device to perform a natural pressure release. Release the steam manually in order to perform a quick pressure release. Make sure to release any remaining pressure before removing the lid. Never try to force the lid open. You can push the valve to vent to make sure all the pressure is released.

Cooking Fix-It and Forget-It Recipes in the Instant Pot

As an essential part of the modern kitchen, the Instant Pot does its job pretty well. You can make a surprising variety of easy homemade dishes in your Instant Pot. When it comes to the types of food, there are a few tips and tricks to keep in mind before starting this adventure.

1. Root vegetables cook wonderfully in your electric pressure cooker. You can cook them straight from the freezer, without thawing! For most vegetables, you should use "Steam" setting to retain nutrients and preserve natural color and texture. Carrots, artichokes, green beans and broccoli turn out great every time!

2. If you tend to cook a homemade soup, just press the "Sauté" button to cook vegetables and sear the meat; then, use the "Soup" mode to simmer a liquid; afterwards, use "Sauté" function again to finish your soup by reducing the cooking liquid if desired.

3. Hearty beans and grains cook up perfectly in no time in the pressure cookers. This is the cooking secret your grandma knew very well. You can soak dried beans overnight to reduce cooking time or not, it's up to you. To cook perfect grains, from oats and quinoa to rice and barley, pay attention to a water to grain ratio. It's not the same as it is for the standard cooking methods.

4. Not only can you have succulent meat in record time with the Instant Pot, but it's arguably the best way to cook inexpensive and large cuts such as back ribs, beef skirt, or ham hock. Pressure cooking breaks down the tough meat fast and easy, while keeping it juicy and meltingly tender.

5. Before pressure cooking, you can sear the meat until it is delicately browned to enhance its natural flavors. Finishing the meat in the oven gives them a nice coating and great flavor.

6. When it comes to the seafood, it is possible to cook the best fish in the Instant Pot. Mussels, shrimp, and squid cook to perfection in a bath of chicken broth, cooking wine, garlic, and lemon in just a few minutes. If using frozen seafood, just add 2 minutes to the cook time.

The Top 5 Benefits of Using the Instant Pot

1. A smart way to eat healthier and lose weight.

"Let food be thy medicine and medicine be thy food" ~ Hippocrates. We all heard this quote. In spite of that, we continue to eat junk food and buy processed food on a regular basis. Furthermore, many people look for shortcuts to lose weight, making unhealthy choices. Luckily, the Instant Pot might help you shed those obstinate pounds in an easy and healthy way.

Researches have shown that cooking in a pressure cooker tends to keep nutrients better than standard cooking methods. Liquids come to a boil under a sealed lid; they cannot escape from the sealed environment while keeping the flavors concentrated. In other words, the super-heated steam and "trapped" pressure prevent the evaporation that occurs with conventional cooking.

This cooking method also requires less oil and liquid so valuable nutrients are not dissolved away by water.

Certain studies have found that pressure cooking can boost your digestion. It means that digestibility of pressure-cooking food is higher in comparison with food that is cooked normally.

Nobody has to tell you that cooking method is extremely important, but your eating habits matter a lot. There are so many benefits of making home-cooked meals. Portion control, bringing a family together, saving time and money, controlling your diet and cutting costs are just a few of benefits that you can receive.

This cookbook promotes a well-balanced diet and traditional values. These recipes call for good fats, lots of fruits and vegetables, healthy fish, nuts, fresh herbs, and so forth. Every recipe contains the nutritional information so you will be able to maintain nutrition and control the amount of food you consume.

2. Cheap but satisfying dishes.

Eating on a budget with minimal cleanup! It sounds like a dream! Luckily, once you start cooking at home using your Instant Pot, you will save your money in the long-term and you don't have to sacrifice taste.

Thanks to its revolutionary technology, the Instant Pot can cook budget-friendly dishes to perfection. You can use the food you already have in your refrigerator and pantry. Moreover, you will stop wasting food because the Instant Pot is the perfect cooker for cheap beans and grains, as well as stocks, soups, desserts with stale bread, tough cuts of meat, and so forth.

3. Time is priceless.

The Instant Pot, with its advanced, one-touch technology, prepares ultra-fast, one-pot meals that otherwise would take hours. It is one of the best time-saving home appliances! It cooks quick family meals on busy nights so you can (finally) relax. This multicooker has proven to be the useful kitchen appliance of those home cooks who want to create healthy and delicious meals for their families with minimum time. No mess, no stress!

4. Go green! Save Mother Earth!

Besides being economical, the Instant Pot is also eco-friendly electric device; it uses two to three times less electricity!

5. Declutter your kitchen.

From this day forward, you don't need too much cookware and you will free up space in your cupboards. It is extremely important since most of us have tiny kitchens. To be honest, besides basic utensils, you will need only one multi-cooker. In fact, minimalism gives you the time and space to create a meaningful life. It's such a relief!

How You Can Benefit From our Recipe Collection

We have got five hundred recipes ahead that are separated into ten different categories. These recipes contain the ingredients that are available everywhere; they are hugely diverse, starting from old-fashioned grandma's dishes to contemporary creations. You will explore five hundred of the best pressure cooker recipes ever! Each recipe offers the ingredient list, the number of servings, approximate cooking time, and step-by-step directions. Regardless of whether you are a newbie or a skilled cook, you will find a lot of inspiration, useful information and creative ideas. It would be a huge motivation for every home cook!

Once you get the hang of it, you will be able to take some of your favorite traditional recipes and adapt them to be made in the Instant Pot. Cooking is a lifelong adventure; it is a form of art that is constantly revamping itself with new, revolutionary ideas.

To sum up, the best way to learn is from experience so go ahead and give this cookbook a whirl. Eventually, you may fall in love with your Instant Pot!

VEGETABLES & SIDE DISHES

1. Buttery Steamed Sweet Potatoes

(Ready in about 35 minutes | Servings 4)

Sweet potatoes are an excellent source of vitamin B6, vitamin C, vitamin D, potassium, carotenoids, and so on. They can improve bone health and nerve function as well as boost your immune system.

Per serving: *154 Calories; 5.9g Fat; 23.5g Carbs; 2.3g Protein; 7.3g Sugars*

Ingredients

1 pound whole small sweet potatoes, cleaned
1/4 teaspoon salt
1/4 teaspoon freshly grated nutmeg
2 tablespoons light butter

Directions

- Add 1 cup of water and a steamer basket to the Instant Pot. Arrange sweet potatoes in the steamer basket.
- Secure the lid and choose the "Steam" mode. Cook for 10 minutes under High pressure. Once cooking is complete, use a natural release for 20 minutes; carefully remove the lid.
- Toss steamed sweet potatoes with salt, nutmeg and butter. Eat warm. Bon appétit!

---

2. Artichokes with Avocado Feta Dip

(Ready in about 20 minutes | Servings 3)

Are you looking for a way to give your artichoke a little more edge? Cook them in your Instant Pot and serve with creamy and silky avocado dip.

Per serving: *282 Calories; 17.7g Fat; 26.3g Carbs; 10.9g Protein; 4.2g Sugars*

Ingredients

1 cup water
3 globe artichokes
1/2 lemon
For the Sauce:
1 avocado, peeled, pitted and diced
3 ounces feta cheese
1/2 lemon, juiced
1/2 yellow onion, chopped
2 tablespoons fresh parsley leaves, chopped
1/2 teaspoon sea salt
1/3 teaspoon black pepper

Directions

- Add 1 cup of water and a steamer basket to the base of your Instant Pot. Now, discard the damaged leaves of the artichokes.
- Cut the bottoms to be flat. Cut off excess stem and remove the tough ends of the leaves; rub with a lemon half.
- Arrange the artichokes in the steamer basket.
- Secure the lid. Choose the "Manual" mode, High pressure and 11 minutes. Once cooking is complete, use a natural release; carefully remove the lid.
- In a mixing bowl, combine all the sauce ingredients. Serve the artichokes with the sauce on the side. Bon appétit!

3. Moong Dal and Green Bean Soup
(Ready in about 45 minutes | Servings 6)

Moong dal, also known as yellow lentils are high in nutrition. They can lower cholesterol levels, improve cardiovascular system and increase your energy. Consequently, if you are looking for a way to balance your diet, consider eating yellow lentils at least once a week.
Per serving: *221 Calories; 4.3g Fat; 34.7g Carbs; 12.8g Protein; 2.1g Sugars*

Ingredients

1 ½ tablespoons olive oil
2 shallots, chopped
2 garlic cloves, minced
1 teaspoon cilantro, ground
1/2 teaspoon ground allspice
1/2 teaspoon smoked paprika
1 teaspoon celery seeds

1/2 teaspoon fennel seeds
1/2 teaspoon ground cumin
1 ½ cups moong dal
7 cups water
Sea salt and ground black pepper, to your liking
2 cups green beans, fresh

Directions

- Press the "Sauté" button to heat up your Instant Pot. Then, heat olive oil and cook the shallots until just tender.
- Now, add garlic and cook 30 to 40 seconds more or until it is aromatic and slightly browned. Stir in all seasonings; cook until aromatic or 2 minutes more, stirring continuously.
- Add the moong dal and water. Secure the lid. Select the "Manual" mode and cook for 17 minutes under High pressure.
- Once cooking is complete, use a natural pressure release for 20 minutes; carefully remove the lid.
- Season with sea salt and black pepper; add green beans and secure the lid again. Select the "Manual" mode one more time and cook for 2 minutes under High pressure.
- Once cooking is complete, use a quick pressure release; carefully remove the lid. Serve immediately with garlic croutons. Bon appétit!

---

4. French-Style Onion Soup
(Ready in about 35 minutes | Servings 6)

Every home cook needs a homemade chicken stock. Make your stock today and keep it in your refrigerator for up to 4 days.
Per serving: *353 Calories; 15.4g Fat; 40.5g Carbs; 15.4g Protein; 20.2g Sugars*

Ingredients

3 tablespoons ghee
6 sweet onions, sliced
2 garlic cloves
Kosher salt and ground black pepper, to taste
1/2 teaspoon cayenne pepper
1 tablespoon granulated sugar
1/3 cup sherry wine
1/2 cup water

5 cups chicken stock, preferably homemade
2 fresh rosemary sprigs
1 loaf French bread, cut into slices and toasted
1 ½ cups Munster cheese, shaved

Directions

- Press the "Sauté" button to heat up the Instant Pot. Then, melt the ghee; sauté the onions until translucent, about 5 minutes.
- Add garlic and sauté it for 1 to 2 minutes more. Reduce the heat to low; add the salt, black pepper, cayenne pepper, and white sugar. Continue to cook, stirring frequently, until sweet onions are slightly browned.
- Pour in sherry wine, and scrape off any brown bits from the bottom of your Instant Pot. Now, pour in the water and chicken stock; add rosemary and stir to combine.
- Secure the lid. Select the "Manual" setting; cook for 8 minutes under High pressure. Once cooking is complete, use a quick pressure release; carefully remove the lid.
- Then, preheat your oven to broil.
- Divide the soup among ovenproof bowls; top with toasted bread and shaved Munster cheese; place your soup under the broiler for 5 to 6 minutes, or until the cheese is bubbly. Serve warm and enjoy!

5. Mashed Potatoes with Spring Garlic and Sour Cream
(Ready in about 15 minutes | Servings 4)

Yukon Gold potatoes and spring onions are magically transformed into a creamy and flavorful side dish that your family will love!
Per serving: *230 Calories; 14g Fat; 23.3g Carbs; 3.8g Protein; 1.7g Sugars*

Ingredients

1 cup water
1 pound Yukon Gold potatoes, peeled and cubed
1/2 stick butter, softened
2 tablespoons spring garlic, minced
1/4 cup milk
1/3 cup sour cream
1/2 teaspoon dried oregano
1/2 teaspoon dried rosemary
1/2 teaspoon paprika
Salt and ground black pepper, to taste

Directions

- Add 1 cup of water and steamer basket to the base of your Instant Pot.
- Place cubed potatoes in the steamer basket; transfer it to the Instant Pot. Secure the lid. Select the "Manual" mode; cook for 4 minutes under High pressure.
- Once cooking is complete, use a quick release; carefully remove the lid.
- Meanwhile, heat a pan over a moderate heat. Melt the butter and cook spring garlic until it is tender and aromatic.
- Add the milk and scrape up any browned bits with a spatula. Allow it to cool slightly.
- In a mixing bowl, mash the cooked potatoes. Add the butter/garlic mixture along with the other ingredients.
- Taste, adjust the seasonings and serve warm. Bon appétit!

---

6. Bok Choy with Black Sesame and Olives
(Ready in about 10 minutes | Servings 4)

Cooking Bok choy in the Instant Pot is simple and fun. Everyone can become an awesome cook with an Instant Pot electric pressure cooker!
Per serving: *178 Calories; 10.8g Fat; 14.3g Carbs; 12.8g Protein; 2.1g Sugars*

Ingredients

1 pound Bok choy, leaves separated
2 teaspoons canola oil
3 tablespoons black sesame seeds
2 tablespoons soy sauce
1/2 teaspoon smoked paprika
Salt and ground black pepper, to taste
1/2 cup Kalamata olives, pitted and sliced

Directions

- Prepare the Instant Pot by adding 1 ½ cups of water and a steamer basket to the bottom. Place the Bok choy in the steamer basket.
- Secure the lid. Select the "Manual" mode and cook for 4 minutes under High pressure. Once cooking is complete, use a quick pressure release; carefully remove the lid.
- Transfer the Bok choy to a bowl and toss with the remaining ingredients. Bon appétit!

7. Russet Potato Bites
(Ready in about 15 minutes | Servings 6)

Russet potatoes are chock-full of valuable nutrients. Serve this dish as a main vegetarian dish or as an appetizer with dry white wine.
Per serving: *221 Calories; 11.2g Fat; 27.9g Carbs; 3.4g Protein; 1g Sugars*

Ingredients

2 pounds russet potatoes, peeled and diced
1/2 stick butter, melted
2 garlic cloves, pressed
1/2 teaspoon mustard powder
1/2 teaspoon sea salt
1/4 teaspoon ground black pepper
1/2 teaspoon cayenne pepper
1 teaspoon thyme
2 tablespoons mayonnaise
2 tablespoons balsamic vinegar

Directions

- Add a metal rack and 1 cup of water to your Instant Pot. Place the potatoes on the rack.
- Secure the lid. Select the "Steam" mode and cook for 10 minutes under High pressure. Once cooking is complete, use a quick pressure release; carefully remove the lid.
- Cut your potatoes into wedges and toss them with the remaining ingredients. Serve at room temperature. Bon appétit!

8. Steamed Root Veggies with Spicy Horseradish Mayo
(Ready in about 10 minutes | Servings 4)

Try this vegetable dish for a quick and nutritious weeknight meal. It goes great with a horseradish mayo.
Per serving: *116 Calories; 9.7g Fat; 5.2g Carbs; 2.4g Protein; 2.6g Sugars*

Ingredients

1 1/3 cups water
1 celery with leaves, chopped
1 turnip, sliced
1 carrot, sliced
1 red onion, sliced
1/4 teaspoon dried dill weed
1 teaspoon garlic powder
1/2 teaspoon sea salt
1/2 teaspoon ground pepper
2 tablespoons fresh parsley

For the Horseradish Mayo:
1 tablespoon horseradish, well drained
1/2 cup mayonnaise
2 teaspoons Dijon mustard

Directions

- Add 1 1/3 cups of water and steamer basket to the Instant Pot.
- Arrange celery, turnip, carrot, and onion in the steamer basket. Season the vegetables with dried dill weed, garlic powder, sea salt, and ground pepper.
- Secure the lid and choose the "Manual" mode, High pressure and 3 minutes. Once cooking is complete, use a quick release; remove the lid carefully.
- In a mixing bowl, combine the horseradish, mayonnaise, and Dijon mustard. Garnish steamed vegetables with fresh parsley; serve with the horseradish mayo on the side. Bon appétit!

9. Steamed Broccoli with Seeds
(Ready in about 10 minutes | Servings 4)

This steamed broccoli is one of the tastiest and healthiest things that you can prepare in the Instant Pot. You can experiment with seasonings, if desired.
Per serving: *199 Calories; 15.6g Fat; 9.9g Carbs; 8.7g Protein; 2.9g Sugars*

Ingredients

1 head (1 ½-pound) broccoli, broken into florets
2 tablespoons extra-virgin olive oil
2 garlic cloves, pressed
2 tablespoons mayonnaise
2 tablespoons balsamic vinegar
1 teaspoon Dijon mustard
Salt and black pepper, to taste
1/2 teaspoon dried basil
1/2 teaspoon dried oregano
1 teaspoon dried parsley flakes
2 tablespoons pepitas
2 tablespoons sunflower seeds
2 tablespoons sesame seeds

Directions

- Add 1 cup of water and a steamer basket to the bottom of your Instant Pot. Place broccoli florets in the steamer basket.
- Secure the lid and choose the "Steam" mode; cook for 6 minutes under High pressure. Once cooking is complete, use a quick release; carefully remove the lid.
- While the broccoli is still hot, add the remaining ingredients. Toss to combine and serve at room temperature.

---

10. Buttery Wax Beans with Sunflower Kernels
(Ready in about 10 minutes | Servings 6)

Wax beans are made unbelievable tasty in no time thanks to the magic of pressure cooking.
Per serving: *115 Calories; 6.8g Fat; 11.2g Carbs; 4.2g Protein; 3.1g Sugars*

Ingredients

2 pounds wax beans
1 red onion, finely chopped
1 teaspoon garlic, smashed
1 ½ cups chicken stock
Black pepper, to taste
1/2 teaspoon cayenne pepper
2 tablespoons butter, melted
1 tablespoon fresh Italian parsley, roughly chopped
2 tablespoons toasted sunflower kernels

Directions

- Add wax beans, onion, garlic, stock, black pepper, cayenne pepper, and butter to the Instant Pot.
- Secure the lid and choose the "Steam" mode; cook for 3 minutes under High pressure. Once cooking is complete, use a quick release; carefully remove the lid.
- Transfer cooked beans to a serving bowl; garnish with parsley and sunflower kernels and serve right now. Bon appétit!

11. Buttery Brussels Sprouts and Carrots
(Ready in about 15 minutes | Servings 4)

Healthy food seems a lot harder to make than it actually is. Use the Instant pot and cook your vegetables in a homemade stock for the best flavor.
Per serving: *211 Calories; 14.4g Fat; 17.8g Carbs; 6g Protein; 5.6g Sugars*

Ingredients

1/2 stick butter, softened
1/2 cup shallots, chopped
2 cloves garlic, minced
1 pound Brussels sprouts
4 carrots, chunked
1/4 cup lager beer
1/4 cup stock, preferably homemade
1/4 cup fresh chives, for garnish

Directions

- Press the "Sauté" button to heat up the Instant Pot. Melt the butter; now, sweat the shallots until tender and fragrant, about 4 minutes.
- Add garlic and continue to cook for 30 seconds more. Stir in Brussels sprouts, carrots, beer, and stock.
- Secure the lid and choose the "Manual" setting, High pressure and 8 minutes. Once cooking is complete, use a quick release; carefully remove the lid.
- Serve garnished with the fresh chives. Enjoy!

12. Mustard Cipollini Onions
(Ready in about 15 minutes | Servings 4)

Onions cook up perfectly in an Instant Pot, making it a must-cook appetizer for a dinner party. In addition, delicate Cipollini onions look great on a dining table.
Per serving: *96 Calories; 0.9g Fat; 19.9g Carbs; 3.4g Protein; 12.1g Sugars*

Ingredients

1 ½ pounds Cipollini onions, outer layer eliminated
3/4 cup roasted vegetable stock
Sea salt and ground black pepper, to taste
2 bay leaves
1 rosemary sprig
1 thyme sprig
2 teaspoons honey
1 tablespoon mustard
1 ½ tablespoons corn starch

Directions

- Add all ingredients to your Instant Pot. Secure the lid and choose the "Steam" mode. Cook for 10 minutes at High pressure.
- Once cooking is complete, use a quick release; carefully remove the lid.
- Arrange the onions on a serving platter and serve warm. Enjoy!

13. Spicy Eggplant with Steamed Eggs
(Ready in about 50 minutes | Servings 4)

Eggs pair wonderfully with sautéed vegetables. Jalapeño pepper adds just the right amount of spiciness to this appetizing family dish.
Per serving: *235 Calories; 15.8g Fat; 13.5g Carbs; 11.4g Protein; 7.7g Sugars*

Ingredients

1 pound eggplant, peeled and cut pieces
2 teaspoons salt
2 tablespoons butter, at room temperature
2 garlic cloves, smashed
1/2 cup scallions, chopped
1 red bell pepper, chopped
1 jalapeño pepper, minced

2 ripe tomatoes, chopped
Sea salt, to taste
1/2 teaspoon freshly ground black pepper
4 eggs

Directions

- Toss the eggplant with the salt and allow it to sit for 30 minutes; then, drain and rinse the eggplant.
- Press the "Sauté" button to heat up the Instant Pot. Once hot, melt the butter. Stir in the eggplant and cook for 3 to 5 minutes, stirring periodically.
- Add the garlic, scallions, peppers, and tomatoes; cook an additional 4 minutes. Season with salt and pepper.
- Secure the lid. Select the "Manual" setting; cook for 8 minutes at HIGH pressure. Once cooking is complete, use a quick release; carefully remove the lid. Reserve.
- Add 1 cup of water and metal rack to the Instant Pot. Crack the eggs into ramekins; lower the ramekins onto the rack.
- Secure the lid. Select the "Steam" setting; cook for 5 minutes under High pressure. Serve with the eggplant mixture on the side. Bon appétit!

---

14. Colby Cheese and Beer Mashed Cauliflower
(Ready in about 20 minutes | Servings 5)

Cauliflower is one of the most versatile vegetables ever! Colby cheese and beer turn this simple mashed vegetable into a decadent side dish.
Per serving: *297 Calories; 23.6g Fat; 8.9g Carbs; 12.8g Protein; 1.4g Sugars*

Ingredients

1 1/3 cups water
1 cauliflower head
1/2 teaspoon cayenne pepper
Sea salt and freshly ground black pepper
2 tablespoons butter
1 ½ tablespoons arrowroot powder
1/2 cup beer

1 teaspoon garlic powder
1 ½ cup Colby cheese, shredded
1/2 cup sour cream

Directions

- Add 1 1/3 cups of water to your Instant Pot.
- Put the cauliflower head into the steaming basket. Transfer the steaming basket to the Instant Pot.
- Secure the lid and choose the "Manual" button, High pressure and 5 minutes. Once cooking is complete, use a quick release; carefully remove the lid.
- Season cooked cauliflower with cayenne pepper, salt, and ground black pepper. Mash cooked cauliflower with a potato masher.
- Next, melt butter in a pan that is preheated over moderate heat. Whisk in the arrowroot powder and cook for 40 seconds, stirring continuously.
- Gradually pour in beer, stirring continuously. Add the garlic powder and cook until the sauce has thickened, for 3 to 4 minutes.
- Remove from heat and stir in Colby cheese and sour cream; stir until the cheese has melted. Add mashed cauliflower and stir until everything is well incorporated. Bon appétit!

15. Zuppa di Pomodoro
(Ready in about 30 minutes | Servings 4)

A thick, flavorful and Italian-inspired tomato soup is super easy to prepare in your Instant Pot. It is loaded with fiber and lycopene and gets an extra boost of flavor from a double cream.
Per serving: *175 Calories; 11.1g Fat; 12.5g Carbs; 7.7g Protein; 6.7g Sugars*

Ingredients

1 tablespoon olive oil
A bunch of scallions, chopped
1 garlic clove, minced
2 carrots, grated
1 celery, chopped
1 pounds tomatoes, seeded and chopped
4 cups roasted-vegetable broth

Sea salt, to taste
1/4 teaspoon freshly ground black pepper
1/2 teaspoon cayenne pepper
1/2 teaspoon dried basil
1/2 teaspoon dried oregano
1/2 cup double cream
1 tablespoon fresh Italian parsley, roughly chopped

Directions

- Press the "Sauté" button to heat up the Instant Pot. Now, heat the oil; sauté the scallions, garlic, carrot, and celery approximately 5 minutes.
- Stir in the tomatoes, broth, salt, black pepper, cayenne pepper, basil, and oregano.
- Secure the lid. Select the "Soup" setting; cook for 20 minutes at High pressure. Once cooking is complete, use a natural pressure release; carefully remove the lid.
- Fold in the cream and purée the soup with an immersion blender. Serve topped with fresh parsley. Bon appétit!

---

16. Broccoli with Two-Cheese and Chili Dip
(Ready in about 15 minutes | Servings 6)

Relax and look forward to the incredible side dish ahead! Serve with Frascati wine.
Per serving: *246 Calories; 14.5g Fat; 13.6g Carbs; 17.1g Protein; 2.8g Sugars*

Ingredients

1 cup water
1 ½ pounds broccoli, broken into florets

For the Sauce:
1 (15-ounces) can of chili
1 cup Ricotta cheese, crumbled
1 ¼ cups Gruyère cheese shredded
1/4 cup salsa

Directions

- Add water to the base of your Instant Pot.
- Put the broccoli florets into the steaming basket. Transfer the steaming basket to the Instant Pot.
- Secure the lid. Choose the "Manual" mode and High pressure; cook for 3 minutes. Once cooking is complete, use a quick pressure release; carefully remove the lid.
- Now, cook all sauce ingredients in a sauté pan that is preheated over medium-low flame. Cook for 7 minutes or until everything is incorporated.
- Serve steamed broccoli with the sauce on the side. Bon appétit!

17. Winter Root Vegetable Soup
(Ready in about 45 minutes | Servings 8)

This family soup features root veggies cooked with high-quality aromatics. The Instant Pot turns dull vegetables into something magnificent!
Per serving: *150 Calories; 6.7g Fat; 18.9g Carbs; 4.7g Protein; 3.3g Sugars*

Ingredients

2 stalks celery, chopped
2 parsnips, chopped
2 carrots, chopped
1 pound potatoes, cubed
1/2 pound turnip, chopped
1 onion, chopped
2 garlic cloves, minced
4 cups water, or as needed

3 cups chicken stock
1/2 stick butter, at room temperature
1/2 teaspoon mustard seeds
2 bay leaves
1 teaspoon paprika
1/2 teaspoon ground black pepper
Salt, to taste

Directions

- Place the celery, parsnip, carrots, potatoes, turnip, onion and garlic in the Instant Pot; now, pour in the water and stock.
- Secure the lid. Select the "Soup" setting; cook for 25 minutes at High pressure. Once cooking is complete, use a quick pressure release; carefully remove the lid.
- Stir in the butter and seasonings; press the "Sauté" button and continue to cook the soup for 14 to 16 minutes more or until everything is heated through. Discard bay leaves and serve hot.

---

18. Broccoli and Celery Chowder
(Ready in about 35 minutes | Servings 6)

This good-for-you chowder is loaded with vegetables, dairy and simple seasonings. Moreover, it is a cinch to make in the Instant Pot.
Per serving: *193 Calories; 5.5g Fat; 28.6g Carbs; 9.2g Protein; 2.1g Sugars*

Ingredients

1/2 cup leeks, chopped
1 pound broccoli, broken into small florets
1/2 pound celery, chopped
1 carrot, sliced
2 potatoes, peeled and diced
3 cups water
2 cups roasted-vegetable stock
Kosher salt, to taste
1/4 teaspoon ground black pepper
1/4 teaspoon red pepper flakes, crushed
1 cup sour cream

Directions

- Simply place all of the above ingredients, except for sour cream, in your Instant Pot.
- Secure the lid. Select the "Soup" setting; cook for 30 minutes at High pressure. Once cooking is complete, use a quick pressure release; carefully remove the lid.
- Then, puree the soup with an immersion blender. Serve in individual bowls, garnished with a dollop of sour cream. Bon appétit!

19. Golden Potato and Cauliflower Soup
(Ready in about 35 minutes | Servings 6)

Widely used in Indian cuisine as a spice, turmeric is a medicinal herb that has antioxidant and anti-inflammatory properties too. It also can treat depression and obstipation.
Per serving: *175 Calories; 8.2g Fat; 13.9g Carbs; 11.7g Protein; 2.7g Sugars*

Ingredients

1 pound cauliflower, broken into florets
1/2 pound yellow potatoes, diced
1 carrot, sliced
1 celery, chopped
2 garlic cloves, pressed
1/2 cup yellow onion, chopped
4 cups vegetable broth

1 cup water
1/2 teaspoon turmeric powder
1/4 teaspoon ground black pepper
1/2 teaspoon sea salt
1/2 teaspoon mustard seeds
1 cup yellow Swiss cheese, shredded

Directions

- Throw all of the above ingredients, except for Swiss cheese, into the Instant Pot.
- Secure the lid. Select the "Soup" setting; cook for 30 minutes at High pressure. Once cooking is complete, use a quick pressure release; carefully remove the lid.
- After that, puree the soup with an immersion blender. Divide the soup among six soup bowls; top each serving with shredded Swiss cheese. Bon appétit!

20. Chinese-Style Vegetable Soup
(Ready in about 15 minutes | Servings 4)

A vegetable soup made with mushrooms and milk for an extra flavor. In addition, it is cooked in minutes in the Instant Pot.
Per serving: *117 Calories; 8.7g Fat; 7.6g Carbs; 3.4g Protein; 4.6g Sugars*

Ingredients

2 tablespoons sesame oil, softened
2 shallots, chopped
2 cloves garlic, smashed
1/2 pound mushroom, sliced
2 carrots, trimmed and chopped
Sea salt and freshly ground pepper, to taste
1/2 teaspoon dried dill
1 teaspoon smoked paprika
2 tablespoons mijiu (rice wine)
3 cups water
1/2 cup milk
1 tablespoon light soy sauce
2 tablespoons fresh parsley, roughly chopped

Directions

- Press the "Sauté" button and heat the oil. Once hot, sweat the shallots and garlic until tender and translucent.
- Add mushrooms and carrots. Season with salt, ground pepper, dill, and paprika. Sauté for 3 more minutes more or until the carrots have softened. Add rice wine to deglaze the pan.
- Add water, milk, and light soy sauce. Secure the lid. Choose the "Manual" function, High pressure and 5 minutes.
- Once cooking is complete, use a quick release; carefully remove the lid. Taste, adjust the seasonings and serve in individual bowls, garnished with fresh parsley. Bon appétit!

21. Vegetarian Mushroom Stroganoff
(Ready in about 45 minutes | Servings 8)

Are you looking for a classic family lunch? This recipe will fit the bill. You can use Italian or crimini mushroom in this recipe.
Per serving: *137 Calories; 3.9g Fat; 23g Carbs; 4.5g Protein; 2.8g Sugars*

Ingredients

2 tablespoons olive oil
1 cup shallots, chopped
2 garlic cloves, minced
2 russet potatoes, chopped
1 celery with leaves, chopped
1 bell pepper, seeded and thinly sliced
1 habanero pepper, minced
14 ounces brown mushrooms, thinly sliced
1 cup water

1 cup vegetable stock
Sea salt and ground black pepper, to taste
1/2 teaspoon Hungarian paprika
1/2 teaspoon cayenne pepper
2 bay leaves
1 ripe tomato, seeded and chopped
2 tablespoons corn flour, plus 3 tablespoons of water

Directions

- Press the "Sauté" button to heat up the Instant Pot. Then, heat the olive oil and sauté the shallot, garlic, potatoes, and celery until they are softened; add a splash of vegetable stock, if needed.
- Stir in the mushrooms, water, stock, paprika, cayenne pepper, bay leaves, and tomatoes.
- Secure the lid. Select the "Meat/Stew" setting; cook for 35 minutes at High pressure. Once cooking is complete, use a quick pressure release; carefully remove the lid.
- Make the slurry by whisking the corn flour with 3 tablespoons of water. Add the slurry back to the Instant Pot and press the "Sauté" button one more time.
- Allow it to cook until the liquid has thickened. Discard bay leaves and serve warm.

---

22. Acorn Squash and Candy Onion Soup
(Ready in about 25 minutes | Servings 6)

Is there anything better than a thick vegetable soup during weekdays? Buttery texture and slightly sweet flavor of acorn squash pair wonderfully with a sweet and mild flavor of candy onions.
Per serving: *365 Calories; 23.3g Fat; 32.1g Carbs; 8.8g Protein; 16.8g Sugars*

Ingredients

2 tablespoons ghee, melted
1 cup candy onions, chopped
1 garlic clove, minced
2 bell peppers, deveined and chopped
1 ½ pounds acorn squash, shredded
1 carrot, chopped
1 celery, chopped
6 ounces cream cheese

1 bay leaf
2 cups water
4 cups vegetable stock

Directions

- Press the "Sauté" button to heat up the Instant Pot; melt the ghee and sauté candy onions, garlic and peppers until they are softened.
- Add the remaining ingredients.
- Secure the lid. Select the "Soup" setting; cook for 20 minutes at High pressure. Once cooking is complete, use a quick pressure release; carefully remove the lid.
- Afterwards, purée the soup with an immersion blender and serve hot. Enjoy!

23. Aromatic Snow Peas
(Ready in about 10 minutes | Servings 4)

There are many recipes for classic snow peas out there. However, this is one of the testiest pea recipe dishes you will ever try.
Per serving: *126 Calories; 5.4g Fat; 16.9g Carbs; 3.6g Protein; 8.1g Sugars*

Ingredients

1 ½ tablespoons coconut oil
1 pound snow peas, frozen
2 carrots, sliced
1 parsnip, sliced
Seasoned salt, to taste
1 cup water
1/2 teaspoon ground black pepper
1/2 teaspoon red pepper flakes, crushed
1 tablespoon white sugar

Directions

- Add all of the above ingredients to your Instant Pot.
- Secure the lid. Select the "Steam" setting; cook for 4 minutes at High pressure. Once cooking is complete, use a quick pressure release; carefully remove the lid.
- Transfer everything to a serving dish. Enjoy!

24. Easy and Delicious Petite Potatoes
(Ready in about 30 minutes | Servings 4)

Petite potatoes are simply irresistible. Simply toss them with aromatics and wow your family! You can use another combo of aromatics, if desired.
Per serving: *220 Calories; 9.2g Fat; 30.4g Carbs; 5g Protein; 1.3g Sugars*

Ingredients

3 tablespoons butter, melted
2 garlic cloves, minced
2 tablespoons parsley, finely chopped
1 ½ pounds baby potatoes
2 sprigs rosemary, leaves only
1/2 teaspoon ginger powder
1/2 teaspoon lime zest, grated
1 cup chicken stock
1/2 teaspoon turmeric powder
Coarse sea salt and ground black pepper, to taste

Directions

- Press the "Sauté" button to heat up the Instant Pot. Warm the butter and add garlic, parsley, potatoes, rosemary, ginger, and lime zest.
- Sauté the potatoes, turning them periodically, about 8 minutes. Add the stock, turmeric powder, salt, and black pepper.
- Secure the lid. Select the "Manual" setting; cook for 12 minutes at High pressure. Once cooking is complete, use a quick pressure release; carefully remove the lid.
- Serve warm and enjoy!

25. Creamed Cabbage with Ham

(Ready in about 20 minutes | Servings 4)

This soup is so versatile, you can add whatever vegetable you have on hand! Use carrots, yams, parsnip, turnip, bell peppers, sweet corn, and so forth.

Per serving: *292 Calories; 19.5g Fat; 16.6g Carbs; 14.6g Protein; 7.9g Sugars*

Ingredients

1 ½ tablespoons olive oil
1 leek, chopped
1 celery rib, chopped
2 garlic cloves, chopped
1 pound cabbage, shredded
3 ½ cups broth, preferably homemade

Sea salt, to taste
1/2 teaspoon black peppercorns
2 bay leaves
1 cup fully cooked ham, cubed
1 cup double cream
1/4 cup fresh chives, chopped

Directions

- Press the "Sauté" button on your Instant Pot; add olive oil. Once hot, cook leeks for 3 minutes or until they are softened.
- Stir in celery and cook for 3 minutes more. Add a splash of broth if needed. Now, add garlic and cook for 30 seconds more or until it is fragrant.
- Add cabbage, broth, salt, black peppercorns, and bay leaves. Secure the lid.
- Choose the "Manual" mode and cook for 3 minutes at High pressure. Once cooking is complete, use a quick release; carefully remove the lid.
- Fold in ham and double cream and continue to cook in the residual heat for 5 minutes longer.
- Taste, adjust the seasonings and serve in individual bowls, garnished with fresh chopped chives. Enjoy!

---

26. Chinese-Style Glazed Baby Carrots

(Ready in about 20 minutes | Servings 4)

Baby carrots are a good source of vitamin A, antioxidants, and dietary fiber. These carrots are tossed with soy sauce, ghee and honey and served with toasted sesame seeds. Lovely!

Per serving: *175 Calories; 10.3g Fat; 19.4g Carbs; 1.8g Protein; 12.6g Sugars*

Ingredients

3 tablespoons ghee
1/4 cup champagne vinegar
2 teaspoons honey
3/4 cup water
2 tablespoons soy sauce
1/2 teaspoon kosher salt
1/2 teaspoon ground white pepper
1/2 teaspoon paprika
1 ½ pounds baby carrots
2 tablespoons sesame seeds, toasted

Directions

- Press the "Sauté" button on your Instant Pot. Place all of the above ingredients, except for the carrots and sesame seeds, in your Instant Pot.
- Cook this mixture for 1 minute, stirring frequently. Stir in baby carrots.
- Secure the lid. Select the "Steam" setting; cook for 10 minutes at High pressure. Once cooking is complete, use a quick pressure release; carefully remove the lid.
- Press the "Sauté" button one more time. Let it simmer until the sauce has reduced and thickened. Sprinkle with sesame seeds and serve at room temperature. Enjoy!

27. Springtime Broccoli Salad
(Ready in about 10 minutes | Servings 4)

This make-ahead, colorful and rich broccoli salad is sure to please your family and guests! This is one of the best tricks to get your kids to eat more veggies; just make sure to serve it in nice and appealing bowls.
Per serving: *302 Calories; 21.1g Fat; 18.2g Carbs; 14.2g Protein; 7.4g Sugars*

Ingredients

1 large (1 ½-pound) head broccoli, cut into small florets
1 teaspoon Dijon seeds
1/4 cup extra-virgin olive oil
1 tablespoon tahini paste
2 tablespoons lemon juice
2 spring garlic stalks, smashed

2 green onions, chopped
1 cup radishes, sliced
2 tablespoons parsley leaves, roughly chopped
Salt and ground black pepper, to taste
1 ½ cups feta cheese, crumbled

Directions

- Prepare your Instant Pot by adding 1 cup of water and a steamer basket to its bottom.
- Place the broccoli in the steamer basket.
- Secure the lid. Choose the "Manual" mode and High pressure; cook for 5 minutes. Once cooking is complete, use a quick pressure release; carefully remove the lid.
- Afterwards, toss your broccoli with the remaining ingredients. Serve at room temperature with garlic croutons if desired. Enjoy!

28. Classic Green Artichoke Dip
(Ready in about 20 minutes | Servings 10)

Here's a completely new way to eat your artichokes and greens! Greens are so funny and delicious!
Per serving: *219 Calories; 19g Fat; 5.5g Carbs; 7.6g Protein; 1.7g Sugars*

Ingredients

1 can (14-ounce) artichoke hearts, drained and roughly chopped
1/2 pound kale leaves, fresh or frozen torn into pieces
1 cup cream cheese
1 cup Colby cheese, shredded
1 cup mayonnaise
1 teaspoon yellow mustard
2 garlic cloves, minced
1 teaspoon shallot powder
1 teaspoon fennel seeds
Sea salt and ground black pepper, to taste

Directions

- Place 1 cup of water and a metal rack in your Instant Pot.
- Then, thoroughly combine all ingredients in a casserole dish that is previously greased with a nonstick cooking spray; cover the casserole dish with a piece of aluminum foil, making a foil sling if needed.
- Lower the casserole dish onto the rack.
- Secure the lid. Select the "Steam" setting; cook for 10 minutes at High pressure. Once cooking is complete, use a quick pressure release; carefully remove the lid.
- Serve with chips or pita wedges. Enjoy!

29. Cheesy Sweet Potatoes with Spring Onions
(Ready in about 15 minutes | Servings 4)

Steaming vegetables in the Instant Pot has a number of advantages to the traditional methods of cooking. See it for yourself!
Per serving: *109 Calories; 5.9g Fat; 10g Carbs; 5.6g Protein; 0.2g Sugars*

Ingredients

1 cup water
1 ½ pounds sweet potatoes, cubed
1/2 cup spring onions, roughly chopped
2 tablespoons extra-virgin olive oil
1/2 cup Romano cheese, freshly grated
1/2 teaspoon cayenne pepper
Kosher salt and freshly ground black pepper, to taste

Directions

- Pour 1 cup of water into the base of your Instant Pot. Put the sweet potatoes into the steaming basket. Transfer the steaming basket to the Instant Pot.
- Secure the lid and choose the "Manual" button, High pressure and 9 minutes. Once cooking is complete, use a natural release; carefully remove the lid.
- Toss warm potatoes with spring onions, olive oil, Romano cheese, cayenne pepper, salt, and black pepper. Serve immediately and enjoy!

---

30. Classic Belgian Endive
(Ready in about 6 minutes | Servings 2)

Endive is an excellent source of ß-carotenes, manganese, B vitamin, and dietary fiber. Belgians call their endive "white gold".
Per serving: *203 Calories; 15.6g Fat; 13g Carbs; 4.1g Protein; 2.9g Sugars*

Ingredients

2 tablespoons sesame oil
2 garlic cloves, minced
1/2 cup scallions, chopped
1 pound Belgian endive, halved lengthwise
1/4 cup champagne vinegar
1 teaspoon lime juice
1 teaspoon Dijon mustard
1 tablespoon soy sauce
1 cup water
1/2 teaspoon crushed red pepper flakes
Sea salt and ground black pepper, to taste
1 bay leaf

Directions

- Press the "Sauté" button to heat up the Instant Pot; heat the sesame oil. Once hot, cook the garlic and scallions for 40 seconds to a minute or until aromatic.
- Add Belgian endive, vinegar, lime juice, mustard, soy sauce water, red pepper, salt, black pepper, and bay leaf.
- Secure the lid. Choose the "Manual" mode and Low pressure; cook for 2 minutes or until tender when pierced with the tip of a knife.
- Once cooking is complete, use a quick pressure release; carefully remove the lid. Serve immediately.

31. Spicy Chanterelles with Purple Cabbage
(Ready in about 15 minutes | Servings 4)

You deserve more for lunch than boring vegetables. Chanterelle mushrooms are a powerhouse of protein, vitamin B6, thiamine, selenium, manganese, and copper.
Per serving: *121 Calories; 3.8g Fat; 20.3g Carbs; 4g Protein; 10.1g Sugars*

Ingredients

3 teaspoons olive oil
1/2 pound Chanterelle mushrooms, thinly sliced
1 pound purple cabbage, cut into wedges
2 red onions, cut into wedges
2 garlic cloves, smashed
1/3 cup Worcestershire sauce

2 tablespoons champagne vinegar
1 teaspoon cayenne pepper
Salt, to taste
1/2 teaspoon ground bay leaf
1/3 teaspoon white pepper
1/2 teaspoon adobo seasoning

Directions

- Press the "Sauté" button to heat up the Instant Pot; heat the oil. Once hot, add the mushrooms; cook until they are lightly browned, about 4 minutes.
- Add the other ingredients in the order listed above. Gently stir to combine and secure the lid.
- Now, choose the "Manual" setting, High pressure and 4 minutes.
- Once cooking is complete, use a quick release; remove the lid carefully. Bon appétit!

32. Greek-Style Vegetables with Halloumi Cheese
(Ready in about 10 minutes | Servings 4)

Try an authentic Greek dish and enjoy Mediterranean aromas in the comfort of your own home. You can use Crimini mushrooms instead of button mushrooms in this recipe.
Per serving: *305 Calories; 20.8g Fat; 18.4g Carbs; 15.2g Protein; 10.4g Sugars*

Ingredients

1 tablespoon olive oil
1 tablespoon butter
2 garlic cloves, minced
1/2 cup shallots, chopped
12 ounces button mushrooms, thinly sliced
1 pepperoncini pepper, minced
1/2 pound eggplant, sliced
1/2 pound zucchini, sliced

1 teaspoon dried basil
2 rosemary sprigs, leaves picked
1 thyme sprig, leaves picked
2 tomatoes, chopped
1/3 cup water
1/2 cup dry Greek wine
8 ounces Halloumi cheese, cubed
1/2 cup Kalamata olives, pitted and halved

Directions

- Press the "Sauté" button to heat up your Instant Pot; heat the olive oil and butter. Cook the garlic and shallots for 1 to 2 minutes, stirring occasionally.
- Stir in the mushrooms, pepper, eggplant, and zucchini and continue to sauté an additional 2 to 3 minutes.
- After that, add basil, rosemary, thyme, tomatoes, water, and wine.
- Secure the lid. Choose the "Manual" mode and Low pressure; cook for 3 minutes. Once cooking is complete, use a quick pressure release; carefully remove the lid.
- Garnish each serving with cheese and olives; serve warm or at room temperature.

33. Herbed Zucchini Appetizer
(Ready in about 10 minutes | Servings 4)

Zucchini appetizer with an outstanding flavor of extra-virgin olive oil and oregano. Zucchini is a powerhouse of many minerals and vitamin so you can snack without guilt.
Per serving: *88 Calories; 5.9g Fat; 5.9g Carbs; 5.3g Protein; 0g Sugars*

Ingredients

1 ½ tablespoons olive oil
2 garlic cloves, minced
1 ½ pounds zucchini, cut into thick slices
1/2 cup water
1/2 cup vegetable broth
1/2 teaspoon dried oregano
1 teaspoon basil, fresh or dried
1 teaspoon rosemary, fresh or dried
1/3 teaspoon smoked paprika
1/3 teaspoon ground black pepper
Coarse sea salt, to taste

Directions

- Press the "Sauté" button to heat up your Instant Pot; heat the olive oil. Once hot, cook the garlic for 1 minute.
- Add the remaining ingredients.
- Secure the lid. Choose the "Manual" mode and Low pressure; cook for 3 minutes. Once cooking is complete, use a quick pressure release; carefully remove the lid. Bon appétit!

---

34. Italian-Style Potatoes
(Ready in about 20 minutes | Servings 6)

Roast amazing cheesy and herby potatoes without turning on the oven! The flavors are fantastic!
Per serving: *270 Calories; 9g Fat; 38.8g Carbs; 9.2g Protein; 1.6g Sugars*

Ingredients

6 white potatoes, cut into cubes
1/2 teaspoon shallot powder
1 teaspoon garlic powder
1 teaspoon oregano, dried
2 sprigs rosemary, leaves picked
Coarse salt, to taste
1/2 teaspoon freshly ground black pepper
1/4 cup extra-virgin olive oil
3/4 cup beef broth
1/4 cup brown ale

1 cup Pecorino Romano cheese, grated
1/4 cup Italian flat-leaf parsley, chopped

Directions

- Toss potato cubes with shallot powder, garlic powder, oregano, rosemary, salt, and black pepper.
- Press the "Sauté" button and heat the oil. Now, cook the potatoes for 5 minutes, stirring periodically.
- Add broth and brown ale; secure the lid. Choose the "Manual" mode and cook for 9 minutes at High pressure.
- Once cooking is complete, use a quick release; carefully remove the lid. Toss warm potatoes with Pecorino Romano and serve garnished with Italian parsley. Enjoy!

35. Green Beans with Pancetta
(Ready in about 10 minutes | Servings 4)

Your family will love a fresh and rich taste of this side dish. Add a few sprinkles of pumpkin seeds just before serving!
Per serving: *177 Calories; 12.1g Fat; 9.9g Carbs; 8.8g Protein; 2.3g Sugars*

Ingredients

2 tablespoons sesame oil
2 garlic cloves, pressed
1 yellow onion, chopped
5 ounces pancetta, diced
1 ½ pounds green beans, cut in half
Kosher salt, to taste
1/4 teaspoon ground black pepper

1/2 teaspoon cayenne pepper
1/2 teaspoon dried oregano
1/2 teaspoon dried dill
1 cup water

Directions

- Press the "Sauté" button to heat up your Instant Pot. Now, heat the sesame oil and sauté the garlic and onion until softened and fragrant; set it aside.
- After that, stir in pancetta and continue to cook for a further 4 minutes; crumble with a fork and set it aside.
- Add the remaining ingredients; stir to combine.
- Secure the lid. Choose the "Manual" mode and Low pressure; cook for 3 minutes. Once cooking is complete, use a quick pressure release; carefully remove the lid.
- Serve warm, garnished with the reserved onion/garlic mixture and pancetta. Bon appétit!

36. Kid-Friendly Stuffed Peppers
(Ready in about 10 minutes | Servings 4)

Your kids will love these mini peppers! They are so easy to make in an Instant Pot and they have a rich taste thanks to the spices and Cheddar cheese.
Per serving: *168 Calories; 8.8g Fat; 15.8g Carbs; 8.2g Protein; 8.2g Sugars*

Ingredients

8 baby bell peppers, seeded and sliced lengthwise
1 tablespoon peanut oil
6 ounces Cheddar cheese, grated
2 ounces sour cream
2 garlic cloves, smashed
1/2 white onion, finely chopped
Sea salt and ground black pepper, to taste
1/2 teaspoon paprika
1/2 teaspoon dill, fresh or dried

Directions

- Start by adding 1 cup of water and a steamer basket to the Instant Pot.
- Then, thoroughly combine all ingredients, except for peppers. Then, stuff the peppers with this mixture.
- Arrange the peppers in the steamer basket.
- Secure the lid. Choose the "Manual" mode and High pressure; cook for 5 minutes. Once cooking is complete, use a quick pressure release; carefully remove the lid.
- Serve immediately and enjoy!

37. Greek-Style Veggie Souvlaki
(Ready in about 10 minutes | Servings 4)

Discover a great way to eat Greek food on a vegetarian diet. Try these traditional Greek skewers and enjoy their wonderful taste!
Per serving: *224 Calories; 14.3g Fat; 22.5g Carbs; 6.4g Protein; 13.4g Sugars*

Ingredients

1 head broccoli, broken into florets and blanched
2 bell peppers, seeded and diced
2 medium zucchinis, cut into 1-inch slices
8 ounces button mushrooms, whole
2 cups cherry tomatoes
4 tablespoons olive oil
Fresh juice of 1/2 lemon
Sea salt and ground black pepper, to taste

1 teaspoon dried oregano
1 teaspoon dried rosemary
1/4 teaspoon ground bay leaves
1/2 teaspoon crushed red pepper

Directions

- Prepare your Instant Pot by adding 1 cup of water and a metal rack to its bottom.
- Thread the vegetables onto bamboo or wooden skewers.
- Drizzle them with olive oil and fresh lemon juice; add seasonings.
- Secure the lid. Choose the "Manual" mode and High pressure; cook for 3 minutes. Once cooking is complete, use a quick pressure release; carefully remove the lid. Bon appétit!

---

38. Ranch Cauliflower Dipping Sauce
(Ready in about 10 minutes | Servings 8)

Are you looking for a party dip that takes 10 minutes from start to finish? This dipping sauce goes perfectly with vegetable sticks, crackers, or tortilla chips.
Per serving: *176 Calories; 13.7g Fat; 7.4g Carbs; 6.5g Protein; 2.8g Sugars*

Ingredients

1 head cauliflower, cut into florets
1 cup tomato puree
1/2 cup red onion, chopped
1 teaspoon fresh garlic, pressed
1 tablespoon fresh cilantro, chopped
1/2 tablespoon fresh rosemary, chopped
Sea salt, to taste
1/4 teaspoon ground black pepper, or more to taste
1 teaspoon crushed red pepper
1 teaspoon Ranch seasoning mix
1 cup mayonnaise
1 cup Ricotta cheese, at room temperature

Directions

- Prepare your Instant Pot by adding 1 cup of water and a steamer basket to its bottom.
- Arrange cauliflower florets in the steamer basket.
- Secure the lid. Choose the "Manual" mode and Low pressure; cook for 5 minutes. Once cooking is complete, use a quick pressure release; carefully remove the lid.
- Add the cauliflower to your food processor; add the remaining ingredients. Process until everything is well incorporated.
- Place in your refrigerator until ready to use. Bon appétit!

39. Farmhouse Vegetable Stew
(Ready in about 35 minutes | Servings 4)

Here's a hearty vegetable stew you don't have to cook for hours. Sauté your veggies briefly, add the remaining ingredients and set your Instant Pot. Easy as 1, 2, 3!
Per serving: *181 Calories; 7.3g Fat; 24.1g Carbs; 6.1g Protein; 5.1g Sugars*

Ingredients

2 tablespoons butter, at room temperature
1 leek, chopped
2 carrots, trimmed and chopped
2 cups white mushrooms, thinly sliced
1 teaspoon garlic, minced
2 sprigs rosemary, leaves picked
2 sprigs thyme, leaves picked

2 ½ cups stock, preferably homemade
3 ripe tomatoes, pureed
1 jalapeno pepper, deveined and chopped
1/2 pound white potatoes, peeled and diced
Sea salt, to taste
1/2 teaspoon ground black pepper
1 ½ tablespoons cornstarch

Directions

- Pres the "Sauté" button and melt the butter. Now, sauté the leek and carrots until they are tender, about 3 minutes.
- Add the mushrooms, garlic, rosemary, and thyme; cook an additional 3 minutes or until they are aromatic and tender.
- Add a splash of homemade stock to deglaze the pan. Add the remaining stock, pureed tomatoes, jalapeno pepper, potatoes, salt, and black pepper.
- Secure the lid and choose "Soup" mode. Cook for 20 minutes at High pressure. Once cooking is complete, use a quick release; carefully remove the lid.
- Meanwhile, make the cornstarch slurry by whisking 1 ½ tablespoons of cornstarch with 2 tablespoons of water. Add the slurry to the Instant Pot.
- Cook the cooking liquid in the residual heat for 5 minutes longer or until it has thickened. Ladle into individual bowls and serve warm. Enjoy!

40. Saucy and Sticky Portobellos
(Ready in about 10 minutes | Servings 4)

The recipe works best with portobello mushrooms, but you can use any type of brown mushrooms you have on hand.
Per serving: *89 Calories; 2.1g Fat; 14.2g Carbs; 6.2g Protein; 9.2g Sugars*

Ingredients

1 ½ pounds portobello mushrooms
1 cup vegetable stock
2 ripe tomatoes, chopped
2/3 teaspoon porcini powder
Sea salt and ground black pepper, to taste
2 garlic cloves, minced
1/2 teaspoon mustard seeds
1 teaspoon celery seeds

1 tablespoon apple cider vinegar
1 tablespoon dark soy sauce
1 tablespoon brown sugar
1/2 teaspoon liquid smoke

Directions

- Add all of the above ingredients to your Instant Pot; stir to combine well.
- Secure the lid. Choose the "Manual" mode and High pressure; cook for 4 minutes. Once cooking is complete, use a natural pressure release; carefully remove the lid. Serve warm and enjoy!

41. Spicy Cauliflower with Yogurt Sauce

(Ready in about 10 minutes | Servings 4)

This is not a typical one-pot dish! Cauliflower is cooked with herbs, habanero pepper, and tomatoes. To serve, drop a tablespoon or two into center of each serving bowl. Use tip of a sharp knife to make swirls and serve.

Per serving: *121 Calories; 6.6g Fat; 13.4g Carbs; 4.8g Protein; 5.8g Sugars*

Ingredients

1 tablespoon peanut oil
1 yellow onion, chopped
1 clove garlic, pressed
1 teaspoon curry powder
1 habanero pepper, minced
1 tablespoon fresh cilantro, chopped
1 tablespoon fresh parsley, chopped

1/2 teaspoon ground black pepper
1/2 teaspoon red pepper flakes
Sea salt, to taste
2 tomatoes, puréed
1 ½ pounds cauliflower, broken into florets
1/2 cup vegetable stock, preferably homemade
1/2 cup Greek-style yogurt

Directions

- Press the "Sauté" button to heat up your Instant Pot. Now, heat the oil and sauté the onion for 1 to 2 minutes.
- Add garlic and continue to cook until fragrant.
- Stir in the remaining ingredients, except the yogurt; stir to combine well.
- Secure the lid. Choose the "Manual" mode and High pressure; cook for 3 minutes. Once cooking is complete, use a quick pressure release; carefully remove the lid.
- Pour in yogurt, stir well, and serve immediately.

---

42. Old-Fashioned Italian Pepperonata

(Ready in about 15 minutes | Servings 4)

Thanks to the Instant Pot, you can create this traditional Italian dish with peppers in less than 15 minutes. Just like nonna used to make!

Per serving: *97 Calories; 4.1g Fat; 10g Carbs; 3.1g Protein; 4.1g Sugars*

Ingredients

1 tablespoon olive oil
1 red onion, chopped
1 pepperoncini, seeded and minced
1 red bell pepper, seeded and chopped
1 yellow bell pepper, seeded and chopped
1 green bell peppers, seeded and chopped
2 ripe Roma tomatoes, pureed
1 teaspoon ginger-garlic paste
1 teaspoon dried rosemary

1 teaspoon dried oregano
1 teaspoon dried sage
1 cup vegetable broth
1/4 cup Italian dry white wine
1/2 teaspoon ground black pepper
1/2 teaspoon red pepper flakes, crushed
Sea salt, to taste

Directions

- Press the "Sauté" button to heat up your Instant Pot. Heat the olive oil and sauté the onion until it is softened.
- Add the remaining ingredients to your Instant Pot.
- Secure the lid. Choose the "Manual" mode and High pressure; cook for 3 minutes. Once cooking is complete, use a quick pressure release; carefully remove the lid.
- Press the "Sauté" button one more time and thicken the liquid about 4 minutes, stirring periodically.
- Serve warm in individual bowls. Bon appétit!

43. Classic Cream of Celery Soup
(Ready in about 10 minutes | Servings 4)

Get ready for this fabulous soup that combines fresh leeks, young galangal, jalapeño peppers, and coconut cream!
Per serving: *200 Calories; 15.9g Fat; 9.5g Carbs; 7.7g Protein; 3.7g Sugars*

Ingredients

1 tablespoon sesame oil
1 teaspoon garlic, minced
1/2 cup leeks, chopped
1 pound celery with leaves, chopped
1 (2-inch) piece young galangal, peeled and chopped
1/2 teaspoon ground bay leaves

1 fresh jalapeño peppers, seeded and finely chopped
4 cups roasted vegetable stock, preferably homemade
Sea salt and freshly ground black pepper, to taste
1/4 teaspoon grated nutmeg
1/2 cup coconut cream, unsweetened

Directions

- Press the "Sauté" button to heat up your Instant Pot. Heat the sesame oil and sauté the garlic and leeks until tender about 1 minute 30 seconds.
- Stir in the celery and galangal; continue to cook for a further 2 minutes.
- Next, add ground bay leaves, jalapeño peppers, stock, salt, black pepper and nutmeg.
- Secure the lid. Choose the "Manual" mode and High pressure; cook for 3 minutes. Once cooking is complete, use a quick pressure release; carefully remove the lid.
- Then, purée the soup with an immersion blender until smooth and creamy. Return the pureed soup to the Instant Pot; fold in the coconut cream.
- Afterwards, press the "Sauté" button. Allow your soup to simmer until thoroughly warmed. Ladle into soup bowls and serve hot. Bon appétit!

44. Dad's Gourmet Beet Salad
(Ready in about 15 minutes + chilling time | Servings 6)

Here is the perfect, nutritious salad that you can serve for any occasion. It is packed with extremely healthy red beets and baby spinach, which make it a vitamin bomb!
Per serving: *182 Calories; 11.1g Fat; 19.7g Carbs; 2.6g Protein; 15.1g Sugars*

Ingredients

2 cups water
1 ½ pounds red beets, washed, stems and leaves removed
2 tablespoons gourmet mustard
2 tablespoons honey
1/4 cup balsamic vinegar
1/4 cup olive oil
2 cups baby spinach
2 garlic cloves, pressed
2 tablespoons pecan halves, toasted

Directions

- Add water to the base of the Instant Pot. Put the beets into the steaming basket. Transfer the steaming basket to the Instant Pot.
- Secure the lid and choose "Manual" button, High pressure and 8 minutes. Once cooking is complete, use a natural release; remove the lid carefully.
- Let the beets cool enough to handle. Peel the cooked beets and cut them into thin slices.
- Meanwhile, whisk the mustard, honey, vinegar, and olive oil. Toss the beats with this vinaigrette and add baby spinach and garlic; stir to combine.
- Garnish with toasted pecan halves and serve well-chilled. Bon appétit!

45. Indian-Style Vegetables with Naan
(Ready in about 20 minutes | Servings 6)

Indian-inspired vegetables pair wonderfully with naans, Indian flatbread. Homemade pillowy naans will amaze your family.
Per serving: 319 Calories; 12.7g Fat; 43.5g Carbs; 7.6g Protein; 1.7g Sugars

Ingredients

1 tablespoon sesame oil
2 bell pepper, seeded and sliced
1 red chili pepper, seeded and sliced
1 teaspoon garlic paste
1/2 teaspoon fresh ginger, grated
1 tablespoon garam masala
1/2 teaspoon dhania
1/2 teaspoon haldi
1/2 teaspoon ground black pepper
Sea salt, to taste

Naan:
1 tablespoon dry active yeast
1 teaspoon sugar
2/3 cup warm water
2 ½ cups all-purpose flour
1/2 teaspoon salt
1/4 cup vegetable oil
1 egg

Directions

- Press the "Sauté" button to heat up your Instant Pot. Heat the oil until sizzling. Once hot, sauté peppers, garlic, ginger, and spices.
- Secure the lid. Choose the "Manual" mode and Low pressure; cook for 4 minutes. Once cooking is complete, use a quick pressure release; carefully remove the lid.
- Meanwhile, make naan by mixing the yeast, sugar and 2 tablespoons of warm water; allow it sit for 5 to 6 minutes.
- Add the remaining ingredients for naans; let it rest for about 1 hour at room temperature.
- Now, divide the dough into six balls; flatten the balls on a working surface.
- Heat up a large-sized pan over moderate heat. Cook naans until they are golden on both sides. Serve these naans with the reserved vegetables and enjoy!

46. Swiss Chard with Caciocavallo
(Ready in about 15 minutes | Servings 4)

Fresh Swiss chard, mellow Caciocavallo cheese and crispy Canadian bacon combine very well in this appetizing family meal. Enjoy!
Per serving: *214 Calories; 12.1g Fat; 5.8g Carbs; 22.1g Protein; 2.4g Sugars*

Ingredients

1/2 pound Canadian bacon, chopped
12 ounces Swiss chard, torn into pieces
1/2 cup vegetable broth
1/4 cup water
1/4 cup rose wine
1 teaspoon paprika
1/2 teaspoon dried basil
1/2 teaspoon dried marjoram
Sea salt and ground black pepper, to taste
1 cup Caciocavallo cheese, shredded

Directions

- Press the "Sauté" button to heat up your Instant Pot. Once hot, cook Canadian bacon until crisp; crumble with a fork and set it aside.
- Stir in the remaining ingredients, except for Caciocavallo cheese.
- Secure the lid. Choose the "Manual" mode and Low pressure; cook for 4 minutes. Once cooking is complete, use a quick pressure release; carefully remove the lid.
- Add Caciocavallo cheese, cover with the lid and allow it to sit for a further 4 minutes or until your cheese is melted. Top each serving with reserved bacon and serve warm.

47. Root Vegetable Sticks
(Ready in about 10 minutes | Servings 6)

These fun-to-eat vegetable sticks can be served on any occasion. Knives and forks are completely optional when serving this appetizer.
Per serving: *99 Calories; 4.7g Fat; 14.4g Carbs; 1g Protein; 6.7g Sugars*

Ingredients

2 tablespoons sesame oil
2 parsnips, peeled and halved lengthwise
2 carrots, cut into sticks
1 turnip, cut into sticks
1/2 teaspoon baking soda
1 tablespoon agave nectar
1/2 teaspoon kosher salt
1/2 teaspoon white pepper, ground
1/2 teaspoon fresh ginger, grated
1 teaspoon grated orange peel
1 cup water

Directions

- Press the "Sauté" button to heat up your Instant Pot; heat the oil.
- Sauté vegetables until aromatic and tender. Now, add the remaining ingredients and gently stir to combine.
- Secure the lid. Choose the "Manual" mode and High pressure; cook for 4 minutes. Once cooking is complete, use a quick pressure release; carefully remove the lid.
- Serve warm or at room temperature.

---

48. Cheesy Brussels Sprouts
(Ready in about 15 minutes | Servings 4)

Accompany your dinner with cheesy Brussels sprouts! You can also serve this fabulous dish as a complete vegetarian meal.
Per serving: *261 Calories; 16.2g Fat; 20.1g Carbs; 13.2g Protein; 4.1g Sugars*

Ingredients

1 ½ pounds Brussels sprouts, trimmed
3 tablespoons ghee
2 garlic cloves, minced
1/2 cup scallions, finely chopped
Salt, to taste
1/2 teaspoon freshly ground black pepper
1/2 teaspoon red pepper flakes
1 cup Romano cheese, grated

Directions

- Place 1 cup of water and a steamer basket on the bottom of your Instant Pot. Place Brussels sprouts in the steamer basket.
- Secure the lid. Choose the "Steam" mode and High pressure; cook for 5 minutes. Once cooking is complete, use a quick pressure release; carefully remove the lid.
- While Brussels sprouts are still hot, add ghee, garlic, scallions, salt, black pepper, red pepper, and Romano cheese; toss to coat well and serve.

49. Red Beet Salad with Goat Cheese
(Ready in about 30 minutes | Servings 6)

Red beets can improve your stamina, blood pressure and the brain's function. You can add freshly crushed garlic to this salad if desired.
Per serving: *222 Calories; 16.1g Fat; 12.9g Carbs; 7.5g Protein; 9.1g Sugars*

Ingredients

1 ½ pounds red beets
1/4 cup apple cider vinegar
1 teaspoon yellow mustard
1 teaspoon honey
Kosher salt and ground black pepper, to taste
1 teaspoon cumin seeds
1/4 cup extra-virgin olive oil
1 cup goat cheese, crumbled

Directions

- Add 1 ½ cups of water and beets to your Instant Pot.
- Secure the lid. Choose "Manual" mode and High pressure; cook for 25 minutes. Once cooking is complete, use a quick pressure release; carefully remove the lid.
- After that, rub off skins; cut the beets into wedges. Transfer them to a serving bowl.
- Thoroughly combine the vinegar, mustard, honey, salt, black pepper, cumin seeds, and olive oil. Dress the salad, top with goat cheese and serve well chilled.

---

50. Holiday Mashed Carrots
(Ready in about 10 minutes | Servings 6)

Make a quick and easy side dish that goes well with meatballs, grilled steak or fish fillets. A heavy cream adds dimension to the mashed carrots.
Per serving: *113 Calories; 6g Fat; 14.6g Carbs; 1.5g Protein; 7.3g Sugars*

Ingredients

1 cup water
2 pounds carrots, chopped
2 tablespoons butter, room temperature
1 teaspoon paprika
1 teaspoon coriander
Kosher salt, to taste
1/2 teaspoon ground black
1/4 cup heavy cream

Directions

- Add water to the base of your Instant Pot.
- Put the carrots into the steaming basket. Transfer the steaming basket to the Instant Pot.
- Secure the lid and choose the "Manual" button, High pressure and 3 minutes. Once cooking is complete, use a natural release; remove the lid carefully.
- Mash the carrots with a fork or potato masher. Add butter, paprika, coriander, salt, ground black, and heavy cream.
- Taste, adjust the seasonings and serve immediately. Bon appétit!

POULTRY

51. Turkey and Green Bean Soup
(Ready in about 25 minutes | Servings 4)

One of the easiest ways to make the most comforting meal such as a poultry soup is to use your Instant Pot. Do not forget to add a pinch of love to each serving.
Per serving: *295 Calories; 12.2g Fat; 16.4g Carbs; 30.6g Protein; 8.4g Sugars*

Ingredients

1 pound turkey breasts, boneless, skinless and diced
2 cups water
2 cups chicken stock
2 tablespoons apple cider vinegar
1 (28-ounce) can diced tomatoes
1 yellow onion, chopped
2 cloves garlic, minced
2 carrots, diced

1 teaspoon dried oregano
1/2 teaspoon dried marjoram
1/2 teaspoon dried thyme
1/2 teaspoon ground cumin
Salt and ground black pepper, to taste
12 ounces green beans, cut into halves

Directions

- Place all of the above ingredients, except for green beans, into the Instant Pot.
- Secure the lid. Choose the "Poultry" mode and High pressure; cook for 15 minutes. Once cooking is complete, use a quick pressure release; carefully remove the lid.
- Then, stir in the green beans. Seal the lid again; let it sit for 5 minutes to blanch the green beans. Bon appétit!

---

52. Grandma's Chicken Stew with Beans
(Ready in about 20 minutes | Servings 4)

An old-fashioned hearty stew for cold winter nights. Adding canned beans takes this classic recipe to the next level.
Per serving: *463 Calories; 23.6g Fat; 19.8g Carbs; 41.1g Protein; 3.6g Sugars*

Ingredients

1 tablespoon olive oil
1/2 cup shallots, chopped
2 carrots, trimmed and chopped
1 celery stalk, chopped
2 garlic cloves, minced
1/2 pound potatoes, peeled and quartered
2 ripe tomatoes, chopped
1 (15-ounce) can red kidney beans, rinsed and drained

1 cup chicken broth
1/2 cup dry white wine
1/2 cup water
4 chicken drumsticks
1/2 teaspoon salt
1/4 teaspoon ground black pepper
1 teaspoon cayenne pepper

Directions

- Press the "Sauté" button to preheat your Instant Pot.
- Then, heat the oil and cook the shallots, carrots, and celery until they are tender.
- Stir in the garlic; cook for another minute. Add the remaining ingredients.
- Secure the lid. Choose the "Poultry" mode and High pressure; cook for 15 minutes. Once cooking is complete, use a natural pressure release; carefully remove the lid.
- Then, pull the meat off the bones; return the chicken to the Instant Pot. Serve warm and enjoy!

53. Saucy Duck with Wild Mushrooms
(Ready in about 30 minutes | Servings 4)

Cook this satisfying poultry recipe with all of your favorites: duck breasts, Port wine, and wild mushrooms. Amazing!
Per serving: *203 Calories; 8.5g Fat; 5.5g Carbs; 26.5g Protein; 2.7g Sugars*

Ingredients

1 pound duck breast, sliced
1/2 teaspoon red chili pepper
1 teaspoon cayenne pepper
1/2 teaspoon sea salt
1/2 teaspoon mustard powder
1/2 teaspoon freshly ground black pepper
1 tablespoon tallow, melted

1/4 cup Port wine
2 medium-sized shallots, sliced
2 garlic cloves, minced
1 (1-inch) piece fresh ginger, peeled and grated
1 pound wild mushrooms, sliced
1 cup water
1 mushroom soup cube

Directions

- Season duck breast with chili pepper, cayenne pepper, salt, mustard powder, and black pepper.
- Press the "Sauté" button to heat up your Instant Pot. Then, melt the tallow. Sear the seasoned duck for 4 to 6 minutes, turning periodically; set it aside.
- Pour in Port wine to scrape up any brown bits from the bottom of the Instant Pot. Stir in the remaining ingredients.
- Secure the lid. Choose the "Poultry" mode and High pressure; cook for 20 minutes. Once cooking is complete, use a quick pressure release; carefully remove the lid. Serve immediately.

---

54. Classic Coq au Vin
(Ready in about 25 minutes | Servings 4)

Earthy chestnut mushrooms, shallots, tomatoes, and aromatics make this amazingly juicy chicken dish. You can replace red wine with chicken broth and add two tablespoons of cognac.
Per serving: *255 Calories; 12.1g Fat; 6.9g Carbs; 29.2g Protein; 2.7g Sugars*

Ingredients

2 teaspoons peanut oil
2 chicken drumettes
1 chicken breast
2 shallots, chopped
2 cloves garlic, crushed
1/2 pound chestnut mushrooms, halved
1 cup vegetable stock

1/3 cup red wine
Sea salt and ground black pepper, to your liking
1/2 teaspoon red pepper flakes
1/4 teaspoon curry powder
1/4 cup tomato puree
2 teaspoons all-purpose flour
2 sprigs fresh thyme, leaves picked

Directions

- Press the "Sauté" button and heat peanut oil. Add the chicken, skin-side down, and cook for 7 minutes or until browned; reserve.
- Now, add the shallots and sauté until they're tender and fragrant. Now, stir in the garlic and mushrooms, and cook until aromatic.
- Add 1/2 cup of vegetable stock and red wine, and scrape the bottom of your Instant Pot to loosen any stuck-on bits.
- Add the salt, black pepper, red pepper flakes, and curry powder; continue to cook, stirring constantly.
- Now, add the reserved chicken, tomato puree and the remaining 1/2 cup of vegetable stock. Sprinkle with all-purpose flour and fresh thyme leaves.
- Secure the lid. Choose the "Manual" and cook at High pressure for 11 minutes. Once cooking is complete, use a quick pressure release; carefully remove the lid. Bon appétit!

55. Christmas Chicken Cutlets
(Ready in about 20 minutes | Servings 4)

What could be better than pressure-cooked chicken cutlets topped with zingy, buttery sauce?! Serve with polenta or warm egg noodles.
Per serving: *190 Calories; 8.4g Fat; 4.3g Carbs; 23.6g Protein; 2g Sugars*

Ingredients

1 pound chicken cutlets, pounded to 1/4-inch thickness
2 garlic cloves, peeled and halved
1/3 teaspoon salt
Ground black pepper and cayenne pepper, to taste
2 teaspoons sesame oil
3/4 cup water
1 ½ tablespoons dry sherry

1 chicken bouillon cube
2 tablespoons fresh lime juice
1 teaspoon dried thyme
1 teaspoon dried marjoram
1 teaspoon mustard powder
3 teaspoons butter, softened

Directions

- Rub the chicken with garlic halves; then, season with salt, black pepper, and cayenne pepper. Press the "Sauté" button.
- Once hot, heat sesame oil and sauté chicken cutlets for 5 minutes, turning once during cooking. Add water and dry sherry and stir; scrape the bottom of the pan to deglaze.
- Secure the lid. Choose the "Manual" mode and High pressure; cook for 4 minutes. Once cooking is complete, use a quick pressure release; carefully remove the lid. Reserve the chicken cutlets, keeping them warm.
- Stir bouillon cube, lime juice, thyme, marjoram, and mustard powder into the cooking liquid.
- Press the "Sauté" button and simmer for 6 minutes or until the cooking liquid has reduced and concentrated.
- Add the butter to the sauce, stir to combine, and adjust the seasonings. Pour the prepared sauce over reserved chicken cutlets and serve warm. Bon appétit!

---

56. Easy Autumn Chicken Soup
(Ready in about 40 minutes | Servings 6)

This is the perfect meal for cold fall days. All of the comfort with minimal effort.
Per serving: *245 Calories; 14.6g Fat; 9.8g Carbs; 18.5g Protein; 2.7g Sugars*

Ingredients

1 pound chicken thighs
2 carrots, trimmed and chopped
2 parsnips, chopped
1 celery with leaves, chopped
1 leek, chopped
2 garlic cloves, minced
6 cups chicken stock, preferably homemade
1 teaspoon dried basil
1/2 teaspoon sea salt
Freshly ground black pepper, to taste
1 tablespoon fresh coriander leaves, chopped

Directions

- Simply throw all of the above ingredients into your Instant Pot.
- Secure the lid. Choose the "Meat/Stew" mode and High pressure; cook for 35 minutes. Once cooking is complete, use a quick pressure release; carefully remove the lid.
- Serve in individual bowls garnished with garlic croutons. Enjoy!

57. Hot Chicken Drumsticks with Parsley Dip
(Ready in about 1 hour 15 minutes | Servings 6)

This parsley dipping sauce makes chicken drumsticks exciting again. And remember – anything pork can do, chicken can do better!
Per serving: *468 Calories; 37.8g Fat; 2.1g Carbs; 28.7g Protein; 0.7g Sugars*

Ingredients

2 garlic cloves, minced
1 cup dry white wine
1 red chili pepper
Sea salt and ground black pepper, to taste
1/4 cup sesame oil
6 chicken drumsticks

Parsley Dip:
1/2 cup fresh parsley leaves, chopped
1/3 cup cream cheese
1/3 cup mayonnaise
1 garlic clove, minced
1/2 teaspoon cayenne pepper
1 tablespoon fresh lime juice

Directions

- Place garlic, whine, chili pepper, salt, black pepper, and sesame oil in a ceramic container. Add chicken drumsticks; let them marinate for 1 hour in your refrigerator.
- Add the chicken drumsticks, along with the marinade, to the Instant Pot.
- Secure the lid. Choose the "Poultry" setting and cook for 10 minutes. Once cooking is complete, use a quick pressure release; carefully remove the lid.
- In a mixing bowl, thoroughly combine parsley, cream cheese mayonnaise, garlic, cayenne pepper, and lime juice.
- Serve chicken drumsticks with the parsley sauce on the side. Bon appétit!

58. Chèvre Stuffed Turkey Tenderloins
(Ready in about 35 minutes | Servings 4)

This classic turkey dish is elegant enough to serve for a festive Thanksgiving dinner but simple enough for an everyday lunch.
Per serving: *475 Calories; 25.4g Fat; 8.2g Carbs; 50g Protein; 2.9g Sugars*

Ingredients

3 tablespoons olive oil
2 shallots, chopped
2 garlic cloves, smashed
1 carrot, chopped
1 parsnip, chopped
2 tablespoons fresh coriander, chopped
Sea salt and freshly ground black pepper, to your liking
1 teaspoon paprika

1 cup dried bread flakes
1/2 teaspoon garlic powder
1/2 teaspoon cumin powder
1/3 teaspoon turmeric powder
2 ½ cups turkey stock, preferably homemade
4 ounces chèvre cheese
2 pounds turkey breast tenderloins

Directions

- Press the "Sauté" button to preheat your Instant Pot. Now, heat 1 tablespoon of olive oil and sauté the shallots, garlic, carrot, and parsnip until they have softened.
- Add coriander, salt, black pepper, paprika, dried bread flakes, garlic powder, cumin, and turmeric powder; stir to combine well.
- Now, slowly and gradually pour in 1/2 cup of turkey stock. Add chèvre and mix to combine well.
- Place the turkey breast on a work surface and spread the stuffing mixture over it. Tie a cotton kitchen string around each tenderloin.
- Press the "Sauté' button on High heat.
- Once hot, add the remaining 2 tablespoons of olive oil. Sear turkey about 4 minutes on each side. Add the remaining turkey stock and secure the lid.
- Choose "Manual", High pressure and 25 minutes cooking time. Use a natural pressure release; carefully remove the lid. Transfer stuffed turkey tenderloins to a serving platter.
- Press the "Sauté" button again and thicken the cooking liquid. Serve with stuffed turkey tenderloins and enjoy!

59. Chicken Breasts with Gruyère Sauce
(Ready in about 15 minutes | Servings 4)

Prepare this chicken recipe and start your week off right! Seriously, chicken breast with cheese sauce will blow your mind.
Per serving: *268 Calories; 14.9g Fat; 1.5g Carbs; 30.5g Protein; 0.8g Sugars*

Ingredients

1 tablespoon olive oil
4 chicken breasts halves
1/4 teaspoon ground black pepper, or more to taste
1/4 teaspoon ground bay leaf
1/2 teaspoon dried basil
Salt, to taste
1 teaspoon dried marjoram
1 cup water

Cheese Sauce:
2 tablespoons mayonnaise
1/2 cup Gruyère cheese, grated
1/2 cup Cottage cheese, at room temperature
1 teaspoon garlic powder
1/2 teaspoon porcini powder

Directions

- Press the "Sauté" button to heat up your Instant Pot; heat the oil. Once hot, sear the chicken breasts for 2 minutes per side.
- Add black pepper, ground bay leaf, dried basil, salt, and marjoram; pour in the water.
- Secure the lid. Choose the "Poultry" setting and cook for 5 minutes at High pressure. Once cooking is complete, use a natural pressure release; carefully remove the lid.
- Clean the Instant Pot and press the "Sauté" button again. Add the sauce ingredients and stir until everything is heated through.
- Top the chicken with the sauce and serve immediately. Bon appétit!

---

60. Festive Turkey and Cheese Meatloaf
(Ready in about 35 minutes | Servings 8)

This cheesy meatloaf is pressure cooked with tomato paste and Italian seasonings. Comfort food at its finest.
Per serving: *387 Calories; 24g Fat; 5g Carbs; 36.9g Protein; 1.7g Sugars*

Ingredients

1 ½ pounds ground turkey
1 pound ground pork
1 cup breadcrumbs
1 cup Romano cheese, grated
1 tablespoon Worcestershire sauce
1 egg, chopped
Salt and ground black pepper, to taste
1/2 cup scallions, chopped

2 garlic cloves, minced
6 ounces tomatoes, puréed
2 tablespoons tomato ketchup
1/2 cup water
1 teaspoon Old Sub Sailor seasoning

Directions

- Prepare your Instant Pot by adding a metal rack and 1 ½ cups of water to the bottom.
- In a large mixing bowl, thoroughly combine ground turkey, pork, breadcrumbs, Romano cheese, Worcestershire sauce, egg, salt, black pepper, scallions, and garlic.
- Shape this mixture into a meatloaf; place the meatloaf in a baking dish and lower the dish onto the rack.
- Then, in a mixing bowl, thoroughly combine puréed tomatoes, ketchup, water, and Old Sub Sailor seasoning. Spread this mixture over the top of your meatloaf.
- Secure the lid. Choose the "Meat/Stew" setting and cook for 20 minutes at High pressure. Once cooking is complete, use a natural pressure release; carefully remove the lid.
- You can place the meatloaf under the preheated broiler for 4 to 6 minutes if desired. Bon appétit!

61. Holiday Chicken Salad
(Ready in about 15 minutes + chilling time | Servings 6)

A good chicken salad is a must have during the holiday season. Luckily, you don't need to be an expert chef to make the chicken salad.
Per serving: *337 Calories; 23.7g Fat; 3.1g Carbs; 26.4g Protein; 0.9g Sugars*

Ingredients

1 ½ pounds chicken breasts
1 cup water
1 fresh or dried rosemary sprig
1 fresh or dried thyme sprig
2 garlic cloves
1/2 teaspoon seasoned salt
1/3 teaspoon black pepper, ground

2 bay leaves
1 teaspoon yellow mustard
1 cup mayonnaise
2 tablespoons sour cream
1 yellow onion, thinly sliced
1 carrot, grated
2 stalks celery, chopped

Directions

- Place the chicken, water, rosemary, thyme, garlic, salt, black pepper, and bay leaves in the Instant Pot.
- Secure the lid. Choose the "Poultry" setting and cook for 10 minutes under High pressure. Once cooking is complete, use a natural pressure release; carefully remove the lid.
- Remove the chicken breasts from the Instant Pot and allow them to cool.
- Slice the chicken breasts into strips; place the chicken in a salad bowl. Add the remaining ingredients; stir to combine well. Serve well-chilled.

---

62. Hungarian Turkey Paprikash
(Ready in about 20 minutes | Servings 4)

Traditional Hungarian Paprikash will please the whole family. The turkey legs, vegetables, and seasonings all cook in the Instant Pot for a memorable flavor. The recipe is generous with meat and root veggies for your well-balanced diet.
Per serving: *403 Calories; 18.5g Fat; 17.1g Carbs; 40.9g Protein; 6g Sugars*

Ingredients

2 tablespoons butter, at room temperature
1 pound turkey legs
Sea salt and ground black pepper, to taste
2 cups turkey stock
1/2 cup leeks, chopped
2 garlic cloves, minced
1 red bell pepper, chopped
1 green bell pepper, chopped

1 Serrano pepper, chopped
1 parsnip, chopped
1 cup turnip, chopped
1/2 pound carrots, chopped
2 tablespoons fresh cilantro leaves, chopped
1/2 teaspoon Hungarian paprika

Directions

- Press the "Sauté" button to preheat your Instant Pot and melt the butter. Now, sear the turkey, skin side down, 3 minutes on each side.
- Sprinkle turkey legs with salt and black pepper as you cook them.
- Stir the remaining ingredients into the Instant Pot. Secure the lid and select the "Manual" mode. Cook for 15 minutes at High pressure.
- Once cooking is complete, use a natural pressure release. Transfer the turkey legs to a bowl and let them cool. Then, strip the meat off the bones, cut it into small pieces and return to the Instant Pot.
- Serve hot and enjoy!

63. Thai-Style Chicken with Mushrooms
(Ready in about 20 minutes | Servings 6)

Make an authentic-tasting Thai chicken in the Instant Pot. Serve over hot wild rice.
Per serving: *296 Calories; 19.6g Fat; 4.9g Carbs; 26.3g Protein; 0.2g Sugars*

Ingredients

1 tablespoon peanut oil
1 ½ pounds chicken breast, cubed
1 stalk lemongrass
1/2 teaspoon cayenne pepper
Salt and freshly ground black pepper, to taste
1 tablespoon red Thai curry paste
1 ½ cups button mushrooms, sliced

2 garlic cloves, minced
1 cup vegetable broth
1 tablespoon fish sauce
1 cup coconut cream
1 tablespoon fresh coriander

Directions

- Press the "Sauté" button to heat up the Instant Pot; heat the oil. Once hot, cook the chicken for 5 minutes, stirring periodically.
- Add the lemongrass, cayenne pepper, salt, black pepper, and Thai curry paste, mushrooms, and garlic. Continue to sauté for 3 minutes more or until the mushrooms are fragrant.
- Now, stir in vegetable broth and fish sauce.
- Secure the lid. Choose the "Manual" setting and cook for 10 minutes at High pressure. Once cooking is complete, use a quick pressure release; carefully remove the lid.
- Afterwards, fold in the coconut cream; press the "Sauté" button and stir until the sauce is reduced and thickened. Serve garnished with fresh coriander. Bon appétit!

---

64. Crispy Chicken Carnitas
(Ready in about 25 minutes | Servings 6)

Here is a perfect chicken recipe for your weekend fiesta. The Instant Pot makes it faster than take-out.
Per serving: *227 Calories; 9g Fat; 3.1g Carbs; 31.9g Protein; 1.7g Sugars*

Ingredients

2 pounds chicken stew meat, cut into pieces
2 cloves garlic, pressed
1 teaspoon chili powder
1 teaspoon dried Mexican oregano
2 tablespoons olive oil
2/3 cup vegetable stock
Sea salt and ground black pepper, to taste
1/2 teaspoon paprika
1/3 cup apple juice
2 tablespoons fresh coriander, chopped

Directions

- Simply throw all of the above ingredients, except for coriander, in the Instant Pot.
- Secure the lid. Choose the "Poultry" setting and cook for 15 minutes. Once cooking is complete, use a quick pressure release; carefully remove the lid.
- Shred the chicken with two forks. Spread chicken on a sheet pan and broil for 7 minutes until crispy.
- Add fresh coriander leaves. Serve in taco shells and enjoy!

65. Old-Fashioned Chicken Soup
(Ready in about 25 minutes | Servings 4)

Two words: Chicken Soup. This recipe might become your go-to!
Per serving: *263 Calories; 9.9g Fat; 15.2g Carbs; 27.7g Protein; 3.3g Sugars*

Ingredients

1 ½ tablespoons butter, softened
1 cup leeks, thinly sliced
Sea salt and freshly ground black pepper, to taste
1 pound chicken wings, halved
2 carrots, chopped
1 celery with leaves, chopped
2 garlic cloves, finely minced

3 cups water
1 tablespoon chicken granulated bouillon
1 tablespoon flaxseed meal
1 tablespoon champagne vinegar
1/2 cup garlic croutons, to garnish

Directions

- Press the "Sauté" button to preheat your Instant Pot. Now, melt the butter; sauté the leeks until just tender and fragrant.
- Now, add the salt, pepper, chicken, carrots, celery, and garlic. Continue to sauté until the chicken is no longer pink and the vegetables are softened.
- Add a splash of water to prevent burning and sticking. Press the "Cancel" button. Add water and chicken granulated bouillon. Secure the lid.
- Choose the "Poultry" setting, High pressure. Cook for 20 minutes. Once cooking is complete, use a natural release.
- Then, press the "Sauté" button again. Make the slurry by whisking flaxseed meal with a few tablespoons of the cooking liquid. Return the slurry to the instant Pot and stir to combine.
- Add champagne vinegar and cook for 1 to 2 minutes more. Serve in individual bowls with garlic croutons. Bon appétit!

---

66. Turkey and Cheese Meatballs
(Ready in about 15 minutes | Servings 6)

Kids of all ages will love these meatballs! Don't forget to add your favorite chili powder for some extra oomph.
Per serving: *404 Calories; 24.9g Fat; 9.6g Carbs; 35.3g Protein; 3.1g Sugars*

Ingredients

1 ½ pounds ground turkey
2 eggs
1 yellow onion, chopped
2 garlic cloves, minced
1 cup tortilla chips, crumbled
1/2 teaspoon paprika
Kosher salt, to taste
1/4 teaspoon freshly ground black pepper
1/2 teaspoon dried basil

1/2 teaspoon dried oregano
8 ounces Swiss cheese, cubed
1 tablespoon olive oil
1/2 cup tomato, pureed
1/2 cup water
1 tablespoon sugar
1/2 teaspoon chili powder

Directions

- Thoroughly combine ground turkey, eggs, onion, garlic, crumbled tortilla chips, paprika, salt, pepper, basil, and oregano.
- Roll the mixture into meatballs. Press 1 cheese cube into center of each meatball, sealing it inside.
- Press the "Sauté" button to heat up your Instant Pot; now, heat the olive oil. Brown the meatballs for a couple of minutes, turning them periodically. Add the tomato sauce, water, sugar, and chili powder.
- Secure the lid. Choose the "Manual" setting and cook for 9 minutes under High pressure. Once cooking is complete, use a quick pressure release; carefully remove the lid. Bon appétit!

67. Stuffed Peppers with Yogurt
(Ready in about 20 minutes | Servings 6)

Using Greek-style yogurt, it's next level ingredient your stuffed peppers deserve. In addition, you only have one pot to clean up.
Per serving: *321 Calories; 19.7g Fat; 8.8g Carbs; 27.9g Protein; 5.1g Sugars*

Ingredients

2 teaspoons olive oil
1 ½ pounds ground chicken
1 red onion, chopped
1 teaspoon garlic, minced
Sea salt and ground black pepper, to taste
1 teaspoon cayenne pepper
1/4 teaspoon ground cumin
5 ounces Colby cheese, grated
6 bell peppers, tops, membrane and seeds removed
1 cup Greek-Style yogurt

Directions

- Press the "Sauté" button to heat up the Instant Pot. Then, heat the oil until sizzling.
- Cook the chicken with onion and garlic for 3 minutes, stirring periodically. Add the salt, black pepper, cayenne pepper, and cumin; stir to combine.
- Fold in Colby cheese, stir, and reserve.
- Wipe down the Instant Pot with a damp cloth. Add 1 ½ cups of water and a metal rack to the Instant Pot.
- Fill the peppers with the meat/cheese mixture; don't pack the peppers too tightly.
- Place the peppers on the rack and secure the lid. Choose the "Poultry" mode and High pressure; cook for 15 minutes.
- Once cooking is complete, use a natural pressure release; carefully remove the lid. Serve with Greek-style yogurt and enjoy!

---

68. Spicy Mexican-Style Chicken Drumettes
(Ready in about 15 minutes | Servings 3)

Spice up your weeknight dinner with these Mexican-inspired chicken drumettes. Mexican oregano with its citrus notes is slightly different than Mediterranean oregano, but you can use them interchangeably in this recipe.
Per serving: *199 Calories; 4.3g Fat; 7.1g Carbs; 32.2g Protein; 3.4g Sugars*

Ingredients

6 chicken drumettes, skinless and boneless
Seasoned salt and ground black pepper, to taste
1/2 teaspoon red pepper flakes, crushed
1/2 teaspoon Mexican oregano
2 ripe tomatoes, chopped
2 garlic cloves, minced

1 teaspoon fresh ginger, grated
1 Cascabel chili pepper, minced
1/2 cup scallions, chopped
1 tablespoon fresh coriander, minced
1 tablespoon fresh lime juice

Directions

- Press the "Sauté" button to heat up your Instant Pot. Sear the chicken drumettes for 3 minutes on each side or until they are browned.
- In a bowl, mix the remaining ingredients. Spoon the mixture over the browned chicken.
- Secure the lid. Choose the "Manual" mode and High pressure; cook for 10 minutes. Once cooking is complete, use a natural pressure release; carefully remove the lid. Bon appétit!

69. Chicken-and-Bacon Meatballs

(Ready in about 15 minutes | Servings 6)

Here are elegant and flavorsome chicken-bacon meatballs for the perfect dinner party. Serve these irresistible balls over hot rice.
Per serving: *412 Calories; 23.1g Fat; 21.2g Carbs; 26g Protein; 7.2g Sugars*

Ingredients

1 ¼ pounds ground chicken
4 slices bacon, chopped
1 cup seasoned breadcrumbs
1 onion, finely chopped
3 garlic cloves, minced
1/2 tablespoon fresh rosemary, finely chopped
2 eggs, beaten
Salt and ground black pepper, to taste

1/2 teaspoon paprika
2 tablespoons olive oil
2 cups tomato purée
2 tablespoons Dijon mustard
1 tablespoon Worcestershire sauce
2 tablespoons ruby port
1/4 cup chicken broth

Directions

- Thoroughly combine the ground chicken, bacon, breadcrumbs, onion, garlic, rosemary, eggs, salt, black pepper, and paprika.
- Shape the mixture into meatballs and reserve.
- Press the "Sauté" button on High heat to preheat your Instant Pot. Heat olive oil and sear the meatballs until they are browned on all sides; work in batches.
- Add the other ingredients. Choose the "Manual" setting and cook at High pressure for 7 minutes. Use a quick pressure release and carefully remove the lid. Bon appétit!

---

70. Cheddar and Chicken Bake

(Ready in about 30 minutes | Servings 6)

This cheese and chicken bake might earn a permanent spot in your weekly meal plan. Regular, full-fat mayonnaise is a perfect addition to this surprisingly delicious dish.
Per serving: *424 Calories; 28.7g Fat; 7.2g Carbs; 33.2g Protein; 2.8g Sugars*

Ingredients

2 tablespoons butter
1 ½ pounds chicken breasts
2 garlic cloves, halved
1 teaspoon cayenne pepper
1/2 teaspoon mustard powder
Sea salt, to taste
1/2 teaspoon ground black pepper
8 ounces Cheddar cheese, sliced
1/2 cup mayonnaise
1 cup Parmesan cheese, grated

Directions

- Press the "Sauté" button to heat up the Instant Pot. Melt the butter; sear the chicken for 2 to 3 minutes per side.
- Add garlic and continue to sauté for 30 seconds more. Season with cayenne pepper, mustard powder, salt, and black pepper.
- Add cheddar cheese and mayonnaise; top with grated Parmesan cheese.
- Secure the lid. Choose the "Meat/Stew" mode and High pressure; cook for 20 minutes. Once cooking is complete, use a quick pressure release; carefully remove the lid. Bon appétit!

71. Chicken Sandwiches with Mayo and Cheese
(Ready in about 20 minutes | Servings 4)

Chicken sandwiches are one of the most popular recipes in the world. Thanks to the Instant Pot, you can make them in just 20 minutes.
Per serving: *439 Calories; 20.1g Fat; 24.1g Carbs; 38.6g Protein; 4.5g Sugars*

Ingredients

1 pound chicken breasts
Sea salt and ground black pepper, to taste
2 bay leaves
1 cup vegetable stock
4 hamburger buns
1 tablespoon Dijon mustard
4 tablespoons mayonnaise
4 ounces goat cheese, crumbled
1/2 cup tomatoes, sliced

Directions

- Add the chicken, salt, black pepper, bay leaves, and stock to the Instant Pot.
- Secure the lid. Choose the "Poultry" setting and cook for 15 minutes under High pressure. Once cooking is complete, use a quick pressure release; carefully remove the lid.
- Assemble your sandwiches with chicken, hamburger buns, mustard, mayo, goat cheese, and tomatoes. Serve and enjoy!

---

72. Sloppy Joe with a Twist
(Ready in about 15 minutes | Servings 6)

Comforting and full of flavor, Sloppy Joe is the perfect weekday autumn meal. Could it be any more vintage?
Per serving: *329 Calories; 23.3g Fat; 3.2g Carbs; 25.1g Protein; 1.7g Sugars*

Ingredients

1 tablespoon olive oil
1 pound ground chicken
1/2 pound ground pork
2 garlic cloves, minced
1 yellow onion, chopped
2 tomatoes, chopped
1 cup chicken broth
Sea salt and ground black pepper, to taste
1/2 teaspoon paprika
1/2 teaspoon porcini powder
1/2 teaspoon fennel seeds
2 bay leaves

Directions

- Press the "Sauté" button to heat up your Instant Pot; heat the oil. Now, cook the ground meat until it is delicately browned; reserve.
- Sauté the garlic and onion in pan drippings for 2 to 3 minutes. Stir in the remaining ingredients.
- Now, secure the lid. Choose the "Poultry" setting and cook for 5 minutes under High pressure.
- Once cooking is complete, use a natural pressure release; carefully remove the lid.
- Spoon the mixture on toasted slider buns and serve.

73. Asian Honey-Glazed Chicken with Peanuts
(Ready in about 25 minutes | Servings 4)

Take your chicken from blah to extraordinary by using the Instant Pot and the best ingredients!
Per serving: *435 Calories; 12.3g Fat; 55.2g Carbs; 30g Protein; 41.9g Sugars*

Ingredients

1 pound chicken, cubed
1 teaspoon paprika
Salt and black pepper, to taste
1/2 teaspoon cassia
1 tablespoon butter, melted
1/2 cup honey
4 garlic cloves, minced

1 ¼ cups water
1/2 cup Worcestershire sauce
1/2 pound mushrooms, sliced
1 teaspoon Sriracha
1 ½ tablespoons lemongrass
1 ½ tablespoons arrowroot powder
1/4 cup peanuts, chopped

Directions

- Press the "Sauté" button to preheat your Instant Pot. Toss chicken cubes with paprika, salt, black pepper, and cassia.
- Heat the butter and sauté the chicken for 4 minutes, stirring periodically. After that, stir in honey, garlic, water, Worcestershire sauce, mushrooms, Sriracha, and lemongrass; stir well to combine.
- Secure the lid and choose the "Poultry" mode. Cook for 12 minutes. Afterwards, use a natural release and carefully remove the lid.
- Press the "Sauté" button.
- To make a thickener, add arrowroot powder to a small bowl; add a cup or so of the hot cooking liquid and whisk until they're combined.
- Add the thickener to the Instant Pot and cook for 4 to 5 minutes more or until the sauce has thickened. Garnish with chopped peanuts. Bon appétit!

---

74. Bacon Wrapped Chicken with Bourbon Sauce
(Ready in about 35 minutes | Servings 3)

Here's a delicious and sophisticated holiday recipe. However, you'll be making this out-of-this-world dish on repeat all year long.
Per serving: *414 Calories; 24.8g Fat; 8.3g Carbs; 38.5g Protein; 5.3g Sugars*

Ingredients

3 chicken breast halves, butterflied
2 garlic cloves, halved
Sea salt and ground black pepper, to taste
1 teaspoon cayenne pepper
1 teaspoon dried parsley flakes
1 teaspoon mustard powder
1/4 teaspoon ground allspice
6 slices bacon
1/2 cup BBQ sauce
2 tablespoons bourbon whiskey

Directions

- Add 1 ½ cups of water and metal trivet to the Instant Pot.
- Then, rub chicken breasts with garlic. Sprinkle the chicken with seasonings.
- Then, wrap each chicken breast into 2 bacon slices; secure with toothpicks. Lower wrapped chicken onto the metal trivet.
- Secure the lid. Choose the "Poultry" setting and cook for 15 minutes under High pressure. Once cooking is complete, use a natural pressure release; carefully remove the lid.
- Then, baste the chicken with BBQ Sauce and bourbon whiskey; bake in your oven for 15 minutes. Bon appétit!

75. Turkey, Pepper and Zucchini Bake
(Ready in about 15 minutes | Servings 4)

You can't go wrong with a combinations of vegetables, ground turkey and tomato paste. Cooked with minimal oil, this meat/veggie bake will fit into your weight-loss plan.

Per serving: *464 Calories; 24.4g Fat; 11.2g Carbs; 43.2g Protein; 1.8g Sugars*

Ingredients

1 tablespoon sesame oil
1 pound ground turkey
1/2 cup Romano cheese, grated
1/4 cup breadcrumbs
Salt and ground black pepper, to taste
1 teaspoon serrano pepper, minced
1 teaspoon garlic, smashed

1/2 teaspoon dried thyme
1 teaspoon dried basil
2 zucchini, thinly sliced
2 red bell pepper, sliced lengthwise into strips
1 cup tomato paste
1 teaspoon brown sugar
5 ounces Swiss cheese, freshly grated

Directions

- Press the "Sauté" button to heat up the Instant Pot. Now, heat the oil until sizzling.
- Then, sauté ground turkey until it is delicately browned, crumbling it with a spoon. Now, stir in cheese, crumbs, salt, black pepper, serrano pepper, garlic, thyme, and basil.
- Cook for 1 to 2 minutes more; reserve.
- Wipe down the Instant Pot with a damp cloth; brush the inner pot with a nonstick cooking spray. Arrange 1/2 of zucchini slices on the bottom.
- Spread 1/3 of meat mixture over zucchini. Place the layer of bell peppers; add ground meat mixture. Repeat the layering until you run out of ingredients.
- Next, thoroughly combine tomato paste and sugar. Pour this tomato mixture over the layers.
- Secure the lid. Choose the "Manual" mode and High pressure; cook for 10 minutes. Once cooking is complete, use a quick pressure release; carefully remove the lid.
- Afterwards, top your casserole with grated Swiss cheese; allow Swiss cheese to melt in the residual heat. Bon appétit!

---

76. Chicken Soup with Green Beans
(Ready in about 20 minutes | Servings 6)

Only one pot to clean! This is an easy and quick way to make a family chicken soup just like grandma used to make.

Per serving: *354 Calories; 10.8g Fat; 11.4g Carbs; 51.3g Protein; 5.3g Sugars*

Ingredients

4 chicken thighs
Kosher salt and ground black pepper, to taste
2 tablespoons ghee
2 shallots, chopped
4 cloves garlic minced
1 (1-inch) piece ginger root, finely chopped
2 carrots, thinly sliced
1 turnip, chopped
1/2 teaspoon dried oregano

1 teaspoon cayenne pepper
1/2 teaspoon dried rosemary
2 cups tomato puree
1 cup green beans
6 cups water
1 ½ tablespoons chicken bouillon granules
2 bay leaves
1/3 cup crumbled crackers, for garnish

Directions

- Season the chicken thighs with salt and black pepper to your liking. Press the "Sauté" button to preheat your Instant Pot.
- Once hot, melt the ghee and sear the chicken thighs for 3 minutes per side.
- Add the shallots, garlic, chopped ginger, carrot, and turnip; continue to sauté until just tender, about 4 minutes.
- Now, add oregano, cayenne pepper, and rosemary. Stir for 30 seconds more.
- Add tomato puree, green beans, water, chicken bouillon granules, and bay leaves. Secure the lid.
- Choose the "Manual", High pressure and 10 minutes. Once cooking is complete, use a natural release and carefully remove the lid. Discard bay leaves.
- Ladle into individual bowls and serve garnished with crumbled crackers.

77. Chicken Wings with Sesame Coleslaw
(Ready in about 25 minutes | Servings 4)

When you're looking for just the right thing to serve for family dinner, simply cook the chicken wings in the Instant Pot and serve them with the coleslaw. Simple but effective!
Per serving: *424 Calories; 28.3g Fat; 7.7g Carbs; 34.3g Protein; 3.9g Sugars*

Ingredients

2 teaspoons sesame oil
1 ½ pounds chicken wings, bone-in, skin-on
2 garlic cloves, minced
Sea salt and ground black pepper, to taste
1 teaspoon paprika
1 cup chicken bone broth

Sesame Cole Slaw:
1 cup white cabbage

1 red onion, thinly sliced
1 garlic clove, minced
1 ½ tablespoons sesame oil
1 tablespoon soy sauce
1 teaspoon honey
1 teaspoon mustard
1 tablespoon lemon juice, freshly squeezed
1 tablespoon toasted sesame seeds

Directions

- Press the "Sauté" button to heat up your Instant Pot. Then, heat 2 teaspoons sesame oil and sear the chicken wings for 2 to 3 minutes per side.
- Add a splash of chicken broth to scrape off any brown bits from the bottom of your Instant Pot.
- Secure the lid. Choose the "Poultry" mode and High pressure; cook for 15 minutes. Once cooking is complete, use a natural pressure release; carefully remove the lid.
- Meanwhile, mix all ingredients for the sesame coleslaw; place in your refrigerator until ready to serve. Serve with warm chicken wings. Bon appétit!

78. Rainbow Veggie Chicken Soup
(Ready in about 25 minutes | Servings 5)

Here's a rich, colorful and nourishing chicken soup your family will love for sure! Rose wine is the perfect addition that compliments this chicken dish.
Per serving: *238 Calories; 17g Fat; 5.4g Carbs; 16.4g Protein; 2.6g Sugars*

Ingredients

2 tablespoons olive oil
1 pound chicken drumettes
1 yellow onion, chopped
2 cloves garlic, minced
1 red bell peppers, seeded and sliced
1 green bell pepper, seeded and sliced
1 orange bell pepper, seeded and sliced
1 carrot, thinly sliced

1 parsnip, thinly sliced
1/4 cup Rose wine
Sea salt and ground black pepper, to your liking
1/2 teaspoon dried dill
1/2 teaspoon dried oregano
1 tablespoon granulated chicken bouillon
4 cups water

Directions

- Press the "Sauté" button to heat up your Instant Pot; now, heat the oil until sizzling. Then, sauté the onion and garlic until tender and fragrant.
- Add the peppers, carrots and parsnip; cook an additional 3 minutes or until the vegetables are softened. Add a splash of rose wine to deglaze the bottom of your Instant Pot.
- Then, stir in the remaining ingredients; stir to combine well.
- Secure the lid. Choose the "Soup" mode and High pressure; cook for 20 minutes. Once cooking is complete, use a quick pressure release. Carefully remove the lid.
- Remove the chicken wings from the cooking liquid; discard the bones and chop the meat.
- Add the chicken meat back to the Instant Pot, stir, and serve hot. Bon appétit!

79. Cavatappi and Meatball Soup
(Ready in about 20 minutes | Servings 6)

Pasta and soup can taste great together! With the help of your Instant Pot, you can come up with this last-minute soup that will make the whole family happy.
Per serving: *408 Calories; 18.4g Fat; 27.4g Carbs; 33.8g Protein; 2.8g Sugars*

Ingredients

1 pound ground turkey
1/2 pound ground pork
2 tablespoons fresh coriander, chopped
1/2 white onion, finely chopped
2 garlic cloves, minced
1 tablespoon oyster sauce
Sea salt and ground black pepper, to your liking
1 teaspoon cayenne pepper

1 whole egg
2 teaspoons sesame oil
1 pound cavatappi pasta
1 teaspoon dill weed
1 cup tomato puree
1 carrot, thinly sliced
1 celery with leaves, chopped
6 cups chicken stock

Directions

- Thoroughly combine ground meat, coriander, onion, garlic, oyster sauce, salt, black pepper, and cayenne pepper. Shape the mixture into meatballs; set aside.
- Press the "Sauté" button to heat up the Instant Pot. Heat the oil and sear the meatballs until they are browned on all sides.
- Now, stir in the remaining ingredients.
- Secure the lid. Choose the "Manual" setting and cook for 12 minutes under High pressure. Once cooking is complete, use a quick pressure release; carefully remove the lid. Bon appétit!

---

80. Sunday Turkey and Sausage Meatloaf
(Ready in about 25 minutes | Servings 6)

Make a juicy turkey meatloaf loaded with ground meat, flavorful sausage, eggs, and aromatics. Satisfying and delicious!
Per serving: *273 Calories; 14.8g Fat; 14.5g Carbs; 22.6g Protein; 4.5g Sugars*

Ingredients

3/4 pound ground turkey
1/2 pound cooked beef sausage, crumbled
1/2 cup tortilla chips, crushed
1/2 cup dried bread flakes
1 tablespoon oyster sauce
2 eggs
1 onion, chopped

2 garlic cloves, chopped
Salt and ground black pepper, to taste
1 teaspoon cayenne pepper
1 cup tomato puree
3 teaspoons brown sugar

Directions

- In a mixing bowl, thoroughly combine ground turkey, beef sausage, tortilla chips, dried bread flakes, oyster sauce, eggs, onion, and garlic.
- Season with salt, black pepper, and cayenne pepper; stir until everything is well incorporated.
- Add 1 ½ cups of water to the bottom of your Instant Pot. Shape the meat mixture into a log that will fit into the steamer rack.
- Place the aluminum foil sling on the rack and carefully lower the meatloaf onto the foil. Mix tomato puree with 3 teaspoons of brown sugar. Spread this mixture over the top of your meatloaf.
- Secure the lid and choose the "Manual" mode. Cook at High pressure for 20 minutes or to an internal temperature of 160 degrees F.
- Once cooking is complete, use a natural release and carefully remove the lid. Bon appétit!

81. Chicken Sausage Chowder with Spinach
(Ready in about 15 minutes | Servings 8)

This rich chowder calls for chicken sausage, cauliflower and spinach. Serve with garlic croutons or a toasted cheese sandwich for a complete meal.

Per serving: *360 Calories; 28.1g Fat; 7.8g Carbs; 19.1g Protein; 2.7g Sugars*

Ingredients

1 tablespoon lard, melted
8 ounces chicken sausage, cooked and thinly sliced
1/2 cup scallions, chopped
1 teaspoon ginger garlic paste
1 pound cauliflower, chopped into florets
4 cups vegetable broth
1 pinch red pepper flakes
Kosher salt, to taste
1/2 teaspoon freshly ground black pepper, to taste
1 cup spinach, torn into pieces

Directions

- Add all ingredients, except for spinach, to your Instant Pot.
- Secure the lid. Choose the "Manual" setting and cook for 9 minutes under High pressure. Once cooking is complete, use a quick pressure release; carefully remove the lid.
- Puree the mixture in your food processor.
- Afterwards, add spinach and seal the lid. Let it stand until the spinach is wilted. Serve in individual bowls. Enjoy!

82. The Best Turkey Beer Chili
(Ready in about 25 minutes | Servings 4)

Your next go-to chili recipe! If you are in a hurry, you can skip searing the ground turkey and just add it to the Instant Pot with the remaining ingredients.

Per serving: *484 Calories; 29.3g Fat; 14.1g Carbs; 41.5g Protein; 4.4g Sugars*

Ingredients

1 tablespoon olive oil
2 garlic cloves, finely minced
1/2 cup shallots, finely chopped
1 carrot, sliced
1 bell pepper, chopped
1 jalapeño pepper, chopped
1 pound ground turkey
1 cup chicken bone broth
6 ounces beer
1 tablespoon cacao powder

1 tablespoon apple butter
1 teaspoon dried basil
1 (14-ounce) can tomatoes
1 (14-ounce) can kidney beans, drained and rinsed

Directions

- Press the "Sauté" button to heat up your Instant Pot. Then, heat the oil; cook garlic, shallot, carrot, and bell peppers for about 5 minutes.
- Stir in the ground turkey and cook for 3 minutes more, crumbling with a fork.
- Secure the lid. Choose the "Poultry" setting and cook for 5 minutes under High pressure. Once cooking is complete, use a quick pressure release; carefully remove the lid. Serve hot and enjoy!

83. Spicy Chicken Lasagna
(Ready in about 20 minutes | Servings 6)

Here is a great twist to a classic lasagna. This chicken version is spicy, light, and diet-friendly.
Per serving: *335 Calories; 19.4g Fat; 17.6g Carbs; 23.8g Protein; 5.1g Sugars*

Ingredients

1 tablespoon olive oil
1 onion, chopped
1 serrano pepper, seeded and chopped
1 bell pepper, seeded and chopped
2 garlic cloves, minced
1 pound ground chicken
2 slices bacon, chopped

Sea salt and ground black pepper, to taste
1 (28-ounce) can tomatoes, crushed
1 cup chicken stock
8 ounces lasagna noodles
1 cup Pepper-Jack cheese, grated

Directions

- Press the "Sauté" button to heat up your Instant Pot. Heat the oil until sizzling. Then, sauté onion, peppers, and garlic about 5 minutes or until they are fragrant and tender.
- Stir in the ground chicken; continue to cook an additional 3 minutes.
- Stir in the bacon, salt, pepper, tomatoes, stock, and noodles.
- Secure the lid. Choose the "Poultry" setting and cook for 10 minutes under High pressure. Once cooking is complete, use a quick pressure release; carefully remove the lid.
- Top with Pepper-Jack cheese and seal the lid. Let it sit in the residual heat until it is melted. Bon appétit!

---

84. Juicy Turkey Breasts with Apricot Sauce
(Ready in about 20 minutes | Servings 8)

Forget boring turkey recipes during holidays! Enjoy the comfort of a sophisticated turkey dish with minimal effort.
Per serving: *256 Calories; 10.2g Fat; 5.9g Carbs; 33.1g Protein; 5.2g Sugars*

Ingredients

2 teaspoons sesame oil
2 pounds turkey breasts, cubed
Sea salt and freshly ground black pepper, to taste
1 teaspoon red pepper flakes, crushed
1 teaspoon dried rosemary
1/2 teaspoon dried sage
1/3 cup Port wine
1/3 cup chicken stock, preferably homemade

For the Sauce:
1/3 cup all-natural apricot jam
1 ½ tablespoons rice vinegar
1 teaspoon fresh ginger root, minced
1/2 teaspoon chili powder
1/2 teaspoon soy sauce
3 teaspoons honey

Directions

- Press the "Sauté" button and preheat your Instant Pot. Now, heat the oil; sear turkey breasts, stirring occasionally, for 3 to 4 minutes.
- Season turkey breasts with salt, black pepper, red pepper flakes, rosemary, and sage.
- Add Port wine and chicken stock to the Instant Pot and deglaze the bottom.
- Return turkey to the Instant Pot and secure the lid. Choose the "Manual" setting and High pressure. Cook for 10 minutes.
- Once cooking is complete, use a natural release and carefully remove the lid. Transfer turkey breasts to a platter.
- Add the sauce ingredients to the Instant Pot. Cook until the sauce reaches preferred consistency. Pour over turkey and serve immediately. Bon appétit!

85. Mediterranean Chicken Drumsticks
(Ready in about 20 minutes | Servings 4)

This homemade meal turns our perfect every time. Grab your Instant Pot and make this recipe tonight.
Per serving: *273 Calories; 14.4g Fat; 8.5g Carbs; 27.6g Protein; 3.6g Sugars*

Ingredients

1 pound chicken drumsticks
1 cup chicken stock
1 cup tomato puree
1 rosemary sprig, chopped
2 thyme sprigs, chopped
2 garlic cloves, minced
Sea salt and ground black pepper, to taste
1/2 teaspoon smoked paprika
1 bay leaf
1/2 cup Kalamata olives, pitted and sliced

Directions

- Add all ingredients to the Instant Pot; gently stir to combine well.
- Secure the lid. Choose the "Poultry" setting and cook for 15 minutes under High pressure. Once cooking is complete, use a quick pressure release; carefully remove the lid.
- You can thicken the sauce on the "Sauté" setting for a couple of minutes if desired.
- Divide chicken drumsticks among serving plates. Top with the sauce and enjoy!

---

86. Elegant Chicken Fillets with Apples
(Ready in about 20 minutes | Servings 4)

These tender chicken fillets are glazed with a sweet apple-flavored sauce. Your Instant Pot helps dinner come together easily.
Per serving: *341 Calories; 16.6g Fat; 19.1g Carbs; 28.9g Protein; 14.6g Sugars*

Ingredients

1 pound chicken fillets
Sea salt and ground black pepper, to taste
1/2 teaspoon smoked paprika
1/2 teaspoon ground bay leaf
1 teaspoon garlic powder
1 teaspoon shallot powder
1 tablespoon butter
1 tablespoon honey
1 tablespoon tamari sauce
2 cooking apples, cored, peeled and diced

Directions

- Place the chicken fillets on the bottom of the Instant Pot. Sprinkle the seasonings over the chicken fillets.
- Add the remaining ingredients.
- Secure the lid. Choose the "Manual" setting and cook for 7 minutes under High pressure. Once cooking is complete, use a quick pressure release; carefully remove the lid.
- Transfer to a serving platter and serve warm. Bon appétit!

87. Turkey and Arborio Rice Delight
(Ready in about 25 minutes | Servings 4)

Perfect for hectic days, this casserole is on the dining table in no time! Any white short-grain rice works well in this recipe.
Per serving: *498 Calories; 21.2g Fat; 25.4g Carbs; 59g Protein; 7.1g Sugars*

Ingredients

1 tablespoon butter, melted
2 chicken breasts, cut into slices
2 slices bacon, chopped
1 onion, chopped
1 serrano pepper, chopped
2 cloves garlic, finely minced
1/2 cup dry white wine

1 (28-ounce) can diced tomatoes
1 ½ cups water
1 cup Arborio rice
Sea salt and ground black pepper, to taste
1/2 teaspoon dried rosemary
1 teaspoon dried oregano

Directions

- Press the "Sauté" button to preheat your Instant Pot. Melt the butter. Then, sear the chicken breasts for 5 minutes. Set them aside.
- Stir in the bacon, onion, serrano pepper, and garlic; cook until the vegetables are tender.
- Stir in the remaining ingredients. Return the reserved chicken to the Instant Pot.
- Secure the lid. Choose the "Poultry" setting and cook for 15 minutes under High pressure. Once cooking is complete, use a quick pressure release; carefully remove the lid. Bon appétit!

---

88. Ranch Chicken Drumettes
(Ready in about 25 minutes | Servings 6)

These tender chicken drumettes take only about 25 minutes prep and cook time from start to finish. And they are surprisingly easy to fix in your Instant Pot!
Per serving: *189 Calories; 7.2g Fat; 6.3g Carbs; 23.5g Protein; 4.8g Sugars*

Ingredients

1 ½ pounds chicken drumettes
1 teaspoon celery salt
1/4 teaspoon freshly ground black pepper, or more to taste
1 ½ tablespoons butter, melted
1/4 cup tamari sauce
3 tablespoons brown sugar
2 tablespoons champagne vinegar
1 packet dry ranch salad dressing mix
1/2 cup onion, sliced
4 cloves garlic, smashed

Directions

- Season the chicken drumettes with celery salt and black pepper. Press the "Sauté" button and warm the butter.
- Now, sear the chicken pieces for 6 minutes or until browned on all sides.
- Add the remaining ingredients in the order listed above. Secure the lid.
- Choose the "Manual" setting and cook for 10 minutes at High pressure. Once cooking is complete, use a natural release and carefully remove the lid.
- You can thicken the sauce on the "Sauté" mode. Serve over hot cooked pasta and enjoy!

89. Chicken Legs with Shallots and Port Wine
(Ready in about 25 minutes | Servings 4)

As simple as it is delicious, this chicken meal appeals to everyone! It's a true family pleaser.
Per serving: *308 Calories; 17.6g Fat; 12.9g Carbs; 24.4g Protein; 6.2g Sugars*

Ingredients

1 pound chicken legs, bone-in
1 cup tomato puree
1 cup vegetable broth
1/4 cup Port wine
2 shallots, cut into wedges
1 teaspoon fresh ginger, grated

2 cloves garlic, chopped
Salt and freshly ground black pepper, to taste
1 teaspoon dried oregano
1 teaspoon dried rosemary

Directions

- Place the chicken legs in the Instant Pot. Pour in the tomato puree, vegetable broth, and Port wine.
- Secure the lid. Choose the "Poultry" setting and cook for 15 minutes under High pressure. Once cooking is complete, use a quick pressure release; carefully remove the lid.
- Stir in the remaining ingredients. Secure the lid. Choose the "Manual" setting and cook for 3 minutes under High pressure.
- Once cooking is complete, use a quick pressure release; carefully remove the lid. Serve warm and enjoy!

90. Turkey Fillets with Coconut-Mushroom Sauce
(Ready in about 30 minutes | Servings 6)

This good-for-you dish can be on your plate quicker than take-out! In addition, these turkey fillets turn out delicious and juicy every single time.
Per serving: *289 Calories; 18.3g Fat; 4.7g Carbs; 28g Protein; 0.6g Sugars*

Ingredients

1 tablespoon olive oil
1 ½ pounds turkey fillets
A bunch of scallions, chopped
2 cups Crimini mushrooms, halved or quartered
2 cloves garlic, peeled and crushed
Sea salt and freshly ground black pepper, to taste
1/2 teaspoon brown yellow mustard
1/2 teaspoon turmeric powder
1 cup water
1 cup coconut cream
1 teaspoon fresh coriander, minced

Directions

- Press the "Sauté" button to preheat your Instant Pot. Heat the oil and sear the turkey fillets for 2 to 3 minutes per side.
- Stir in the scallion, mushrooms and garlic; sauté them for 2 minutes more or until they are tender and fragrant.
- Next, add the salt, black pepper, mustard, turmeric powder, and water to the Instant Pot.
- Secure the lid. Choose the "Meat/Stew" setting and cook for 20 minutes under High pressure. Once cooking is complete, use a quick pressure release; carefully remove the lid.
- Then, fold in coconut cream and seal the lid. Let it sit in the residual heat until everything is thoroughly warmed. Garnish with coriander. Bon appétit!

91. Easy Chicken Française
(Ready in about 15 minutes | Servings 6)

These chicken wings are addictive! The recipe calls for Pinot Grigio, but feel free to use any dry white wine that you enjoy drinking.
Per serving: *273 Calories; 14.1g Fat; 5.3g Carbs; 27.8g Protein; 2.9g Sugars*

Ingredients

1 tablespoon butter, melted
2 pounds chicken wings, skin-on
2 garlic cloves, sliced
1 teaspoon mustard powder
1 teaspoon smoked paprika
Sea salt and ground black pepper, to taste
1/2 cup Pinot Grigio
1 cup tomato puree
1/2 cup water
1 cup cream cheese
1/2 lemon, cut into slices

Directions

- Press the "Sauté" button to preheat the Instant Pot. Melt the butter and brown the chicken wings for 1 to 2 minutes on each side.
- Stir in the garlic, mustard powder, paprika, salt, black pepper, Pinot Grigio, tomato puree, and water.
- Secure the lid. Choose the "Manual" mode and High pressure; cook for 10 minutes. Once cooking is complete, use a natural pressure release; carefully remove the lid.
- Serve with cream cheese and lemon slices. Bon appétit!

92. Classic Chicken Chasseur
(Ready in about 25 minutes | Servings 4)

With fragrant brown mushrooms and spices, the chicken chasseur is super addicting! You can skip the alcohol if desired.
Per serving: *343 Calories; 21.1g Fat; 14.4g Carbs; 24.4g Protein; 7g Sugars*

Ingredients

1 tablespoon olive oil
4 chicken drumsticks, skinless and boneless
1 red onion, chopped
1 celery with leaves, chopped
1 carrot, trimmed and chopped
3 garlic cloves, minced
1 teaspoon dried thyme
1/2 pound brown mushrooms, sliced

2 cups water
2 chicken bouillon cubes
Salt and ground black pepper, to taste
1 teaspoon paprika
2 bay leaves
1 tablespoon flour
4 tablespoons dry vermouth

Directions

- Press the "Sauté" button to preheat the Instant Pot. Now, heat the oil; cook the chicken until delicately browned on all sides; reserve.
- Then, sauté the onion, celery and carrot in pan drippings; sauté until tender or about 4 minutes.
- Now, stir in the garlic, thyme, mushrooms, water, bouillon cubes, salt, black pepper, paprika, and bay leaves; stir to combine well. Add the reserved chicken.
- Secure the lid. Choose the "Poultry" setting and cook for 15 minutes at High pressure. Once cooking is complete, use a natural pressure release; carefully remove the lid.
- Add flour and dry vermouth. Press the "Sauté" button again and let it simmer until the cooking liquid has reduced. Enjoy!

93. Dilled Turkey Thighs
(Ready in about 30 minutes | Servings 6)

If you enjoy spice food, add Sriracha, Tabasco sauce, or Tapatio. You can substitute a low-sodium chicken or vegetable broth for turkey bone broth.
Per serving: *257 Calories; 13.3g Fat; 5.6g Carbs; 27.2g Protein; 3.8g Sugars*

Ingredients

2 tablespoons lard, melted
1 ½ pounds turkey thighs
Sea salt, to taste
1/2 teaspoon ground black pepper
1/2 teaspoon paprika
1 teaspoon dried dill weed

1 shallot, chopped
1 cup turkey bone broth
1 tablespoon maple syrup
1/2 cup dry white wine

Directions

- Press the "Sauté" button to preheat the Instant Pot; melt the lard. Now, brown turkey thighs for 4 to 5 minutes on each side.
- Add the remaining ingredients.
- Secure the lid. Choose the "Meat/Stew" setting and cook for 20 minutes. Once cooking is complete, use a natural pressure release; carefully remove the lid.
- Press the "Sauté" button again to thicken the cooking liquid. Spoon the sauce over turkey thighs and serve warm.

94. Saucy Chicken Legs with Crimini Mushrooms
(Ready in about 20 minutes | Servings 4)

Here is one of the easiest ways to make the most comforting chicken dish. Chicken legs go perfectly with Cremini mushrooms.
Per serving: *384 Calories; 13.7g Fat; 10.5g Carbs; 51.8g Protein; 3.7g Sugars*

Ingredients

2 teaspoons sesame oil
4 chicken legs, skinless, bone-in
Salt, to your liking
2 garlic cloves, crushed
2 tablespoons spring onion, chopped
1 cup brown mushrooms, chopped
2 tablespoons dry sherry

1 teaspoon dried rosemary
1 cup water
1 tablespoon chicken bouillon granules
1 teaspoon brown sugar
2 tablespoons Worcestershire sauce
2 tablespoons arrowroot powder
4 tablespoons cold water

Directions

- Press the "Sauté" button to heat up your Instant Pot. Heat the oil; season the chicken with salt.
- Brown the chicken in the hot oil on all sides; reserve. Cook the garlic, onion, and mushrooms in pan drippings until they are tender and aromatic.
- Add dry sherry and deglaze the bottom of your Instant Pot with a wooden spoon.
- Add the rosemary, water, chicken bouillon granules, brown sugar, and Worcestershire sauce. Return the reserved chicken to the Instant Pot.
- Secure the lid. Choose the "Manual" setting and cook at High Pressure for 6 minutes. Once cooking is complete, use a natural release and carefully remove the lid.
- Meanwhile, whisk the arrowroot powder with cold water. Add the slurry to the Instant Pot to thicken the cooking liquid. Press the "Sauté" button and cook until the sauce has thickened.
- Spoon the sauce over the chicken and mushrooms and serve on individual plates. Enjoy!

95. Chicken Drumsticks with Aioli
(Ready in about 1 hour 15 minutes | Servings 4)

The flavors of this dish are bright, tangy, and irresistible. Minimal work but maximum pay-off. Enjoy!
Per serving: *441 Calories; 34.8g Fat; 3.4g Carbs; 27.1g Protein; 0.5g Sugars*

Ingredients

4 chicken drumsticks, bone-in, skin-on
2 teaspoons olive oil
1 tablespoon oyster sauce
1 cup water
1 tablespoon chicken bouillon granules
1/2 teaspoon freshly ground black pepper
1/2 cup dry white wine
3/4 cup mayonnaise
3 cloves garlic, minced
2 tablespoons lemon juice

Directions

- Place the chicken, olive oil, oyster sauce, water, chicken bouillon granules, black pepper and wine in a ceramic bowl.
- Allow it to marinate for 1 hour in your refrigerator. Add the chicken and marinade to the Instant Pot.
- Secure the lid. Now, press the "Manual" button. Cook for 12 minutes under High pressure.
- Once cooking is complete, use a natural pressure release; carefully remove the lid.
- In the meantime, mix mayonnaise with garlic and lemon juice until well combined. Serve chicken drumsticks with the aioli on the side. Bon appétit!

---

96. Turkey Tacos with Pico de Gallo
(Ready in about 15 minutes | Servings 6)

All of the comfort with minimal work. In addition, there is literally only one dirty pot to clean.
Per serving: *323 Calories; 12g Fat; 15.2g Carbs; 37.1g Protein; 2.8g Sugars*

Ingredients

2 pounds turkey breasts
1/2 cup turkey stock
2 garlic cloves, smashed
1/2 teaspoon seasoned salt
1/4 teaspoon ground black pepper
1/2 teaspoon crushed red pepper flakes
1/4 cup fresh cilantro leaves, chopped
6 corn tortillas, warmed
1 cup Pico de Gallo

Directions

- Put the turkey breast into your Instant Pot. Now, pour in the stock.
- Add garlic, salt, black pepper, red pepper flakes, and cilantro leaves. Secure the lid. Choose the "Manual" setting and cook for 10 minutes at High pressure.
- Once cooking is complete, use a natural release and carefully remove the lid. Shred the turkey breasts.
- Serve shredded turkey breasts over corn tortillas garnished with Pico de Gallo. Bon appétit!

97. Cheesy and Peppery Chicken Pottage
(Ready in about 15 minutes | Servings 4)

Rich and spicy, this chicken pottage calls for a crusty bread! If you prefer mild-tasting dishes, omit a jalapeño pepper.
Per serving: *463 Calories; 32.3g Fat; 11.1g Carbs; 32.6g Protein; 6.1g Sugars*

Ingredients

1 tablespoon olive oil
1 pound chicken fillets
2 cloves garlic, smashed
1 jalapeño pepper, seeded and chopped
1 white onion, chopped
1 red bell pepper, seeded and sliced
1 green bell pepper, seeded and sliced
1 orange bell pepper, seeded and sliced
1/2 teaspoon dried basil

1/2 teaspoon dried oregano
1 teaspoon dried sage
Kosher salt and ground black pepper, to taste
1 teaspoon cayenne pepper
1 cup roasted vegetable broth
1 cup heavy cream
1/2 cup cream cheese
1/2 cup Cheddar cheese, grated

Directions

- Press the "Sauté" button to preheat your Instant Pot. Now, heat the oil and cook chicken for 2 to 3 minutes per side.
- Stir in the garlic, jalapeño pepper, onion, and peppers.
- Add seasonings and gently stir to combine. Pour in the roasted vegetable broth.
- Secure the lid. Choose the "Poultry" setting and cook for 5 minutes at High pressure. Once cooking is complete, use a natural pressure release; carefully remove the lid.
- Now, add heavy cream, cream cheese and Cheddar cheese; press the "Sauté" button again and cook until cheesy is melted and everything is thoroughly heated. Serve immediately and enjoy!

---

98. Peasant Turkey Thigh Soup
(Ready in about 25 minutes | Servings 5)

Everyone will love this belly-warming soup. Serve with mashed cauliflower swirled into each serving.
Per serving: *194 Calories; 7.9g Fat; 12.7g Carbs; 18.8g Protein; 7.4g Sugars*

Ingredients

1 tablespoon peanut oil
1 medium-sized leek, chopped
1/2 teaspoon ginger-garlic paste
1 (28-ounce) can diced tomatoes
1 celery stalk, chopped
1 carrot, chopped
1/2 teaspoon dried rosemary

2 bay leaves
Sea salt and ground black pepper
1/2 teaspoon cayenne pepper
1 pound turkey thighs
5 cups turkey bone broth
2 tablespoons fresh coriander, roughly chopped

Directions

- Press the "Sauté" button to preheat your Instant Pot. Heat the peanut oil until sizzling. Cook the leek until tender.
- Add the ginger-garlic paste, tomatoes, celery, carrot, rosemary, bay leaves, salt, black pepper, cayenne pepper, turkey thighs, and broth.
- Secure the lid. Choose the "Soup" setting and cook for 20 minutes at High pressure. Once cooking is complete, use a quick pressure release; carefully remove the lid.
- Remove turkey thighs from the soup, shred the meat and discard the bones. After that, return the meat to the Instant Pot.
- Divide among five soup bowls. Top each bowl with fresh coriander and serve immediately.

99. Southwestern Chicken Salad
(Ready in about 15 minutes | Servings 5)

Not sure what to make for dinner? Here's the recipe for the easiest and most delicious chicken salad ever!
Per serving: *441 Calories; 30.2g Fat; 14.1g Carbs; 27.1g Protein; 3.7g Sugars*

Ingredients

2 chicken breasts, boneless and skinless
Seasoned salt and ground black pepper, to taste
1/2 teaspoon taco seasoning
1 sprig thyme
1 sprig rosemary
1 sprig sage
2 garlic cloves, pressed
1 cup green onions, sliced
1/2 cup sour cream

1/2 cup mayonnaise
1 teaspoon Dijon mustard
1 cup frozen corn, thawed
1 carrot, shredded
1 bell pepper, sliced
1/2 cup radishes, sliced
1 cucumber, chopped
2 tablespoons cilantro, chopped

Directions

- Add 1 ½ cups of water and a metal trivet to your Instant Pot.
- Then, season chicken breast with salt, black pepper and taco seasoning. Place the seasoned chicken breast onto the trivet. Top with thyme, rosemary, sage, and garlic.
- Now, secure the lid. Choose the "Poultry" setting and cook for 5 minutes under High pressure. Once cooking is complete, use a natural pressure release; carefully remove the lid.
- Allow the chicken to cool and cut it into strips. Stir in the remaining ingredients; gently stir to combine well. Serve well-chilled.

---

100. Four-Cheese Italian Butter Chicken
(Ready in about 15 minutes | Servings 4)

Here's an ideal, family dish for a weeknight! 4 -Cheese Italian cheese is a blend of smoked Provolone, Mozzarella, Romano and Asiago cheese.
Per serving: *193 Calories; 12.5g Fat; 5g Carbs; 15.8g Protein; 2.3g Sugars*

Ingredients

2 tablespoons butter, softened
3 garlic cloves, minced
2 rosemary sprigs, leaves picked
2 ripe tomatoes, chopped
1/2 teaspoon cumin, ground
1 teaspoon paprika

1/2 teaspoon curry powder
Salt and ground black pepper, to taste
4 chicken fillets, boneless and skinless
Water
1/2 cup 4-Cheese Italian, shredded
1/4 cup fresh chives, chopped

Directions

- Press the "Sauté" button to heat up your Instant Pot. Now, melt the butter.
- Add the garlic and rosemary, and sauté until they are fragrant.
- Now, stir in chopped tomatoes, ground cumin, paprika, curry powder, salt, and black pepper. Top with chicken fillets and pour in water to cover the chicken.
- Secure the lid and select the "Poultry" mode. Cook for 6 minutes. Once cooking is complete, use a natural release and carefully remove the lid.
- Press the "Sauté" button. Add shredded cheese and cook 2 to 3 minutes more or until cheese is melted. Serve right away garnished with fresh chopped chives. Bon appétit!

PORK

101. Summer Barbeque Pork Loin
(Ready in about 30 minutes | Servings 6)

Throwing a family lunch is easier than you thought. If you are in a hurry, feel free to use a store-bought barbecue sauce.
Per serving: *435 Calories; 18.9g Fat; 15.1g Carbs; 48.8g Protein; 12.4g Sugars*

Ingredients

3 pounds pork butt roast
1/2 cup water
1 cup ketchup
1/4 cup champagne vinegar
3 tablespoons brown sugar
1/2 teaspoon sea salt
1/2 tablespoon fresh ground black pepper.
1 teaspoon ground mustard
1 teaspoon garlic powder

Directions

- Add all of the above ingredients to your Instant Pot.
- Secure the lid and select the "Meat/Stew" mode. Cook for 20 minutes under High pressure. Once cooking is complete, use a natural pressure release; carefully remove the lid.
- Shred the meat and return it back to the Instant Pot. Serve the pork loin with the sauce and enjoy!

---

102. Pork Shoulder with Gravy
(Ready in about 45 minutes | Servings 4)

Here is an elegant pork recipe that is surprisingly easy to make. Using a fatty, flavorful pork shoulder guarantees an extraordinary dish.
Per serving: *379 Calories; 26.4g Fat; 3.2g Carbs; 30.3g Protein; 2.5g Sugars*

Ingredients

1 pound pork shoulder, cut into 4 pieces
Salt and ground black pepper, to taste
1/2 teaspoon cayenne pepper
1 ½ tablespoons lard, at room temperature
1 onion, thinly sliced
1 ½ teaspoons garlic paste
3/4 cup plain milk
1/2 teaspoon agar agar
2 tablespoons fresh cilantro leaves, chopped

Directions

- Add pork shoulder, salt, black pepper, cayenne pepper to a resealable plastic bag. Shake until the meat is coated on all sides.
- Press the "Sauté" button and heat the lard; once hot, sear the pork for 4 minutes on each side; reserve.
- Then, cook the onion in pan drippings until translucent. Now, add garlic paste and top with reserved pork.
- Secure the lid. Choose the "Manual" setting and cook at High pressure for 35 minutes. Once cooking is complete, use a natural release; carefully remove the lid.
- Remove the pork to a serving plate. Press the "Sauté" button again; add plain milk to the cooking liquid. Now, stir in agar-agar and whisk until it is dissolved.
- Allow it to simmer for 4 minutes or until the sauce has thickened. Serve pork shoulder, carrots, and broccoli garnished with the gravy and cilantro leaves. Bon appétit!

103. Creamy Smothered Pork Cutlets
(Ready in about 15 minutes | Servings 4)

Pork cutlets cook perfectly in the Instant Pot; in addition, you can turn cooking juices into a delicious sauce and ladle it over each serving.
Per serving: *334 Calories; 18.3g Fat; 5.8g Carbs; 34.2g Protein; 0.4g Sugars*

Ingredients

1 cup water
2 chicken bouillon cubes
2 cloves garlic, finely chopped
Sea salt and freshly ground black pepper, to taste
2/3 teaspoon cayenne pepper
1 pound pork cutlets
1 ½ tablespoons cornstarch, plus 2 tablespoons water
6 ounces Ricotta cheese

Directions

- Add water, bouillon cubes, garlic, salt, black pepper, cayenne pepper, and pork cutlets to the Instant Pot.
- Secure the lid. Choose the "Manual" setting and cook at High pressure for 8 minutes. Once cooking is complete, use a quick pressure release; carefully remove the lid.
- Then, whisk the cornstarch and water in a mixing bowl; add the slurry to the cooking liquid. Press the "Sauté" button and let it cook until thickened.
- Afterwards, fold in Ricotta cheese and serve immediately. Bon appétit!

104. Maple Mustard Pork Belly
(Ready in about 50 minutes | Servings 8)

Impress your family with this fork-tender and appetizing pork belly. If you tend to simplify things, this recipe will be your next family favorite.
Per serving: *475 Calories; 45.1g Fat; 6.1g Carbs; 8.1g Protein; 4.9g Sugars*

Ingredients

1 ½ pounds pork belly, scored and patted dry
1 teaspoon garlic paste
Sea salt and ground black pepper, to taste
1/2 teaspoon dried marjoram
1/2 teaspoon red pepper flakes, crushed
1/2 cup water
1/2 dry white wine
3 tablespoons maple syrup
1 teaspoon stone-ground mustard
1/2 teaspoon ground allspice

Directions

- Spread garlic paste over the pork belly; sprinkle with salt, black pepper, dried marjoram and red pepper flakes.
- Press the "Sauté" button to preheat your Instant Pot. Then, sear the pork belly for 3 minutes per side.
- In a mixing bowl, thoroughly combine water, wine, maple syrup, mustard, and allspice. Pour this mixture over the pork belly in the Instant Pot.
- Secure the lid. Choose the "Meat/Stew" setting and cook at High pressure for 40 minutes. Once cooking is complete, use a natural pressure release; carefully remove the lid.
- Cut the prepared pork belly into pieces; serve with some extra mustard, if desired. Bon appétit!

105. Boston Butt with Home-Style Sauce
(Ready in about 1 hour 5 minutes | Servings 8)

Boston butt, also known as pork butt, becomes exceptionally juicy and flavorful when it is cooked in the Instant Pot and then, soaked in home-style, zingy sauce.
Per serving: *333 Calories; 8.6g Fat; 55.5g Carbs; 10.8g Protein; 27.1g Sugars*

Ingredients

3 pounds Boston butt
1 teaspoon salt
1/2 teaspoon whole black peppercorns
1 bay leaf
1 teaspoon celery seeds
1 teaspoon fennel seeds

For the Sauce:

1 cup water
1 ½ cups ketchup
1/4 cup balsamic vinegar
4 tablespoons brown sugar
1 teaspoon shallot powder
1 teaspoon chipotle powder
1 tablespoon Worcestershire sauce

Directions

- Season Boston butt with salt and add it to the Instant Pot that is previously greased with a nonstick cooking spray.
- Add enough water to cover the meat. Stir in black peppercorns, bay leaf, celery seeds, and fennel seeds.
- Secure the lid and select the "Manual" mode. Cook for 55 minutes at High pressure.
- In the meantime, in a saucepan, place the remaining ingredients for the sauce. Bring this mixture to a boil, and then, immediately, reduce heat to medium-low.
- Cook until it is thickened and heated through, stirring continuously.
- Once cooking is complete, use a quick pressure release; remove the lid; reserve about 1 cup of cooking liquid. Shred the pork with two forks, add cooking liquid and stir to combine well.
- Serve with the prepared sauce.

---

106. Vermouth Pork Shanks with Vegetables
(Ready in about 40 minutes | Servings 4)

You can experiment with seasonings in this recipe because it is hard to fail! Here are some ideas: mustard seeds, thyme, marjoram, sage, ground allspice, and so forth.
Per serving: *348 Calories; 25.1g Fat; 12.1g Carbs; 17.3g Protein; 4.5g Sugars*

Ingredients

2 teaspoons olive oil
1 pound pork shanks, trimmed of skin
1 teaspoon turmeric powder
2 tablespoons vermouth
1 carrot, sliced
1 celery stalk, chopped
1 parsnip, sliced

1 bell pepper, deveined and sliced
1 serrano pepper, deveined and sliced
Sea salt and ground black pepper, to taste
1 teaspoon red pepper flakes, crushed
1 teaspoon garlic powder
1 cup beef bone broth
2 bay leaves

Directions

- Press the "Sauté" button to preheat your Instant Pot; heat the olive oil. Once hot, cook the pork shanks until they are delicately browned.
- Stir in the remaining ingredients.
- Secure the lid. Choose the "Meat/Stew" setting and cook at High pressure for 35 minutes. Once cooking is complete, use a natural pressure release; carefully remove the lid.
- Serve warm over mashed potatoes and enjoy!

107. Herbed Pork Steaks
(Ready in about 15 minutes | Servings 6)

A great pork steak is not just about the recipe. It's also about the reliable cooker. You could also try adding some chili peppers to give this pork an extra kick.

Per serving: *476 Calories; 44.2g Fat; 0.1g Carbs; 21.2g Protein; 0.1g Sugars*

Ingredients

2 teaspoons lard
1 ½ pounds pork steaks
1 cup roasted vegetable broth
2 sprigs rosemary
1 sprig thyme
1 tablespoon fresh parsley
Salt, to taste
1/2 teaspoon mixed peppercorns

Directions

- Press the "Sauté" button to preheat your Instant Pot; melt the lard. Once hot, sear the pork until delicately browned.
- Stir in the remaining ingredients.
- Secure the lid. Choose the "Manual" setting and cook at High pressure for 8 minutes. Once cooking is complete, use a quick pressure release; carefully remove the lid.
- Press the "Sauté" button to thicken the sauce. Serve warm and enjoy!

---

108. Sticky Pork Ribs
(Ready in about 30 minutes | Servings 8)

Pork ribs are a staple in the pressure cooker kitchen. Instant Pot turns pork ribs into a flavorful meal that everyone will love!

Per serving: *268 Calories; 8.9g Fat; 19.7g Carbs; 26.7g Protein; 15.1g Sugars*

Ingredients

2 pounds pork ribs
1/2 teaspoon ground black pepper
Sea salt, to taste
1 teaspoon garlic powder
1/2 teaspoon shallot powder
1 teaspoon paprika
1 cup tomato paste
1 (12-ounce) bottle light beer
1 tablespoon honey
1/2 cup beef bone broth
1 tablespoon ground cumin

Directions

- Add all ingredients to your Instant Pot.
- Secure the lid. Choose the "Meat/Stew" setting and cook at High pressure for 20 minutes. Once cooking is complete, use a natural pressure release; carefully remove the lid.
- Serve over roasted potatoes and enjoy!

109. Family Pork Stew
(Ready in about 15 minutes | Servings 5)

Your family will ever guess that this stew has not cooked all afternoon. Habanero pepper can lower your cholesterol and blood pressure as well as protect against prostate cancer.
Per serving: *279 Calories; 10.1g Fat; 18.1g Carbs; 30g Protein; 8.2g Sugars*

Ingredients

2 teaspoons olive oil
1 pound pork stew meat, cubed
1 cup tomato paste
2 tablespoons fresh cilantro, chopped
2 tablespoons fresh parsley, chopped
1 leek, chopped
1 habanero pepper, deveined and minced

1 teaspoon ginger-garlic paste
1 teaspoon ground cumin
1 teaspoon paprika
Kosher salt and black pepper, to taste
5 cups beef bone broth
1 cup sour cream, for garnish

Directions

- Press the "Sauté" button to preheat your Instant Pot; heat the oil. Now, sear the meat until it is delicately browned.
- Add tomato paste, cilantro, parsley, leek, habanero pepper, ginger-garlic paste, cumin, paprika, salt, black pepper, and broth.
- Secure the lid. Choose the "Manual" setting and cook at High pressure for 8 minutes. Once cooking is complete, use a quick pressure release; carefully remove the lid.
- Divide your stew among serving bowls; top each serving with sour cream. Enjoy!

---

110. Country-Style Spare Ribs
(Ready in about 30 minutes + marinating time | Servings 6)

An extraordinary blend of honey and three types of sauces caramelizes to create sticky ribs that will melt in your mouth.
Per serving: *388 Calories; 14.7g Fat; 19.2g Carbs; 42.2g Protein; 16.3g Sugars*

Ingredients

1/4 cup honey
1/4 cup soy sauce
2 tablespoons hoisin sauce
1/4 cup tomato sauce
2 garlic cloves, smashed
1 teaspoon fresh ginger, finely grated
2 teaspoons sesame oil
6 country-style spare rib rashes

1 teaspoon chili powder
Salt and black pepper, to your liking
1/2 teaspoon ground allspice
1 teaspoon whole grain mustard
1 teaspoon smoked paprika

Directions

- Thoroughly combine the honey, soy sauce, hoisin sauce, tomato sauce, garlic, ginger, and sesame oil in a bowl.
- Place the spare rib rashes in a large ceramic dish and pour over the honey/sauce. Cover with a plastic wrap and transfer to your refrigerator; let it sit at least 4 hours to develop the flavors.
- Add spare rib rashes to the Instant Pot; add the remaining ingredients, along with the reserved marinade.
- Secure the lid. Select the "Manual" button and cook for 23 minutes at High pressure.
- Once cooking is complete, use a natural release; remove the lid carefully. Now, press the "Sauté" button and continue to cook, uncovered, until the liquid is concentrated. Serve warm and enjoy!

111. Garden Vegetable Soup with Pork
(Ready in about 40 minutes | Servings 4)

Pork soup with vegetable is the ultimate comfort food. You can make a double batch and easily freeze the leftovers for later.
Per serving: *264 Calories; 8.6g Fat; 6.6g Carbs; 38.2g Protein; 2.5g Sugars*

Ingredients

1 tablespoon olive oil
1 pound pork stew meat, cubed
4 cups beef bone broth
1 cup scallion, chopped
1 carrot, sliced
1 celery, sliced
1 turnip, peeled and sliced
Sea salt and ground black pepper, to taste
2 cups spinach

Directions

- Press the "Sauté" button to preheat your Instant Pot; heat the oil. Now, sear the meat until it is delicately browned.
- Add the remaining ingredients, except for spinach.
- Secure the lid. Choose the "Soup" setting and cook at High pressure for 30 minutes. Once cooking is complete, use a quick pressure release; carefully remove the lid.
- Add spinach to the Instant Pot; seal the lid and allow it to sit in the residual heat until wilted.
- Ladle the soup into individual bowls and serve right away. Bon appétit!

---

112. Pork in Sweet Wine Sauce
(Ready in about 30 minutes | Servings 6)

A great-tasting pork shoulder dish that combines Riesling, honey, and herbs. Serve it with green beans.
Per serving: 483 Calories; 31g Fat; 7.3g Carbs; 38g Protein; 6.1g Sugars

Ingredients

2 tablespoons lard, melted
2 pounds pork shoulder, cut into four pieces
2 garlic cloves, chopped
2 tablespoons honey
1/2 cup Riesling
1/2 cup water
1 tablespoon Worcestershire sauce
2 sprigs rosemary
1 sprig thyme
Kosher salt and ground black pepper, to taste

Directions

- Press the "Sauté" button to preheat your Instant Pot. Melt the lard. Then, sear the meat for 2 to 3 minutes, stirring frequently.
- Add the remaining ingredients and gently stir to combine.
- Secure the lid. Choose the "Meat/Stew" setting and cook at High pressure for 20 minutes. Once cooking is complete, use a quick pressure release; carefully remove the lid. Bon appétit!

113. Texas-Style Pulled Pork Sandwiches
(Ready in about 1 hour 5 minutes + marinating time | Servings 6)

If you prefer the subtle flavor of your pulled pork, opt for salt, ground pepper, and paprika. If you want to take the flavor up a notch, don't be shy with seasonings!
Per serving: *518 Calories; 17.5g Fat; 72.5g Carbs; 15.6g Protein; 23.1g Sugars*

Ingredients

2 pounds Boston butt, cut into 4 pieces
1 teaspoon chipotle powder
Seasoned salt and ground black pepper, to your liking
1 teaspoon shallot powder
1/2 teaspoon granulated garlic
1 teaspoon mustard powder
1 teaspoon paprika
2 tablespoons lard, at room temperature

1 (16-ounce) bottle BBQ sauce
2 cloves garlic, peeled and pressed
6 burger buns, split
2 tablespoons butter, softened

Directions

- Place Boston butt, chipotle powder, salt, ground black pepper, shallot powder, granulated garlic, mustard powder, and paprika in a resealable plastic bag; shake to coat on all sides.
- Place seasoned Boston butt in your refrigerator for 3 hours.
- Now, press the "Sauté" button and add lard; once hot, sear the pork on all sides until it is just browned.
- Add BBQ sauce and garlic; secure the lid. Select the "Manual" button and cook for 55 minutes at High pressure.
- Once cooking is complete, use a natural release; remove the lid carefully.
- Remove the pork from the Instant Pot, and shred the meat with Bear Paws or two forks. Return the shredded pork to the Instant Pot, and stir it into the hot cooking juices.
- Spread the halves of burger buns with butter; then, toast the buns. Spoon pork into the toasted burger buns and eat warm. Bon appétit!

---

114. Saucy Pork Sausage with Macaroni
(Ready in about 15 minutes | Servings 6)

Sausages and macaroni are cooked in tomato purée and topped with sharp, yellow cheese. This dish might win your heart!
Per serving: *495 Calories; 15.2g Fat; 60g Carbs; 27.8g Protein; 4.5g Sugars*

Ingredients

1 tablespoon olive oil
1 yellow onion, finely chopped
2 cloves garlic, minced
1 pound pork sausage, casing removed, coarsely chopped
Salt, to taste
1/2 teaspoon ground black pepper
1/2 teaspoon red pepper flakes, crushed

1 teaspoon dried basil
1 teaspoon dried oregano
1 teaspoon stone-ground mustard
1 cup water
1 cup tomato purée
1 pound macaroni
4 ounces Colby cheese, shredded

Directions

- Press the "Sauté" button to preheat your Instant Pot. Then, heat the oil; now, cook the onion until translucent.
- Now, add garlic and sausage; continue to cook for 4 minutes more. Stir in the seasonings, mustard, water, tomato purée, and macaroni
- Secure the lid. Choose the "Manual" setting and cook at High pressure for 6 minutes. Once cooking is complete, use a quick pressure release; carefully remove the lid.
- Top with Colby cheese; seal the lid and let it sit in the residual heat until the cheese is melted. Bon appétit!

115. Apple Maple Pulled Pork
(Ready in about 35 minutes | Servings 8)

With Instant pot pulled pork, your family dinner becomes a breeze! Serve on hamburger buns with coleslaw on the side.
Per serving: *434 Calories; 25.2g Fat; 13.6g Carbs; 36.1g Protein; 10.5g Sugars*

Ingredients

2 ½ pounds pork butt, cut into bite-sized cubes
1/2 cup vegetable broth
1/2 cup barbecue sauce
Sea salt and ground black pepper
1 teaspoon dried oregano
1/2 teaspoon dried basil
1 tablespoon maple syrup
1 red chili pepper, minced
1 cooking apple, cored and diced
1 lemon, sliced

Directions

- Add pork, broth, barbecue sauce, salt, black pepper, oregano, basil, maple syrup, chili pepper, and apple to your Instant Pot.
- Secure the lid. Choose the "Soup" setting and cook at High pressure for 30 minutes. Once cooking is complete, use a natural pressure release; carefully remove the lid.
- Shred the pork with two forks. Return it back to the Instant Pot. Serve with lemon slices. Bon appétit!

116. Holiday Pork Ham Hock
(Ready in about 55 minutes | Servings 6)

Go gourmet with this pork recipe by adding ale beer and dried sage to the Instant Pot. Thanks to the Instant pot, you will keep a great texture and tenderness of the ham hocks. Enjoy!
Per serving: *304 Calories; 19.1g Fat; 2.6g Carbs; 30.5g Protein; 0.6g Sugars*

Ingredients

- 1 cup water
- 1/2 cup ale beer
- Sea salt and ground black pepper, to taste
- 1/2 teaspoon cayenne pepper, or more to taste
- 1/2 teaspoon marjoram
- 1/2 teaspoon dried sage, crushed
- A bunch of scallions, chopped
- 2 pounds pork ham hocks
- 2 bay leaves
- 2 garlic cloves, minced

Directions

- Place all of the above ingredients in the Instant Pot.
- Secure the lid. Choose the "Meat/Stew" setting and cook at High pressure for 45 minutes. Once cooking is complete, use a natural pressure release; carefully remove the lid.
- Remove ham hocks from the Instant Pot; allow them to cool enough to be handled. Remove meat from ham hocks and return it to the cooking liquid.
- Serve on individual plates and enjoy!

117. Old-Fashioned Pork Stew
(Ready in about 50 minutes | Servings 6)

Opt for a pork meat that will stay juicy even after a sear. Consequently, you will be rewarded with a super-juicy meat after pressure cooking.
Per serving: *307 Calories; 17.2g Fat; 4.8g Carbs; 31.1g Protein; 2.5g Sugars*

Ingredients

1 ½ tablespoons lard, at room temperature
1 ½ pounds pork stew meat, cubed
Hickory smoked salt and ground black pepper, to taste
1 cup leeks, chopped
2 garlic cloves, minced
1 (1-inch) piece fresh ginger root, grated
1 teaspoon mustard seeds
1 teaspoon fennel seeds
2 tablespoons soy sauce
1/4 cup dry red wine
5 cups beef bone broth
1/4 cup fresh parsley leaves, roughly chopped

Directions

- Press the "Sauté" button and melt the lard. Now, brown pork stew meat for 4 to 6 minutes, stirring occasionally.
- Season the pork with salt and black pepper to taste and set it aside. In pan drippings, cook the leeks along with garlic and ginger until tender and aromatic.
- Add the pork back to the Instant Pot; add the remaining ingredients and gently stir to combine. Secure the lid.
- Choose "Meat/Stew" mode and cook at High pressure for 40 minutes. Once cooking is complete, use a quick release; remove the lid carefully.
- Ladle into individual bowls and serve garnished with fresh parsley leaves. Bon appétit!

---

118. Mexican-Style Meatballs
(Ready in about 15 minutes | Servings 6)

Here is a great idea for your next fiesta party! Serve with hot cooked rice or pasta.
Per serving: *476 Calories; 24.5g Fat; 33.2g Carbs; 27.9g Protein; 19.5g Sugars*

Ingredients

1 pound ground pork
2 slices bacon, chopped
1 white onion, minced
1 teaspoon garlic, minced
1/3 cup tortilla chips, crushed
1/2 cup Romano cheese, freshly grated
1 egg

Sea salt and ground black pepper, to taste
1 teaspoon dried marjoram
1 cup ketchup
2 cups tomato sauce
2 chipotle chile in adobo
2 tablespoons fresh cilantro

Directions

- Thoroughly combine ground pork, bacon, onion, garlic, tortilla chips, Romano cheese, egg, salt, black pepper, and marjoram. Shape the mixture into balls.
- Now, add ketchup, tomato sauce, and chipotle chile in adobo to the Instant Pot. Place the meatballs in your Instant Pot.
- Secure the lid. Choose the "Manual" setting and cook at High pressure for 6 minutes. Once cooking is complete, use a quick pressure release; carefully remove the lid.
- Serve warm garnished with fresh cilantro. Enjoy!

119. Easy Pork Soup with Corn
(Ready in about 15 minutes | Servings 4)

If you like rich soups, try this recipe that is both delicious and satisfying. Serve with a homemade crusty bread.
Per serving: *358 Calories; 9.1g Fat; 32.4g Carbs; 36.1g Protein; 0.8g Sugars*

Ingredients

1 tablespoon olive oil
1/2 cup onion, chopped
1 pound pork stew meat, cubed
4 cups water
1/4 teaspoon bay leaf, ground
1/2 teaspoon dried basil
1 teaspoon celery seeds
1 cup corn, torn into pieces

Directions

- Press the "Sauté" button to preheat your Instant Pot. Heat the olive oil; cook the onion until tender and translucent.
- Add pork and continue to cook until it is delicately browned. Add water, ground bay leaf, basil, and celery seeds to the Instant Pot.
- Secure the lid. Choose the "Manual" setting and cook at High pressure for 8 minutes. Once cooking is complete, use a quick pressure release; carefully remove the lid.
- Stir in corn kernels; seal the lid and allow it to sit in the residual heat until the corn is warmed through. Serve in individual bowls and enjoy!

---

120. Pork with Raisin and Port Sauce
(Ready in about 35 minutes | Servings 6)

Prepare this dish ahead of time and warm it in your Instant Pot just before the guests arrive. You can use port wine to deglaze the bottom of the cooker and easily make this 5-star sauce.
Per serving: *395 Calories; 15.9g Fat; 21.4g Carbs; 40.9g Protein; 16.7g Sugars*

Ingredients

1 tablespoon canola oil
2 pounds pork loin roast, boneless
Kosher salt, to taste
1/2 teaspoon ground black pepper
1 teaspoon paprika
1/2 teaspoon mustard powder
1 teaspoon dried marjoram
2 cloves garlic, crushed
4 ounces raisins
1/2 cup port wine
1 cup pomegranate juice
1/2 teaspoon fresh ginger, grated

Directions

- Press the "Sauté" button to preheat your Instant Pot. Now, heat the oil; sear the pork loin for 3 minutes on each side.
- Then, add the remaining ingredients to your Instant Pot.
- Secure the lid. Choose the "Poultry" setting and cook at High pressure for 15 minutes. Once cooking is complete, use a natural pressure release; carefully remove the lid.
- Serve the pork topped with raisin-port sauce. Bon appétit!

121. Chipotle Pork with Salsa
(Ready in about 35 minutes | Servings 6)

Mouth-tingling and satisfying. That's all you need for good family lunch.
Per serving: *398 Calories; 19.4g Fat; 8.1g Carbs; 45.5g Protein; 5.9g Sugars*

Ingredients

1 ½ pounds pork loin, boneless and well-trimmed
Kosher salt and ground black pepper, to your liking
1 teaspoon grainy mustard
1 (1-inch) piece fresh ginger root, grated
1/3 teaspoon ground allspice
1/2 teaspoon ground bay leaf
2 tablespoons brown sugar
1 tablespoon chipotle paste
1 cup broth

For the Salsa Sauce:
2 ripe tomatoes, peeled, seeds removed, chopped
2 tablespoons onion, finely chopped
1 clove garlic, minced
1 mild chile pepper
2 tablespoons cilantro, chopped
1 ½ tablespoons lime juice
Salt, to your liking

Directions

- Sprinkle pork loin with all seasonings. Spritz the Instant Pot with a nonstick cooking spray.
- Press the "Sauté" button to heat up your Instant Pot. Sear pork loin on both sides until just browned.
- Add brown sugar, chipotle paste, and broth. Secure the lid. Choose the "Manual" setting and cook for 25 minutes at High Pressure.
- Once cooking is complete, use a natural release; remove the lid carefully.
- Meanwhile, make the salsa by mixing all ingredients. Serve pork loin with fresh salsa on the side. Bon appétit!

---

122. Pork Carnitas Taquitos
(Ready in about 1 hour | Servings 8)

Chock-full of tender meat, tomato sauce and seasonings, these taquitos are sure to please. You can thicken the cooking liquid by adding the slurry.
Per serving: *417 Calories; 24.4g Fat; 16.6g Carbs; 32.3g Protein; 11.8g Sugars*

Ingredients

1 tablespoon lard, melted
2 pounds pork shoulder
1 tablespoon granulated sugar
1 teaspoon shallot powder
1 teaspoon granulated garlic
Salt and black pepper, to taste
1 teaspoon ground cumin
1 cup ketchup

1 cup tomato paste
1/2 cup dry red wine
1 teaspoon mixed peppercorns
2 bay leaves
1 teaspoon chipotle powder
1/2 cup Manchego cheese, shredded
16 corn tortillas, warmed

Directions

- Press the "Sauté" button to preheat your Instant Pot. Then, melt the lard. Sear the pork shoulder until it is delicately browned on all sides.
- Add the sugar, shallot powder, garlic, salt, black pepper, cumin, ketchup, tomato paste, wine, peppercorns, bay leaves, and chipotle powder.
- Secure the lid. Choose the "Meat/Stew" setting and cook at High pressure for 45 minutes. Once cooking is complete, use a natural pressure release; carefully remove the lid.
- Shred the meat with two forks. Divide the shredded pork among tortillas. Top with cheese. Roll each tortilla and brush it lightly with oil.
- Arrange tortillas on a cookie sheet. Bake approximately 13 minutes and serve. Enjoy!

123. Pork Chops with Creamed Mustard Sauce
(Ready in about 15 minutes | Servings 4)

There are many recipes for the classic pork chops, but this is one of the tastiest and creamiest that you have ever tried!
Per serving: *433 Calories; 22.7g Fat; 7g Carbs; 48.3g Protein; 0.8g Sugars*

Ingredients

2 tablespoons canola oil
4 pork loin chops
Salt and ground black pepper, to taste
1 teaspoon smoked paprika
1/2 cup cream of celery soup
1/2 cup chicken broth
1 cup sour cream
1 tablespoon Dijon mustard

Directions

- Press the "Sauté" button to preheat your Instant Pot. Then, heat the oil and sear the pork chops for 2 minutes per side.
- Then, stir in salt, black pepper, paprika, cream of celery soup, and chicken broth.
- Secure the lid. Choose the "Manual" setting and cook at High pressure for 9 minutes. Once cooking is complete, use a quick pressure release; carefully remove the lid.
- Remove pork chops from the Instant Pot.
- Fold in sour cream and Dijon mustard. Press the "Sauté" button again and let it simmer until the sauce is reduced and heated through. Bon appétit!

124. French-Style Pork and Bean Casserole
(Ready in about 40 minutes | Servings 6)

With this recipe, you can turn ordinary pork and beans into something fantastic, adding good quality seasonings and sour cream for garnish.
Per serving: *491 Calories; 27g Fat; 25.5g Carbs; 36.1g Protein; 7.1g Sugars*

Ingredients

1 tablespoon olive oil
1 pound pork shoulder, cut into cubes
1/2 pound pork sausage, sliced
1 cup water
1 tablespoon beef bouillon granules
1 pound dry cannellini beans
1 cloves garlic, finely minced
1 yellow onion, sliced

1 parsnip, sliced
1 carrots, sliced
1 teaspoon celery seeds
1/2 teaspoon mustard seeds
1/2 teaspoon cumin powder
Sea salt and ground black pepper, to taste
1 ½ cups sour cream

Directions

- Press the "Sauté" button to preheat your Instant Pot. Heat olive oil until sizzling.
- Then, brown the meat and sausage for 3 to 4 minutes, stirring periodically.
- Add water, beef bouillon granules, cannellini beans, garlic, onion, parsnip, carrot, and seasonings.
- Secure the lid. Choose the "Bean/Chili" setting and cook at High pressure for 30 minutes. Once cooking is complete, use a natural pressure release; carefully remove the lid.
- Serve topped with sour cream. Enjoy!

125. Tender Aji Panca Pork
(Ready in about 55 minutes | Servings 6)

This fancy pork dish might become your holiday favorite. With its specific mild flavor, Aji Panca chili will add just the right amount of excitement to your dish.
Per serving: *511 Calories; 30.7g Fat; 17.5g Carbs; 39.2g Protein; 16.4g Sugars*

Ingredients

1 tablespoon lard
2 pounds pork shoulder
3/4 cup broth, preferably homemade
1/3 cup honey
2 tablespoons champagne vinegar
1 teaspoon garlic, minced
2 tablespoons soy sauce
1 teaspoon aji panca powder
Kosher salt and ground black pepper, to your liking
1 tablespoon flaxseed, ground

Directions

- Press the "Sauté" button, and melt the lard. Once hot, sear pork shoulder on all sides until just browned.
- Add the broth, honey, vinegar, garlic, soy sauce, aji panca powder, salt, and pepper. Secure the lid. Select the "Manual" mode, High pressure and 50 minutes.
- Once cooking is complete, use a natural release; remove the lid carefully. Set the pork shoulder aside keeping it warm.
- Now, press the "Sauté" button again and add ground flaxseed to the cooking liquid. Let it simmer until the sauce has thickened.
- Taste, adjust the seasoning and pour the sauce over the reserved pork shoulder. Bon appétit!

126. Southwestern-Style Cheese Meatloaf
(Ready in about 35 minutes | Servings 6)

Get ready for a top-rated Southwestern meatloaf! Use crushed tortilla chips instead of breadcrumbs for extra taste and texture.
Per serving: *352 Calories; 22.1g Fat; 13.2g Carbs; 24.8g Protein; 3.7g Sugars*

Ingredients

1 pound ground pork
1 egg
1/2 cup scallions, minced
2 garlic cloves, minced
1/2 cup whole grain tortilla chips, finely crushed
1/2 cup Cotija cheese, crumbled
Sea salt and ground black pepper, to taste

1 teaspoon smoked paprika
1 cup bottled chipotle salsa
2 tablespoons ketchup
1 teaspoon fresh lime juice

Directions

- Prepare your Instant Pot by adding 1 cup of water and a metal rack to its bottom.
- Thoroughly combine ground pork, egg, scallions, garlic, crushed tortilla chips, Cotija cheese, salt, black pepper, paprika, and 1/2 cup of salsa in a mixing bowl.
- Now, shape the mixture into a meatloaf. Transfer the meatloaf to a lightly greased baking pan. Lower the baking pan onto the rack.
- In a bowl, mix the remaining 1/2 cup of salsa with ketchup and lime juice. Brush the salsa mixture over top of the meatloaf.
- Secure the lid. Choose the "Bean/Chili" setting and cook at High pressure for 30 minutes. Once cooking is complete, use a quick pressure release; carefully remove the lid. Bon appétit!

127. Easy Louisiana Ribs
(Ready in about 30 minutes | Servings 6)

Whether you like your ribs the classic way, glazed or crispy, we've got the recipe that you have to try.
Per serving: *365 Calories; 25g Fat; 3.7g Carbs; 3.1g Protein; 2.6g Sugars*

Ingredients

2 pounds baby back ribs
2 slices fresh ginger
1/2 cup dry wine
1 tablespoon brown sugar
2 cloves garlic, sliced
2 tablespoons soy sauce
1 cup beef bone broth
1 teaspoon Cajun seasoning
Sat, to taste

Directions

- Add all of the above ingredients to your Instant Pot.
- Secure the lid. Choose the "Meat/Stew" setting and cook at High pressure for 20 minutes. Once cooking is complete, use a natural pressure release; carefully remove the lid.
- Serve warm and enjoy!

128. Pork Steaks Marchand de Vin
(Ready in about 15 minutes | Servings 6)

Marchand de Vin is the classic red wine reduction sauce that is widely used in French cooking. Awaken the French chef in you!
Per serving: *330 Calories; 22.2g Fat; 1.7g Carbs; 28.7g Protein; 0.6g Sugars*

Ingredients

1 tablespoon lard, melted
1 ½ pounds pork steaks
1 cup demi-glace
1/2 cup red wine
2 bay leaves
Sea salt and ground black pepper, to taste
1 teaspoon dried oregano

Directions

- Press the "Sauté" button to preheat your Instant Pot. Melt the lard. Now, sear the pork steaks approximately 3 minutes per side.
- Add the remaining ingredients to the Instant Pot.
- Secure the lid. Choose the "Manual" setting and cook at High pressure for 8 minutes. Once cooking is complete, use a quick pressure release; carefully remove the lid.
- Press the "Sauté" button one more time and continue simmering until the cooking liquid has reduced by three-fourths. Bon appétit!

129. Filipino Pork Soup
(Ready in about 40 minutes | Servings 4)

Here is a complete meal in a bowl. This hearty soup is loaded with market-fresh vegetables and succulent pork chops for a well-balanced meal.

Per serving: *444 Calories; 16.9g Fat; 42.2g Carbs; 31.6g Protein; 5.1g Sugars*

Ingredients

2 tablespoons vegetable oil
3/4 pound bone-in pork chops
1/2 cup sweet onion, chopped
1 teaspoon fresh garlic, crushed
2 sweet peppers, deveined and chopped
4 potatoes, peeled and diced
2 carrots, trimmed and thinly sliced
1 parsnip, trimmed and thinly sliced

4 cups vegetable broth, preferably homemade
Salt and freshly ground black pepper, to taste
1/2 teaspoon paprika
1 teaspoon dried thyme
1 (1/2-inch) piece fresh ginger, grated
1 (1.41-ounce) package tamarind soup base

Directions

- Preheat your Instant Pot on "Sauté" setting. Then, heat the vegetable oil and brown pork chops for 4 minutes on each side.
- Add the remaining ingredients and secure the lid. Choose the "Soup" mode and cook for 30 minutes at High pressure.
- Once cooking is complete, use a natural pressure release; remove the lid carefully. Serve hot with toasted bread. Bon appétit!

---

130. Kid-Friendly Pork Sandwiches
(Ready in about 50 minutes | Servings 6)

Pork sandwiches are easy to prepare and fun to eat! Use extra soft rolls to assemble the sandwiches. Enjoyment guaranteed!

Per serving: *480 Calories; 18.4g Fat; 30.1g Carbs; 45.1g Protein; 3.3g Sugars*

Ingredients

2 teaspoons lard, at room temperature
2 pounds pork shoulder roast, rind removed, boneless
2 garlic cloves, chopped
1 (1-inch) piece fresh ginger, peeled and grated
1 tablespoon maple syrup
1/4 cup dry red wine
1 cup water
1/2 tablespoon Worcestershire sauce

Sea salt, to taste
1/3 teaspoon ground black pepper
2 sprig thyme
2 whole star anise
1 tablespoon arrowroot powder
12 soft lunch rolls, warmed
1 cup pickles, sliced

Directions

- Press the "Sauté" button to preheat your Instant Pot. Now, melt the lard. Once hot, sear the pork shoulder roast for 3 minutes per side.
- Add the garlic, ginger, maple syrup, wine, water, Worcestershire sauce, and seasonings to the Instant Pot.
- Secure the lid. Choose the "Meat/Stew" setting and cook at High pressure for 45 minutes. Once cooking is complete, use a natural pressure release; carefully remove the lid.
- Transfer the pork shoulder to a chopping board. Shred the meat and return it back to the Instant Pot.
- Whisk the arrowroot powder with 2 tablespoons of water; press the "Sauté" button again and add the slurry. Let it simmer until thickened.
- Assemble the sandwiches with pork and pickles. Bon appétit!

131. Pork Roast with Fresh Avocado Sauce

(Ready in about 35 minutes | Servings 6)

Pork roast with fresh, creamy sauce! This dish will be gone as soon as it hits the table!
Per serving: *442 Calories; 26.4g Fat; 8.7g Carbs; 42.3g Protein; 1.4g Sugars*

Ingredients

2 pounds pork roast, cut into cubes
1 cup water
1 tablespoon beef bouillon granules
1 tablespoon fish sauce
1 habanero pepper, minced
1/2 cup scallions, chopped
1 teaspoon ginger-garlic paste
2 teaspoons olive oil
Freshly ground black pepper, to taste
Avocado Sauce:
1 avocado, pitted and peeled
2 tablespoons mayonnaise
2 garlic cloves, pressed
1 tablespoon fresh lime juice

Directions

- Add pork roast, water, beef bouillon granules, fish sauce, habanero pepper, scallions, ginger-garlic paste, olive oil, and ground black pepper to the Instant Pot.
- Secure the lid. Choose the "Meat/Stew" setting and cook at High pressure for 30 minutes. Once cooking is complete, use a natural pressure release; carefully remove the lid.
- Meanwhile, whisk all of the sauce ingredients in a mixing bowl. Serve with pork roast and enjoy!

---

132. Thai Pork Medallion Curry

(Ready in about 15 minutes | Servings 4)

Thai-style pork is an elegant and sophisticated dish that can be served on any occasion. Pork curry is a cinch to make in the Instant Pot.
Per serving: *286 Calories; 15.3g Fat; 5.8g Carbs; 30.5g Protein; 1.7g Sugars*

Ingredients

2 teaspoons coconut oil
1 pound pork medallions
1/2 teaspoon cumin seeds
1 jalapeño pepper, seeded and minced
1 bay leaf
1 ½ tablespoons fish sauce
1 cup beef bone broth
2 cloves garlic, minced

2 tablespoons Thai green curry paste
1 tablespoon apple cider vinegar
Salt and ground black pepper, to taste
1/2 teaspoon cayenne pepper
Zest and juice of 1 lime

Directions

- Press the "Sauté" button to preheat the Instant Pot. Heat the coconut oil. Once hot, sear the pork medallions for 2 to 3 minutes.
- Add the remaining ingredients, including roasted seasonings.
- Secure the lid. Choose the "Manual" setting and cook at High pressure for 8 minutes. Once cooking is complete, use a quick pressure release; carefully remove the lid.
- Serve with basmati rice and enjoy!

133. Easy Pork Sliders
(Ready in about 1 hour 10 minutes + marinating time | Servings 6)

Embrace your inner child and prepare these delicious pork sliders! Choose your favorite fixings and enjoy!
Per serving: *433 Calories; 18.8g Fat; 20.9g Carbs; 43.9g Protein; 6g Sugars*

Ingredients

2 pounds pork loin roast, cut into cubes
4 cloves garlic, smashed
2 tablespoons fresh scallions, chopped
1/2 cup pineapple juice
Salt and black pepper, to taste
1 teaspoon cayenne pepper
1/4 teaspoon mustard seeds
1/4 teaspoon cumin
1 ½ tablespoons olive oil
1 head fresh Iceberg lettuce, leaves separated
2 tablespoons Dijon mustard
6 dinner rolls

Directions

- Place the pork, garlic, scallions, pineapple, juice, salt, black pepper, cayenne pepper, mustard seeds, and cumin in a mixing bowl; wrap with a foil and transfer to your refrigerator for 2 hours.
- Press the "Sauté" button and heat olive oil. Now, cook the pork, working in batches, until it is well browned.
- Secure the lid. Now, select the "Manual" mode, High pressure and 60 minutes. Once cooking is complete, use a natural release; carefully remove the lid.
- Serve over dinner rolls, garnished with fresh lettuce and Dijon mustard. Bon appétit!

---

134. Five-Star Picnic Shoulder
(Ready in about 50 minutes | Servings 4)

A minimum internal temperature of picnic shoulder should be 175 degrees F. For the complete experience, serve with roasted new potatoes.
Per serving: *288 Calories; 12.7g Fat; 6.1g Carbs; 35.2g Protein; 3.2g Sugars*

Ingredients

1 ½ pounds pork picnic shoulder
1 teaspoon garlic powder
1/2 teaspoon cumin powder
1/4 teaspoon cinnamon, ground
1 teaspoon celery seeds
1 teaspoon oregano, dried
Sea salt and ground black pepper, to taste
1/2 cup fresh orange juice
1 cup beef bone broth

Directions

- Place all of the above ingredients in the Instant Pot.
- Secure the lid. Choose the "Meat/Stew" setting and cook at High pressure for 45 minutes. Once cooking is complete, use a natural pressure release; carefully remove the lid.
- Test for doneness and thinly slice the pork; transfer to a serving platter. Serve warm and enjoy!

135. Goan Pork Vindaloo
(Ready in about 15 minutes + marinating time | Servings 6)

Pork rib chops are one of the favorite main dishes that cook perfectly in the Instant Pot. They combine with Kashmiri chili peppers and red wine very well.

Per serving: 340 Calories; 14.8g Fat; 9.5g Carbs; 39.8g Protein; 7.7g Sugars

Ingredients

1 cup water
1/4 cup dry red wine
2 tablespoons white vinegar
Salt and ground black pepper, to taste
1 teaspoon garlic, minced
2 tablespoons honey
1 bay leaf
1 tablespoon lard, melted
2 pounds pork rib chops
4 dried Kashmiri chili peppers, stemmed and chopped
1 cinnamon stick

Directions

- Place water, wine, vinegar, salt, black pepper, garlic, honey and bay leaf in a ceramic dish. Add the rib chops and let them marinate for 2 hours in the refrigerator.
- Press the "Sauté" button to preheat your Instant Pot. Melt the lard and sear the pork until it is delicately browned.
- Then, transfer the pork along with the marinade to the Instant Pot. Add Kashmiri chili peppers and cinnamon stick.
- Secure the lid. Now, select the "Manual" mode, High pressure and 8 minutes. Once cooking is complete, use a quick release; carefully remove the lid. Serve warm.

136. Pork Soup with Queso Fresco Cheese
(Ready in about 25 minutes | Servings 6)

Pork stew meat inspires us in so many ways! In this recipe, it is pressure cooked with Mexican chilies and topped with Queso fresco.

Per serving: 334 Calories; 10.6g Fat; 10g Carbs; 48.4g Protein; 6.1g Sugars

Ingredients

2 pounds pork stew meat, cubed
2 garlic cloves, smashed
1 teaspoon fresh ginger, grated
1/2 cup yellow onion, chopped
1 fresh poblano chile, minced
5 cups water
1 cup tomato paste

2 bouillon cubes
1 teaspoon dried oregano
1 teaspoon dried basil
Sea salt, to taste
1/4 teaspoon freshly ground pepper, or more to taste
1 cup Queso fresco cheese, crumbled

Directions

- Place all of the above ingredients, except for Queso fresco cheese, in your Instant Pot.
- Secure the lid. Choose the "Soup" setting and cook at High pressure for 20 minutes. Once cooking is complete, use a quick pressure release; carefully remove the lid.
- Divide warm soup among serving bowls; top each serving with crumbled cheese and serve immediately.

137. Pork Tacos with Tomatillo Sauce
(Ready in about 45 minutes | Servings 6)

Tacos por favor! Make your taco night "muy bueno" with these flavorful pork bites! You can replace morita chiles with chipotles if desired.
Per serving: *477 Calories; 20g Fat; 27.7g Carbs; 43.8g Protein; 3.2g Sugars*

Ingredients

2 pounds meaty pork belly, skin-on
4 cloves garlic, halved
Seasoned salt and freshly ground black pepper, to taste
1 teaspoon mustard powder
1/2 teaspoon dried sage, crushed
1 teaspoon dried marjoram
1 cup stock
1 bay leaf

6 large tortillas, warmed

For the Sauce:
1 cup tomatillos, finely chopped
2 morita chiles, finely chopped
1 red onion, finely chopped
1/4 cup fresh lime juice
Salt, to your liking

Directions

- Rub pork belly with garlic halves. Sprinkle pork belly with salt, black pepper, mustard powder, sage, and marjoram.
- Brush the bottom of the Instant Pot with a nonstick cooking oil.
- Press the "Sauté" button; add the pork belly, skin side down. Cook until it is browned on all sides.
- Add stock and bay leaf; secure the lid. Now, select the "Manual" mode, High pressure and 35 minutes.
- Once cooking is complete, use a quick release; remove the lid carefully.
- Meanwhile, make the sauce by mixing all the sauce ingredients.
- Allow pork belly to cool slightly. Place the pork belly, skin side up, on a cutting board. Slice across the grain.
- Divide sliced pork among warm tortillas, add the sauce and serve warm.

138. Hungarian Pork Paprikash
(Ready in about 30 minutes | Servings 8)

Here is a comfort food you will cook again and again! Thanks to the Instant Pot, you can enjoy a home-cooked meal even when you don't have time for cooking!
Per serving: *549 Calories; 22.6g Fat; 9.6g Carbs; 72.9g Protein; 3.1g Sugars*

Ingredients

2 tablespoons olive oil
1 cup red onions, chopped
2 garlic cloves, minced
1 cup button mushrooms, sliced
2 pounds pork stew meat, cubed
2 bell pepper, deveined and thinly sliced
1 chili pepper, deveined and minced

2 carrots, peeled and cut into large pieces
1 can tomatoes, crushed
6 cups chicken broth
Salt and ground black pepper, to taste
1 teaspoon Hungarian paprika
1 bay leaf
1 cup sour cream

Directions

- Press the "Sauté" button to preheat your Instant Pot. Now, heat the oil until sizzling. Then, sauté the onion until tender and translucent.
- Stir in the garlic and mushrooms; continue to sauté an additional 2 minute or until they are fragrant. Reserve.
- Cook the meat for 2 to 3 minutes, stirring frequently; add the reserved onion/mushroom mixture to your Instant Pot.
- Add the pepper, carrots, tomatoes, chicken broth, salt, pepper, paprika, and bay leaf.
- Secure the lid. Choose the "Soup" setting and cook at High pressure for 20 minutes. Once cooking is complete, use a quick pressure release; carefully remove the lid.
- Garnish each serving with a dollop of sour cream and serve.

139. Mexican Posole Rojo
(Ready in about 35 minutes | Servings 8)

This Mexican-inspired dish provides a unique menu opportunity for you and your family! Really tasty!
Per serving: *503 Calories; 30.4g Fat; 11.6g Carbs; 42.6g Protein; 2.9g Sugars*

Ingredients

1 heaping tablespoon lard, melted
1 cup shallots, chopped
2 cloves garlic, sliced
2 pounds pork butt, cut into 2-inch pieces
2 sprigs thyme, leaves chopped
1/2 teaspoon cumin
1 teaspoon Mexican oregano
Sea salt and ground black pepper, to taste

4 cups chicken bone broth
1/2 cup fresh ripe tomato, puréed
2 bay leaves
1 celery with leaves, chopped
2 dried ancho chiles, chopped
1 red bell pepper, thinly sliced
1 (15-ounce) can white hominy, drained and rinsed

Directions

- Press the "Sauté" button to preheat your Instant Pot. Now, melt the lard. Once hot, sauté the shallots and garlic until they are tender and fragrant.
- Add the pork and cook an additional 3 minutes or until it is delicately browned. Add the remaining ingredients and gently stir to combine.
- Secure the lid. Choose the "Poultry" setting and cook at High pressure for 30 minutes. Once cooking is complete, use a natural pressure release; carefully remove the lid.
- Divide between individual bowls and serve warm. Enjoy!

---

140. Traditional Pork Ragù
(Ready in about 30 minutes | Servings 6)

If you've never tried a pork ragù in the Instant Pot, you're missing out! Cooking traditional pork ragù to perfection has never been easier!
Per serving: *385 Calories; 25.4g Fat; 6.7g Carbs; 31.2g Protein; 3.7g Sugars*

Ingredients

2 tablespoons olive oil
1 ½ pounds pork stew meat, cubed
1 onion, chopped
2 garlic cloves, chopped
2 cups roasted vegetable stock
1/4 cup red wine
1/2 (15-ounce) can tomato sauce
2 carrots, sliced
1 celery with leaves, chopped
1 teaspoon Italian seasoning
Salt and ground black pepper, to taste

Directions

- Press the "Sauté" button to preheat your Instant Pot. Heat the oil and sauté the pork and onions until the meat is delicately browned.
- Add the remaining ingredients.
- Secure the lid. Choose the "Soup" setting and cook at High pressure for 20 minutes. Once cooking is complete, use a quick pressure release; carefully remove the lid.
- Serve topped with shredded cheese if desired. Bon appétit!

141. Pork Medallions with Root Vegetables
(Ready in about 25 minutes | Servings 4)

Turn pork medallions into something deeply satisfying using the Instant Pot, a revolutionary kitchen appliance. Serve with coleslaw.
Per serving: *438 Calories; 22.3g Fat; 16.9g Carbs; 41g Protein; 4.4g Sugars*

Ingredients

4 pork medallions
1 teaspoon cayenne pepper
1 teaspoon cumin, ground
Salt and black pepper, to taste
1 ½ tablespoons olive oil
2 shallots, chopped
1 garlic cloves, minced

1 cup vegetable stock
2 sprigs rosemary
2 parsnips, thinly sliced
1 turnip, thinly sliced
2 carrots, thinly sliced
1 tablespoon cornstarch

Directions

- Season pork medallions with cayenne pepper, cumin, salt, and black pepper. Press the "Sauté" button and heat the olive oil.
- Sear pork medallions for 4 minutes on each side; reserve. Cook shallots in pan drippings until just tender and fragrant.
- Return pork medallions to the Instant Pot along with garlic, stock, and rosemary. Secure the lid. Choose the "Manual" setting and cook for 10 minutes at High pressure.
- Once cooking is complete, use a quick release; remove the lid carefully.
- Select the "Manual" mode again and cook root vegetables for 4 minutes; use a quick release again. Remove the vegetables from the Instant Pot.
- Add cornstarch and 1 tablespoons of cold water to a small bowl; stir until smooth paste forms.
- Add the slurry to your Instant Pot, press the "Sauté" button and cook until the sauce is concentrated. Serve the sauce over reserved pork and root vegetables.

---

142. Braised Pork Leg with Green Onions
(Ready in about 2 hours 50 minutes | Servings 8)

You can serve this pork dish on any occasion. Leftovers can find their way to your sandwich as well.
Per serving: *287 Calories; 10g Fat; 10.8g Carbs; 38.2g Protein; 6.8g Sugars*

Ingredients

2 garlic cloves, minced
1 ½ tablespoons honey
1 teaspoon Aleppo red pepper
Sea salt and ground black pepper, to taste
2 star anise
3 pounds pork leg

2 tablespoons tamari sauce
1/4 cup tomato paste
1/4 cup shaoxing rice wine
1/2 cup water
2 tablespoons olive oil
A bunch of green onions, chopped

Directions

- Add all ingredients, except for olive oil and green onions, to a ceramic dish. Cover the dish and place in your refrigerator for 2 hours.
- Then, press the "Sauté" button to preheat your Instant Pot. Heat the oil until sizzling. Now, cook the pork until delicately browned on all sides, about 10 minutes. Then, add the marinade.
- Secure the lid. Choose the "Meat/Stew" setting and cook at High pressure for 35 minutes. Once cooking is complete, use a natural pressure release; carefully remove the lid.
- Add green onions to the Instant Pot; seal the lid and let it sit approximately 5 minutes. Serve warm.

143. Momofuku Bo Ssam (Korean-Style Pork)
(Ready in about 1 hour 5 minutes | Servings 10)

This pork dish is very popular in Korea. Doenjang is authentic Korean soybean paste while Gochugaru are ground chilies with moderate spiciness.
Per serving: *512 Calories; 37.2g Fat; 4.2g Carbs; 38.2g Protein; 2.3g Sugars*

Ingredients

1 heaping tablespoon lard, at room temperature
3 pounds pork shoulder
1/2 cup yellow onions, chopped
2 garlic cloves, minced
1/2 cup chicken bone broth
1/2 cup orange juice
1 tablespoon tamari sauce
Sea salt and ground black pepper, to taste

1/2 teaspoon Gochugaru
1 tablespoon castor sugar
1 stick butter
2 bay leaves
1/4 cup doenjang (korean soybean paste)
2 tablespoons walnuts, ground

Directions

- Press the "Sauté" button to preheat your Instant Pot. Melt the lard and brown the pork shoulder for 5 minutes, turning once or twice.
- Add the onions, garlic, broth, orange juice, tamari sauce, salt, black pepper, teaspoon Gochugaru, and sugar.
- Secure the lid. Choose the "Manual" setting and cook at High pressure for 50 minutes. Once cooking is complete, use a natural pressure release; carefully remove the lid.
- Transfer the pork shoulder to a cutting board; allow it to cool; then, cut into slices.
- Then, press the "Sauté" button again. Add the remaining ingredients and let it simmer for 5 to 6 minutes or until the sauce is thoroughly heated and reduced by half.
- Spoon the sauce over the pork and serve. Bon appétit!

144. Provençal Sausage Casserole
(Ready in about 15 minutes | Servings 4)

What's the secret to the best sausage casserole? Combine a high-quality sausage with carefully selected seasonings and fresh vegetables.
Per serving: *376 Calories; 29.6g Fat; 12.9g Carbs; 15g Protein; 3.1g Sugars*

Ingredients

2 tablespoons olive oil
1 pound pork sausages, sliced
1 leek, thinly sliced
2 garlic cloves, crushed
2 ripe tomatoes, chopped
1 cup vegetable broth
2 tablespoons white wine

1 tablespoon oyster sauce
1 tablespoon Herbs de Provence
1 (15-ounce) can black beans
Sea salt, to taste
1/4 teaspoon freshly ground black pepper
1 teaspoon cayenne pepper
1/2 teaspoon ground bay leaf

Directions

- Press the "Sauté" button to preheat your Instant Pot. Then, heat the oil until sizzling. Brown the sausage for 2 to 3 minutes.
- Add the remaining ingredients and gently stir to combine.
- Secure the lid. Choose the "Manual" setting and cook at High pressure for 8 minutes. Once cooking is complete, use a quick pressure release; carefully remove the lid.
- Divide among individual bowls and serve warm. Bon appétit!

145. Sunday Beer-Braised Ribs
(Ready in about 40 minutes | Servings 8)

This easy recipe for pork ribs will help you get through a long, lazy Sunday. Gather your family around the dinner table and enjoy memorable moments!
Per serving: 405 Calories; 24.1g Fat; 3.2g Carbs; 40.5g Protein; 0.7g Sugars

Ingredients

1/2 cup chicken stock
1 (12-ounce) bottle dark beer
2 ripe tomatillos, chopped
2 garlic cloves, minced
1 bell pepper, deveined and chopped
1 jalapeno pepper, deveined and chopped
2 ½ pounds baby back ribs
Salt and ground black pepper, to taste
1/2 teaspoon ground allspice
1 teaspoon fennel seeds
Lime wedges, for serving

Directions

- Simply throw all of the above ingredients, except for lime wedges, into your Instant Pot. Secure the lid.
- Choose the "Manual" setting and cook for 35 minutes at High pressure.
- Once cooking is complete, use a natural release; remove the lid carefully. Serve garnished with lime wedges. Bon appétit!

---

146. Fancy Pork Pâté
(Ready in about 55 minutes + chilling time | Servings 10)

Prepare this fancy recipe in your Instant Pot and wow your party guests! Keep in your refrigerator for up to 1 week.
Per serving: *147 Calories; 6.4g Fat; 2.5g Carbs; 18.2g Protein; 0.9g Sugars*

Ingredients

1 tablespoon olive oil
1 ½ pounds boneless pork shoulder, cubed
4 ounces pork liver
1 red onion, chopped
2 cloves garlic, minced
1 teaspoon dried basil
1 teaspoon mustard powder

Sea salt and ground black pepper, to taste
1 teaspoon ground nutmeg
1/2 teaspoon ground ginger
1 teaspoon ground coriander
2 tablespoons brandy
1/2 cup heavy cream

Directions

- Press the "Sauté" button to preheat your Instant Pot. Heat the olive oil; once hot, sear the pork shoulder and pork liver until they are delicately browned; reserve.
- Add the onion and garlic and continue to sauté them in pan drippings. Return the meat and pork liver back to the Instant Pot.
- Add the remaining ingredients, except for heavy cream.
- Secure the lid. Choose the "Manual" setting and cook at High pressure for 50 minutes. Once cooking is complete, use a natural pressure release; carefully remove the lid.
- Fold in heavy cream. Give it a good stir and seal the lid. Let it sit in the residual heat until thoroughly warmed. Refrigerate until it is completely chilled.

147. Two-Cheese and Bacon Bread Pudding
(Ready in about 40 minutes | Servings 6)

Undoubtedly, this is a very versatile recipe. A fancy bread pudding is much simpler to prepare than you might expect!
Per serving: *385 Calories; 25.3g Fat; 17.1g Carbs; 21.8g Protein; 4.1g Sugars*

Ingredients

1 loaf of sourdough bread, cut into chunks
2 tablespoons butter, melted
6 slices Canadian bacon, chopped
6 ounces Monterey-Jack cheese, grated
3 eggs, beaten
1/2 cup milk

1/2 cup cream cheese
1/4 teaspoon marjoram
1 teaspoon onion powder
Garlic salt and ground black pepper, to taste

Directions

- Prepare your Instant Pot by adding 1 ½ cups of water and a metal rack to its bottom.
- Spritz the bottom and sides of a soufflé dish with a nonstick cooking spray. Add 1/2 of bread cubes to the bottom of the dish; drizzle the melted butter over them.
- Add bacon and grated Monterey-Jack cheese. Add the remaining 1/2 of bread cubes.
- In a mixing bowl, thoroughly combine the eggs, milk, cheese marjoram, onion powder, garlic salt, and black pepper. Pour this mixture over the top.
- Lower the soufflé dish onto the prepared metal rack. Cover with a piece of foil.
- Secure the lid. Choose the "Bean/Chili" setting and cook at High pressure for 25 minutes. Once cooking is complete, use a quick pressure release; carefully remove the lid.
- Allow it to stand on a cooling rack for 10 to 15 minutes before cutting and serving. Bon appétit!

148. Spicy Sausages with Beans and Cubanelle Peppers
(Ready in about 15 minutes | Servings 4)

Try an addictive Instant Pot meal that is easy to make and fun to eat. The recipe is inexpensive, practical and a real time saver.
Per serving: *322 Calories; 24.4g Fat; 12.4g Carbs; 14.2g Protein; 2g Sugars*

Ingredients

1/2 tablespoon shortening
4 pork spicy sausages, without casing
2 shallots, chopped
2 garlic cloves, minced
1/2 cup Cubanelle peppers, chopped
25 ounces canned black beans, rinsed and drained
1/3 cup water
1/2 teaspoon paprika
Sat, to taste
1 bay leaf

Directions

- Press the "Sauté" button to preheat your Instant Pot. Once hot, warm the shortening. Now, cook the sausage, crumbling them with a spatula; reserve.
- Next, cook the shallots and garlic in pan drippings until tender and fragrant. Add the other ingredients, along with reserved pork sausages.
- Secure the lid. Choose the "Manual" mode, High heat, and 6 minutes.
- Once cooking is complete, use a natural release; remove the lid carefully. Discard bay leaf and serve over hot cooked rice. Bon appétit!

149. Pork Chops in Creamy Herbed Sauce
(Ready in about 15 minutes + marinating time | Servings 6)

Prepare these juicy, pork chops with a finger-licking creamy sauce. Spend your afternoon surrounded by the irresistible aromas of the kitchen!
Per serving: *405 Calories; 24g Fat; 1.9g Carbs; 42.9g Protein; 0.6g Sugars*

Ingredients

2 tablespoons fresh lemon juice
2 garlic cloves, smashed
1 teaspoon mustard powder
1/2 teaspoon ground cumin
1 teaspoon rosemary, minced
1 teaspoon thyme, minced

Sea salt and ground black pepper, to taste
2 tablespoons olive oil
6 pork chops
1/2 cup dry white wine
1/2 cup beef bone broth
2 tablespoons fresh parsley, chopped

Directions

- Place the lemon juice, garlic, mustard powder, ground cumin, rosemary, thyme, salt, black pepper, 1 tablespoon of olive oil, and pork chops in a ceramic dish. Allow the pork to marinate at least 2 hours.
- Press the "Sauté" button to preheat the Instant Pot. Heat the remaining tablespoon of olive oil. Then, brown the pork for 3 minutes per side.
- Deglaze the bottom of the inner pot with the white wine. Pour in the broth.
- Secure the lid. Choose the "Manual" setting and cook at High pressure for 8 minutes. Once cooking is complete, use a quick pressure release; carefully remove the lid. Serve garnished with fresh parsley. Bon appétit!

---

150. Classic Pasta Bolognese
(Ready in about 30 minutes | Servings 4)

In a rush? Don't worry, you can have an amazing family meal in 30 minutes.
Per serving: *677 Calories; 39.5g Fat; 37.9g Carbs; 43.3g Protein; 2.5g Sugars*

Ingredients

1 ½ tablespoons olive oil
1 cup leeks, chopped
2 garlic cloves, minced
1 pound ground pork
1/2 pound ground beef
1 celery stick, diced small
1 sweet pepper, finely chopped
1 jalapeno, finely chopped
1 ½ cups broth, preferably homemade
1 (28-ounce) can Italian tomatoes, finely chopped
2 pounds penne rigate
1/4 cup heavy cream

Directions

- Press the "Sauté" button. Preheat your Instant Pot and add the oil. Once hot, sweat the leeks for 3 to 4 minutes, stirring frequently.
- Add the garlic and cook for 30 seconds more. Add ground meat and cook for 3 minutes more or until it is just browned.
- Add celery, peppers, broth, tomatoes, and penne rigate. Secure the lid. Choose the "Manual" setting and cook for 15 minutes at High pressure.
- Once cooking is complete, use a quick release; remove the lid carefully. Press the "Sauté" button and fold in heavy cream; stir until heated through.
- Divide among individual bowls and eat warm. Bon appétit!

BEEF

151. Spicy Beef in White Rum Sauce
(Ready in about 25 minutes | Servings 6)

Whether you are planning an elegant dinner party or Sunday family lunch, this saucy beef makes the perfect main dish. Serve over spaghetti.
Per serving: *293 Calories; 15.6g Fat; 4.3g Carbs; 27.3g Protein; 0.9g Sugars*

Ingredients

2 tablespoons olive oil
1 ½ pounds beef flank steak
Sea salt and freshly ground black pepper, to taste
1 teaspoon cayenne pepper
1 teaspoon dried marjoram
1/2 teaspoon dried thyme
1/2 teaspoon dried basil

1/4 cup white rum
1 cup water
2 bell peppers, deveined and chopped
1 Chile de Arbol, deveined and minced
1 shallot, halved and sliced
1 cup sour cream

Directions

- Press the "Sauté" button to preheat your Instant Pot. Then, heat the oil until sizzling. Once hot, cook the beef until browned on all sides.
- Add seasonings. Deglaze the inner pot with white rum and add water, peppers, and shallot.
- Secure the lid. Choose the "Poultry" setting and cook at High pressure for 15 minutes. Once cooking is complete, use a quick pressure release; carefully remove the lid.
- Transfer the meat to a cutting board; slice the beef against the grain.
- Now, fold in sour cream and press the "Sauté" button; let it simmer until the cooking liquid is thoroughly warmed and reduced. Serve warm.

---

152. Traditional Beef Biryani
(Ready in about 25 minutes | Servings 6)

Beef Biryani is a traditional Indian dish that consists of beef chunks, authentic spices, hard-boiled eggs, and natural yogurt. Serve over basmati rice.
Per serving: *370 Calories; 16g Fat; 9.4g Carbs; 49g Protein; 5.5g Sugars*

Ingredients

1 ½ pounds braising steak, cut into bite-sized cubes
1 (28-ounce) can tomatoes, crushed
1 cup shallot, chopped
2 garlic cloves, peeled and chopped
1 teaspoon coriander seeds
1/2 teaspoon ground cumin
1 tablespoon Garam Masala

1 teaspoon saffron strands
Kosher salt and ground black pepper, to taste
1 heaping teaspoon caster sugar
8 ounces natural yoghurt
4 hard-boiled eggs, peeled and sliced
2 ounces almonds, flaked

Directions

- Add beef steak, canned tomatoes, shallot, garlic, coriander seeds, cumin, Garam Masala, saffron strands, salt, black pepper, and sugar to the Instant Pot.
- Secure the lid. Choose the "Meat/Stew" setting and cook at High pressure for 20 minutes. Once cooking is complete, use a natural pressure release; carefully remove the lid.
- Add yogurt and seal the lid. Let it sit in the residual heat until everything is heated through. Serve garnished with eggs and flaked almonds. Enjoy!

153. Lavash Beef Wraps
(Ready in about 20 minutes | Servings 4)

Lavash is a type of soft bread, popular throughout the Middle East. Actually, it is a thin unleavened flatbread made of flour, water, and salt.
Per serving: *521 Calories; 22.6g Fat; 35.4g Carbs; 44.8g Protein; 6.2g Sugars*

Ingredients

1 ½ tablespoons olive oil
1 ¼ pounds ground beef
2 garlic cloves, chopped
1/2 cup scallions, chopped
1 small Habanero pepper, deveined and minced
1 cup tomato puree
Salt and pepper, to taste
1 teaspoon coriander
1/2 teaspoon caraway seeds
1/4 teaspoon chipotle powder
1/4 teaspoon cloves, ground
1/3 cup chicken stock
4 lavash, warmed
1/2 cup baba ghanoush

Directions

- Press the "Sauté" button to heat up your Instant Pot; heat the oil.
- Once hot, sauté ground beef along with garlic, scallions, and Habanero pepper; cook until ground beef is no longer pink.
- Add tomato puree and continue to cook 3 minutes longer. Add seasonings and chicken stock.
- Secure the lid. Choose the "Manual" mode; cook for 6 minutes at High pressure. Once cooking is complete, use a natural release and carefully remove the lid.
- Spread the meat mixture evenly across the lavash. Top with baba ghanoush. Now, gently wrap the lavash and serve. Bon appétit!

154. Beef with Sweet Apricot-Riesling Sauce
(Ready in about 1 hour 5 minutes | Servings 6)

The beef brisket, as one of the beef primal cuts, cooks perfectly in the Instant Pot. Sweet Riesling sauce makes a great addition to the braised beef brisket.
Per serving: *338 Calories; 21.7g Fat; 15.5g Carbs; 18.4g Protein; 10.4g Sugars*

Ingredients

2 tablespoons olive oil
1 ½ pounds beef brisket
3 cloves garlic, minced or pressed
1 tablespoon Worcestershire sauce
1 celery, diced
1 carrot, diced

1 onion, cut into wedges
1 cup vegetable broth
1 tablespoon honey
1/4 cup late-harvest Riesling
1/3 cup dried apricots, chopped

Directions

- Press the "Sauté" button to preheat your Instant Pot. Heat the olive oil. Once hot, cook beef brisket until it is delicately browned on all sides.
- Add the remaining ingredients, except for dried apricots, to the Instant Pot.
- Secure the lid. Choose the "Manual" setting and cook at High pressure for 60 minutes. Once cooking is complete, use a natural pressure release; carefully remove the lid.
- Garnish with dried apricots and serve immediately. Bon appétit!

155. Roast Beef in Sage-Merlot Sauce
(Ready in about 50 minutes | Servings 6)

The combination of roast beef, vegetables, Merlot and herbs is marvelous! A perfect mix of flavor and textures!
Per serving: *283 Calories; 12.2g Fat; 5.4g Carbs; 30.9g Protein; 2.1g Sugars*

Ingredients

2 teaspoons lard, at room temperature
1 ½ pounds beef roast
1 red onion, chopped
2 garlic cloves, smashed
1 carrot, chopped
1 celery stalk, diced
1 cup water
1/2 cups Merlot

Sea salt, to taste
1/2 teaspoon ground black pepper
1 teaspoon paprika
2 bay leaves
1 tablespoon fresh sage
1 tablespoon soy sauce
1 teaspoon butter
1/4 cup fresh chives, chopped

Directions

- Press the "Sauté" button to preheat the Instant Pot. Melt the lard and sear the beef until it is browned on all sides.
- Add the onion, garlic, carrot, celery, water, merlot, salt, black pepper, paprika, bay leaves, sage, and soy sauce.
- Secure the lid. Choose the "Meat/Stew" mode and High pressure; cook for 40 minutes. Once cooking is complete, use a natural pressure release; carefully remove the lid.
- Transfer roast to a cutting board; allow it to cool slightly before slicing.
- Press the "Sauté" button and let it simmer until the sauce is reduced. Stir in the butter and press the "Cancel" button.
- Spoon the sauce over the sliced beef. Serve garnished with fresh chives and enjoy!

---

156. Classic Mississippi Roast
(Ready in about 45 minutes | Servings 8)

Make the ultimate comfort food in your Instant Pot and delight your family for Sunday dinner. Serve with lots of fresh salad.
Per serving: *313 Calories; 8.1g Fat; 24.8g Carbs; 34.6g Protein; 3.1g Sugars*

Ingredients

1 tablespoon tallow, at room temperature
3 pounds shoulder roast
1 teaspoon ginger garlic paste
Sea salt and ground black pepper, to taste
1 packet ranch dressing mix
1 ½ cups vegetable broth
4 pepperoncini peppers
2 pounds russet potatoes, peeled and quartered

Directions

- Press the "Sauté" button to preheat your Instant Pot. Now, melt the tallow. Sear the roast until it is delicately browned on all sides.
- Then, add the ginger garlic paste, salt, black pepper, ranch dressing mix, and vegetable broth. Top with pepperoncini peppers.
- Secure the lid. Choose the "Meat/Stew" mode and High pressure; cook for 35 minutes. Once cooking is complete, use a natural pressure release; carefully remove the lid. Shred the meat with two forks.
- Add potatoes and secure the lid. Choose "Manual" mode and High pressure; cook for 5 minutes. Once cooking is complete, use a quick pressure release; carefully remove the lid.
- Serve pulled beef with potatoes and enjoy!

157. Ground Beef Sirloin Soup
(Ready in about 45 minutes | Servings 4)

Here is an amazing beef soup featuring ground sirloin, root vegetables, and Mediterranean herbs. Take it up a notch with the cubes of sharp cheese and garlic croutons.

Per serving: *276 Calories; 11.8g Fat; 22.6g Carbs; 19.3g Protein; 4.4g Sugars*

Ingredients

1 tablespoon olive oil
1/2 pound beef sirloin, ground
1/2 teaspoon salt
1/2 teaspoon ground black pepper
4 cups bone broth
2 teaspoons dark soy sauce
1/2 cup shallots, chopped
1 teaspoon garlic, minced

2 carrots, chopped
2 Yukon Gold potatoes, chopped
1/2 cup tomato puree
2 bay leaves
1/2 teaspoon dried basil
1 teaspoon dried marjoram
1 teaspoon celery seeds

Directions

- Press the "Sauté" button to heat up your Instant Pot. Heat olive oil and brown ground beef sirloin, crumbling with a fork. Season with salt and black pepper.
- Add bone broth to deglaze the pot. Stir in the remaining ingredients.
- Secure the lid and choose the "Soup" button.
- Cook for 30 minutes at High pressure. Once cooking is complete, use a natural release for 10 minutes; carefully remove the lid. Bon appétit!

---

158. Delicious Keema Curry
(Ready in about 10 minutes | Servings 6)

You are going to fall in love with this Indian-inspired dish! Feel free to add green peas or potatoes if desired.

Per serving: *265 Calories; 12.5g Fat; 6g Carbs; 3.7g Protein; 4.4g Sugars*

Ingredients

1 tablespoon olive oil
2 pounds beef, ground
1/2 cup onion, chopped
2 cloves garlic, smashed
1 ripe tomato, diced
1 red chili pepper
Salt and ground black pepper, to taste

1/2 teaspoon ground cumin
1/2 teaspoon mustard seeds
1 teaspoon chili paste
1 teaspoon curry powder
1 cup water
1/2 cup light plain yogurt
2 tablespoons fresh green onions, chopped

Directions

- Press the "Sauté" button to preheat your Instant Pot. Heat olive oil and cook ground beef for 2 to 3 minutes.
- Then, process onion, garlic, tomato and chili pepper in your blender. Add this mixture to the Instant Pot.
- Next, add the salt, black pepper, cumin, mustard seeds, chili paste, curry powder, and water.
- Secure the lid. Choose the "Manual" mode and High pressure; cook for 5 minutes. Once cooking is complete, use a natural pressure release; carefully remove the lid.
- After that, fold in yogurt and seal the lid. Let it sit in the residual heat until thoroughly heated. Serve garnished with fresh green onions. Bon appétit!

159. Cheesy Meatballs in Mushroom Sauce

(Ready in about 10 minutes | Servings 6)

Drop meatballs into a sauce that features condensed mushroom soup and thick tomato paste; then, cook for 6 minutes. Ta-da!
Per serving: *450 Calories; 24g Fat; 26.7g Carbs; 27.8g Protein; 9.9g Sugars*

Ingredients

1 pound ground beef
2 slices bacon, chopped
1/2 cup Romano cheese, grated
1 cup seasoned breadcrumbs
1/2 cup scallions, chopped
2 garlic cloves, crushed

2 large eggs, beaten
1/3 cup milk
1 tablespoon canola oil
1 (10 ¼-ounce) can condensed mushroom soup
1 cup tomato paste

Directions

- Thoroughly combine ground beef, bacon, cheese, breadcrumbs, scallions, garlic, eggs, and milk. Roll the mixture into meatballs.
- Press the "Sauté" button to preheat the Instant Pot. Heat the oil and sear the meatballs until they are browned on all sides.
- Add canned mushroom soup and tomato paste to the Instant Pot.
- Secure the lid. Choose the "Manual" mode and High pressure; cook for 6 minutes. Once cooking is complete, use a quick pressure release; carefully remove the lid.
- Serve warm, garnished with mashed potatoes. Bon appétit!

---

160. Chili-Beef Tacos

(Ready in about 25 minutes | Servings 6)

What's for dinner? The answer is simple – tacos! Give a classic ground meat a Mexican spin!
Per serving: *361 Calories; 14.6g Fat; 34.5g Carbs; 24.1g Protein; 3.8g Sugars*

Ingredients

2 teaspoons lard
1 pound ground chuck
2 onions, diced
3 garlic cloves, smashed
2 ripe tomatoes, pureed
1 cup beef bone broth
1 envelope (1-ounce) taco seasoning mix
2 cans (16-ounce) pinto beans, drained
1 tablespoon chipotle powder
1 teaspoon cumin, ground

1/2 teaspoon mustard seeds
1 teaspoon dried marjoram
1/2 teaspoon dried basil
Salt and pepper, to taste
2 tablespoons tamari sauce
3/4 teaspoon cocoa powder, unsweetened
6 medium store-bought taco shells
1/2 cup sour cream
2 tablespoons fresh cilantro leaves, chopped

Directions

- Press the "Sauté" button to heat up your Instant Pot and melt the lard. Once hot, cook the ground chuck, crumbling with a fork. Set aside.
- Cook the onions and garlic in pan drippings, stirring occasionally; add a splash of bone broth, if necessary, to prevent sticking.
- Now, stir in tomatoes, beef bone broth, and taco seasoning mix; cook, stirring continuously, an additional minute or until warmed through.
- Next, stir in canned beans, chipotle powder, cumin, mustard seeds, marjoram, basil, salt, pepper, tamari sauce, and cocoa powder. Secure the lid.
- Select the "Manual" mode and cook at High Pressure for 12 minutes. Once cooking is complete, use a natural release and carefully remove the lid.
- To assemble, divide the beef/bean mixture among taco shells; top each with sour cream and fresh chopped cilantro. Bon appétit!

161. Muffin-Topped Beef Stew
(Ready in about 45 minutes | Servings 6)

Enjoy delicious one-pot meals! Muffin-topped stew is the perfect family dinner, both easy and gourmet!
Per serving: *404 Calories; 15.5g Fat; 31.1g Carbs; 34.4g Protein; 7g Sugars*

Ingredients

1 heaping tablespoon lard, at room temperature
1 ½ pounds beef steak, thinly sliced
1 large-sized leek, chopped
2 garlic cloves, crushed
1 cup celery with leaves
1 cup carrots, chopped
1 cup parsnip, chopped
2 bell peppers, chopped
1 (14-ounce) can tomatoes, diced

4 cups water
4 bouillon cubes
1 bay leaf
Topping:
1 cup plain flour
1 teaspoon baking powder
1 cup Swiss cheese, grated
1/2 cup full-fat milk

Directions

- Press the "Sauté" button to preheat your Instant Pot. Melt the lard and brown the beef for 3 to 4 minutes, stirring occasionally.
- Then, add the leeks and cook an additional 2 minutes or until it has softened. Add the garlic, celery, carrot, parsnip, peppers, tomatoes, water, bouillon cubes, and bay leaf.
- Secure the lid. Choose the "Meat/Stew" mode and High pressure; cook for 20 minutes. Once cooking is complete, use a quick pressure release; carefully remove the lid.
- In a mixing bowl, thoroughly combine all of the topping ingredients. Spread the topping over the top of your stew. Seal the lid and press the "Sauté" button.
- Let it simmer for 15 minutes longer or until golden. Serve immediately.

---

162. Mexican-Style Beef Carnitas
(Ready in about 50 minutes | Servings 8)

This recipe calls for salsa, preferably homemade. Other taco fixings include diced avocado, Guacamole, sour cream, pickled cabbage, Pico de Gallo and so forth.
Per serving: *250 Calories; 11.6g Fat; 6.1g Carbs; 31.4g Protein; 3.1g Sugars*

Ingredients

1 tablespoon corn oil
2 pounds chuck roast, cut into pieces
1 red onion, chopped
2 garlic cloves, minced
1 teaspoon ancho chili powder
Sea salt and ground black pepper, to taste
1 teaspoon Mexican oregano

1/2 teaspoon coriander seeds
1/2 teaspoon fennel seeds
1 teaspoon mustard powder
2 cups tomato purée
1 cup water
2 beef bouillon cubes
1 cup salsa, to serve

Directions

- Press the "Sauté" button to preheat your Instant Pot. Then, heat the oil. Brown the chuck roast for 3 minutes.
- Add onion and garlic and cook an additional 2 minutes, stirring continuously. Stir in the remaining ingredients, except for salsa.
- Secure the lid. Choose the "Soup" mode and High pressure; cook for 40 minutes. Once cooking is complete, use a natural pressure release; carefully remove the lid.
- Remove beef from the Instant Pot and let it cool slightly. After that, shred the meat using two forks.
- Meanwhile, press the "Sauté" button again and simmer the cooking liquid until the sauce has reduced and thickened. Adjust the seasonings and return the shredded meat back to the Instant Pot.
- Serve with salsa. Enjoy!

163. Quinoa Meatball Biscuit Sliders
(Ready in about 20 minutes | Servings 5)

Here's an exciting way to make and eat beef meatballs. They are loaded with quinoa and fresh herbs and served on dinner rolls.
Per serving: *577 Calories; 26.2g Fat; 44.9g Carbs; 40g Protein; 8.4g Sugars*

Ingredients

1 pound lean beef, ground
1/2 pound ground pork
1 cup quinoa, cooked
2 garlic cloves, chopped
4 tablespoons scallions, chopped
1 tablespoon fresh cilantro, chopped
1 cup breadcrumbs
1 egg, beaten
1/4 cup milk
Salt and black pepper, to taste

1/2 teaspoon crushed red pepper flakes
1/2 teaspoon dried rosemary, chopped
2 tablespoons olive oil
2 ½ cups tomato sauce
1/4 cup brown sugar
2 tablespoons vinegar
1 dash allspice
1/2 teaspoon chili powder
16 dinner rolls

Directions

- In a mixing bowl, combine ground beef, pork, quinoa, garlic, scallions, cilantro, breadcrumbs egg, and milk; now, season with salt, black pepper, red pepper, and rosemary.
- Shape the meat mixture into 16 meatballs. Press the "Sauté" button to preheat your Instant Pot. Now, heat the oil until sizzling. Once hot, brown your meatballs on all sides.
- Add tomato sauce, sugar, vinegar, allspice and chili powder.
- Select the "Manual" mode and cook for 12 minutes. Once cooking is complete, use a quick release.
- Place one meatball on top of the bottom half of a dinner roll. Spoon the sauce on top of your meatball. Top with the other half of the dinner roll.
- Repeat until you run out of ingredients. Bon appétit!

---

164. Sloppy Joe Soup
(Ready in about 25 minutes | Servings 4)

This hearty and meaty soup is a perfect idea on cold autumn days. Serve with enough crusty, sauce-sopping bread.
Per serving: *340 Calories; 16.3g Fat; 15.7g Carbs; 31.9g Protein; 7.2g Sugars*

Ingredients

1 tablespoon olive oil
1 pound ground beef
1 onion, peeled and finely chopped
Sea salt and ground black pepper, to taste
1 teaspoon cayenne pepper
1 parsnip, thinly sliced
2 carrots, thinly sliced

4 cups beef bone broth
2 garlic cloves, minced
1/2 cup tomato purée

Directions

- Press the "Sauté" button to preheat your Instant Pot. Heat the olive oil and brown the ground beef and onions until the meat is no longer pink.
- Add the remaining ingredients to your Instant Pot
- Secure the lid. Choose the "Soup" mode and High pressure; cook for 20 minutes. Once cooking is complete, use a quick pressure release; carefully remove the lid.
- Ladle into individual bowls and serve hot. Bon appétit!

165. Chipolata Sausage and Cheese Casserole
(Ready in about 25 minutes | Servings 6)

This simple recipe is all you need to take holiday dinner to the next level. A feast for the eyes and the belly!
Per serving: *498 Calories; 40.5g Fat; 11.2g Carbs; 21.8g Protein; 2.6g Sugars*

Ingredients

1 tablespoon olive oil
1 ½ pounds lean beef chipolata sausages
1 leek, thinly sliced
2 garlic cloves, minced
1 cup tomato purée
1/2 cup beef bone broth
2 tablespoons ketchup
1 tablespoon tamari sauce
1 teaspoon cocoa powder

2 bay leaves
1 (20-ounce) can red kidney beans
1 teaspoon red pepper flakes
Salt, to taste
1/3 teaspoon freshly ground black pepper
1 teaspoon dried saffron
3/4 cup Colby cheese, grated

Directions

- Press the "Sauté" button to preheat your Instant Pot. Now, heat the oil until sizzling. Brown the sausage for 2 minutes; reserve.
- Then, sauté the leeks and garlic in pan drippings for 2 more minutes; return the sausage back to the Instant Pot.
- Add tomato purée, broth, ketchup, tamari sauce, cocoa powder, bay leaves, beans, red pepper flakes, salt, black pepper, and saffron to the Instant Pot.
- Secure the lid. Choose the "Poultry" mode and High pressure; cook for 15 minutes. Once cooking is complete, use a quick pressure release; carefully remove the lid.
- Top with grated cheese and seal the lid again. Let it sit until cheese is melted. Serve warm.

166. Country-Style Ribs with Green Beans
(Ready in about 1 hour 5 minutes | Servings 10)

Green beans can help manage diabetes symptoms, boost your immune system and improve bone health. If you could find pasture-raised beef ribs, you will have a completely healthy and nutritious meal.
Per serving: *520 Calories; 43g Fat; 7.8g Carbs; 24.2g Protein; 4g Sugars*

Ingredients

3 pounds Country-style ribs
2 tablespoons sesame oil
1 shallot, diced
4 garlic cloves, minced
1 (1-inch) piece fresh ginger, grated
1 cup vegetable broth
1/4 cup hoisin sauce

2 tablespoons tamari sauce
1 tablespoon honey
1 tablespoon five-spice powder
Salt, to taste
1/2 teaspoon ground black pepper
1 pound green beans

Directions

- Add all of the above ingredients, except for green beans, to the Instant Pot.
- Secure the lid. Choose the "Manual" mode and High pressure; cook for 55 minutes. Once cooking is complete, use a natural pressure release; carefully remove the lid.
- Then, add green beans. Secure the lid. Choose the "Steam" mode and High pressure; cook for 3 minutes. Once cooking is complete, use a quick pressure release; carefully remove the lid.
- Transfer the ribs along with green beans to a nice serving platter and serve immediately.

167. New York Strip with Sweet Peppers

(Ready in about 25 minutes | Servings 4)

Making an elegant beef dinner just got even easier. This dish features New York strip, three sauces, and peppers.
Per serving: *322 Calories; 12.7g Fat; 25.5g Carbs; 27g Protein; 14.3g Sugars*

Ingredients

1 pound New York strip, cut into pieces
Salt and ground black pepper, to taste
1 teaspoon paprika
1 tablespoon lard, melted
2 sweet onions, chopped
2 cloves garlic, smashed
1 sweet red bell pepper, chopped
1 sweet green bell pepper, chopped

1/2 cup beef broth
1/2 cup tomato sauce
2 tablespoons Worcestershire sauce
1 tablespoon oyster sauce
2 tablespoons flaxseed meal
2 tablespoons toasted pine nuts, for garnish

Directions

- Toss beef with salt, black pepper, and paprika. Press the "Sauté" button on your Instant Pot. Once hot, melt the lard.
- Brown beef for 4 to 5 minutes, stirring periodically; add a splash of beef broth, if necessary; reserve.
- Then, cook sweet onions, garlic, and bell peppers until they are softened.
- Add beef broth, tomato sauce, Worcestershire, and oyster sauce to the Instant Pot. Return browned beef to the Instant Pot.
- Choose "Manual" setting, High pressure, and 15 minutes. Once cooking is complete, use a quick release.
- Press the "Sauté" button, stir in flaxseed meal, and cook until the sauce is concentrated. Serve garnished with toasted pine nuts. Bon appétit!

---

168. Thai-Style Beef Salad

(Ready in about 45 minutes | Servings 6)

You're about to cook the best beef salad you've ever eaten! Beef pairs well with citrus dressing, red chilies, and Thai herbs.
Per serving: *318 Calories; 17.7g Fat; 5.1g Carbs; 33.4g Protein; 1.9g Sugars*

Ingredients

2 pounds beef rump steak
1/2 cup vegetable broth
1/2 cup water
1 tablespoon black peppercorns
2 bay leaves
1 tablespoon tamari sauce
1/4 cup lemon juice, freshly squeezed
1/4 cup sesame oil
Sea salt flakes, to taste

1 cup red onions, thinly sliced
1 fresh tomato, diced
1 large-sized cucumber, sliced
2 long fresh red chilies, chopped
2 cups arugula
1 tablespoon Dijon mustard
1 bunch fresh Thai basil, leaves picked
3 kaffir lime leaves, shredded

Directions

- Add the beef, vegetable broth, water, black peppercorns, and bay leaves to your Instant Pot.
- Secure the lid. Choose the "Meat/Stew" mode and High pressure; cook for 35 minutes. Once cooking is complete, use a natural pressure release; carefully remove the lid.
- Thinly slice beef across the grain and add to the salad bowl. In a small mixing bowl, make the dressing by whisking tamari sauce, lemon juice, sesame oil, and salt.
- Add the remaining ingredients to the salad bowl; dress the salad. Serve at room temperature.

169. Beef Roast with Vegetables
(Ready in about 55 minutes | Servings 6)

Add vegetables and Chianti to the Instant Pot, and you will turn an ordinary roast into something spectacular! This recipe calls for Chianti but you can use Merlot and Pinot Noir and even white wines such as Pinot Grigio and Sancerre.
Per serving: *363 Calories; 17.6g Fat; 6.1g Carbs; 41.6g Protein; 1.8g Sugars*

Ingredients

2 tablespoons olive oil
2 pounds beef roast
1 cup vegetable broth
1/2 cup Chianti
Sea salt and ground black pepper, to taste
1 teaspoon red pepper flakes, crushed
1 cup shallots, chopped
2 cloves garlic, pressed
2 bay leaves
2 carrots, sliced
1 parsnip, sliced

Directions

- Add the olive oil, beef, broth, Chianti, salt, black pepper, red pepper, shallots, garlic, and bay leaves to the Instant Pot.
- Secure the lid. Choose the "Meat/Stew" mode and High pressure; cook for 45 minutes. Once cooking is complete, use a quick pressure release; carefully remove the lid.
- Then, add the carrots and parsnip to the Instant Pot.
- Secure the lid. Choose the "Manual" mode and High pressure; cook for 5 minutes. Once cooking is complete, use a quick pressure release; carefully remove the lid.
- You can thicken the cooking liquid on "Sauté" function if desired. Bon appétit!

---

170. Deluxe Beef Sandwich
(Ready in about 45 minutes | Servings 6)

Select a great beef roast and good quality dry vermouth to make these extraordinary and satisfying sandwiches for your family. With lots of fresh salad, these sandwiches are addictive!
Per serving: *503 Calories; 23.7g Fat; 36.2g Carbs; 34.3g Protein; 19.8g Sugars*

Ingredients

1 tablespoon olive oil
2 pounds sirloin
1/2 cup vegetable broth
1/2 cup water
1/4 cup dry vermouth
1 tablespoon Dijon mustard

1 tablespoon tamari sauce
Salt and black pepper, to taste
1/2 teaspoon cayenne pepper
2 cloves garlic, minced
1 red chili pepper
6 sandwich buns, split

Directions

- Press the "Sauté" button to preheat your Instant Pot. Then, heat the oil until sizzling. Sear the beef until browned on all sides.
- Add broth, water, vermouth, mustard, tamari sauce, salt, black pepper, cayenne pepper, garlic, and red chili pepper.
- Secure the lid. Choose the "Soup" mode and High pressure; cook for 40 minutes. Once cooking is complete, use a natural pressure release; carefully remove the lid.
- Then, pull the cooked beef apart into chunks. Return it back to the Instant Pot and stir well to combine. Assemble the sandwiches with buns and serve. Enjoy!

171. Melt in Your Mouth Beef Rump Roast
(Ready in about 40 minutes | Servings 8)

A classic rump roast is made simple with rich herbs, Chinese cooking wine, and root vegetables. Simple but effective. Enjoy!
Per serving: *269 Calories; 11.5g Fat; 10g Carbs; 31.7g Protein; 3.7g Sugars*

Ingredients

2 pounds beef rump roast
2 garlic cloves, halved
Salt and pepper, to your liking
1 teaspoon dried rosemary
1 teaspoon dried thyme
1 tablespoon olive oil
1 cup leeks, chopped
4 carrots, peeled
2 parsnips, chopped
1/3 cup Shaoxing wine
1 ½ cups vegetable stock

Directions

- Rub beef rump roast with garlic halves. Now, cut it into cubes. Season with salt, pepper, rosemary, and thyme.
- Then, press the "Sauté" button and heat olive oil. Sauté the leeks together with carrot and parsnips.
- Add a splash of Shaoxing wine to deglaze the pan. Place beef pieces in a single layer on top of sautéed vegetables.
- Pour in the vegetable stock and the remaining Shaoxing wine. Secure the lid. Select the "Manual" mode and cook for 35 minutes.
- Once cooking is complete, use a quick release. Serve warm. Bon appétit!

---

172. Classic Hungarian Goulash
(Ready in about 40 minutes | Servings 4)

Use well-marbled beef chuck for this recipe. Serve with sourdough bread and cream cheese.
Per serving: *336 Calories; 16.6g Fat; 10.5g Carbs; 36.5g Protein; 1.2g Sugars*

Ingredients

1/3 cup all-purpose flour
Sea salt and freshly ground pepper, to taste
1 teaspoon garlic powder
1 ½ pounds boneless beef chuck, cut into cubes
2 tablespoons sesame oil
4 cups water
4 bullion cubes

1/4 cup rose wine
1 bay leaf
2 shallots, chopped
1 celery with leaves, chopped
2 carrots, sliced
1 red bell pepper, sliced
1 teaspoon Hungarian paprika

Directions

- In a mixing bowl, thoroughly combine the flour, salt, black pepper, and garlic powder. Now add the beef cubes to the flour mixture; toss to coat well.
- Press the "Sauté" button. Heat the oil and sear the meat for 4 to 6 minutes.
- Add the remaining ingredients and stir to combine.
- Secure the lid. Choose the "Soup" mode and High pressure; cook for 30 minutes. Once cooking is complete, use a natural pressure release; carefully remove the lid.
- Serve in individual bowls and enjoy!

173. Saucy and Cheesy Beef Brisket

(Ready in about 1 hour 5 minutes | Servings 6)

This is the next level brisket recipe! A fork-tender beef brisket pairs perfectly with Monterey Jack cheese. Enjoy!
Per serving: *434 Calories; 33.7g Fat; 3.2g Carbs; 28g Protein; 0.7g Sugars*

Ingredients

2 tablespoons lard, at room temperature
2 pounds beef brisket
Sea salt, to taste
1/2 teaspoon ground black pepper
1/2 teaspoon cayenne pepper
1/2 teaspoon ground bay leaf
1/2 teaspoon celery seeds

1 teaspoon mustard seeds
2 garlic cloves, chopped
1 leek, chopped
1 cup beef bone broth
1 cup Monterey Jack cheese, freshly grated

Directions

- Press the "Sauté" button to preheat your Instant Pot. Then, melt the lard.
- Once hot, sear the brisket for 2 to 3 minutes on each side. Then, add seasonings, garlic, leek, and beef bone broth.
- Secure the lid. Choose the "Manual" mode and High pressure; cook for 60 minutes. Once cooking is complete, use a natural pressure release; carefully remove the lid.
- Slice the beef into strips and top with cheese.
- Press the "Sauté" button once again and allow it to simmer until cheese is melted. Serve warm.

174. Beef Stew with Sweet Corn

(Ready in about 30 minutes | Servings 6)

This stew will make your kitchen smell wonderful! It will be a good match with rice noodles.
Per serving: *223 Calories; 5.6g Fat; 14.4g Carbs; 28.1g Protein; 3.4g Sugars*

Ingredients

2 pounds beef stewing meat, cut into cubes
4 cups bone broth
1/2 cup Pinot Noir
1 yellow onion, chopped
2 bell peppers, chopped
1 red chili pepper, chopped
1/2 pound carrots, chopped
Sea salt and ground black pepper, to taste
1/2 teaspoon mustard powder
1 teaspoon celery seeds
1 cup sweet corn kernels, frozen

Directions

- Add all ingredients, except for sweet corn, to the Instant Pot.
- Secure the lid. Choose the "Soup" mode and High pressure; cook for 20 minutes. Once cooking is complete, use a quick pressure release; carefully remove the lid.
- Stir in sweet corn kernels and press the "Sauté" button. Let it simmer until thoroughly heated. Taste, adjust the seasonings and serve. Bon appétit!

175. Hoisin Sirloin Steak
(Ready in about 1 hour | Servings 8)

Here's the recipe for busy days when you don't have time to cook, but you want something special for your family.
Per serving: *283 Calories; 14.9g Fat; 10.9g Carbs; 24.8g Protein; 4.6g Sugars*

Ingredients

1 tablespoon lard, at room temperature
2 pounds boneless sirloin steak, thinly sliced
Sea salt and ground black pepper, to your liking
1 teaspoon chili powder
2 tablespoons fresh parsley, chopped

1/2 cup red onion, sliced
2 garlic cloves, minced
2 sweet peppers, deveined and sliced
1/2 cup beef bone broth
1/2 cup hoisin sauce

Directions

- Press the "Sauté" button and preheat the Instant Pot; melt the lard. Once hot, brown the sirloin steak for 6 minutes, flipping halfway through cooking time.
- Season with salt and pepper; add chili powder, parsley, onion, garlic, and peppers. Pour in beef bone broth and secure the lid.
- Select "Manual" setting, High pressure and 50 minutes. Once cooking is complete, use a natural release and carefully remove the lid.
- Shred the beef and return it to the Instant Pot; stir to combine. Afterwards, pour hoisin sauce over shredded beef and vegetables and serve immediately. Bon appétit!

---

176. Beef Brisket with Quick Cabbage Slaw
(Ready in about 1 hour 10 minutes | Servings 6)

Make sure to save some leftovers because cold sandwiches with beef brisket are so good.
Per serving: *397 Calories; 29.4g Fat; 10.9g Carbs; 21.4g Protein; 5.1g Sugars*

Ingredients

2 teaspoons olive oil
1 ½ pounds beef brisket
4 bacon slices, chopped
2 garlic cloves, pressed
1 carrot, chopped
1/2 cup dry red wine
1/2 cup water
2 sprigs rosemary
1/2 teaspoon mixed peppercorns, whole
1/4 cup tomato purée

1/2 teaspoon sea salt
1/2 teaspoon ground black pepper
1/2 teaspoon cayenne pepper
Cole Slaw:
1 head cabbage
1 yellow onion, thinly sliced
1 carrot, grated
4 tablespoons sour cream
4 tablespoons mayonnaise
Salt, to taste

Directions

- Press the "Sauté" button to preheat your Instant Pot. Then, heat the oil until sizzling. Sear the beef for 3 to 4 minutes or until it is delicately browned; reserve.
- Add the bacon to the Instant Pot; sear the bacon approximately 3 minutes; reserve. Then, cook the garlic for 1 minute or until fragrant.
- Add carrot, wine, water, rosemary, mixed peppercorns, tomato purée, salt, black pepper, and cayenne pepper. Return the beef brisket and bacon back to the Instant Pot.
- Secure the lid. Choose the "Manual" mode and High pressure; cook for 60 minutes. Once cooking is complete, use a quick pressure release; carefully remove the lid.
- Meanwhile, make the cabbage slaw by mixing the remaining ingredients. Serve and enjoy!

177. Country-Style Steak Soup

(Ready in about 25 minutes | Servings 4)

An old-fashioned soup with root vegetables and canned tomato sauce. Get ready to a pot full of comfort!
Per serving: *278 Calories; 7.6g Fat; 22.3g Carbs; 30.4g Protein; 9.7g Sugars*

Ingredients

1 pound beef steak, cut into cubes
1 cup water
2 (8-ounce) cans tomato sauce
1 cup roasted vegetable broth
1 shallot, diced
2 carrots, chopped
1 parsnip, chopped
1 turnip, chopped
2 bell peppers, deveined and chopped
2 cloves garlic, minced
Sea salt and ground black pepper, to taste
1 bay leaf

Directions

- Simply throw all of the above ingredients in your Instant Pot that is previously greased with a nonstick cooking spray.
- Secure the lid. Choose the "Soup" mode and High pressure; cook for 20 minutes. Once cooking is complete, use a quick pressure release; carefully remove the lid.
- Divide the soup among four serving bowls and serve warm.

178. Hungarian Marha Pörkölt

(Ready in about 30 minutes | Servings 4)

Full of comforting flavors, this traditional beef stew is loaded with vegetables and stewing meat, and garnished with a dollop of refreshing sour cream.
Per serving: *487 Calories; 19g Fat; 11.3g Carbs; 65g Protein; 2.7g Sugars*

Ingredients

1 tablespoon sesame oil
1 ½ pounds beef stewing meat, cut into bite-sized chunks
1 cup scallions, chopped
2 cloves garlic, minced
Kosher salt, to taste
1/4 teaspoon freshly ground black pepper, or more to taste
2 carrots, sliced
1 jalapeño pepper, minced

4 cups beef bone broth
1 cup tomato purée
2 sprigs thyme
1 teaspoon dried sage, crushed
2 tablespoons sweet Hungarian paprika
1/2 teaspoon mustard seeds
2 bay leaves
1 cup sour cream

Directions

- Press the "Sauté" button to preheat your Instant Pot. Then, heat the sesame oil. Sear the beef for 3 to 4 minutes or until it is delicately browned; reserve.
- Cook the scallions and garlic in pan drippings until tender and fragrant. Now, add the remaining ingredients, except for sour cream.
- Secure the lid. Choose the "Soup" mode and High pressure; cook for 20 minutes. Once cooking is complete, use a quick pressure release; carefully remove the lid.
- Divide your stew among four soup bowls; serve with a dollop of sour cream and enjoy!

179. Creamy and Saucy Beef Delight
(Ready in about 30 minutes | Servings 6)

Some beef recipes can get really, really complicated. With a few basic ingredients dumped into the Instant Pot, this one is oh-so-simple! Serve with crisp, fresh lettuce.
Per serving: *485 Calories; 30.9g Fat; 12.8g Carbs; 37.1g Protein; 2.4g Sugars*

Ingredients

1 tablespoon lard, at room temperature
1 shallot, diced
1 ½ pounds beef brisket, cut into 2-inch cubes
Sea salt and freshly ground pepper, to taste
1 teaspoon red pepper flakes, crushed
2 garlic cloves, minced
2 sprigs dried rosemary, leaves picked

2 sprigs dried thyme, leaves picked
1 teaspoon caraway seeds
1 ½ tablespoons flaxseed meal
1/2 cup chicken stock
6 ounces wonton noodles
3/4 cup cream cheese
2 tablespoons toasted sesame seeds

Directions

- Press the "Sauté" button to preheat your Instant Pot. Now, melt the lard; once hot, sweat the shallot for 2 to 3 minutes.
- Toss beef brisket with salt, ground pepper, and red pepper flakes. Add beef to the Instant pot; continue cooking for 3 minutes more or until it is no longer pink.
- After that, stir in garlic, rosemary, thyme, and caraway seeds; cook an additional minute, stirring continuously.
- Add the flaxseed meal, chicken stock, and wonton noodles. Stir to combine well and seal the lid. Choose the "Meat/Stew" setting and cook at High pressure for 20 minutes.
- Once cooking is complete, use a quick release; remove the lid. Divide the beef mixture among 6 serving bowls.
- To serve, stir in cream cheese and garnish with toasted sesame seeds. Bon appétit!

---

180. Sunday Hamburger Pilaf
(Ready in about 15 minutes | Servings 4)

Pilaf recipes seem complicated at first glance. The truth is that you do not have to spend hours in the kitchen to create this amazing one-pot meal. It takes only 15 minutes in the Instant Pot electric pressure cooker.
Per serving: *493 Calories; 28.8g Fat; 34.9g Carbs; 42.1g Protein; 3.3g Sugars*

Ingredients

1 tablespoon sesame oil
1/2 cup leeks, chopped
1 teaspoon garlic, minced
1 jalapeño pepper, minced
1 (1-inch) piece ginger root, peeled and grated
1 ½ pounds ground chuck

1 cup tomato purée
Sea salt, to taste
1/3 teaspoon ground black pepper, or more to taste
1 teaspoon red pepper flakes
2 cups Arborio rice
1 ½ cups roasted vegetable broth

Directions

- Press the "Sauté" button to preheat your Instant Pot. Now, heat the sesame oil and sauté the leeks until tender.
- Then, add the garlic, jalapeño and ginger; cook for 1 minute more or until aromatic.
- Add the remaining ingredients; stir well to combine.
- Secure the lid. Choose the "Manual" mode and High pressure; cook for 7 minutes. Once cooking is complete, use a quick pressure release; carefully remove the lid. Serve immediately.

181. Italian-Style Steak Pepperonata
(Ready in about 1 hour 10 minutes | Servings 6)

If you like beef and bell peppers, you should try this Italian classic. Serve on Semelle rolls just like Italian nonna used to make.
Per serving: *309 Calories; 7.4g Fat; 10.8g Carbs; 46.9g Protein; 5.1g Sugars*

Ingredients

2 teaspoons lard, at room temperature
2 pounds top round steak, cut into bite-sized chunks
1 red onion, chopped
1 pound mixed bell peppers, deveined and thinly sliced
2 cloves garlic, minced
1 tablespoon Italian seasoning blend
Sea salt and ground black pepper, to taste
1 tablespoon salt-packed capers, rinsed and drained
1/2 cup dry red wine
1 cup water

Directions

- Press the "Sauté" button to preheat your Instant Pot. Then, melt the lard. Cook the round steak approximately 5 minutes, stirring periodically; reserve.
- Then, sauté the onion for 2 minutes or until translucent.
- Stir in the remaining ingredients, including the reserved beef.
- Secure the lid. Choose the "Manual" mode and High pressure; cook for 60 minutes. Once cooking is complete, use a natural pressure release; carefully remove the lid. Bon appétit!

182. Wine-Braised Beef Shanks
(Ready in about 45 minutes + marinating time | Servings 6)

The beef is incredibly tender and delicious in the Instant Pot. You can prepare beef shank that tastes like it is simmered all day, while it only takes 35 minutes.
Per serving: *329 Calories; 10.5g Fat; 25.8g Carbs; 32g Protein; 2.7g Sugars*

Ingredients

1 ½ pounds beef shanks, cut into pieces
1/2 cup port
1 cup wine
2 garlic cloves, crushed
1 teaspoon celery seeds
12 teaspoon dried thyme
1 tablespoon olive oil

1/2 cup leeks, chopped
2 potatoes, diced
2 carrots, chopped
1 1/3 cups vegetable stock
Salt and black pepper, to taste

Directions

- Add beef shanks to a bowl; now, add port, red wine, garlic, celery seeds, and dried thyme. Let it marinate overnight.
- On an actual day, preheat your Instant Pot on "Sauté" function. Add olive oil; once hot, brown marinated shanks on all sides; reserve.
- Now, cook leeks, potatoes and carrots in pan drippings until they have softened. Add vegetable stock, salt, and pepper to taste.
- Pour in the reserved marinade and secure the lid.
- Select the "Meat/Stew" and cook for 35 minutes at High pressure. Once cooking is complete, use a quick release; remove the lid.
- Now, press the "Sauté" button to thicken the cooking liquid for 5 to 6 minutes. Taste, adjust the seasonings and serve right away!

183. Holiday Osso Buco
(Ready in about 30 minutes | Servings 8)

Take holiday dinner to the next level with these saucy veal shanks. Rose wine is a must in this recipe.
Per serving: *302 Calories; 7.2g Fat; 21.7g Carbs; 34.3g Protein; 3g Sugars*

Ingredients

2 tablespoons olive oil
1 ½ pounds Osso buco
2 carrots, sliced
1 celery with leaves, diced
1 cup beef bone broth
1/2 cup rose wine
2 garlic cloves, chopped
1 onion, chopped
2 bay leaves
1 sprig dried rosemary
1 teaspoon dried sage, crushed
1/2 teaspoon tarragon
Sea salt and ground black pepper, to taste

Directions

- Press the "Sauté" button to preheat your Instant Pot. Now, heat the olive oil. Sear the beef on all sides.
- Add the remaining ingredients.
- Secure the lid. Choose the "Meat/Stew" mode and High pressure; cook for 25 minutes. Once cooking is complete, use a natural pressure release; carefully remove the lid. Bon appétit!

---

184. Tagliatelle with Beef Sausage and Cheese
(Ready in about 10 minutes | Servings 6)

A great recipe dish for a typical weeknight. Cooking pasta in the Instant Pot has a number of advantages to the traditional methods of boiling.
Per serving: *596 Calories; 32.6g Fat; 52.1g Carbs; 26.5g Protein; 11.3g Sugars*

Ingredients

2 teaspoons canola oil
1 pound beef sausage, sliced
1 ½ pounds tagliatelle pasta
3 cups water
2 cups tomato paste

Sea salt and ground black pepper, to taste
8 ounces Colby cheese, grated
5 ounces Ricotta cheese, crumbled
2 tablespoons fresh chives, roughly chopped

Directions

- Press the "Sauté" button to preheat your Instant Pot. Now, heat the oil. Cook the sausages until they are no longer pink; reserve.
- Then, stir in the pasta, water, tomato paste, salt, and black pepper.
- Secure the lid. Choose the "Manual" mode and High pressure; cook for 4 minutes. Once cooking is complete, use a quick pressure release; carefully remove the lid.
- Next, fold in the cheese; seal the lid and let it sit in the residual heat until heated through. Add the reserved sausage and stir; serve garnished with fresh chives. Bon appétit!

185. Balkan-Style Beef Stew
(Ready in about 35 minutes | Servings 6)

A hearty stew that will nourish and energize your body and soul. This traditional dish can be served in less than 35 minutes. Amazing!
Per serving: *403 Calories; 21.3g Fat; 16.4g Carbs; 36.8g Protein; 8.7g Sugars*

Ingredients

1 tablespoon olive oil
2 pounds beef sirloin steak, cut into bite-sized chunks
1 cup red onion, chopped
2 garlic cloves, minced
1 pound bell peppers, seeded and sliced
1 cup vegetable broth
4 Italian plum tomatoes, crushed
Salt and ground black pepper, to taste
1 teaspoon paprika
1 egg, beaten

Directions

- Press the "Sauté" button to preheat your Instant Pot. Now, heat the oil. Cook the beef until it is no longer pink.
- Add onion and cook an additional 2 minutes. Stir in the minced garlic, peppers, broth, tomatoes, salt, black pepper, and paprika.
- Secure the lid. Choose the "Soup" mode and High pressure; cook for 20 minutes. Once cooking is complete, use a quick pressure release; carefully remove the lid.
- Afterwards, fold in the egg and stir well; seal the lid and let it sit in the residual heat for 8 to 10 minutes.
- Serve in individual bowls with mashed potatoes. Enjoy!

186. Bacon and Blade Roast Sandwiches
(Ready in about 1 hour 30 minutes | Servings 8)

Here's a flavor-packed twist on beef sandwiches. Soaked with lager and herbs mixture, gently cooked, and served with mellow cheese, these hearty sandwiches will hit all the best flavor notes.
Per serving: *698 Calories; 40.1g Fat; 36.9g Carbs; 46g Protein; 19g Sugars*

Ingredients

2 center-cut bacon slices, chopped
2 1/2 pounds top blade roast
Salt and ground black pepper, to taste
1 teaspoon dried marjoram
1/2 teaspoon dried rosemary
1 teaspoon Juniper berries

1 (12-ounce) bottle lager
1 ½ cups unsalted beef stock
8 slices Cheddar cheese
2 tablespoons Dijon mustard
8 burger buns

Directions

- Press the "Sauté" button and preheat the Instant Pot. Cook the bacon for 4 minutes or until crisp; reserve.
- Add beef and sear 8 minutes, turning to brown on all sides.
- In the meantime, mix salt, pepper, marjoram, rosemary, Juniper berries, lager, and beef stock. Pour the mixture over the seared top blade roast and seal the lid.
- Choose the "Manual" setting and cook for 1 hour 10 minutes at High pressure. Once cooking is complete, use a quick release; remove the lid.
- Now, shred the meat and return to the cooking liquid; stir to soak well. Return the reserved bacon to the Instant Pot.
- Assemble sandwiches with meat/bacon mixture, cheddar cheese, mustard, and burger buns. Enjoy!

187. Tuscan-Style Cassoulet
(Ready in about 35 minutes | Servings 6)

If you are short on time, prepare this traditional cassoulet in your Instant pot for dinner! You can add a touch of hot paprika for extra flavor.
Per serving: 376 Calories; 19.3g Fat; 18.1g Carbs; 36.3g Protein; 1.6g Sugars

Ingredients

1 tablespoon olive oil
1 ½ pounds beef shoulder, cut into bite-sized chunks
1/2 pound beef chipolata sausages, sliced
1 onion, chopped
2 garlic cloves, minced
1 cup beef stock
1/2 cup tomato purée
1/2 tablespoon ancho chili powder
Sea salt and ground black pepper, to taste
1 tablespoon fresh thyme leaves
1 (15-ounce) can white beans, drained and rinsed
1 cup sour cream

Directions

- Press the "Sauté" button and preheat the Instant Pot. Heat the oil and sear the meat and sausage until they are delicately browned; reserve.
- Then, sauté the onion in pan drippings for 3 to 4 minutes.
- Stir in garlic, stock, tomato purée, ancho chili powder, salt, black pepper, thyme leaves and beans.
- Secure the lid. Choose the "Bean/Chili" mode and High pressure; cook for 25 minutes. Once cooking is complete, use a quick pressure release; carefully remove the lid.
- Garnish each serving with sour cream and serve. Bon appétit!

---

188. Barbecued Beef Round with Cheese
(Ready in about 50 minutes | Servings 6)

Serve on over mashed potatoes in pita bread, and so forth. This barbecued beef makes great leftovers for the lunchbox.
Per serving: *336 Calories; 9.5g Fat; 23.4g Carbs; 37.5g Protein; 17.6g Sugars*

Ingredients

2 pounds bottom round
1 cup beef stock
1 cup barbecue sauce
2 tablespoons tamari sauce
1 cup scallions, chopped
2 cloves garlic, minced

2 teaspoons olive oil
1 teaspoon chili powder
1 cup Cheddar cheese, grated

Directions

- Place all of the above ingredients, except for Cheddar cheese, in your Instant Pot.
- Secure the lid. Choose the "Meat/Stew" mode and High pressure; cook for 45 minutes. Once cooking is complete, use a quick pressure release; carefully remove the lid.
- Top with freshly grated cheese and serve immediately. Enjoy!

189. Home-Style Beef Tikka Kebabs
(Ready in about 30 minutes | Servings 4)

Because beef on a flatbread is just more fun! This traditional Turkish dish features lean steak with seasonings, pickled slaw, and Bazlama flatbread.
Per serving: *590 Calories; 29g Fat; 22.5g Carbs; 58g Protein; 1.8g Sugars*

Ingredients

2 tablespoons olive oil
1 ½ pounds lean steak beef, cubed
1/2 cup onion, sliced
2 cloves garlic, minced
2 tablespoons fresh cilantro, chopped
Salt and ground black pepper, to taste
1 teaspoon Aleppo chili flakes
1/2 teaspoon sumac

1/2 teaspoon turmeric powder
1/3 cup chicken stock
1 tablespoon champagne vinegar
1/3 cup mayonnaise
4 tablespoons pickled slaw
4 Bazlama flatbread

Directions

- Press the "Sauté" button to heat up the Instant Pot. Now, heat olive oil and brown beef cubes, stirring frequently.
- Add onion, garlic, and seasonings to the Instant Pot. Cook an additional 4 minutes or until onion is translucent.
- Pour chicken stock and champagne vinegar over the meat. Seal the lid.
- Choose the "Meat/Stew" setting and cook for 20 minutes at High pressure. Once cooking is complete, use a quick release; remove the lid.
- Assemble sandwiches with mayonnaise, pickled slaw, the meat mixture, and Bazlama bread. Bon appétit!

---

190. Favorite Tex-Mex Tacos
(Ready in about 15 minutes | Servings 8)

This authentic dish is both delicious and super affordable! You can use taco bowls instead of tortillas and take your taco night to a whole new level.
Per serving: *566 Calories; 33.4g Fat; 38.6g Carbs; 30.7g Protein; 6.5g Sugars*

Ingredients

1 tablespoon olive oil
1/2 cup shallots, chopped
2 cloves garlic, pressed
2 pounds ground sirloin
1/2 teaspoon ground cumin
1/2 cup roasted vegetable broth
1/2 ketchup
Sea salt, to taste
1/2 teaspoon fresh ground pepper
1 teaspoon paprika

1 can (16-ounces) diced tomatoes, undrained
2 canned chipotle chili in adobo sauce, drained
12 whole-wheat flour tortillas, warmed
1 head romaine lettuce
1 cup sour cream

Directions

- Press the "Sauté" button and preheat the Instant Pot. Heat the oil and cook the shallots and garlic until aromatic.
- Now, add the ground sirloin and cook an additional 2 minutes or until it is no longer pink.
- Add ground cumin, broth, ketchup, salt, black pepper, paprika, tomatoes, and chili in adobo sauce to your Instant Pot.
- Secure the lid. Choose the "Poultry" mode and High pressure; cook for 5 minutes. Once cooking is complete, use a natural pressure release; carefully remove the lid.
- Divide beef mixture between tortillas. Garnish with lettuce and sour cream and serve.

191. Traditional Beef Pho Noodle Soup
(Ready in about 15 minutes | Servings 4)

Traditional pho is so easy to reinvent in your Instant Pot. Some other garnish ideas include lime slices avocado, Tsang classic stir-fry sauce, and so on.
Per serving: *417 Calories; 14g Fat; 27.5g Carbs; 43.1g Protein; 3.6g Sugars*

Ingredients

1 tablespoon sesame oil
1 pound round steak, sliced paper thin
4 cups roasted vegetable broth
1 tablespoon brown sugar
Kosher salt and ground black pepper, to taste
2 carrots, trimmed and diced
1 celery stalk, trimmed and diced
1 cinnamon stick
3 star of anise
1/2 (14-ounce) package rice noodles
1 bunch of cilantro, roughly chopped
2 stalks scallions, diced

Directions

- Press the "Sauté" button and preheat the Instant Pot. Heat the oil and sear the round steak for 1 to 2 minutes.
- Add the broth, sugar, salt, black pepper, carrots, celery, cinnamon stick, and star anise. Top with rice noodles so they should be on top of the other ingredients.
- Secure the lid. Choose the "Manual" mode and High pressure; cook for 3 minutes. Once cooking is complete, use a quick pressure release; carefully remove the lid.
- Serve in individual bowls, topped with cilantro and scallions. Enjoy!

---

192. Ground Beef Taco Bowls
(Ready in about 15 minutes | Servings 4)

You can make your own homemade taco bowls using the underside of a muffin tin and store-bought corn tortillas. Garnish with ripe black olives and reduced-fat sour cream, if desired.
Per serving: *409 Calories; 15.7g Fat; 37.5g Carbs; 29.5g Protein; 6.6g Sugars*

Ingredients

1 tablespoon peanut oil
1 pound ground chuck
1 cup beef bone broth
1 bell pepper, seeded and chopped
1 red chili pepper, seeded and chopped
1 onion, chopped

1 (1.25-ounce) package taco seasoning
4 tortilla bowls, baked
1 (15-ounce) can beans, drained and rinsed
2 fresh tomatoes, chopped

Directions

- Press the "Sauté" button and preheat the Instant Pot. Heat the oil and cook the ground chuck until it is no longer pink.
- Add the broth, bell pepper, chili pepper, onion, and taco seasoning.
- Secure the lid. Choose the "Manual" mode and High pressure; cook for 5 minutes. Once cooking is complete, use a quick pressure release; carefully remove the lid.
- Divide the mixture between tortilla bowls. Top with beans and tomatoes. Enjoy!

193. Barbeque Chuck Roast
(Ready in about 45 minutes | Servings 6)

Here's a cheap, delicious and satisfying roast dinner. You can substitute beef broth for teriyaki sauce. Enjoy!
Per serving: *252 Calories; 9.9g Fat; 9g Carbs; 30.1g Protein; 5.9g Sugars*

Ingredients

2 tablespoons lard, at room temperature
2 pounds chuck roast
4 carrots, sliced
1/2 cup leek, sliced
1 teaspoon garlic, minced
3 teaspoons fresh ginger root, thinly sliced
Salt and pepper, to taste
1 ½ tablespoons fresh parsley leaves, roughly chopped
1 cup barbeque sauce
1/2 cup teriyaki sauce

Directions

- Press the "Sauté" button on your Instant Pot. Now, melt the lard until hot.
- Sear chuck roast until browned, about 6 minutes per side. Add the other ingredients.
- Choose "Manual" setting and cook for 35 minutes at High pressure or until the internal temperature of the chuck roast is at least 145 degrees F.
- Once cooking is complete, use a quick release; remove the lid.
- Serve with crusty bread and fresh salad of choice. Bon appétit!

---

194. Beef Pad Thai
(Ready in about 20 minutes | Servings 6)

Skirt steak cooks perfectly with peanut oil, Thai chili and shallots in this traditional Thai dish.
Per serving: *418 Calories; 24.1g Fat; 5.2g Carbs; 46.1g Protein; 1.2g Sugars*

Ingredients

2 tablespoons peanut oil
2 pounds skirt steak, cut into thin 1-inch-long slices
1 small Thai chili, finely chopped
1 cup beef bone broth
1/2 cup shallots, chopped
2 tablespoons oyster sauce
1/4 cup peanuts, finely chopped

Directions

- Press the "Sauté" button to preheat your Instant Pot. Heat the oil and sear the beef until it is delicately browned on all sides.
- Add Thai chili, broth, shallots, and oyster sauce.
- Secure the lid. Choose the "Poultry" mode and High pressure; cook for 15 minutes. Once cooking is complete, use a quick pressure release; carefully remove the lid.
- Garnish with chopped peanuts and serve warm.

195. Easy Balsamic Beef
(Ready in about 50 minutes | Servings 6)

This one-pot meal is super easy to prepare in your Instant Pot. If you want leftovers of this fabulous beef dish, feel free to double the recipe.
Per serving: *282 Calories; 13.3g Fat; 9.1g Carbs; 32.5g Protein; 5.4g Sugars*

Ingredients

2 tablespoons sesame oil
2 pounds beef chuck, cut into bite-sized pieces
1/4 cup balsamic vinegar
1/2 teaspoon dried basil
1 teaspoon dried rosemary, crushed
1/2 teaspoon cayenne pepper
1/2 teaspoon ground black pepper
Sea salt, to taste
1 onion, chopped
2 cloves garlic, minced
1 tablespoon cilantro, finely chopped
1/2 cup water
1/2 cup tomato paste
1 jalapeño pepper, finely minced

Directions

- Press the "Sauté" button to preheat your Instant Pot. Heat the sesame oil until sizzling.
- Once hot, cook the beef for 2 to 3 minutes. Add the remaining ingredients.
- Secure the lid. Choose the "Meat/Stew" mode and High pressure; cook for 45 minutes. Once cooking is complete, use a natural pressure release; carefully remove the lid.
- Afterwards, thicken the sauce on the "Sauté" function. Serve over hot macaroni and enjoy!

---

196. Juicy Round Steak
(Ready in about 55 minutes | Servings 8)

The succulent and juicy steak that is seared in hot olive oil, then, pressure-cooked in red wine, marinara sauce, and bone broth. Yummy!
Per serving: *363 Calories; 17.9g Fat; 3.1g Carbs; 44.5g Protein; 1.1g Sugars*

Ingredients

2 ½ pounds round steak, cut into 1-inch pieces
Kosher salt and freshly ground black pepper, to taste
1/2 teaspoon ground bay leaf
3 tablespoons chickpea flour
1/4 cup olive oil
2 shallots, chopped

2 cloves garlic, minced
1 cup red wine
1/4 cup marinara sauce
1/3 cup bone broth
1 celery with leaves, chopped

Directions

- Press the "Sauté" button to preheat your Instant Pot. Toss round steak with salt, pepper, ground bay leaf, and chickpea flour.
- Once hot, heat olive oil and cook the beef for 6 minutes, stirring periodically; reserve.
- Stir in the shallots and garlic and cook until they are tender and aromatic. Pour in the wine to deglaze the bottom of the pan. Continue to cook until the liquid has reduced by half.
- Add the other ingredients, stir, and seal the lid. Choose the "Meat/Stew" setting and cook at High pressure for 45 minutes.
- Once cooking is complete, use a natural release; remove the lid. Taste, adjust the seasonings and serve warm.

197. Ground Beef Bulgogi
(Ready in about 15 minutes | Servings 6)

This bulgogi is loaded with a delicious seared beef, tangy sour cream, and fresh leeks. The secret ingredient is a freshly grated ginger.
Per serving: *274 Calories; 17.5g Fat; 4.1g Carbs; 25.4g Protein; 0.8g Sugars*

Ingredients

2 tablespoons canola oil
1/2 cup leeks, chopped
1 (2-inch) knob ginger, grated
2 garlic cloves, finely chopped
1 ½ pounds ground chuck
Sea salt and ground black pepper, to taste
2 cups roasted vegetable broth
1/2 cup sour cream
1 ½ tablespoons flax seed meal
2 tablespoons sesame seeds

Directions

- Press the "Sauté" button to preheat your Instant Pot. Heat the oil and sweat the leeks until tender.
- Then, add ginger and garlic; continue to sauté an additional 2 minutes or until fragrant.
- Add the ground meat and cook for 2 more minutes or until it is no longer pink. Add the salt, black pepper, and broth to the Instant Pot.
- Secure the lid. Choose the "Manual" mode and High pressure; cook for 5 minutes. Once cooking is complete, use a natural pressure release; carefully remove the lid.
- Lastly, fold in sour cream and flax seed meal; seal the lid again; let it sit until thoroughly heated.
- Ladle into individual bowls and top with sesame seeds. Bon appétit!

198. Classic Beef Stroganoff
(Ready in about 25 minutes | Servings 6)

This hearty classic beef dish made with stewing meat, peppers, mushrooms, tomatoes can simmer all day or it can be ready in 20 minutes in the Instant Pot.
Per serving: *536 Calories; 19.6g Fat; 45g Carbs; 50g Protein; 8.5g Sugars*

Ingredients

2 tablespoons sesame oil
1/2 cup shallots, chopped
1 teaspoon minced garlic
1 bell pepper, seeded and chopped
1 ½ pounds stewing meat, cubed
1 celery with leaves, chopped
1 parsnip, chopped

1/2 cup rose wine
1 cup tomato paste
1/2 cup ketchup
1 can (10 ¾-ounce) condensed golden mushroom soup
9 ounces fresh button mushrooms, sliced
6 ounces cream cheese
1/4 cup fresh chives, coarsely chopped

Directions

- Press the "Sauté" button to preheat your Instant Pot. Heat the oil and sauté the shallots until they have softened.
- Stir in the garlic and pepper; continue to sauté until tender and fragrant.
- Add meat, celery, parsnip, wine, tomato paste, ketchup, mushroom soup, and mushrooms.
- Secure the lid. Choose the "Meat/Stew" mode and High pressure; cook for 20 minutes. Once cooking is complete, use a quick pressure release; carefully remove the lid.
- Stir cream cheese into beef mixture; seal the lid and let it sit until melted. Serve garnished with fresh chives. Enjoy!

199. Pepper Jack Beef and Cauliflower Casserole
(Ready in about 35 minutes | Servings 4)

Casserole in an ultimate family dish! Ground beef goes perfectly with spicy sausage, cauliflower, and Pepper Jack cheese.
Per serving: *523 Calories; 39.6g Fat; 10.9g Carbs; 30.8g Protein; 5.3g Sugars*

Ingredients

1 head cauliflower, chopped into small florets
2 tablespoons olive oil
1/2 cup yellow onion, chopped
2 garlic cloves, minced
1/2 pound ground beef
2 spicy sausages, chopped
2 ripe tomatoes, chopped
1 ½ tablespoons brown sugar

2 tablespoons tamari sauce
Salt and freshly ground black pepper, to your liking
1 teaspoon cayenne pepper
1/2 teaspoon celery seeds
1/2 teaspoon fennel seeds
1 teaspoon dried basil
1/2 teaspoon dried oregano
1 cup Pepper Jack cheese, shredded

Directions

- Parboil cauliflower in a lightly salted water for 3 to 5 minutes; remove the cauliflower from the water with a slotted spoon and drain.
- Press the "Sauté" button to preheat your Instant Pot. Now, heat the oil and sweat the onions and garlic.
- Then, add ground beef and sausage and continue to cook for 4 minutes more or until they are browned.
- Stir in the remaining ingredients, except for shredded cheese, and cook for 4 minutes more or until heated through. Add cauliflower florets on top.
- Secure the lid and choose the "Manual" mode, High pressure and 6 minutes. Once cooking is complete, use a quick release; remove the lid.
- Top with shredded cheese and let it melt for 5 to 6 minutes. Bon appétit!

---

200. Hayashi Rice Stew
(Ready in about 30 minutes | Servings 6)

If you like Japanese flavors, you will love this Western-style Japanese beef and rice. You can use Asian mushrooms and Japanese rice for an authentic experience.
Per serving: *368 Calories; 16.1g Fat; 30.9g Carbs; 25.5g Protein; 3g Sugars*

Ingredients

1 tablespoon lard, at room temperature
1 ½ pounds ribeye steaks, cut into bite-sized pieces
1/2 cup shallots, chopped
4 cloves garlic, minced
Salt and black pepper, to taste
1/2 teaspoon sweet paprika
1 sprig dried thyme, crushed
1 sprig dried rosemary, crushed
1 carrot, chopped

1 celery stalk, chopped
1/4 cup tomato paste
2 cups beef bone broth
1/3 cup rice wine
1 tablespoon Tonkatsu sauce
1 cup brown rice

Directions

- Press the "Sauté" button to preheat your Instant Pot. Now, heat the oil and cook the beef until it is delicately browned.
- Add the remaining ingredients; stir to combine.
- Secure the lid. Choose the "Bean/Chili" mode and High pressure; cook for 25 minutes. Once cooking is complete, use a natural pressure release; carefully remove the lid. Bon appétit!

FISH & SEAFOOD

201. Elegant Trout Salad
(Ready in about 15 minutes | Servings 4)

Good-quality ocean trout fillets are high in brain-loving omega-3 fatty acids. Combine it with tomatoes, egg noodles and cucumbers for a quick healthy lunch.
Per serving: *506 Calories; 13.6g Fat; 56g Carbs; 39.1g Protein; 12.1g Sugars*

Ingredients

2 tablespoons olive oil
1 yellow onion, chopped
2 garlic cloves, minced
1 green chili, seeded and minced
2 pieces ocean trout fillets, deboned and skinless
1 cup water
1/2 cup dry vermouth

Sea salt and ground black pepper, to taste
1/2 teaspoon sweet paprika
2 ripe Roma tomatoes, diced
8 ounces dry egg noodles
2 Lebanese cucumbers, chopped
1/2 bunch coriander, leaves picked, roughly chopped
1/4 cup freshly squeezed lime juice

Directions

- Press the "Sauté" button to preheat your Instant Pot. Now, heat the olive oil and sauté the onion until translucent.
- Stir in the garlic and chili; continue to sauté until they are fragrant.
- Add the fish, water, vermouth, salt, black pepper, sweet paprika, tomatoes, and noodles.
- Secure the lid. Choose the "Manual" mode and Low pressure; cook for 10 minutes. Once cooking is complete, use a quick pressure release; carefully remove the lid.
- Flake the fish and allow the mixture to cool completely. Add cucumbers and coriander. Drizzle fresh lime juice over the salad and serve. Bon appétit!

---

202. Tuna Fillets with Eschalots
(Ready in about 10 minutes | Servings 4)

Turn ordinary fish fillets into something spectacular, adding carefully selected seasonings and eschalots.
Per serving: *249 Calories; 9.1g Fat; 11.7g Carbs; 29.5g Protein; 5.6g Sugars*

Ingredients

2 lemons, 1 whole and 1 freshly squeezed
1 pound tuna fillets
Sea salt and ground black pepper, to taste
1 tablespoon dried parsley flakes
2 tablespoons butter, melted
2 eschalots, thinly sliced

Directions

- Place 1 cup of water and lemon juice in the Instant Pot. Add a steamer basket too.
- Place the tuna fillets in the steamer basket. Sprinkle the salt, pepper, and parsley over the fish; drizzle with butter and top with thinly sliced eschalots.
- Secure the lid. Choose the "Steam" mode and Low pressure; cook for 3 minutes. Once cooking is complete, use a quick pressure release; carefully remove the lid.
- Serve immediately with lemon. Bon appétit!

203. Calamari with Roasted Pimentos
(Ready in about 1 hour | Servings 4)

Calamari has a significant amount of vitamin B2, B6 and B12, as well as phosphorus, magnesium, zinc, and calcium. You can double this recipe and serve over spaghetti if desired.
Per serving: *325 Calories; 10.7g Fat; 17.2g Carbs; 38.6g Protein; 6.5g Sugars*

Ingredients

3 Pimentos, stem and core removed
2 tablespoons olive oil
1/2 cup leeks, chopped
2 cloves garlic chopped
1 ½ cups stock, preferably homemade
2 tablespoons fish sauce
1/3 cup dry sherry

Seas salt and ground black pepper, to taste
1/2 teaspoon red pepper flakes, crushed
1 teaspoon dried rosemary, chopped
1 teaspoon dried thyme, chopped
1 ½ pounds frozen calamari, thawed and drained
2 tablespoons fresh chives, chopped

Directions

- Split your Pimentos into halves and place them over the flame. Cook, turning a couple of times, until the skin is blistering and blackened.
- Allow them to stand for 30 minutes; peel your Pimentos and coarsely chop them.
- Press the "Sauté" button to heat up your Instant Pot; add olive oil. Once hot, cook the leeks until tender and fragrant, about 4 minutes.
- Now, stir in the garlic and cook an additional 30 seconds or until just browned and aromatic.
- Add stock, fish sauce, dry sherry, salt, pepper, red pepper flakes, rosemary, and thyme. Add roasted Pimentos. Lastly, place calamari on top. Pour in 3 cups of water.
- Secure the lid. Select the "Manual" mode. Cook for 20 minutes at High pressure. Once cooking is complete, use a quick release; remove the lid carefully.
- Serve warm garnished with fresh chopped chives. Enjoy!

204. Curried Halibut Steaks
(Ready in about 15 minutes | Servings 4)

Alaskan halibut is a good choice for your health and the planet. It is loaded with protein, vitamin B-complex, selenium, magnesium, potassium, phosphorus, and omega-3 fatty acids.
Per serving: *325 Calories; 10.7g Fat; 17.2g Carbs; 38.6g Protein; 6.5g Sugars*

Ingredients

1 tablespoon olive oil
1 cup scallions, chopped
1/2 cup beef bone broth
1 pound halibut steaks, rinsed and cubed
1 cup tomato purée
1 jalapeño pepper, seeded and minced

1 teaspoon ginger garlic paste
1 tablespoon red curry paste
1/2 teaspoon ground cumin
1 cup coconut milk, unsweetened
Salt and ground black pepper, to taste

Directions

- Press the "Sauté" button to preheat your Instant Pot. Now, heat the olive oil; cook the scallions until tender and fragrant.
- Then, use the broth to deglaze the bottom of the inner pot. Stir in the remaining ingredients.
- Secure the lid. Choose the "Manual" mode and Low pressure; cook for 7 minutes. Once cooking is complete, use a quick pressure release; carefully remove the lid.
- Taste, adjust the seasonings and serve right now.

205. Fisherman's Carp Pilaf
(Ready in about 15 minutes | Servings 4)

The easiest way to make lunch is with one-pot meals. A teaspoon of capers will elevate this pilaf from simple to extraordinary.
Per serving: *336 Calories; 16.7g Fat; 28.4g Carbs; 28.6g Protein; 8.8g Sugars*

Ingredients

1 tablespoon olive oil
1 cup chicken stock
1 cup tomato paste
1 teaspoon dried rosemary, crushed
1 tablespoon dried parsley
1/2 teaspoon dried marjoram leaves
Sea salt and ground black pepper, to taste
1/2 teaspoon dried oregano leaves
1 cup Arborio rice
1 pound carp, chopped

Directions

- Simply throw all of the above ingredients into your Instant Pot.
- Secure the lid. Choose the "Manual" mode and High pressure; cook for 6 minutes. Once cooking is complete, use a quick pressure release; carefully remove the lid.
- Serve in individual serving bowls, garnished with fresh lemon slices.

206. Tilapia Fillets with Cremini Mushrooms
(Ready in about 15 minutes | Servings 3)

Tilapia can improve bone health, protect your cardiovascular system and regulate metabolic activities. Make the most of your food!
Per serving: *218 Calories; 12.9g Fat; 2.2g Carbs; 23.6g Protein; 0.7g Sugars*

Ingredients

3 tilapia fillets
1/2 teaspoon sea salt
Freshly ground black pepper, to taste
1 teaspoon cayenne pepper
1 cup Cremini mushrooms, thinly sliced
1/2 cup yellow onions, sliced
2 cloves garlic, peeled and minced
2 sprigs thyme, leaves picked
2 sprigs rosemary, leaves picked
2 tablespoons avocado oil

Directions

- Season tilapia fillets with salt, black pepper, and cayenne pepper on all sides. Place tilapia fillets in the steaming basket fitted for your Instant Pot.
- Place the sliced mushroom and yellow onions on top of the fillets. Add the garlic, thyme, and rosemary; drizzle avocado oil over everything.
- Add 1 ½ cups of water to the base of your Instant Pot. Add the steaming basket to the Instant Pot and secure the lid.
- Select the "Manual" mode. Cook for 8 minutes at Low pressure.
- Once cooking is complete, use a quick release; remove the lid carefully. Serve immediately.

207. Shrimp in Herbed Tomato Sauce
(Ready in about 15 minutes | Servings 4)

If you love light family meals, shrimp is a good choice for you. Shrimp is a staple food in the pressure cooker kitchen so take advantage of this simple and delicious recipe.
Per serving: *214 Calories; 5.4g Fat; 3.9g Carbs; 35.5g Protein; 2.5g Sugars*

Ingredients

1 tablespoon butter, at room temperature
1 cup green onion, chopped
1 teaspoon garlic, minced
1 ½ pounds shrimp, peeled and deveined
1 tablespoon tamari sauce
1 sprig thyme
1 sprig rosemary
2 ripe tomatoes, chopped

Directions

- Press the "Sauté" button to preheat your Instant Pot. Melt the butter and cook green onions until they have softened.
- Now, stir in the garlic and cook an additional 30 seconds or until it is aromatic. Add the rest of the above ingredients.
- Secure the lid. Choose the "Manual" mode and Low pressure; cook for 3 minutes. Once cooking is complete, use a quick pressure release; carefully remove the lid.
- Serve over hot jasmine rice and enjoy!

---

208. Chunky Tilapia Stew
(Ready in about 15 minutes | Servings 4)

This fish stew is made delicious in no time thanks to the Instant Pot. If you like spicy food, feel free to add a few serrano peppers to the stew.
Per serving: *221 Calories; 9.3g Fat; 4.9g Carbs; 25g Protein; 1.8g Sugars*

Ingredients

2 tablespoons sesame oil
1 cup scallions, chopped
2 garlic cloves, minced
1/3 cup dry vermouth
1 cup shellfish stock
2 cups water
2 ripe plum tomatoes, crushed
Sea salt, to taste

1/4 teaspoon freshly ground black pepper, or more to taste
1 teaspoon hot paprika
1 pound tilapia fillets, boneless, skinless and diced
1 tablespoon fresh lime juice
1 teaspoon dried rosemary
1/2 teaspoon dried oregano
1/2 teaspoon dried basil

Directions

- Press the "Sauté" button to preheat your Instant Pot. Heat the oil and sauté the scallions and garlic until fragrant.
- Add a splash of vermouth to deglaze the bottom of the inner pot.
- Secure the lid. Choose the "Manual" mode and High pressure; cook for 5 minutes. Once cooking is complete, use a quick pressure release; carefully remove the lid.
- Serve with some extra lime slices if desired. Bon appétit!

209. Halibut Steaks with Sautéed Tomatoes
(Ready in about 40 minutes | Servings 4)

Make perfectly steamed and delicate fish steaks in your Instant Pot! A great idea for your next family dinner.
Per serving: *166 Calories; 3.8g Fat; 5g Carbs; 21.7g Protein; 1.5g Sugars*

Ingredients

2 tablespoons Worcestershire sauce
2 tablespoons oyster sauce
1/2 cup dry white wine
1 tablespoon Dijon mustard
1 (1-inch) piece fresh ginger, grated
4 halibut steaks
2 teaspoons olive oil
2 tomatoes, sliced
2 spring onions, sliced
2 garlic cloves, crushed
1 cup mixed salad greens, to serve

Directions

- In a mixing bowl, whisk Worcestershire sauce, oyster sauce, white wine, mustard, and ginger. Add fish steaks and let them marinate for 30 minutes in your refrigerator.
- Meanwhile, press the "Sauté" button on your Instant Pot. Now, heat olive oil and sauté the tomatoes with spring onions and garlic until they are tender.
- Add 2 cups of water to the base of your Instant Pot. Add the metal steamer insert to the Instant Pot.
- Now, place the halibut steaks on top of the steamer insert. Secure the lid. Select the "Manual" mode. Cook for 5 minutes at Low pressure.
- Once cooking is complete, use a quick release; remove the lid carefully. Serve warm halibut steaks with sautéed vegetables and mixed salad greens. Enjoy!

---

210. Creamy Shrimp Salad
(Ready in about 10 minutes | Servings 4)

The shorter cooking time retains all valuable nutrients in your food. This salad is perfect for a sandwich!
Per serving: *220 Calories; 10.5g Fat; 7.3g Carbs; 25.4g Protein; 2.9g Sugars*

Ingredients

1 pound shrimp, deveined and peeled
Fresh juice of 2 lemons
Salt and black pepper, to taste
1 red onion, chopped
1 stalk celery, chopped
1 tablespoon fresh dill, minced
1/2 cup mayonnaise
1 teaspoon Dijon mustard

Directions

- Prepare your Instant Pot by adding 1 cup of water and steamer basket to the Instant Pot. Now, add shrimp to the steamer basket.
- Top with lemon slices.
- Secure the lid. Choose the "Manual" mode and Low pressure; cook for 2 minutes. Once cooking is complete, use a quick pressure release; carefully remove the lid.
- Add the remaining ingredients and toss to combine well. Serve well chilled and enjoy!

211. Risotto with Sea Bass and Leeks

(Ready in about 10 minutes | Servings 4)

This risotto is perfect for a potluck since it is easily transported. Feel free to use another combo of seasonings.
Per serving: *432 Calories; 22.2g Fat; 32.2g Carbs; 42g Protein; 1.1g Sugars*

Ingredients

2 tablespoons butter, melted
1/2 cup leeks, sliced
2 garlic cloves, minced
2 cups basmati rice
1 ½ pounds sea bass fillets, diced
2 cups vegetable broth
1 cup water
Salt, to taste
1/2 teaspoon ground black pepper
1 teaspoon fresh ginger, grated

Directions

- Press the "Sauté" button to preheat your Instant Pot. Then, melt the butter and sweat the leeks for 2 to 3 minutes.
- Stir in the garlic; continue to sauté an additional 40 seconds. Add the remaining ingredients.
- Secure the lid. Choose the "Manual" mode and Low pressure; cook for 4 minutes. Once cooking is complete, use a quick pressure release; carefully remove the lid.
- Serve warm in individual bowls and enjoy!

212. Haddock Fillets with Black Beans

(Ready in about 10 minutes | Servings 2)

Here's a summer favorite! Now, you've got to find some crusty bread and your meal is ready!
Per serving: *183 Calories; 4.8g Fat; 1.3g Carbs; 31.8g Protein; 0.8g Sugars*

Ingredients

1 cup water
2 haddock fillets
2 teaspoons coconut butter, at room temperature
Salt and ground black pepper, to taste
2 sprigs thyme, chopped
1/4 teaspoon caraway seeds
1/2 teaspoon tarragon
1/2 teaspoon paprika

4 tomato slices
2 tablespoons fresh cilantro, roughly chopped
1 can black beans, drained

Directions

- Add 1 cup of water to the bottom of your Instant Pot. Add a steamer insert.
- Brush haddock fillets with coconut butter. Now, season haddock fillets with salt and pepper.
- Place the haddock fillets on top of the steamer insert. Add thyme, caraway seeds, tarragon, and paprika. Place 2 tomato slices on each fillet.
- Secure the lid and choose "Manual" setting. Cook for 3 minutes at Low pressure. Once cooking is complete, use a natural release; remove the lid carefully.
- Transfer haddock fillets to serving plates. Scatter chopped cilantro over each fillet and serve garnished with black beans. Bon appétit!

213. Foil-Packet Fish with Aioli

(Ready in about 15 minutes | Servings 2)

Eating healthy doesn't have to be difficult! You can make this light and easy dinner in no time.
Per serving: 397 Calories; 30.1g Fat; 12.3g Carbs; 20.7g Protein; 4.8g Sugars

Ingredients

2 cod fish fillets
1/2 teaspoon seasoned salt
1/4 teaspoon ground black pepper, or more to taste
1/2 teaspoon mustard powder
1/2 teaspoon ancho chili powder
1 shallot, thinly sliced
1 lemon, cut into slices
For Aioli:

1 egg yolk
A pinch of salt
2 garlic cloves, minced
2 teaspoons fresh lemon juice
1/4 cup olive oil

Directions

- Prepare your Instant Pot by adding 1 ½ cups of water and steamer basket to the Instant Pot.
- Place a fish fillet in the center of each piece of foil. Season with salt, pepper, mustard powder, and chili powder.
- Top with shallots and wrap tightly.
- Secure the lid and choose "Manual" setting. Cook for 10 minutes at High pressure. Once cooking is complete, use a natural release; remove the lid carefully.
- In your food processor, mix the egg, salt, garlic, and lemon juice. With the machine running, gradually and slowly add the olive oil.
- Garnish warm fish fillets with lemon slices; serve with aioli on the side. Bon appétit!

---

214. Baked Fish with Parmesan

(Ready in about 15 minutes | Servings 4)

This is the absolute best way to eat mahi-mahi fish. Mahi-mahi fish is loaded with antioxidants, protein, and selenium.
Per serving: *376 Calories; 22.1g Fat; 9.4g Carbs; 34.2g Protein; 0.8g Sugars*

Ingredients

2 ripe tomatoes, sliced
1 teaspoon dried rosemary
1 teaspoon dried marjoram
1/2 teaspoon dried thyme
4 mahi-mahi fillets
2 tablespoons butter, at room temperature
Sea salt and ground black pepper, to taste
8 ounces Parmesan cheese, freshly grated

Directions

- Add 1 ½ cups of water and a rack to your Instant Pot.
- Spritz a casserole dish with a nonstick cooking spray. Arrange the slices of tomatoes on the bottom of the dish. Add the herbs.
- Place mahi-mahi fillets on the top; drizzle the melted butter over the fish. Season it with salt and black pepper. Place the baking dish on the rack.
- Secure the lid. Choose the "Manual" mode and Low pressure; cook for 9 minutes. Once cooking is complete, use a quick pressure release; carefully remove the lid.
- Top with parmesan and seal the lid again; allow the cheese to melt and serve.

215. Salmon Steaks with Kale Pesto Sauce
(Ready in about 15 minutes | Servings 4)

These steamed and herby fish steaks go perfectly with creamy pesto. Serve accompanied by a dry white wine.
Per serving: *366 Calories; 27.1g Fat; 6.6g Carbs; 24.8g Protein; 0.7g Sugars*

Ingredients

1 pound salmon steaks
1 shallot, peeled and sliced
1/2 cup Kalamata olives
2 sprigs rosemary
2 tablespoons olive oil
1/2 teaspoon whole mixed peppercorns
Sea salt, to taste
Kale Pesto Sauce:

1 avocado
1 teaspoon garlic, crushed
2 tablespoons fresh parsley
1 cup kale
2 tablespoons fresh lemon juice
2 tablespoons extra-virgin olive oil

Directions

- Prepare your Instant Pot by adding 1 ½ cups of water and a steamer basket to its bottom.
- Place the salmon steaks in the steamer basket; add the shallots, olives, rosemary, olive oil, peppercorns, and salt.
- Secure the lid. Choose the "Steam" mode and High pressure; cook for 5 minutes. Once cooking is complete, use a quick pressure release; carefully remove the lid.
- Add avocado, garlic, parsley, kale, and lemon juice to your blender. Then, mix on high until a loose paste forms.
- Add olive oil a little at a time and continue to blend until the desired consistency is reached; add a tablespoon or two of water if needed.
- Serve fish fillets with the pesto on the side. Bon appétit!

---

216. Saucy Parmesan Cod with Basmati Rice
(Ready in about 15 minutes | Servings 4)

The Instant Pot ensures you get a quick and tasty fish with rice without losing any nutrition and flavor from your food.
Per serving: *443 Calories; 25.4g Fat; 33.7g Carbs; 36.9g Protein; 1.1g Sugars*

Ingredients

2 cups basmati rice
2 cups water
1 ¼ pounds cod, slice into small pieces
Salt and ground black pepper, to taste
1 teaspoon paprika
2 bay leaves
1 teaspoon coriander
1 teaspoon lemon thyme
2 tablespoons lemon juice
1/2 cup heavy cream
1 cup Parmesan cheese, freshly grated

Directions

- Choose the "Manual" button and cook basmati rice with water for 4 minutes. Once cooking is complete, use a natural release; carefully remove the lid. Reserve.
- Now, press the "Sauté" button on your Instant Pot. Add the remaining ingredients and cook until Parmesan has melted.
- Serve the fish mixture over hot basmati rice and enjoy!

217. Lemon Butter Grouper
(Ready in about 15 minutes | Servings 4)

Fish and seafood are key to a healthy diet. They are protein-packed and they provide vitamins, minerals, and omega 3 fatty acids.
Per serving: 344 Calories; 14.1g Fat; 1.1g Carbs; 50.1g Protein; 0.2g Sugars

Ingredients

4 grouper fillets
4 tablespoons butter
2 tablespoons fresh lemon juice
2 garlic cloves, smashed
1/2 teaspoon sweet paprika
1/2 teaspoon dried basil
Sea salt and ground black pepper, to taste

Directions

- Add 1 ½ cups of water and steamer basket to the Instant Pot. Then, place the fish fillets in the steamer basket.
- Add butter; drizzle with lemon juice; add garlic, paprika, basil, salt, and black pepper.
- Secure the lid. Choose the "Manual" mode and Low pressure; cook for 4 minutes. Once cooking is complete, use a quick pressure release; carefully remove the lid.
- Serve immediately.

---

218. Tuna, Ham and Green Pea Chowder
(Ready in about 15 minutes | Servings 5)

Crispy, fried ham, tuna steaks, and green peas combine to create the perfect seafood chowder that your family will love! Double cream is the perfect thing to thicken the chowder and makes it richer.
Per serving: *360 Calories; 11.2g Fat; 25.7g Carbs; 38.5g Protein; 9.6g Sugars*

Ingredients

2 tablespoons olive oil
4 slices ham, chopped
1 cup shallots, chopped
2 cloves garlic, minced
2 carrots, chopped
5 cups seafood stock
1 ¼ pounds tuna steak, diced

Sea salt and ground black pepper, to taste
1 teaspoon cayenne pepper
1/2 teaspoon ground bay leaf
1/2 teaspoon mustard powder
1 ½ cups double cream
1 ½ cups frozen green peas

Directions

- Press the "Sauté" button to preheat your Instant Pot. Heat the oil and fry the ham until crispy.
- Then, add the shallot and garlic; continue to cook an additional 2 minutes or until tender and fragrant.
- Add the carrot, stock, tuna, salt, black pepper, cayenne pepper, ground bay leaf, and mustard powder.
- Secure the lid. Choose the "Manual" mode and High pressure; cook for 6 minutes. Once cooking is complete, use a natural pressure release; carefully remove the lid.
- Add double cream and frozen peas. Press the "Sauté" button again and cook for a couple of minutes more or until heated through. Bon appétit!

219. Sinfully Delicious Ocean Trout Fillets
(Ready in about 15 minutes | Servings 4)

Ocean Trout is a powerhouse of heart-healthy omega-3 fatty acids. These home-style fish fillets will win your heart!
Per serving: *122 Calories; 2.2g Fat; 1.6g Carbs; 22.7g Protein; 0.5g Sugars*

Ingredients

1 pound ocean trout fillets
Sea salt, to taste
1 teaspoon caraway seeds
1/2 teaspoon mustard seeds
1/2 teaspoon paprika
1/2 cup spring onions, chopped
2 garlic cloves, minced
1 teaspoon mixed peppercorns
2 tablespoons champagne vinegar
1 tablespoon fish sauce
2 ½ cups broth, preferably homemade

Directions

- Place the steaming basket in your Instant Pot. Sprinkle the ocean trout fillets with salt, caraway seeds, mustard seeds, and paprika.
- Place the ocean trout fillet in the steaming basket. Add the other ingredients.
- Secure the lid and choose the "Manual" setting. Cook for 3 minutes at Low pressure. Once cooking is complete, use a quick release; carefully remove the lid.
- You can thicken the sauce using the "Sauté" button. Bon appétit!

---

220. Red Snapper in Tomatillo-Mushroom Sauce
(Ready in about 15 minutes | Servings 4)

This is amazing, belly-filling recipe! Red snapper cooks perfectly with canned tomatillos and fresh brown mushrooms.
Per serving: *242 Calories; 13.6g Fat; 3.7g Carbs; 25.7g Protein; 1.7g Sugars*

Ingredients

1/2 stick butter, at room temperature
2 shallots, peeled and chopped
2 garlic cloves, minced
1 cup brown mushrooms, thinly sliced
2 tablespoons coriander
1 (11-ounce) can tomatillo, chopped
2 tablespoons tomato ketchup
1 cup chicken stock, preferably homemade
1 pound red snapper, cut into bite-sized chunks
Salt and freshly ground black pepper, to taste

Directions

- Press the "Sauté" button to preheat your Instant Pot. Then, melt the butter. Once hot, cook the shallots with garlic until tender and aromatic.
- Stir in the mushrooms; cook an additional 3 minutes or until they have softened.
- Stir the remaining ingredients into your Instant Pot.
- Secure the lid and choose the "Manual" setting. Cook for 6 minutes at High pressure. Once cooking is complete, use a quick release; carefully remove the lid.
- Serve over hot basmati rice if desired. Enjoy!

221. Portuguese-Style Fish Medley
(Ready in about 15 minutes | Servings 4)

Try this all-star recipe for fish medley with a Portuguese twist! This recipe is so simple to make in the Instant Pot and the balance of flavors is amazing.
Per serving: *342 Calories; 20.8g Fat; 14.7g Carbs; 24.6g Protein; 9.2g Sugars*

Ingredients

1 pound fish, mixed pieces for fish soup, cut into bite-sized pieces
1 yellow onion, chopped
1 celery with leaves, chopped
2 carrots, chopped
2 cloves garlic, minced
1 green bell pepper, thinly sliced
2 tablespoons peanut oil
1 ½ cups seafood stock

1/3 cup dry vermouth
2 fresh tomatoes, puréed
1 tablespoon loosely packed saffron threads
Sea salt and ground black pepper, to taste
1 teaspoon Piri Piri
2 bay leaves
1/4 cup fresh cilantro, roughly chopped
1/2 lemon, sliced

Directions

- Simply throw all of the above ingredients, except for cilantro and lemon, into your Instant Pot.
- Secure the lid and choose the "Manual" setting. Cook for 8 minutes at Low pressure. Once cooking is complete, use a quick release; carefully remove the lid.
- Ladle the medley into individual bowls; serve with fresh cilantro and lemon. Enjoy!

---

222. Aromatic Prawns with Basmati Rice
(Ready in about 15 minutes | Servings 5)

This low-fat prawn dish is a healthy meal idea for the whole family. It's flavored with fresh mint leaves. Lovely!
Per serving: *331 Calories; 17.6g Fat; 31.9g Carbs; 26.2g Protein; 4.6g Sugars*

Ingredients

2 tablespoons olive oil
1 cup red onions, thinly sliced
2 cloves garlic, pressed
2 bell peppers, seeded and thinly sliced
1 serrano pepper, seeded and thinly sliced
2 cups basmati rice
1 (14-ounce) can tomatoes, diced
2 ½ cups vegetable stock, preferably homemade

1 tablespoon tamari sauce
1 pound prawns, peeled and deveined
Sea salt and ground black pepper, to taste
1/2 teaspoon sweet paprika
1 teaspoon dried rosemary
1/2 teaspoon dried oregano
2 tablespoons fresh mint, roughly chopped

Directions

- Press the "Sauté" button to preheat your Instant Pot. Then, heat the oil and sauté the onions until tender and translucent.
- Stir in the garlic; continue to sauté until aromatic. Add the rest of the above ingredients, except for mint, to the Instant Pot.
- Secure the lid and choose the "Manual" setting. Cook for 3 minutes at Low pressure. Once cooking is complete, use a natural release; carefully remove the lid.
- Serve garnished with fresh mint leaves. Bon appétit!

223. Tuna Steaks with Lime-Butter Sauce
(Ready in about 15 minutes | Servings 3)

Sit back and relax! Tuna steaks cook perfectly in the Instant Pot so that all you need is a tablespoon of delicate butter-lime sauce to make it magnificent.
Per serving: *316 Calories; 18g Fat; 1g Carbs; 35.4g Protein; 0.3g Sugars*

Ingredients

3 tuna steaks
1 ½ tablespoons sesame oil, melted
1/2 teaspoon salt
1/4 teaspoon black pepper, to taste
1/4 teaspoon smoked paprika
1 cup water
1 tablespoon fresh cilantro, chopped
For the Sauce:
1 tablespoon butter, at room temperature
1 tablespoon fresh lime juice
1 teaspoon Worcestershire sauce

Directions

- Brush tuna steaks with sesame oil. Season tuna steaks with salt, black pepper, and smoked paprika.
- Place the fish in the steaming basket; transfer it to the Instant Pot.
- Pour 1 cup of water into the base of your Instant Pot. Secure the lid.
- Choose "Manual" mode, Low pressure and 4 minutes. Once cooking is complete, use a quick release; carefully remove the lid.
- Meanwhile, warm butter over medium-low heat. Add the lime juice and Worcestershire sauce; remove from heat and stir until everything is well incorporated.
- Spoon sauce over tuna steaks, sprinkle with fresh cilantro leaves and serve. Bon appétit!

224. Spicy Beer-Steamed Mussels
(Ready in about 15 minutes | Servings 4)

This light dish is so simple and quick to make in the Instant Pot and contains great flavors of succulent mussels, fresh tomatoes, and authentic Thai chili peppers.
Per serving: *241 Calories; 7.3g Fat; 15.3g Carbs; 21.9g Protein; 3g Sugars*

Ingredients

1 tablespoon olive oil
1/2 cup scallions, chopped
2 cloves garlic, minced
2 medium-sized ripe tomatoes, puréed
1 (12-ounce) bottles lager beer
1 cup water

1 tablespoon fresh cilantro, chopped
Sea salt and freshly ground black pepper, to taste
2 Thai chili peppers, stemmed and split
1 ½ pounds mussels, cleaned and debearded

Directions

- Press the "Sauté" button to preheat your Instant Pot. Heat the oil and cook the scallions until tender and fragrant.
- Then, stir in the garlic and cook an additional 30 seconds or until fragrant. Add the remaining ingredients.
- Secure the lid and choose the "Manual" setting. Cook for 3 minutes at Low pressure. Once cooking is complete, use a quick release; carefully remove the lid.
- Serve with garlic croutons. Bon appétit!

225. Classic Fish Paprikash
(Ready in about 15 minutes | Servings 4)

Are you looking for a recipe for a relaxed dinner with your family? Look no further! This authentic one-pot meal will be ready in no time.
Per serving: *310 Calories; 13.7g Fat; 14.4g Carbs; 32.3g Protein; 4.5g Sugars*

Ingredients

2 tablespoons butter, at room temperature
1 cup leeks, chopped
2 bell peppers, seeded and sliced
2 garlic cloves, minced
2 sprigs thyme
1 sprig rosemary
1 teaspoon sweet paprika
1 teaspoon hot paprika

Sea salt and ground black pepper, to taste
2 tomatoes, puréed
2 cups vegetable broth
2 cups water
1 ½ pounds cod fish, cut into bite-sized chunks
2 tablespoons fresh cilantro, roughly chopped
1 cup sour cream, well-chilled

Directions

- Press the "Sauté" button to preheat your Instant Pot. Melt the butter and sauté the leeks until fragrant.
- Then, stir in the peppers and garlic and continue to sauté an additional 40 seconds.
- Add thyme, rosemary, paprika, salt, black pepper, tomatoes, broth, water, and fish.
- Secure the lid and choose the "Manual" setting. Cook for 6 minutes at High pressure. Once cooking is complete, use a quick release; carefully remove the lid.
- Ladle into individual bowls and serve garnished with fresh cilantro and well-chilled sour cream. Bon appétit!

---

226. Mahi-Mahi Fish with Cumin Guacamole
(Ready in about 30 minutes | Servings 4)

This one-pot dish is simple: fresh-from-the-sea fish fillets, shallots, and aromatics. Cumin guacamole completes your recipe and adds nutritional value.
Per serving: *324 Calories; 18g Fat; 13.1g Carbs; 29.1g Protein; 4.6g Sugars*

Ingredients

1 cup water
4 mahi-mahi fillets
2 tablespoons olive oil
Sea salt and ground black pepper, to taste
1/2 teaspoon red pepper flakes, crushed
1/2 cup shallots, sliced
2 tablespoons fresh lemon juice
1 teaspoon epazote
1/4 cup fresh coriander, chopped

1 teaspoon dried sage

For Cumin Guacamole:
2 medium tomatoes, chopped
1 large avocado, peeled, pitted and mashed
2 tablespoons salsa verde
1 clove garlic, minced
Fresh juice of 1 lime
Sea salt to taste

Directions

Pour 1 cup of water to the base of your Instant Pot.
Brush mahi-mahi fillets with olive oil; then, sprinkle with salt, black pepper, and red pepper flakes.
Place the mahi-mahi fillets in the steaming basket; transfer it to the Instant Pot. Add shallots on top; add lemon juice, epazote, coriander, and sage.
Secure the lid. Choose "Manual" mode, Low pressure and 3 minutes. Once cooking is complete, use a quick release; carefully remove the lid.
Next, mix all ingredients for cumin guacamole; place in your refrigerator at least 20 minutes. Serve mahi-mahi fillets with fresh cumin guacamole on the side. Bon appétit!

227. Herbed Mackerel Fillets with Peppers
(Ready in about 15 minutes | Servings 5)

These flaky mackerel fillets retain healthy nutrients with the help of the Instant Pot. The recipe utilizes the butter to cook the fillets perfectly.

Per serving: *423 Calories; 7.9g Fat; 1.6g Carbs; 80g Protein; 0.9g Sugars*

Ingredients

5 mackerel fillets, skin on
Sea salt, to taste
1/4 teaspoon ground black pepper, to taste
1/2 teaspoon cayenne pepper
1/2 teaspoon dried rosemary
1 teaspoon marjoram
1 tablespoon butter, melted
1 red bell pepper, deveined and sliced
1 green bell pepper, deveined and sliced

Directions

- Prepare your Instant Pot by adding 1 ½ cups of water and steamer basket to its bottom.
- Season mackerel fillets with the salt, black pepper, cayenne pepper, rosemary, and marjoram.
- Place mackerel fillets in the steamer basket. Drizzle with melted butter. Top with sliced peppers.
- Secure the lid and choose the "Manual" setting. Cook for 3 minutes at Low pressure. Once cooking is complete, use a quick release; carefully remove the lid. Serve immediately.

228. Seafood and Yellow Lentil Gumbo
(Ready in about 15 minutes | Servings 5)

Versatility and quick cook time are just a few of the things that make cooking seafood in the Instant Pot so easy! For this recipe, choose a wine that has a moderate alcohol content.

Per serving: *277 Calories; 9.2g Fat; 8.3g Carbs; 36.7g Protein; 3.1g Sugars*

Ingredients

2 tablespoons butter, at room temperature
2 garlic cloves, minced
1/2 (14-ounce) can diced tomatoes
1/3 cup Sauvignon Blanc
1 cup vegetable broth

1 ½ tablespoons apple cider vinegar
Sea salt and ground black pepper, to taste
1 cup French green lentils
1 ½ pounds shrimp, cleaned and deveined
5 ounces crabmeat

Directions

- Press the "Sauté" button to preheat your Instant Pot. Melt the butter. Then, sauté the garlic until aromatic about 40 seconds.
- Now, add canned tomatoes, Sauvignon Blanc, broth, vinegar, salt, black pepper, and lentils to your Instant Pot.
- Secure the lid and choose the "Manual" setting. Cook for 6 minutes at High pressure. Once cooking is complete, use a quick release; carefully remove the lid.
- Press the "Sauté" button again. Stir in the shrimp and crabmeat; simmer until they become pink. Ladle into soup bowls. Bon appétit!

229. Fish Tikka Masala
(Ready in about 15 minutes | Servings 4)

Tikka masala is a traditional, creamy and aromatic Indian dish. Serve with warm naan and lots of fresh salad.
Per serving: *273 Calories; 9.3g Fat; 13.5g Carbs; 34.9g Protein; 6.6g Sugars*

Ingredients

2 tablespoons olive oil
1/2 cup scallions, chopped
2 garlic cloves, minced
1/4 cup tikka masala curry paste
1/3 teaspoon ground allspice
1 (14-ounce) can diced tomatoes
1 tablespoon brown sugar

1 teaspoon hot paprika
1 cup vegetable broth
1 ½ pounds haddock fillets, cut into bite-sized chunks
1 cup natural yogurt
1 lime, cut into wedges

Directions

- Press the "Sauté" button to preheat your Instant Pot; heat the oil. Then, sauté the scallions until tender and translucent.
- Now, add the garlic; continue to sauté for a further 30 seconds.
- Stir curry paste, allspice, tomatoes, sugar, paprika, broth, and haddock into the Instant Pot.
- Secure the lid and choose the "Manual" setting. Cook for 5 minutes at Low pressure. Once cooking is complete, use a quick release; carefully remove the lid.
- Then, fold in natural yogurt and stir to combine well; seal the lid again and allow it to sit in the residual heat until warmed through.
- Serve in individual bowls, garnished with lime wedges. Enjoy!

230. Shrimp and Ham Hock Soup
(Ready in about 45 minutes | Servings 6)

Here is an easy and delicious soup recipe perfect for a busy weekday. This soup is loaded with vegetables, ham, and shrimp, and finished with double cream.
Per serving: *298 Calories; 13.5g Fat; 10.5g Carbs; 34.1g Protein; 3.7g Sugars*

Ingredients

2 tablespoons olive oil
1/2 cup leeks, chopped
2 garlic cloves, minced
2 carrots, diced
1 parsnip, diced
2 tablespoons chickpea flour
2 tablespoons tomato paste
2 teaspoons chipotle in adobo sauce, chopped
1 ham hock

1 cup water
5 cups broth, preferably homemade
2 sprigs rosemary
1 teaspoon lemon thyme
Sea salt, to taste
1/2 teaspoon mixed peppercorns, freshly cracked
3/4 pound shrimp, peeled and deveined
1/2 cup double cream

Directions

- Press the "Sauté" button and add olive oil. Once hot, sauté the leeks together with garlic, carrots, and parsnips; cook until the vegetables are just tender.
- Add the chickpea flour and cook for a further 1 minute 30 seconds, stirring frequently.
- Stir in tomato paste, chipotle in adobo sauce, ham hock, water, and broth. Season with rosemary, lemon thyme, salt and mixed peppercorns. Secure the lid.
- Choose the "Soup" function, High pressure and 35 minutes. Once cooking is complete, use a natural release; carefully remove the lid.
- Place ham hock on a cutting board; allow it to rest. Pull meat from ham hock bone and shred. Add it back to the Instant Pot.
- Stir in shrimp and double cream. Close the Instant Pot and cook your shrimp in the residual heat for 8 minutes. Bon appétit!

231. Saucy and Spicy Halibut Steaks
(Ready in about 15 minutes | Servings 4)

The Instant Pot is a true lifesaver when it comes to quick and easy fish meals. If your spice shelf is well-stocked, you are on a roll!
Per serving: *174 Calories; 6.5g Fat; 27.7g Carbs; 6.2g Protein; 13.9g Sugars*

Ingredients

2 tablespoons butter, melted
1 yellow onion, chopped
2 garlic cloves, pressed
2 bell peppers, chopped
1/4 cup Chardonnay
2 ripe tomatoes, puréed
1 pound halibut steaks
1 cup fish stock
1 dried red chili, coarsely chopped
1/2 teaspoon nigella seeds
2 bay leaves
1/2 teaspoon ground black pepper, to taste
Sea salt, to taste

Directions

- Press the "Sauté" button to preheat your Instant Pot. Then, melt the butter and sauté the onion until tender and translucent.
- Then, stir in the garlic and bell peppers; continue to cook an additional 2 minutes or until the peppers have softened.
- Add a splash of wine to deglaze the bottom of the inner pot. Add the remaining ingredients and stir to combine.
- Secure the lid and choose the "Manual" setting. Cook for 5 minutes at Low pressure. Once cooking is complete, use a quick release; carefully remove the lid.
- Taste, adjust the seasonings and serve warm. Bon appétit!

232. Simple Fish Mélange
(Ready in about 15 minutes | Servings 4)

This simple seafood mélange features Creole seasoning, cream and vegetables. Serve with mashed potatoes or polenta.
Per serving: *254 Calories; 15.4g Fat; 15.5g Carbs; 13.9g Protein; 7.9g Sugars*

Ingredients

1 tablespoon olive oil
2 shallots, diced
2 garlic cloves, smashed
2 carrots, diced
2 (6-ounce) cans crab, juice reserved
1/2 pound cod, cut into bite-sized chunks
Sea salt, to taste

1/2 teaspoon freshly ground black pepper
2 bay leaves
1 tablespoon Creole seasoning
2 cups water
1 cup double cream
1 tablespoon lemon juice

Directions

- Press the "Sauté" button to preheat your Instant Pot. Then, heat the oil and sauté the shallots until tender.
- Stir in the garlic and carrots; cook an additional minute or so. Add canned crab meat, cod, salt, black pepper, bay leaves, Creole seasoning, and water.
- Secure the lid and choose the "Manual" setting. Cook for 6 minutes at High pressure. Once cooking is complete, use a quick release; carefully remove the lid.
- Lastly, stir in double cream and lemon juice. Press the "Sauté" button one more time; let it simmer until heated through. Enjoy!

233. Easy Fish Burritos
(Ready in about 15 minutes | Servings 4)

These extraordinary burritos will please the whole family. You can also add beans to your tortillas, if desired.
Per serving: *377 Calories; 14.2g Fat; 30.5g Carbs; 31.2g Protein; 5.3g Sugars*

Ingredients

2 tablespoons olive oil
4 catfish fillets
Sea salt to taste
1/3 teaspoon ground black pepper, to taste
1/2 teaspoon cayenne pepper
1/2 teaspoon ground bay leaf
1 teaspoon dried thyme
4 burrito-sized tortillas
1 cup fresh salsa
1 large-sized tomato, sliced

Directions

- Prepare your Instant Pot by adding 1 ½ cups of water and a metal rack to its bottom.
- Place fish fillets in the center of foil. Drizzle olive oil over the fish. Season with salt, black pepper, cayenne pepper, ground bay leaf and dried thyme.
- Wrap tightly and lower it onto the rack.
- Secure the lid and choose "Manual" setting. Cook for 10 minutes at High pressure. Once cooking is complete, use a natural release; carefully remove the lid.
- Divide the fish fillets among tortillas. Top it with salsa and tomatoes. Roll each tortilla into a burrito and serve immediately.

---

234. Easy Saucy Clams
(Ready in about 10 minutes | Servings 5)

Perfectly cooked clams with bacon and tarty white wine. Using the Instant Pot ensures even cooking, which is extremely important for a bright and flavorful seafood dishes. Serve alongside crusty bread and corn on the cob.
Per serving: *157 Calories; 4.6g Fat; 27.7g Carbs; 3.4g Protein; 8.3g Sugars*

Ingredients

1/2 cup bacon, smoked and cubed
2 onions, chopped
3 garlic cloves, minced
1 sprig thyme
3 (6.5-ounce) cans clams, chopped
1/3 cup tarty white wine

1/3 cup water
1/2 cup clam juice
A pinch of cayenne pepper
1 bay leaf
5 lime juice
2 tablespoons fresh chives, roughly chopped

Directions

- Press the "Sauté" button to preheat your Instant Pot. Add cubed bacon. Once your bacon releases its fat, add the onions, garlic, and thyme.
- Cook for 3 minutes more or until the onion is transparent.
- Add the clams, white wine, water, clam juice, cayenne pepper, and bay leaf. Secure the lid. Select "Manual" mode and cook at Low pressure for 4 minutes.
- Once cooking is complete, use a natural release; remove the lid carefully
- Ladle into individual bowls and serve garnished with lime slices and fresh chives. Bon appétit!

235. Sole Fillets with Pickle Mayo
(Ready in about 10 minutes | Servings 4)

Fish fillets taste so great with this mayo sauce! This is the easiest way to dress up a plate of fish fillets.
Per serving: *211 Calories; 12.0g Fat; 3.9g Carbs; 22.3g Protein; 1.1g Sugars*

Ingredients

1 ½ pounds sole fillets
Sea salt and ground black pepper, to taste
1 teaspoon paprika
1/2 cup mayonnaise
1 tablespoon pickle juice
2 cloves garlic, smashed

Directions

- Sprinkle the fillets with salt, black pepper, and paprika.
- Add 1 ½ cups of water and a steamer basket to the Instant Pot. Place the fish in the steamer basket.
- Secure the lid and choose "Manual" setting. Cook for 3 minutes at Low pressure. Once cooking is complete, use a quick release; carefully remove the lid.
- Then, make the sauce by mixing the mayonnaise with pickle juice and garlic. Serve the fish fillets with the well-chilled sauce on the side. Bon appétit!

236. Fish Taco Bowl
(Ready in about 10 minutes | Servings 4)

Taco bowls are so versatile because you can jazz them up with different toppings. For the full experience, serve with corn chips.
Per serving: *245 Calories; 15.7g Fat; 9.3g Carbs; 16.9g Protein; 5.4g Sugars*

Ingredients

1 pound halibut steaks
1/4 cup fresh cilantro leaves chopped
2 garlic cloves, crushed
Sea salt and ground black pepper, to taste
1 cup white cabbage, shredded
1 jalapeño, coarsely chopped
1 can black beans
1 cup Pico de gallo

Directions

- Add 1 ½ cups of water and a steamer basket to the Instant Pot. Place the fish in the steamer basket.
- Top with cilantro and garlic. Season with salt and pepper.
- Secure the lid and choose "Manual" setting. Cook for 4 minutes at High pressure. Once cooking is complete, use a quick release; carefully remove the lid.
- Cut cooked halibut into slices and transfer them to a serving bowl. Garnish with cabbage, jalapeño, black beans, and Pico de gallo. Enjoy!

237. Vietnamese Fish Chowder in a Bread Bowl
(Ready in about 15 minutes | Servings 4)

This creamy cod chowder tastes so delicious! Your family will request it all the time. Good luck!
Per serving: *419 Calories; 29.9g Fat; 17.6g Carbs; 21.2g Protein; 5.4g Sugars*

Ingredients

2 ½ cups water
3 cod fillets
2 sweet potatoes, peeled and diced
1 parsnip, chopped
1 celery with leaves, chopped
2 shallots, chopped
1 green bell pepper, chopped
2 garlic cloves, minced
Salt, to taste

1/3 teaspoon ground black pepper
2 teaspoons capers, liquid reserved
1 teaspoon sumac powder
1 teaspoon fennel seeds
1/2 teaspoon Vietnamese cinnamon
1 ½ cups stock, preferably homemade
2 tablespoons fish sauce
1 ½ cups double cream
4 (8-ounce) round bread loaves

Directions

- Add water, cod fillets, sweet potatoes, parsnip, celery, shallot, bell pepper, garlic, salt, black pepper, capers, sumac powder, fennel seeds, Vietnamese cinnamon, stock, and fish sauce to your Instant Pot.
- Secure the lid and choose "Manual" mode. Cook for 8 minutes at Low pressure.
- Once cooking is complete, use a natural release; remove the lid carefully.
- Fold in double cream, press the "Sauté" button and continue to cook until it is thoroughly cooked.
- Now, cut a slice off the top of each bread loaf. Now, gently pull the inner bread from the round with a tablespoon, leaving a 1/4-inch thick shell.
- Ladle the soup into bread loaves and serve hot.

238. Traditional Creole Jambalaya
(Ready in about 15 minutes | Servings 4)

This Jambalaya combines some of our favorite Spanish and French flavors. It's easy to double this recipe. Serve over hot rice.
Per serving: *366 Calories; 13g Fat; 18.3g Carbs; 45.1g Protein; 4.1g Sugars*

Ingredients

6 ounces Andouille sausage, sliced
1 yellow onion, chopped
1 teaspoon garlic, minced
1 teaspoon fresh ginger, grated
1 ½ pounds shrimp, cleaned and deveined
2 sweet peppers, seeded and sliced
1 red chili pepper, seeded and minced

2 carrots, thinly sliced
Sea salt and ground black pepper, to taste
1 teaspoon Creole seasoning
2 ½ cups water
2 ripe tomatoes, puréed
2 chicken Bouillon cubes

Directions

- Press the "Sauté" button to preheat your Instant Pot. Now, cook the sausage until delicately browned, about 3 minutes; add the onion, garlic, and ginger and continue to cook for a further 2 minutes, stirring periodically.
- Throw the rest of the above ingredients into your Instant Pot.
- Secure the lid. Choose the "Manual" mode and Low pressure; cook for 6 minutes. Once cooking is complete, use a quick pressure release; carefully remove the lid.
- Ladle into individual bowls and serve garnished with fresh lemon slices if desired. Bon appétit!

239. Spanish Chorizo and Seafood Paella
(Ready in about 15 minutes | Servings 6)

This traditional paella comes together so quickly in the Instant Pot. Cooking the rice and seafood under the intense pressure keeps them moist and full of flavors.

Per serving: *335 Calories; 11.8g Fat; 35.8g Carbs; 31.6g Protein; 12.6g Sugars*

Ingredients

3 teaspoons olive oil
1/2 ring of Chorizo sausage, sliced
1 onion, chopped
1 ½ cups basmati rice
2 cups water
1 cup tomato paste
1 red bell pepper, chopped
1 roasted yellow bell pepper, chopped
1 ½ pounds tiger shrimp, cleaned and divined

Sea salt, to taste
1/2 teaspoon ground black pepper
1/2 teaspoon sweet paprika
A pinch of saffron threads
1 bay leaf
1 cup frozen peas
1 cup frozen sweetcorn

Directions

- Press the "Sauté" button to preheat your Instant Pot. Heat the olive oil; now, brown the sausage and onion for 2 to 3 minutes.
- Add the rice and continue to cook an additional 3 minutes or until it starts to turn translucent.
- Stir the remaining ingredients into your Instant Pot.
- Secure the lid. Choose the "Manual" mode and High pressure; cook for 6 minutes. Once cooking is complete, use a quick pressure release; carefully remove the lid. Serve warm.

240. Scallops in Champagne-Butter Sauce
(Ready in about 10 minutes | Servings 3)

The title seems complex, but this recipe is so easy to prepare in the Instant Pot. It requires only a few steps and takes 10 minutes to serve.

Per serving: *165 Calories; 7.6g Fat; 5.7g Carbs; 17.6g Protein; 0.3g Sugars*

Ingredients

1 pound scallops
1 teaspoon ginger garlic paste
Sea salt and ground black pepper, to taste
1/2 teaspoon cayenne pepper
1/4 teaspoon pink peppercorns, crushed
1 cup vegetable broth
1/2 cup Champagne
2 tablespoons butter

Directions

- Add all of the above ingredients to the Instant Pot.
- Secure the lid. Choose the "Manual" mode and Low pressure; cook for 3 minutes. Once cooking is complete, use a quick pressure release; carefully remove the lid.
- Then, press the "Sauté" button and cook the sauce, whisking constantly, until it has reduced by half. Bon appétit!

241. Home-Style Fish Burgers
(Ready in about 20 minutes | Servings 3)

There's something about fish burgers that gather your family around the dinner table. For this recipe, we opted for tuna, but any dense fish will work; consider using cod or salmon.
Per serving: *447 Calories; 17.6g Fat; 48.4g Carbs; 24.7g Protein; 11.9g Sugars*

Ingredients

1 cup water
1/2 pound tuna filets
1 onion, finely chopped
2 garlic cloves, chopped
1 sweet bell pepper, chopped
1 jalapeno pepper, chopped
1 egg
1 cup tortilla chips, crushed

1 teaspoon cayenne pepper
1/4 teaspoon dried dill weed
Salt and black pepper, to taste
3 teaspoons canola oil
3 tablespoons mayonnaise
2 teaspoon Dijon mustard
3 cornichons, diced
3 hamburger buns

Directions

- Pour 1 cup of water into the base of your Instant Pot. Place tuna fillets in the steaming basket; transfer it to the Instant Pot.
- Secure the lid and choose the "Manual" mode, Low pressure and 4 minutes.
- Once cooking is complete, use a quick release; remove the lid carefully. Now, flake steamed fish with a fork.
- Add the onion, garlic, pepper, egg, tortilla chips, cayenne pepper, dill, salt, and black pepper. Now, shape the fish mixture into patties.
- Heat a frying pan over a moderately high heat. Now, heat canola oil. Once hot, fry fish patties until they're crispy and golden brown.
- Pop burger buns in the oven and lightly toast them.
- Assemble the fish burgers, by spreading on a layer of mayo and mustard, followed by cornichons, a fish patty, and then, the bun top. Bon appétit!

---

242. Greek-Style Seafood Dinner
(Ready in about 10 minutes | Servings 4)

A Greek-inspired family dish that features prawns, Kalamata olives, and fresh tomatoes. To make it a complete meal, serve with mashed potatoes.
Per serving: *351 Calories; 16.6g Fat; 11.9g Carbs; 37.8g Protein; 5.6g Sugars*

Ingredients

1 tablespoon olive oil
1/2 cup scallions, chopped
2 garlic cloves, minced
Sea salt and ground black pepper, to taste
1/2 teaspoon cayenne pepper, or more taste
1 teaspoon dried oregano

2 ripe tomatoes, chopped
1 ½ pounds prawns, cleaned
6 ounces Halloumi cheese, sliced
1/2 cup Kalamata olives, pitted and sliced
2 tablespoons fresh cilantro, chopped

Directions

- Press the "Sauté" button to preheat your Instant Pot. Then, heat the oil; sauté the scallions and garlic until tender and fragrant.
- Add the salt, black pepper, cayenne pepper, oregano, tomatoes, and prawns.
- Secure the lid. Choose the "Manual" mode and Low pressure; cook for 3 minutes. Once cooking is complete, use a quick pressure release; carefully remove the lid.
- Ladle into serving bowls; top each serving with cheese, olives and fresh cilantro. Bon appétit!

243. Polenta with Peppers and Fish
(Ready in about 20 minutes | Servings 4)

Pressure-cooked polenta and saucy cod fish take center stage in this outstanding recipe. This recipe may seem complicated but it is easy to cook in the Instant Pot.

Per serving: *389 Calories; 18.1g Fat; 23.6g Carbs; 32.6g Protein; 6.2g Sugars*

Ingredients

4 cups water
2 tablespoons butter
A pinch of salt
1 cup polenta
4 ounces bacon, diced
2 shallots, thinly sliced
2 garlic cloves, minced
2 bell peppers, chopped

2 tomatoes, puréed
1 cup fish stock, preferably homemade
1 sprig thyme
2 sprigs rosemary
1 ½ pounds cod fillets, chopped
Sea salt and ground black pepper, to taste

Directions

- Press the "Sauté" button to preheat the Instant Pot. Then, add the water, butter, and salt; bring to a simmer. Whisk in the polenta.
- Secure the lid. Choose the "Manual" mode and High pressure; cook for 7 minutes. Once cooking is complete, use a natural pressure release; carefully remove the lid.
- Transfer the prepared polenta to a serving bowl. Wipe down the Instant Pot with a damp cloth.
- Press the "Sauté" button to preheat the Instant Pot. Now, cook the bacon until crisp; reserve. Add the shallots and continue to cook for 2 to 3 minutes more or until tender.
- Then, add the garlic and peppers. Continue sautéing for one minute longer. Add the remaining ingredients to the Instant Pot.
- Secure the lid. Choose the "Manual" mode and Low pressure; cook for 3 minutes. Once cooking is complete, use a natural pressure release; carefully remove the lid.
- Add the fish mixture to the serving bowl with polenta. Top with bacon and serve warm. Enjoy!

244. Steamed Oysters with Green Onion Sauce
(Ready in about 10 minutes | Servings 4)

Oysters are a great source of protein, Vitamin B-complex, and selenium. They have a mild taste and go well with pungent green onion sauce. Save this recipe for a special occasion!

Per serving: *443 Calories; 34.1g Fat; 13.4g Carbs; 15.1g Protein; 2.4g Sugars*

Ingredients

2 tablespoons olive oil
1 ½ pounds fresh oysters, shucked
1/2 cup rose wine
1 ¼ cups chicken stock
1 teaspoon sweet paprika
Sea salt and ground black pepper, to taste
1/2 teaspoon fennel seeds

1 teaspoon marjoram
1 teaspoon ginger-garlic paste
Green Onion Sauce:
1/4 cup sour cream
1/2 cup mayonnaise
3 tablespoons fresh green onions, chopped
1 garlic clove, minced

Directions

- Press the "Sauté" button to preheat your Instant Pot. Heat the oil until sizzling; once hot, sauté the oysters for 1 minute.
- Add wine, stock, paprika, salt, black pepper, fennel seeds, marjoram, and ginger-garlic paste.
- Secure the lid. Choose "Manual" mode and Low pressure; cook for 6 minutes. Once cooking is complete, use a quick pressure release; carefully remove the lid.
- Afterwards, make the sauce by mixing sour cream, mayonnaise, green onions, and garlic. Serve the oysters with the sauce on the side. Bon appétit!

245. Old Bay Fish with Gherkin Sauce
(Ready in about 15 minutes | Servings 3)

Mackerel fillets accompanied by rich and fresh tartar-like sauce. You can serve these fantastic fish fillets with hand-cut potato chips.
Per serving: *361 Calories; 20.6g Fat; 10g Carbs; 33.3g Protein; 7.1g Sugars*

Ingredients

1/4 cup white wine
1 ½ teaspoons Old Bay seasoning
Sea salt, to taste
1/4 teaspoon ground black pepper, or more to taste
3/4 pound mackerel fillets
1 cup water
1 lime, sliced

For the Gherkin Sauce:

1/2 cup cream cheese
2 hard-boiled eggs
3 gherkins, chopped
1 tablespoon capers
A pinch of brown sugar
A pinch of cayenne pepper
2 tablespoons fresh cilantro leaves, chopped
Salt, to taste

Directions

- In a mixing bowl, thoroughly combine white wine, Old Bay seasoning, salt, and black pepper. Brush this mixture on both sides of mackerel fillets.
- Add 1 cup of water to the base of your Instant Pot.
- Place mackerel fillets in the steaming basket; transfer it to the Instant Pot. Secure the lid and choose "Manual" mode, Low pressure and 5 minutes.
- Once cooking is complete, use a quick release; remove the lid carefully.
- In the meantime, mix all ingredients for the sauce; place in your refrigerator until ready to serve. Serve steamed fish with the lime and Gherkin sauce on the side. Enjoy!

246. Paprika Seafood Boil
(Ready in about 10 minutes | Servings 4)

Smoked sausage, fish, and paprika make a great blend. Serve with a horseradish sauce if desired.
Per serving: *301 Calories; 14.8g Fat; 10.1g Carbs; 31.4g Protein; 3.9g Sugars*

Ingredients

2 cups chicken stock
8 ounces smoked sausage, cut into bite-sized pieces
1 pound catfish
1 celery with leaves, chopped
1 carrot, chopped
1 leek, thinly sliced
2 garlic cloves, minced
Sea salt and ground black pepper, to taste
1 teaspoon smoked paprika
1 teaspoon hot paprika
1 teaspoon Old Bay seasoning
2 tomatoes, chopped

Directions

- Add all of the above ingredients to your Instant Pot.
- Secure the lid. Choose "Manual" mode and High pressure; cook for 4 minutes. Once cooking is complete, use a quick pressure release; carefully remove the lid.
- Remove all ingredients from the Instant Pot using a slotted spoon; serve immediately.

247. Indian Meen Kulambu
(Ready in about 15 minutes | Servings 6)

Meen Kulambu is a traditional South Indian curry. You can use any type of white fish in this recipe.
Per serving: *335 Calories; 19.9g Fat; 6.2g Carbs; 33.4g Protein; 2.9g Sugars*

Ingredients

1 tablespoon olive oil
1 cup scallions, chopped
1 teaspoon fresh garlic, smashed
2 pounds mackerel fillets, cut into bite-size chunks
1 ½ cups coconut milk
1 cup chicken bone broth, preferably homemade
2 dried red chilies, coarsely chopped
1 teaspoon curry powder
1 teaspoon ground coriander
1 teaspoon cayenne pepper
Sea salt and ground black pepper, to taste
2 tablespoons freshly squeezed lemon juice

Directions

- Press the "Sauté" button to preheat your Instant Pot. Heat the oil until sizzling; once hot, sauté the scallions and garlic until tender and fragrant.
- Add the remaining ingredients, except for lemon juice, to the Instant Pot.
- Secure the lid. Choose "Manual" mode and Low pressure; cook for 6 minutes. Once cooking is complete, use a quick pressure release; carefully remove the lid.
- Divide among individual bowls. Drizzle lemon juice over each serving and enjoy!

---

248. Green Bean and Crab Casserole
(Ready in about 15 minutes | Servings 4)

This seafood and vegetable casserole is absolutely perfect! Juicy, rich and palatable. In addition, it comes together in 15 minutes.
Per serving: *435 Calories; 16.8g Fat; 33.1g Carbs; 32.1g Protein; 10.9g Sugars*

Ingredients

2 tablespoons butter, melted
2 garlic cloves, minced
1/2 cup scallions, chopped
1/2 pound frozen green beans
1/2 cup dry white wine
1 ½ cups stock
1 ½ cups plain milk
1 pound crabmeat
Salt and ground pepper, to taste
1 can cream of mushroom soup
1 teaspoon cayenne pepper
1/2 teaspoon tarragon
1/2 teaspoon dried parsley flakes
1 cup seasoned breadcrumbs

Directions

- Press the "Sauté" button to preheat your Instant Pot. Now, warm butter and add garlic, scallions, and green beans. Cook for 2 to 3 minutes.
- Add a splash of wine to scrape up any browned bits from the bottom of the inner pot. Add the remaining wine, stock, milk, crabmeat, salt, pepper, and cream of mushroom soup.
- Sprinkle with cayenne pepper, tarragon, and parsley flakes. Add seasoned breadcrumbs to the top. Secure the lid.
- Choose the "Manual' mode, Low pressure and 6 minutes. Once cooking is complete, use a quick release; remove the lid carefully.
- Divide between individual serving plates and eat warm. Bon appétit!

249. Moroccan Fish Kebabs
(Ready in about 15 minutes | Servings 4)

Check to ensure ingredients are desired doneness; if not seal the lid again and cook a few minutes more.
Per serving: *263 Calories; 15.1g Fat; 6.4g Carbs; 24.8g Protein; 3.7g Sugars*

Ingredients

1/2 pound yellow squash zucchini, cubed
1 red onion, cut into wedges
2 bell peppers, cut into strips
1 pound salmon, skinned, deboned and cut into bite-sized chunks
2 tablespoons toasted sesame oil
Sea salt and ground black pepper, to taste
1 teaspoon red pepper flakes
8 sticks fresh rosemary, lower leaves removed

Directions

- Prepare your Instant Pot by adding 1½ cups of water and metal rack to its bottom.
- Thread vegetables and fish alternately onto rosemary sticks.
- Drizzle with sesame oil; sprinkle with salt, black pepper, and red pepper flakes. Cover with a piece of foil.
- Secure the lid. Choose "Manual" mode and Low pressure; cook for 6 minutes. Once cooking is complete, use a quick pressure release; carefully remove the lid. Serve immediately.

---

250. Tuna and Buckwheat Salad
(Ready in about 10 minutes + chilling time | Servings 4)

This salad is so fresh and healthy! Simply combine farmer's market veggies, fresh-from-the-sea tuna, and extra-virgin olive oil and dig in!
Per serving: *238 Calories; 6.8g Fat; 14.1g Carbs; 30.1g Protein; 3.3g Sugars*

Ingredients

1 pound tuna, cut into bite-sized pieces
1 cup buckwheat
1/2 teaspoon dried or fresh dill
Salt and black pepper, to taste
2 cups water
1 white onion, thinly sliced
2 bell peppers, seeded and thinly sliced
1 carrot, grated
1 large-sized cucumber, thinly sliced
1/4 cup extra-virgin olive oil
2 tablespoons lemon juice, freshly squeezed

Directions

- Throw the water, buckwheat, dill, salt, black pepper, and water into your Instant Pot
- Secure the lid. Choose the "Manual" mode and Low pressure; cook for 3 minutes. Once cooking is complete, use a quick pressure release; carefully remove the lid.
- Allow the fish and buckwheat to cool completely. Then, toss it with the remaining ingredients and serve well chilled. Bon appétit!

BEANS & GRAINS

251. Classic Navy Beans
(Ready in about 35 minutes | Servings 6)

Navy beans are a great source of dietary fiber, iron, phosphorus, B1, manganese, copper, and protein.
Per serving: *292 Calories; 1.6g Fat; 52.3g Carbs; 19g Protein; 3.6g Sugars*

Ingredients

1 ¼ pounds dry navy beans
6 cups water
2 tablespoons bouillon granules
2 bay leaves
1 teaspoon black peppercorns, to taste

Directions

- Rinse off and drain navy beans. Place navy beans, water, bouillon granules, bay leaves, and black peppercorns in your Instant Pot.
- Secure the lid. Choose the "Manual" mode and cook at High pressure for 20 minutes.
- Once cooking is complete, use a natural release; remove the lid carefully. Bon appétit!

---

252. Coconut Buckwheat Porridge with Sultanas
(Ready in about 20 minutes | Servings 5)

To plump sultanas for this porridge, you can soak them in 2 tablespoons of rum, if desired. You can use gin or vodka as well.
Per serving: *371 Calories; 19.1g Fat; 53.6g Carbs; 3.3g Protein; 42.1g Sugars*

Ingredients

2 teaspoons coconut butter
1 ½ cups buckwheat
1 ½ cups coconut milk
1 ½ cups water
1/2 teaspoon coconut extract
A pinch of salt
A pinch of grated nutmeg
1/2 teaspoon ground cinnamon
3/4 cup agave syrup
2/3 cup sultanas

Directions

- Press the "Sauté" button to preheat your Instant Pot. Now, melt the butter and toast the buckwheat, stirring frequently, until it is aromatic or about 3 minutes.
- Add the remaining ingredients and stir to combine well.
- Secure the lid. Choose the "Manual" mode and High pressure; cook for 3 minutes. Once cooking is complete, use a natural pressure release for 10 minutes; carefully remove the lid. Serve right away.

253. Winter Oatmeal with Walnuts and Figs
(Ready in about 25 minutes | Servings 3)

Add nutty flavor to your oatmeal with a topping of chopped or ground walnuts. We opted for coconut milk, but it doesn't matter what kind of milk you use in this recipe.
Per serving: *270 Calories; 13.3g Fat; 43g Carbs; 9.2g Protein; 19.6g Sugars*

Ingredients

1 cup steel cut oats
1 cup water
1/2 cup coconut milk
2 tablespoons coconut flakes
1/2 teaspoon star anise
2 tablespoons honey
3 fresh or dried figs, chopped
1/2 cup walnuts, chopped or ground

Directions

- Add steel cut oats, water, milk, coconut flakes, anise, and honey to your Instant Pot.
- Secure the lid. Choose the "Manual" mode and High pressure; cook for 10 minutes. Once cooking is complete, use a natural pressure release for 12 minutes; carefully remove the lid.
- Divide the oatmeal among 3 serving bowls; top each serving with chopped figs and walnuts. Bon appétit!

254. Red Bean Soup
(Ready in about 40 minutes | Servings 5)

Thanks to the Instant Pot, making a homemade bean soup is easier than you ever thought. You will go one step further with this recipe and make a hearty family soup in less than 40 minutes.
Per serving: *188 Calories; 9.6g Fat; 16.2g Carbs; 11.9g Protein; 4g Sugars*

Ingredients

2 tablespoons canola oil
1 cup red onions, chopped
1 parsnip, chopped
1 red bell pepper, seeded and chopped
1 carrot, chopped
3 garlic cloves, minced
1 pound dried red beans, soaked and rinsed
5 cups beef bone broth
1 teaspoon dried oregano
1 teaspoon dried sage
1 teaspoon dried rosemary
Kosher salt and freshly ground black pepper, to taste
2 bay leaves

Directions

- Press the "Sauté" button to preheat your Instant Pot. Now, heat the oil and sweat the onions until they are translucent.
- Then, add the parsnip, bell pepper, carrot, and garlic; cook an additional 3 minutes or until the vegetables are softened.
- Stir in the remaining ingredients.
- Secure the lid. Choose the "Bean/Chili" mode and High pressure; cook for 25 minutes. Once cooking is complete, use a natural pressure release for 10 minutes; carefully remove the lid.
- Discard bay leaves. You can purée the soup in your blender if desired; serve in individual bowls. Bon appétit!

255. Oatmeal with Bananas and Walnuts
(Ready in about 25 minutes | Servings 4)

Oatmeal is an ultimate comfort breakfast. Use your favorite fixings and create a unique meal.
Per serving: *244 Calories; 10.1g Fat; 48.4g Carbs; 10.4g Protein; 9.2g Sugars*

Ingredients

2 cups steel cut oats
5 ½ cups water
1/2 teaspoon ground cinnamon
1/4 teaspoon cardamom
1/4 teaspoon grated nutmeg
2 bananas
1/2 cup walnuts, chopped

Directions

- Add steel cut oats to your Instant Pot. Pour in the water. Add cinnamon, cardamom, and nutmeg.
- Secure the lid. Choose the "Manual" mode and cook for 10 minutes under High pressure.
- Once cooking is complete, use a natural release for 10 minutes; remove the lid carefully. Ladle into serving bowls.
- Top with bananas and walnuts. Bon appétit!

---

256. Cuban-Style Black Beans
(Ready in about 30 minutes | Servings 5)

Black beans pack a nutritious punch in every dish. You can top each serving with crispy bacon slices if desired. Ridiculously easy and delicious!
Per serving: *276 Calories; 6.7g Fat; 43.1g Carbs; 13.3g Protein; 9.8g Sugars*

Ingredients

2 tablespoons olive oil
2 red onions, diced
3 cloves garlic, smashed
1 bell pepper, chopped
1/2 teaspoon ancho chili pepper, minced
2 cups tomatoes, puréed
1 ¼ pounds dry black beans, rinsed and drained
2 cups vegetable broth
Morton kosher salt and ground black pepper, to taste
1 teaspoon cayenne pepper
2 bay leaves
2 tablespoons fresh cilantro leaves, roughly chopped

Directions

- Press the "Sauté" button to preheat your Instant Pot. Now, heat the oil and sauté the onions until tender and aromatic.
- Then, add the garlic and peppers; cook an additional 1 minute 30 seconds or until fragrant. After that, stir the puréed tomatoes, black beans, broth, salt, black pepper, cayenne pepper, and bay leaves into your Instant Pot.
- Secure the lid. Choose the "Bean/Chili" mode and High pressure; cook for 25 minutes. Once cooking is complete, use a natural pressure release; carefully remove the lid.
- Garnish with fresh cilantro leaves and serve.

257. Greek-Style Savory Polenta
(Ready in about 15 minutes | Servings 3)

If you don't think you like polenta, try this recipe! Polenta, vegetables, and feta cheese are healthy and full of delicious flavors.
Per serving: *420 Calories; 26.2g Fat; 32.1g Carbs; 17.8g Protein; 6.3g Sugars*

Ingredients

2 tablespoons butter, at room temperature
1 cup scallions, chopped
2 garlic cloves, smashed
1 pound Crimini mushrooms, thinly sliced
1/2 teaspoon dried oregano
1/2 teaspoon dried basil
1/2 teaspoon dried dill weed

Sea salt and freshly ground black pepper, to taste
1 teaspoon cayenne pepper
2 cups water
2 cups vegetable broth
1 cup polenta
1 cup Kalamata olives, pitted and sliced
6 ounces feta cheese, crumbled

Directions

- Press the "Sauté" button to preheat your Instant Pot. Now, melt the butter and cook the scallions until tender.
- Stir in the garlic and mushrooms; cook an additional 40 seconds or until aromatic.
- Then, add herbs, salt, black pepper, and cayenne pepper. Add a splash of water to deglaze the pot; reserve the mushroom mixture. Press the "Cancel" button.
- Add the water and broth. Press the "Sauté" button again. Slowly and gradually, pour the polenta into the liquid; make sure to whisk continuously.
- Secure the lid. Choose the "Manual" mode and High pressure; cook for 5 minutes. Once cooking is complete, use a quick pressure release; carefully remove the lid.
- Top warm polenta with mushroom mixture, olives, and feta cheese. Serve immediately.

---

258. Risotto with Chorizo and Black Olives
(Ready in about 20 minutes | Servings 4)

If your family love rice and sausage, the Instant Pot is a great tool to prepare this all-in-one meal while saving you time in the kitchen.
Per serving: *576 Calories; 34.7g Fat; 44.8g Carbs; 20.5g Protein; 2.3g Sugars*

Ingredients

2 tablespoons butter, melted
1 yellow onion, chopped
2 carrots, trimmed and chopped
1/2 pound Chorizo sausage, sliced
1 cup white long-grain rice
2 cups chicken stock
Sea salt and ground black pepper, to taste
1/4 cup lightly packed fresh coriander, roughly chopped
1 cup black olives, pitted and sliced

Directions

- Press the "Sauté" button to preheat your Instant Pot. Now, melt the butter and cook the onion until aromatic.
- Then, add the carrot and Chorizo; cook an additional 2 minutes. Add the remaining ingredients and stir to combine well.
- Secure the lid. Choose the "Manual" mode and High pressure; cook for 3 minutes. Once cooking is complete, use a natural pressure release for 10 minutes; carefully remove the lid.
- Ladle into individual bowls and serve warm. Bon appétit!

259. Corn on the Cob with Smoky Lime Butter
(Ready in about 15 minutes | Servings 3)

Turn an ordinary corn on the cob into a fantastic snack! Corn on the cob is pressure cooked and then, coated with tangy and smoky butter sauce. Amazing!
Per serving: *263 Calories; 16.2g Fat; 30.9g Carbs; 4.3g Protein; 1.1g Sugars*

Ingredients

1 ¼ cups water
3 ears corn on the cob
1/2 stick butter, softened
A few drops of liquid smoke
1/2 lemon, juiced
1 tablespoon fresh cilantro, minced
A pinch of sugar
Sea salt and white pepper, to taste

Directions

- Pour water into the base of your Instant Pot. Place three ears corn on the cob on a metal trivet. Secure the lid.
- Choose the "Steam" mode and cook for 3 minutes under High pressure. Once cooking is complete, use a natural release; remove the lid carefully. Reserve corn on the cob.
- Press the "Sauté" button to heat up your Instant Pot. Melt the butter and remove from heat. Add the liquid smoke, lemon juice, cilantro, sugar, sea salt, and pepper; stir to combine.
- Toss corn on the cob with smoky lemon butter. Bon appétit!

260. The Best Barley Salad Ever
(Ready in about 15 minutes | Servings 4)

Do you love salads? We've got an easy and delicious salad recipe! Feel free to experiment with grains in this recipe and use wild rice, wheat berries, and buckwheat.
Per serving: *582 Calories; 22.1g Fat; 81g Carbs; 17.6g Protein; 6.4g Sugars*

Ingredients

1 ½ cups pearl barley
3 cups water
Sea salt and ground black pepper, to taste
1 leek, thinly sliced
2 cloves garlic, crushed
4 tablespoons extra-virgin olive oil
1/2 cup fresh parsley, chopped
2 tablespoons lime juice, freshly squeezed
1/2 cup canned chickpea, rinsed
1 cup pickles, diced
4 ounces feta cheese, crumbled

Directions

- Add barley and water to the Instant Pot.
- Secure the lid. Choose the "Manual" mode and High pressure; cook for 9 minutes. Once cooking is complete, use a natural pressure release; carefully remove the lid.
- Allow barley to cool completely; then, transfer it to a salad bowl. Add the remaining ingredients and toss to combine well. Place in your refrigerator until ready to serve. Enjoy!

261. Bulgur Wheat with Pico de Gallo
(Ready in about 25 minutes | Servings 4)

Nothing says comfort like a warm grain bowl with the onion and spicy sauce. It will remind you of an authentic Mexican table.
Per serving: *184 Calories; 10.4g Fat; 17.8g Carbs; 6g Protein; 3.8g Sugars*

Ingredients

2 tablespoons vegetable oil
1 yellow onion, chopped
2 garlic cloves, minced
1 ¼ cups bulgur wheat
3 cups roasted vegetable broth
Sea salt and white pepper, to taste
1 teaspoon smoked paprika
1/2 cup Pico de gallo

Directions

- Press the "Sauté" button to preheat your Instant Pot. Now, sauté the onions with garlic for 1 minute or so.
- Then, stir bulgur wheat, broth, salt, pepper, and paprika into your Instant Pot.
- Secure the lid. Choose the "Manual" mode and High pressure; cook for 12 minutes. Once cooking is complete, use a natural pressure release for 10 minutes; carefully remove the lid.
- Serve topped with chilled Pico de gallo. Bon appétit!

262. Herby Pinto Beans with Rice
(Ready in about 30 minutes | Servings 6)

This simple and surprisingly sophisticated dish will become your favorite weeknight staple! However, it is good enough for an elegant dinner party.
Per serving: *277 Calories; 5.9g Fat; 46.3g Carbs; 9.9g Protein; 2.4g Sugars*

Ingredients

2 tablespoons olive oil
1 cup dry pinto beans
1 cup dry brown rice
2 tomatoes, puréed
3 cups water
3 bouillon cubes
1 tablespoon fresh parsley, chopped
1 tablespoon fresh rosemary, chopped
1 tablespoon fresh mint, chopped
1 ancho chili pepper, chopped
2 tablespoons fresh chives, roughly chopped

Directions

- Add all ingredients, except for chives, to your Instant Pot.
- Secure the lid. Choose the "Bean/Chili" mode and High pressure; cook for 25 minutes. Once cooking is complete, use a natural pressure release; carefully remove the lid.
- Garnish with the chopped chives and enjoy!

263. Chicken and Barley Soup

(Ready in about 40 minutes | Servings 6)

Chicken soup with grains is good for your body and soul. It is the most comforting meal in the world as well.
Per serving: *379 Calories; 5.9g Fat; 48.8g Carbs; 33.2g Protein; 5.3g Sugars*

Ingredients

1 tablespoon butter, melted
1 ½ pounds chicken drumettes
1 onion, chopped
2 parsnips, trimmed and sliced
2 carrots, trimmed and sliced
1 celery stalk, chopped
2 cloves garlic, minced

1/2 teaspoon sea salt
1/3 teaspoon freshly ground black pepper
1/2 cup white wine
6 cups chicken broth, preferably homemade
2 bay leaves
1 1/3 cups barley, pearled

Directions

- Press the "Sauté" button to heat up the Instant Pot. Now, melt the butter. Once hot, sear chicken drumettes on all sides for 3 to 4 minutes. Discard bones and reserve.
- Then, sweat the onion until it is translucent.
- Add parsnips, carrots, and celery; cook an additional 3 minute or until the vegetables have softened. After that, stir in garlic and cook an additional 30 seconds.
- Add the remaining ingredients and secure the lid. Choose "Soup" setting and cook at High pressure for 30 minutes.
- Once cooking is complete, use a natural release; remove the lid carefully. Add reserved chicken and stir to combine. Ladle into individual bowls and serve hot.

---

264. Decadent Baked Beans with Madeira Wine

(Ready in about 40 minutes | Servings 4)

Madeira wine, with its layered character, adds a rich flavor to this family meal, while fresh lime wedges give a hit of bright and refreshing note.
Per serving: *226 Calories; 4.5g Fat; 29.3g Carbs; 12.9g Protein; 10.2g Sugars*

Ingredients

2 red onions, thinly sliced
2 garlic cloves, smashed
1 pound dry Cannellini beans
2 cups tomatoes, puréed
2 tablespoons tomato ketchup
1 teaspoon whole grain mustard
2 bay leaves
2 canned chipotle chilies
1 lime, cut into wedges
1/2 cup Madeira wine

Directions

- Add red onions, garlic, beans, tomatoes, ketchup, mustard, bay leaves, and chilies to the Instant Pot.
- Secure the lid. Choose the "Bean/Chili" mode and High pressure; cook for 30 minutes. Once cooking is complete, use a natural pressure release; carefully remove the lid.
- Ladle into individual bowls; squeeze lime wedges into each serving; add Madeira wine and stir to blend well. Serve warm.

265. Cinnamon Almond Oatmeal
(Ready in about 15 minutes | Servings 4)

Are you looking for a no-fuss family breakfast? This sweet and flavorful oatmeal is ready in 15 minutes!
Per serving: *347 Calories; 12.1g Fat; 51.3g Carbs; 8.7g Protein; 25.1g Sugars*

Ingredients

1 ½ cups regular oats
2 cups water
2 cups almond milk
1 teaspoon cinnamon, ground
2 tablespoons almond butter
1/2 cup chocolate chips

Directions

- Simply throw the oats, water, milk, and cinnamon into the Instant Pot.
- Secure the lid. Choose the "Manual" mode and High pressure; cook for 10 minutes. Once cooking is complete, use a quick pressure release; carefully remove the lid.
- Divide the oatmeal between serving bowls; top with almond butter and chocolate chips. Enjoy!

---

266. Refreshing Farro Salad
(Ready in about 15 minutes | Servings 4)

For the best results, this salad should be refrigerated overnight. Drizzled with fresh lime juice, this is a recipe you won't forget.
Per serving: *329 Calories; 6.8g Fat; 61.3g Carbs; 7.6g Protein; 9.9g Sugars*

Ingredients

1 ¼ cups farro, semi-pearled and rinsed
3 cups water
1 Walla Walla onion, chopped
1 cup cherry tomatoes, halved
2 green garlic stalks, minced
Salt and ground black pepper, to taste
4 tablespoons extra-virgin olive oil
1 tablespoon fresh lime juice
2 tablespoons fresh parsley leaves, chopped

Directions

- Add rinsed farro and water to your Instant Pot.
- Secure the lid. Choose the "Manual" mode and High pressure; cook for 10 minutes. Once cooking is complete, use a quick pressure release; carefully remove the lid.
- Drain well; allow it to cool completely. Add the onion, tomatoes, garlic, salt, and pepper; toss to combine.
- Toss with olive oil, lime juice, and parsley leaves. Bon appétit!

267. Favorite Cremini Mushroom Risotto
(Ready in about 15 minutes | Servings 5)

Cremini mushrooms are a powerhouse of Vitamin B-complex, zinc, potassium, selenium, phosphorus and manganese.
Per serving: *335 Calories; 14.9g Fat; 60g Carbs; 11g Protein; 2.3g Sugars*

Ingredients

2 cups jasmine rice
2 cups water
1/4 teaspoon kosher salt
2 tablespoons butter
1 onion, chopped
2 garlic cloves, minced
1/2 pound Cremini mushrooms, thinly sliced

Directions

- Rinse rice under cold running water and transfer to the Instant Pot; add water and 1/4 teaspoon of salt.
- Secure the lid and select the "Manual" mode. Cook at High pressure for 6 minutes. Once cooking is complete, use a natural release; remove the lid carefully.
- Fluff rice with the rice paddle or fork; reserve.
- Press the "Sauté" button and melt the butter. Now, sauté the onion until tender and translucent. Add garlic and cook an additional minute or until it is fragrant and lightly browned.
- Add Cremini mushrooms and continue to sauté until they are slightly browned. Add reserved jasmine rice, stir and serve warm. Bon appétit!

268. Spicy Japanese Okayu
(Ready in about 15 minutes | Servings 6)

Okayu is a simple Japanese congee recipe. This is a basic recipe, so you can choose your favorite toppings for savory porridge.
Per serving: *288 Calories; 3.3g Fat; 56.8g Carbs; 6.6g Protein; 1.9g Sugars*

Ingredients

1 tablespoon sesame oil
1 cup white onions, chopped
1 teaspoon garlic, minced
1 thumb-size ginger, julienned
1 carrot, chopped
2 cups white short-grain rice, rinsed
1 cup water
2 cups dashi stock
Sea salt and ground black pepper, to taste
1 teaspoon gochujang
2 tablespoons Shoyu sauce

Directions

- Press the "Sauté" button to preheat your Instant Pot. Then, heat the oil and sauté the onions until translucent.
- Add the garlic and ginger; continue to sauté for 30 seconds more. Add the carrot, rice, water, stock, salt, black pepper, and gochujang.
- Secure the lid. Choose the "Manual" mode and High pressure; cook for 8 minutes. Once cooking is complete, use a quick pressure release; carefully remove the lid.
- After that, add Shoyu sauce and stir to combine; divide okayu among 6 serving bowls and serve immediately.

269. Romano Rice with Tomatoes and Cheese

(Ready in about 10 minutes | Servings 5)

Topped with sun-dried tomatoes and cheese, this risotto has all your favorite Italian flavors.
Per serving: *354 Calories; 10.4g Fat; 52.7g Carbs; 11.1g Protein; 2.3g Sugars*

Ingredients

1 tablespoon toasted sesame oil
1 yellow onion, chopped
2 cloves garlic, pressed
1 ½ cups Romano rice
Sea salt and ground black pepper, to taste
1/2 cup tomatoes, puréed
2 tablespoons tomato ketchup
3 cups water
1 teaspoon sweet paprika
2 ounces sun-dried tomatoes
1 cup Pecorino-Romano cheese, freshly grated

Directions

- Press the "Sauté" button to preheat your Instant Pot. Then, heat the oil and sauté the onions until translucent.
- Add the garlic and cook for a further 30 seconds. Add Romano rice, salt, pepper, tomatoes, ketchup, water, and paprika.
- Secure the lid. Choose the "Poultry" mode and High pressure; cook for 5 minutes. Once cooking is complete, use a natural pressure release; carefully remove the lid.
- Ladle into individual bowls; garnish with sun-dried tomatoes and Pecorino-Romano cheese. Bon appétit!

270. Amaranth and Almond Porridge

(Ready in about 15 minutes | Servings 4)

Amaranth is a great source of vitamins, minerals, dietary fiber, and unsaturated fatty acids. It can lower high cholesterol levels, improve your digestion, and prevent atherosclerosis.
Per serving: *347 Calories; 6.3g Fat; 65.5g Carbs; 10.2g Protein; 27.1g Sugars*

Ingredients

1 ¼ cups amaranth
2 cups water
1 cup soy milk
1/3 teaspoon cinnamon, ground
1/2 teaspoon ground cloves
1/3 cup honey
1/2 cup almonds, slivered

Directions

- Place amaranth, water, milk, cinnamon, cloves and honey in your Instant Pot.
- Secure the lid. Choose the "Manual" mode and High pressure; cook for 8 minutes. Once cooking is complete, use a natural pressure release; carefully remove the lid.
- Ladle into individual bowls; top with slivered almonds and serve warm. Bon appétit!

271. Caribbean-Style Chili
(Ready in about 30 minutes | Servings 6)

Rich and flavorful, this chili will win your heart. Raisins and cocoa give this unusual chili a hint of island flavors.
Per serving: *375 Calories; 20g Fat; 24.2g Carbs; 24.6g Protein; 13.3g Sugars*

Ingredients

2 tablespoons olive oil
1/2 pound ground pork
1/2 pound ground beef
1 cup leeks, chopped
2 garlic cloves, minced
1 tablespoon chili powder
1/2 teaspoon ground allspice
1/2 teaspoon ground bay leaf
1 teaspoon dried basil
1 tablespoon brown sugar

1/2 teaspoon celery salt
1/4 teaspoon black pepper, or more to taste
1 ½ cups stock, preferably homemade
2 ripe tomatoes, chopped
2 (15-ounce) cans black beans, rinsed and drained
2 tablespoons soy sauce
1 teaspoon cocoa powder, unsweetened
1/2 cup golden raisins
1/2 cup sour cream

Directions

- Press the "Sauté" button to heat up your Instant Pot. Now, heat olive oil until sizzling.
- Cook ground meat, crumbling it with a spatula, until it is no longer pink; reserve.
- Now, stir in the leeks and garlic; cook until they have softened. Now, add chili powder, ground allspice, ground bay leaf, basil, sugar, salt, and pepper. Continue to sauté for 4 minutes more.
- Now, deglaze the bottom of the inner pot with the stock. Add tomatoes, beans, soy sauce, and cocoa powder.
- Then, choose the "Manual" button, High pressure and 8 minutes. Once cooking is complete, use a natural release; remove the lid carefully.
- Add raisins and cook in the residual heat for 5 to 6 minutes. Ladle into individual bowls and serve garnished with sour cream.

---

272. Herb and Tomato Bulgur Pilaf
(Ready in about 30 minutes | Servings 5)

The next time you plan to make pilaf, consider using bulgur and you will get plenty of bright and nutty flavors.
Per serving: *275 Calories; 7.6g Fat; 48.2g Carbs; 7.3g Protein; 5.3g Sugars*

Ingredients

2 tablespoons olive oil
1 red onion, chopped
1 teaspoon ginger-garlic paste
1 ½ cups bulgur wheat
4 ½ cups roasted vegetable broth
2 Roma tomatoes, seeded and diced

1/3 teaspoon ground turmeric
1/4 teaspoon ground cumin
1/4 cup lightly packed flat-leaf parsley, chopped
1/4 cup lightly packed fresh dill, chopped
Sea salt and freshly ground black pepper, to taste

Directions

- Press the "Sauté" button to preheat the Instant Pot; heat the oil until sizzling.
- Sauté the onion until fragrant or about 2 minutes. Stir the remaining ingredients into your Instant Pot.
- Secure the lid. Choose the "Manual" mode and High pressure; cook for 12 minutes. Once cooking is complete, use a natural pressure release for 10 minutes; carefully remove the lid.
- Ladle into serving bowls and garnish with some extra fresh herbs if desired. Serve immediately.

273. Pear and Almond Couscous
(Ready in about 15 minutes | Servings 4)

This couscous is an autumn comfort food that is sure to please. We used water, which make a lighter porridge, while almond milk will make a richer texture.
Per serving: *207 Calories; 0.3g Fat; 50g Carbs; 2.6g Protein; 31.8g Sugars*

Ingredients

1 ½ cups couscous, well rinsed
3 cups water
A pinch of salt
1/3 cup honey
1/4 teaspoon ground cloves
1/3 teaspoon ground cinnamon
1/2 teaspoon freshly grated nutmeg
1 teaspoon pure vanilla extract
2 medium-sized pears, cored and diced
1/3 cup almonds, slivered

Directions

- Place all of the above ingredients, except for almonds, into your Instant Pot; stir to combine well.
- Secure the lid. Choose the "Manual" mode and High pressure; cook for 8 minutes. Once cooking is complete, use a quick pressure release; carefully remove the lid.
- Serve topped with slivered almonds. Bon appétit!

274. Spicy Millet with Peppers
(Ready in about 20 minutes | Servings 4)

This is one of the most common ways to eat millet. Prepare this savory porridge in no time and enjoy with your family!
Per serving: *339 Calories; 6.6g Fat; 60.6g Carbs; 9.2g Protein; 2.9g Sugars*

Ingredients

1 tablespoon olive oil
1 red onion, chopped
1 red bell pepper, deveined and sliced
1 green bell pepper, deveined and sliced
1 ancho chili pepper, deveined and chopped
1/2 teaspoon granulated garlic
1 teaspoon salt
1/4 teaspoon ground black pepper
1/4 teaspoon cayenne pepper
1 ½ cups millet
3 cups water

Directions

- Press the "Sauté" button to preheat your Instant Pot. Then, heat the oil until sizzling; sauté the onions until they are caramelized.
- Stir in the peppers and continue to sauté an additional 2 minutes or until they are tender and fragrant.
- Add granulated garlic, salt, black pepper, cayenne pepper, millet, and water.
- Secure the lid. Choose the "Manual" mode and High pressure; cook for 5 minutes. Once cooking is complete, use a natural pressure release for 10 minutes; carefully remove the lid.
- Lastly, fluff the millet with a fork. Spoon into individual bowls and serve immediately. Bon appétit!

275. Pepper-Jack and Cilantro Cornbread
(Ready in about 35 minutes | Servings 8)

The perfect mixture of cornmeal, cheese, fresh cilantro, and spices. Salty, sweet, and melty!
Per serving: *318 Calories; 14.3g Fat; 37.2g Carbs; 9.9g Protein; 5.6g Sugars*

Ingredients

1 cup water
1 ½ cups cornmeal
1/2 cup all-purpose flour
1 teaspoon baking soda
1 teaspoon baking powder
1/2 teaspoon kosher salt
1/4 teaspoon black pepper, or more to taste
1/4 teaspoon cayenne pepper
1/2 teaspoon dried basil
1/4 teaspoon dried oregano

1/2 teaspoon ground allspice
1 cup Pepper-Jack cheese, grated
3/4 cup fresh corn kernels
2 tablespoons cilantro, roughly chopped
1 cup milk
1/2 teaspoon lime juice
1/2 stick butter, melted
2 tablespoons pure maple syrup
2 eggs

Directions

- Add water and a metal trivet to the base of your Instant Pot. Lightly grease a baking pan that fits in your Instant Pot.
- In a mixing bowl, thoroughly combine the cornmeal, flour, baking soda, baking powder, salt, black pepper, cayenne pepper, basil, oregano, and allspice.
- Stir in Pepper-Jack cheese, corn kernels, and cilantro. Mix to combine well.
- In another mixing bowl, whisk the remaining ingredients; add this wet mixture to the dry mixture.
- Pour the batter into the prepared baking pan. Cover with a paper towel; then, top with foil.
- Lower the pan onto the trivet and secure the lid. Choose the "Manual" mode, High pressure, and 23 minutes. Once cooking is complete, use a natural release; remove the lid carefully.
- Serve immediately and enjoy!

276. Indian Upma with Mushrooms
(Ready in about 10 minutes | Servings 4)

If you like a super creamy oatmeal, keep this recipe in your back pocket. Indian spices, cream of mushroom soup and bell pepper will add something special to your regular oats.
Per serving: *384 Calories; 12.3g Fat; 75.1g Carbs; 12.8g Protein; 3.6g Sugars*

Ingredients

1 tablespoon ghee
1 small-sized leek, finely diced
1 teaspoon garlic, minced
1/2 pound button mushrooms, chopped
1 red bell pepper, chopped
1 ¼ cups oat bran
2 cups water

2 cups cream of mushroom soup
1 sprig curry leaves
1/2 teaspoon chana dal
1/2 teaspoon urad dal
1/4 teaspoon ground turmeric
1/4 teaspoon dried dill
Sea salt and ground black pepper, to taste

Directions

- Press the "Sauté" button to preheat your Instant Pot. Now, melt the ghee and cook the leek until tender and fragrant.
- Then, stir in the garlic, mushrooms and pepper; cook an additional 2 minutes; reserve.
- Wipe down the Instant Pot with a damp cloth. Stir the remaining ingredients into your Instant Pot.
- Secure the lid. Choose the "Manual" mode and High pressure; cook for 2 minutes. Once cooking is complete, use a natural pressure release; carefully remove the lid.
- Serve in individual bowls topped with the reserved mushroom mixture. Enjoy!

277. Quinoa with Scallions and Peppers
(Ready in about 10 minutes | Servings 4)

The Instant Pot keeps the quinoa plump and moist, a good match for the peppers and scallions. For even more flavor, top with cheese and jazz up your weeknights!
Per serving: *225 Calories; 8.4g Fat; 31.3g Carbs; 6.7g Protein; 1.9g Sugars*

Ingredients

2 tablespoons butter, melted
2 tablespoons scallions, chopped
1 teaspoon garlic, minced
2 bell peppers, chopped
1 carrot, chopped
Salt and ground black pepper, to taste
1/2 teaspoon turmeric powder
1/2 teaspoon paprika
1/2 teaspoon dried rosemary
1 ½ cups water
1 cup quinoa

Directions

- Press the "Sauté" button to preheat your Instant Pot. Melt the butter. Sauté the scallions, garlic, peppers, and carrot until tender.
- Add the salt, black pepper, turmeric, paprika, and rosemary; cook an additional minute or until they are aromatic.
- Wipe down the Instant Pot with a damp cloth. Then, stir in the water and quinoa.
- Secure the lid. Choose the "Manual" mode and High pressure; cook for 1 minute. Once cooking is complete, use a natural pressure release; carefully remove the lid.
- Ladle the prepared quinoa into individual bowls; top with scallion mixture and serve immediately.

278. Creamy Polenta with Bacon
(Ready in about 15 minutes | Servings 4)

Here is an easy way to add layers of flavor to your polenta. Add smoked paprika, a few slices of bacon and a pinch of dried herbs.
Per serving: *165 Calories; 7.6g Fat; 14.3g Carbs; 9.6g Protein; 0.8g Sugars*

Ingredients

2 tablespoons butter, softened
2 cups vegetable broth
1 cup water
1 cup polenta
Ground black pepper, to taste
1/2 teaspoon sweet paprika
1/2 teaspoon smoked paprika

1/2 teaspoon dried basil
1/2 teaspoon dried oregano
1/2 teaspoon mustard powder
4 ounces Canadian bacon, chopped
1/4 cup scallions, chopped
1/4 cup fresh cilantro, chopped

Directions

- Press the "Sauté" button to preheat your Instant Pot. Add the butter, broth, and water; bring to a rolling boil.
- Gradually stir in the polenta, whisking continuously, for 2 minutes. Now, add black pepper, paprika, basil, oregano, and mustard powder.
- Secure the lid. Choose the "Manual" mode and High pressure; cook for 8 minutes. Once cooking is complete, use a natural pressure release; carefully remove the lid.
- Ladle the polenta into four serving bowls; top each serving with Canadian bacon, scallions, and cilantro. Serve warm and enjoy!

279. Decadent Brioche Pudding with Sultanas
(Ready in about 40 minutes | Servings 6)

Prepare this make-ahead bread pudding with subtle white chocolate, buttermilk, sultanas, and amazing coconut oil. Luscious, warm and comforting.
Per serving: *337 Calories; 13g Fat; 42.4g Carbs; 12.1g Protein; 10.8g Sugars*

Ingredients

2 eggs, whisked
1/3 cup buttermilk
1/2 teaspoon ground cinnamon
1/4 teaspoon grated nutmeg
1 teaspoon vanilla paste
2 tablespoons coconut oil, melted
1 large brioche loaf, torn into pieces
1/4 cup white chocolate chips
1/4 cup Turbinado sugar
1/4 cup sultanas, soaked in rum
1 cup water

Directions

* In a mixing dish, thoroughly combine the eggs, buttermilk, cinnamon, nutmeg, vanilla, and melted coconut oil.
* Add brioche and let it soak for 20 minutes; press the bread lightly with the back of a large spoon.
* Stir in chocolate chips, Turbinado sugar, and sultanas; stir gently to combine. Then, lightly grease a baking pan with a nonstick cooking spray.
* Pour water into the base of your Instant Pot; add a metal trivet. Lower the baking pan onto the trivet. Secure the lid.
* Choose the "Manual" mode, High pressure, and 15 minutes. Once cooking is complete, use a quick release; remove the lid carefully. Bon appétit!

---

280. Warming Brown Rice Risotto
(Ready in about 40 minutes | Servings 4)

You might want to consider this risotto to be the next dinner with your vegan friends. They will gobble up this delicious and healthy risotto.
Per serving: *238 Calories; 6.7g Fat; 40.1g Carbs; 4.6g Protein; 2.2g Sugars*

Ingredients

1 tablespoon olive oil
1 shallot, chopped
2 garlic cloves, smashed
1 bell pepper, seeded and chopped
1 cup tomato, puréed
1 cup brown rice, well-rinsed

1/2 cup water
1 teaspoon oregano
1 teaspoon basil
1 teaspoon ancho chili powder
1/2 cup black olives, pitted and sliced

Directions

* Press the "Sauté" button to preheat your Instant Pot. Heat the oil and sauté the onion, garlic, and pepper for 3 minutes.
* Add tomato purée, rice, water, oregano, basil, and chili powder.
* Secure the lid. Choose the "Manual" mode and High pressure; cook for 22 minutes. Once cooking is complete, use a natural pressure release for 10 minutes; carefully remove the lid.
* Serve topped with black olives. Bon appétit!

281. Grandma's Bean Medley
(Ready in about 40 minutes | Servings 4)

This old-fashioned meal is cheap, easy and quick to prepare. If you like spicy food, you can boost flavors with dried chili peppers.
Per serving: *238 Calories; 6.7g Fat; 40.1g Carbs; 4.6g Protein; 2.2g Sugars*

Ingredients

1 tablespoon olive oil
1 cup onions, chopped
4 garlic cloves, minced
1 bell pepper, thinly sliced
2 medium-sized carrots, thinly sliced
3/4 pound white kidney beans
6 cups water
Seasoned salt and ground black pepper, to taste
1 heaping teaspoon cayenne pepper
2 bay leaves

Directions

- Press the "Sauté" button to preheat your Instant Pot. Heat the oil and sauté the onions and garlic for 2 minutes or until tender and fragrant.
- Add the remaining ingredients. Stir to combine well.
- Secure the lid. Choose the "Bean/Chili" mode and High pressure; cook for 30 minutes. Once cooking is complete, use a natural pressure release; carefully remove the lid.
- Ladle into individual bowls and garnish with dried chili peppers if desired. Bon appétit!

282. Elegant Bean Purée
(Ready in about 30 minutes | Servings 4)

Adzuki beans are loaded with protein, antioxidants, iron, potassium and dietary fiber. They can protect your heart and prevent diabetes.
Per serving: *95 Calories; 4.9g Fat; 7.7g Carbs; 6.4g Protein; 0.4g Sugars*

Ingredients

1 tablespoon canola oil
1/2 cup scallions, chopped
4 cloves garlic, smashed
1 ½ cups Adzuki beans
2 cups water
3 cups beef bone broth
Sea salt and freshly ground black pepper, to taste
1 teaspoon paprika

Directions

- Press the "Sauté" button to preheat your Instant Pot. Then, heat the oil and cook the scallions and garlic until tender; reserve.
- Wipe down the Instant Pot with a damp cloth. Add Adzuki beans, water, broth, salt, pepper, and paprika.
- Secure the lid. Choose the "Bean/Chili" mode and High pressure; cook for 20 minutes. Once cooking is complete, use a natural pressure release; carefully remove the lid.
- Transfer to your food processor and add the reserved scallion/garlic mixture. Then, process the mixture, working in batches. Process until smooth and uniform. Serve warm and enjoy!

283. Aromatic Kamut with Sweet Onions
(Ready in about 15 minutes | Servings 4)

Kamut, also known as Oriental wheat, is an excellent source of magnesium, selenium, and zinc as well as dietary fiber and protein.
Per serving: *349 Calories; 8.3g Fat; 62.1g Carbs; 11.5g Protein; 13.7g Sugars*

Ingredients

2 tablespoons olive oil
2 sweet onions, thinly sliced
1/2 teaspoon ground cinnamon
1/2 teaspoon cardamom
1 ½ cups kamut
4 ½ cups water
Sea salt and ground white pepper, to taste

Directions

- Press the "Sauté" button and heat the olive oil. Add sweet onions, together with cinnamon and cardamom; sauté until sweet onions are caramelized.
- Add the kamut, water, salt, and ground pepper. Now, secure the lid. Choose the "Manual" mode and cook at High pressure for 8 minutes.
- Once cooking is complete, use a natural release; remove the lid carefully. Bon appétit!

---

284. Chili Con Carne
(Ready in about 35 minutes | Servings 8)

You can't go wrong with a classic chili because it cooks perfectly in the Instant Pot. Serve over hot rice if desired.
Per serving: *300 Calories; 19.1g Fat; 9.7g Carbs; 22g Protein; 2.9g Sugars*

Ingredients

1 tablespoon lard
1 cup onion, chopped
3 garlic cloves, smashed
1/2 pound ground pork
1/2 pound ground beef
2 pounds red kidney beans, soaked overnight
2 cups tomato, puréed
1 cup onion, chopped
3 garlic cloves, smashed
2 bell peppers, deveined and chopped

1 cup water
1 cup chicken stock
Sea salt and freshly ground black pepper, to taste
1 teaspoon cayenne pepper
1 teaspoon red chili powder
1 teaspoon Mexican oregano
1 bay leaf
1 cup Pepper-Jack cheese, grated

Directions

- Press the "Sauté" button to preheat your Instant Pot. Now, melt the lard and cook the onion until tender and translucent.
- Add the garlic and ground meat; continue to cook until the meat is delicately browned.
- Now, stir in the beans, tomato, onion, garlic, peppers, water, stock, salt, black pepper, cayenne pepper, chili powder, oregano and bay leaf.
- Secure the lid. Choose the "Bean/Chili" mode and High pressure; cook for 30 minutes. Once cooking is complete, use a natural pressure release; carefully remove the lid.
- Ladle into individual bowls; serve topped with grated cheese and enjoy!

285. Red Rice with Smoked Kielbasa
(Ready in about 40 minutes | Servings 4)

Smoked Kielbasa is combined with good-for-you red rice, tangy tomato ketchup, and aromatics. Serve with your favorite red wine.
Per serving: *282 Calories; 20.1g Fat; 21.7g Carbs; 13.1g Protein; 2.3g Sugars*

Ingredients

1 tablespoon canola oil
1/2 pound smoked Kielbasa, sliced
1 leek, chopped
1 cup red rice
1/4 cup tomato, puréed
1 cup vegetable broth
1 tablespoon ketchup
1/2 teaspoon mustard powder
1/2 teaspoon garlic powder
1/2 teaspoon dried marjoram

Directions

- Press the "Sauté" button to preheat your Instant Pot. Now, heat the canola oil; cook the sausage and leek for 2 to 3 minutes.
- Add the remaining ingredients; stir to combine well.
- Secure the lid. Choose the "Porridge" mode and High pressure; cook for 25 minutes. Once cooking is complete, use a natural pressure release for 10 minutes; carefully remove the lid.
- Ladle into serving bowls; serve with some extra mustard if desired and enjoy!

---

286. Carnaroli Rice Risotto with Ground Beef
(Ready in about 15 minutes | Servings 4)

"Superfino" Carnaroli rice meets slightly browned ground beef in this Italian favorite. This risotto reheats well in the Instant Pot.
Per serving: *430 Calories; 26.3g Fat; 37.2g Carbs; 29.6g Protein; 4.2g Sugars*

Ingredients

2 tablespoons butter
1 cup shallots, diced
2 garlic cloves, minced
1/2 pound ground beef
2 bell peppers, seeded and chopped
1 red chili pepper, seeded and minced
2 cups Carnaroli rice, well-rinsed

4 cups beef stock
A pinch of saffron
Kosher salt and ground black pepper, to taste
1 teaspoon sweet paprika

Directions

- Press the "Sauté" button to preheat your Instant Pot. Now, melt the butter; cook the shallots until they are softened.
- Stir the garlic, ground beef, and peppers into your Instant Pot. Continue to cook an additional 2 minutes or until the beef is no longer pink and peppers are tender.
- Add rice, stock and seasonings to your Instant Pot; gently stir to combine.
- Secure the lid. Choose the "Poultry" mode and High pressure; cook for 5 minutes. Once cooking is complete, use a quick pressure release; carefully remove the lid.
- Serve in individual bowls. Bon appétit!

287. Savory Mediterranean Oatmeal
(Ready in about 15 minutes | Servings 3)

Greek feta is a perfect addition to any simple porridge, and oatmeal is no exception. Add Kalamata olives and you will bring the Mediterranean into your home.
Per serving: *244 Calories; 14g Fat; 35.3g Carbs; 13.1g Protein; 1.8g Sugars*

Ingredients

1 ½ cups oats, quick cooking
2 3/4 cups water
2 tablespoons flax seeds
1/3 teaspoon cayenne pepper
1 rosemary sprig, leaves picked and chopped
1/2 teaspoon sea salt
Ground black pepper, to your liking
1/2 cup feta cheese, crumbled
1/2 cup Kalamata olives, pitted and sliced

Directions

- Add quick cooking oats and water to your Instant Pot. Add flax seeds, cayenne pepper, rosemary, salt, and black pepper. Secure the lid.
- Choose the "Manual" button and cook for 6 minutes at High pressure. Once cooking is complete, use a natural release; remove the lid carefully.
- Ladle the prepared oatmeal into individual bowls. Top with crumbled feta cheese and sliced olives and serve. Enjoy!

---

288. Kamut with Cherries and Sour Cream
(Ready in about 45 minutes | Servings 4)

There's no shortage of flavor on this kamut porridge, topped with sour cream and honey. You can use dried figs, cranberries or raisins as well.
Per serving: *473 Calories; 13.4g Fat; 82.1g Carbs; 12.7g Protein; 33.2g Sugars*

Ingredients

1 ½ cups kamut, well-rinsed
4 ½ cups water
A pinch of salt
2 tablespoons butter
1/4 teaspoon grated nutmeg
1/2 teaspoon ground cinnamon
1 cup dried cherries
1 cup sour cream
1/3 cup honey

Directions

- Add kamut, water, and salt to your Instant Pot.
- Secure the lid. Choose the "Multigrain" mode and High pressure; cook for 40 minutes. Once cooking is complete, use a natural pressure release; carefully remove the lid.
- Now, add the butter, nutmeg, cinnamon and cherries to the Instant Pot; stir to combine and divide the porridge between four serving bowls.
- Top each serving with sour cream; drizzle honey over the top and serve. Enjoy!

289. Easy Cheesy Polenta
(Ready in about 15 minutes | Servings 4)

This polenta is easy to make and tastes so good. A great idea for a family dinner! This is the perfect opportunity to break that take out habit!
Per serving: *502 Calories; 22.1g Fat; 54.2g Carbs; 20.3g Protein; 4.6g Sugars*

Ingredients

6 cups roasted vegetable broth
1/2 stick butter, softened
1 ½ cups cornmeal
Sea salt and ground black pepper, to taste
1 cup Cheddar cheese, shredded
1/2 cup Ricotta cheese, at room temperature

Directions

● Press the "Sauté" button to preheat the Instant Pot. Then, add the broth and butter; bring to a boil. Slowly and gradually, whisk in the cornmeal. Season with the salt and pepper.
● Secure the lid. Choose the "Manual" mode and High pressure; cook for 8 minutes. Once cooking is complete, use a natural pressure release; carefully remove the lid.
● Divide between individual bowls; serve topped with cheese. Bon appétit!

290. Italian-Style Baked Beans
(Ready in about 20 minutes | Servings 4)

Super satisfying, comforting and easy to make, these baked beans might become your next favorite lunch. You can use pork or beef sausage in this recipe.
Per serving: *449 Calories; 26.8g Fat; 35.1g Carbs; 25g Protein; 10.2g Sugars*

Ingredients

1 pound pinto beans, soaked overnight
2 tablespoons brown sugar
1 bay leaf
2 tomatoes, puréed
1/2 teaspoon dried rosemary
1 teaspoon dried marjoram
1/2 teaspoon freshly ground black pepper
1/2 teaspoon cayenne pepper
Sea salt, to taste

1 pound smoked Italian sausage, sliced
1 yellow onion, chopped
2 cloves garlic, minced
1 carrot, sliced
1 parsnip, sliced
2 bell peppers, seeded and chopped
1 Pepperoncini, seeded and minced
1/2 cup sour cream

Directions

● Add pinto beans to your Instant Pot; now, pour in enough water to cover the beans completely.
● Next, stir in the sugar, bay leaf, tomatoes, rosemary, marjoram, black pepper, cayenne pepper, and salt; stir to combine well.
● Secure the lid. Choose the "Bean/Chili" mode and High pressure; cook for 10 minutes. Once cooking is complete, use a natural pressure release; carefully remove the lid.
● In the meantime, cook the sausage with the onion, garlic, carrot, parsnip, and peppers for 3 to 4 minutes; transfer the sausage mixture to the Instant Pot.
● Top with well-chilled sour cream and serve. Bon appétit!

291. Hazelnut and Cranberry Buckwheat Porridge
(Ready in about 25 minutes | Servings 3)

Here is the perfect winter breakfast porridge. You can add fresh fruits too. If you are going vegan, just skip the regular milk and use a non-dairy milk instead.
Per serving: *301 Calories; 19.3g Fat; 24.4g Carbs; 10g Protein; 13g Sugars*

Ingredients

3/4 cup raw buckwheat, rinsed
1 cup water
2 cups milk
1/3 cup dried cranberries
1/4 teaspoon cardamom
1/2 teaspoon ground cinnamon
1/2 teaspoon anise seed powder
1 teaspoon vanilla paste
1/2 teaspoon hazelnut extract
1/2 cup hazelnuts, chopped
1 tablespoon orange rind strips, for garnish

Directions

- Add buckwheat to the Instant Pot. Now, pour in water and milk.
- Stir in dried cranberries, cardamom, cinnamon, anise seed powder, vanilla, and hazelnut extract. Secure the lid.
- Choose the "Manual" button and cook for 7 minutes at High pressure. Once cooking is complete, use a natural release for 15 minutes; remove the lid carefully.
- Divide hot porridge among 3 serving bowls and top with hazelnuts; garnish with orange rind strips and serve right now. Bon appétit!

---

292. Lime and Wild Rice Soup
(Ready in about 35 minutes | Servings 4)

This quick and refreshing soup might become a new weeknight favorite! Serve with a slice of rye bread if desired.
Per serving: *236 Calories; 7.7g Fat; 36.7g Carbs; 6.9g Protein; 3.2g Sugars*

Ingredients

2 tablespoons olive oil
1 onion, chopped
2 carrots, halved lengthwise and finely sliced
1 celery stalk, chopped
1 cup wild rice
6 cups water, bone broth, or a combination
1/2 teaspoon granulated garlic
2 tablespoons bouillon granules
1/4 cup freshly squeezed lime juice

Directions

- Press the "Sauté" button to preheat the Instant Pot. Then, heat the oil; sauté the onions until tender and translucent.
- Now, stir in the carrots and celery; continue to sauté until tender.
- Add rice, water, granulated garlic, and bouillon granules to the Instant Pot.
- Secure the lid. Choose the "Soup" mode and High pressure; cook for 30 minutes. Once cooking is complete, use a natural pressure release; carefully remove the lid.
- Ladle into soup bowls; drizzle each serving with fresh lime juice. Enjoy!

293. Barley and Beef Soup with Corn
(Ready in about 55 minutes | Servings 5)

Barley packs a nutritious punch in this soup. It combines well with beef, sweet corn, and root vegetables. Enjoy!
Per serving: *366 Calories; 8.4g Fat; 44.1g Carbs; 30.2g Protein; 3.9g Sugars*

Ingredients

1 tablespoon butter, softened
1 pound beef stew meat
1 shallot, chopped
Sea salt, to taste
1/4 teaspoon freshly ground black pepper, or more to taste
2 carrots, chopped
1 parsnip, chopped
2 celery stalks, chopped
1 teaspoon ginger-garlic paste
1/2 cup port wine
5 cups beef bone broth
1 cup barley, whole
5 ounces sweet corn kernels, frozen and thawed

Directions

- Press the "Sauté" button to preheat the Instant Pot. Then, melt the butter; cook the meat and shallot until the meat is no longer pink.
- Add the salt, pepper, carrots, parsnip, celery, ginger-garlic paste, wine, broth and barley.
- Secure the lid. Choose the "Soup" mode and High pressure; cook for 40 minutes. Once cooking is complete, use a natural pressure release for 10 minutes; carefully remove the lid.
- Add the corn and seal the lid. Allow it to seat until heated through. Ladle into individual bowls and serve right away!

294. Tangy Wheat Berry Salad
(Ready in about 55 minutes | Servings 4)

This refreshing, sweet and tart salad is perfect idea for a light dinner. Serve on a bed of lettuce.
Per serving: *371 Calories; 19.3g Fat; 44.9g Carbs; 8.1g Protein; 8.2g Sugars*

Ingredients

1 ½ cups wheat berries
4 ½ cups water
1/4 teaspoon sea salt
1/4 teaspoon ground white pepper
1 large Fuji apple, unpeeled, diced
1 cucumber, sliced
1 carrot, julienned
1/3 cup almonds, toasted and chopped
2 tablespoons raspberry vinegar
1/4 cup extra-virgin olive oil

Directions

- Add wheat berries and water to the Instant Pot.
- Secure the lid. Choose the "Multigrain" mode and High pressure; cook for 50 minutes. Once cooking is complete, use a natural pressure release; carefully remove the lid.
- Allow wheat berries to cool completely. Toss them with the remaining ingredients and serve well chilled.

295. Savory Millet with Sunflower Seeds
(Ready in about 20 minutes | Servings 4)

Millet is an extremely healthy grain. It is a powerhouse of dietary fiber, vitamin E, B-group vitamins, copper, selenium, magnesium, zinc, iron, and so forth.
Per serving: *275 Calories; 9.1g Fat; 41.5g Carbs; 7.8g Protein; 1.6g Sugars*

Ingredients

2 teaspoons pure sesame oil
1 cup carrots, chopped
A bunch of scallions, roughly chopped
1/2 teaspoon coarse salt
1/4 teaspoon ground white pepper
1/2 teaspoon cayenne pepper
1 teaspoon dried basil

1/2 teaspoon dried oregano
1 bay leaf
1/4 cup sunflower seeds
1 cup millet
1 2/3 cups water
3 tablespoons fresh chives, finely chopped

Directions

- Press the "Sauté" button to preheat your Instant Pot. Now, heat sesame oil until sizzling. After that, cook the carrots and scallions until they are just tender and fragrant, about 3 minutes.
- Add the salt, white pepper, cayenne pepper, basil, oregano, bay leaf, sunflower seeds, and millet. Lastly, pour in the water and secure the lid.
- Select the "Manual" function and cook for 10 minutes under High pressure. Once cooking is complete, use a quick release; remove the lid carefully.
- Serve in individual bowls, garnished with fresh chives. Bon appétit!

---

296. Kamut Pilaf with Olives
(Ready in about 25 minutes | Servings 4)

Nutty kamut goes well with fresh herbs, root vegetables, and olives. If you forgot to soak your kamut, just cook it on high pressure for 40 minutes.
Per serving: *285 Calories; 5g Fat; 53.6g Carbs; 10.8g Protein; 7.4g Sugars*

Ingredients

1 tablespoon olive oil
2 shallots, chopped
2 cloves garlic minced
1 carrot, chopped
1 celery stalk, chopped
1 ½ cups kamut, soaked overnight

3 cups water
Salt and black pepper, to taste
1/2 teaspoon dried rosemary
1/4 cup fresh chives, chopped
1/4 cup fresh parsley, chopped
1/2 cup green olives, pitted and sliced

Directions

- Press the "Sauté" button to preheat your Instant Pot. Now, heat the oil until sizzling; sauté the shallots for 2 minutes or until tender.
- Next, stir in the garlic, carrots and celery; continue to sauté until they are tender. Add kamut, water, salt, black pepper, and rosemary to the Instant Pot.
- Secure the lid. Choose the "Porridge" mode and High pressure; cook for 20 minutes. Once cooking is complete, use a natural pressure release; carefully remove the lid.
- Transfer to a serving bowl; garnish with chives, parsley and olives and serve. Enjoy!

297. Colombian Style Beans
(Ready in about 35 minutes | Servings 5)

These Colombian-style beans also known as Frijoles Colombianos is a common dish from the Antioquia region. You can use cranberry beans as well.

Per serving: *553 Calories; 5.2g Fat; 93.3g Carbs; 37.2g Protein; 8.5g Sugars*

Ingredients

1 tablespoon olive oil
1 purple onion, chopped
2 bell peppers, seeded and chopped
1 serrano pepper, seeded and minced
2 garlic cloves, minced
1/2 green plantain, cut into slices
1 ½ pounds dry Borlotti beans
4 cups roasted vegetable broth

2 ripe tomatoes, puréed
1/2 teaspoon cumin
1/2 teaspoon dried basil
1/2 teaspoon oregano
Salt and freshly ground black pepper, to taste
1 heaping tablespoon fresh parsley leaves, chopped
2 bay leaves

Directions

- Press the "Sauté" button to preheat your Instant Pot. Now, heat the oil until sizzling; sauté the onion for 2 minutes or until tender.
- Then, add the peppers, garlic, and plantain; continue to sauté an additional minute or until they are fragrant; reserve.
- Add the remaining ingredients to your Instant Pot; stir to combine.
- Secure the lid. Choose the "Bean/Chili" mode and High pressure; cook for 25 minutes. Once cooking is complete, use a natural pressure release; carefully remove the lid.
- Add the reserved onion/pepper mixture. Seal the lid and let it sit for 5 minutes more or until everything is thoroughly warmed.
- Discard bay leaves. Taste for salt and serve warm.

298. Pot Barley with Vegetables
(Ready in about 45 minutes | Servings 4)

If you're wondering what to cook with pot barley, try this recipe. Firstly, sauté your veggies to enhance the flavors and then cook all ingredients in the Instant Pot. It's really as simple as that!

Per serving: *286 Calories; 8.3g Fat; 43.3g Carbs; 11.4g Protein; 2.6g Sugars*

Ingredients

1 tablespoon olive oil
1 yellow onion, chopped
2 garlic cloves, minced
1 carrot, chopped
1 ½ cups button mushrooms, thinly sliced
1 cup pot barley

4 cups stock, preferably homemade
1/2 teaspoon salt
1/3 teaspoon freshly ground black pepper
1/4 teaspoon paprika
1/2 teaspoon ground bay leaf

Directions

- Press the "Sauté" button and heat up your Instant Pot. Heat olive oil until sizzling. Once hot, sweat onion until tender.
- Now, add garlic, carrot, and mushrooms; cook until the mushrooms start to release their moisture and carrots are softened.
- Rinse and drain barley; transfer to the Instant Pot. Add the remaining ingredients; stir to combine.
- Select the "Manual" mode and cook for 30 minutes under High pressure. Once cooking is complete, use a natural release for 10 minutes; remove the lid carefully. Bon appétit!

299. Buttermilk and Cottage Cheese Cornbread
(Ready in about 30 minutes | Servings 8)

Olive oil, herbs, buttermilk, and cheese! What more could you ask for in a cornbread?
Per serving: *266 Calories; 13.7g Fat; 27g Carbs; 8.2g Protein; 5.9g Sugars*

Ingredients

1 ½ cups polenta
1 cup all-purpose flour
2 tablespoons honey
1 tablespoon baking powder
1/2 teaspoon baking soda
1/2 teaspoon sea salt
1/3 cup olive oil
3 eggs
1/2 cup buttermilk

2/3 cup Cottage cheese, crumbled
1/2 teaspoon garlic powder
1/2 teaspoon onion powder
1/2 teaspoon oregano
1/2 teaspoon basil
1 teaspoon rosemary
1 teaspoon thyme

Directions

* Begin by adding 1 cup of water and a metal trivet to the bottom of your Instant Pot. Spritz the bottom and sides of a baking pan with a nonstick cooking pan.
* Thoroughly combine dry ingredients in a mixing bowl. In a separate mixing bowl, mix wet ingredients.
* Then, combine the wet mixture with dry mixture; scrape the batter into the prepared baking pan. Place the baking pan on the trivet.
* Secure the lid. Choose the "Porridge" mode and High pressure; cook for 20 minutes. Once cooking is complete, use a natural pressure release; carefully remove the lid.
* Afterwards, transfer the cornbread to a cooling rack; allow it to sit for 5 to 6 minutes before slicing and serving. Enjoy!

---

300. Oatmeal and Purple Onion Soup
(Ready in about 30 minutes | Servings 4)

You'll be obsessed with this oatmeal soup – it is easy to prepare and serve for a family lunch. Add a spicy sausage or bacon bits if desired.
Per serving: *160 Calories; 9.3g Fat; 18.6g Carbs; 7g Protein; 5.2g Sugars*

Ingredients

2 tablespoons ghee
1 purple onion, chopped
2 garlic cloves, minced
2/3 cup oat groat
2 cups water
1 cup milk
1 cup vegetable broth
Sea salt and ground black pepper, to taste
1/2 teaspoon cayenne pepper
1/2 teaspoon turmeric powder
2 cups spinach leaves, roughly chopped

Directions

* Press the "Sauté" button to preheat your Instant Pot. Then, melt ghee and cook the onion and garlic until tender and fragrant.
* Add oat groat, water, milk, broth, salt, black pepper, cayenne pepper, and turmeric powder; stir to combine.
* Secure the lid. Choose the "Manual" mode and High pressure; cook for 22 minutes. Once cooking is complete, use a natural pressure release; carefully remove the lid.
* Add spinach and seal the lid; let it sit until the spinach is wilted. Serve warm and enjoy!

SNACKS & APPETIZERS

301. Chicken Wings with Barbecue Sauce
(Ready in about 20 minutes | Servings 3)

Are you craving barbecued wings? Try juicy, pressure-cooked chicken wings that are ready in 20 minutes.
Per serving: *204 Calories; 6.7g Fat; 23.1g Carbs; 13.2g Protein; 20.1g Sugars*

Ingredients

1 cup water
6 chicken wings
For the Barbecue Sauce:
1/3 cup water
1/3 cup ketchup
2 tablespoons brown sugar
2 tablespoons blackstrap molasses
1 tablespoon mustard

1 tablespoon cider vinegar
1 tablespoon olive oil
1 teaspoon garlic, minced
1 teaspoon chipotle powder
1/4 teaspoon sea salt
1/4 teaspoon freshly ground black pepper
1/4 teaspoon ground allspice

Directions

* Pour 1 cup of water into the base of your Instant Pot.
* Now, arrange the wings in the steaming basket. Transfer the steaming basket to the Instant Pot.
* Secure the lid and choose the "Poultry" function; cook for 15 minutes at High pressure. Once cooking is complete, use a natural release; carefully remove the lid.
* In a pan, combine all of the ingredients for the sauce and bring to a boil. Remove from heat and stir well. Add chicken wings and serve. Bon appétit!

---

302. Hoisin-Glazed White Mushrooms
(Ready in about 10 minutes | Servings 5)

With their natural umami taste, mushrooms go wonderfully with tangy and sweet hoisin sauce. You can also use King Trumpet mushrooms in this recipe.
Per serving: *124 Calories; 8.1g Fat; 10.2g Carbs; 4.4g Protein; 7.7g Sugars*

Ingredients

20 ounces fresh white mushrooms
1/3 cup water
1 tablespoon apple cider vinegar
3 tablespoons soy sauce
1 tablespoon peanut butter
1 tablespoon molasses
2 garlic cloves, minced
2 tablespoons olive oil
1/2 teaspoon hot sauce
Sea salt and ground black pepper, to taste
1 teaspoon paprika

Directions

* Add all ingredients to your Instant Pot.
* Secure the lid. Choose the "Manual" mode and High pressure; cook for 5 minutes. Once cooking is complete, use a quick pressure release; carefully remove the lid; remove the mushrooms from the cooking liquid.
* Then, press the "Sauté" button and continue to simmer until the sauce has reduced and thickened.
* Place the reserved mushrooms in a serving bowl, add the sauce and serve.

303. Easy Brussels Sprout Appetizer
(Ready in about 10 minutes | Servings 4)

Brussels sprouts are loaded with omega-3 fatty acids, vitamin C, vitamin K, vitamin B1, vitamin B6, manganese, copper, and dietary fiber.
Per serving: *145 Calories; 7.7g Fat; 15.5g Carbs; 7.3g Protein; 3.8g Sugars*

Ingredients

2 tablespoons butter
1/2 cup shallots, chopped
1/4 cup dry white wine
1 ½ pounds Brussels sprouts, trimmed and halved
1 cup water
Salt, to taste
1/4 teaspoon ground black pepper, or more to taste

Directions

- Press the "Sauté" button to preheat your Instant Pot. Once hot, melt the butter and sauté the shallots until tender.
- Add a splash of wine to deglaze the bottom of the Instant Pot. Add the remaining ingredients to the Instant Pot.
- Secure the lid. Choose the "Manual" mode and High pressure; cook for 4 minutes. Once cooking is complete, use a quick pressure release; carefully remove the lid. Bon appétit!

304. Appetizer Meatballs with Barbecue Sauce
(Ready in about 15 minutes | Servings 12)

A tangy barbecue sauce gives meatballs the kick you didn't know they needed! If you are in a hurry, any store-bought barbecue sauce will work.
Per serving: *178 Calories; 9.4g Fat; 8.3g Carbs; 15g Protein; 5.1g Sugars*

Ingredients

For the Meatballs:
1 pound ground chuck
1/2 pound ground pork
Seasoned salt and ground black pepper, to taste
1 onion, chopped
2 garlic cloves, minced
1 egg, well-beaten
1/2 cup Romano cheese, preferably freshly grated

2/3 cup tortilla chips, crushed
For the Sauce:
1 cup water
1 cup ketchup
1/4 cup apple cider vinegar
6 tablespoons light brown sugar
1/2 teaspoon onion powder
1 teaspoon ground mustard

Directions

- Mix all ingredients for the meatballs. Spritz a sauté pan with a nonstick cooking spray.
- Heat the sauté pan over a medium-high heat. Then, brown the meatballs until they are delicately browned on all sides.
- In another mixing dish, thoroughly combine all ingredients for the sauce. Add the sauce to the Instant Pot.
- Drop the meatballs into the sauce.
- Secure the lid and choose the "Poultry" function; cook for 5 minutes at High pressure. Once cooking is complete, use a natural release; carefully remove the lid.
- Serve on a nice platter with toothpicks. Enjoy!

305. Honey-Glazed Baby Carrots
(Ready in about 15 minutes | Servings 6)

Make delicate baby carrots for the next family gathering. In this recipe, the herbs are actually sautéed with coconut oil for an extra flavor!
Per serving: *151 Calories; 4.8g Fat; 28g Carbs; 1.3g Protein; 21.1g Sugars*

Ingredients

1 ½ cups water
2 ½ pounds baby carrots, trimmed
1 teaspoon thyme
1 teaspoon dill
Salt and white pepper, to taste
2 tablespoons coconut oil
1/4 cup honey

Directions

- Add 1 ½ cups of water to the base of your Instant Pot.
- Now, arrange baby carrots in the steaming basket. Transfer the steaming basket to the Instant Pot.
- Secure the lid and choose the "Manual" function; cook for 3 minutes at High pressure. Once cooking is complete, use a quick release; carefully remove the lid.
- Strain baby carrots and reserve.
- Then, add the other ingredients to the Instant Pot. Press the "Sauté" button and cook until everything is heated through.
- Add reserved baby carrots and gently stir. Bon appétit!

---

306. Party Dilled Deviled Eggs
(Ready in about 15 minutes + chilling time | Servings 6)

Update the classic deviled eggs with dill pickle and Sriracha. You can garnish these eggs with sweet Hungarian paprika if desired.
Per serving: *277 Calories; 21.9g Fat; 3.7g Carbs; 15.8g Protein; 1.4g Sugars*

Ingredients

10 eggs
1/4 cup extra-virgin olive oil
2 tablespoons mayonnaise
1 teaspoon yellow mustard
1 tablespoon dill pickle juice
1/2 teaspoon Sriracha sauce
Maldon salt and freshly ground black pepper, to taste
1 tablespoon fresh parsley, chopped
2 tablespoons dill pickle, chopped

Directions

- Begin by adding 1 cup of water and steamer basket to your Instant Pot. Place the eggs in the steamer basket.
- Secure the lid and choose the "Manual" function; cook for 5 minutes at High pressure. Once cooking is complete, use a natural release; carefully remove the lid.
- Slice each egg in half lengthwise.
- Transfer egg yolks to your food processor. Now, add the remaining ingredients; process until creamy and smooth.
- Then, pipe the chilled filling mixture into egg whites, overstuffing each. Serve on a nice serving platter and enjoy!

307. Classic Hummus Dip
(Ready in about 45 minutes | Servings 8)

This classic hummus is so tasty, light and diet-friendly! Add a pinch of ground chili pepper for some extra oomph!
Per serving: *206 Calories; 8.1g Fat; 26.1g Carbs; 8.8g Protein; 4.6g Sugars*

Ingredients

1 tablespoon olive oil
1 yellow onion, chopped
2 garlic cloves, minced
1 ½ cups dried chickpeas
4 cups water
3 tablespoons tahini paste
2 tablespoons fresh lemon juice

Directions

- Press the "Sauté" button to preheat your Instant Pot. Once hot, heat the olive oil until sizzling. Then, cook the onion and garlic until tender and fragrant; reserve.
- Wipe down the Instant Pot with a damp cloth. Then, add chickpeas and water to the Instant Pot.
- Secure the lid and choose the "Bean/Chili" function; cook for 40 minutes at High pressure. Once cooking is complete, use a natural release; carefully remove the lid.
- Drain chickpeas, reserving cooking liquid. Now, transfer chickpeas to your blender. Add tahini, lemon juice, and reserved onion/garlic mixture.
- Process until everything is creamy, uniform, and smooth, adding a splash of cooking liquid. Serve with pita bread and vegetable sticks.

308. Ranch-Style Popcorn
(Ready in about 10 minutes | Servings 6)

We can't imagine a movie night or late-night snack without a crunchy, buttery popcorn! You will love this recipe.
Per serving: *177 Calories; 13.9g Fat; 11.1g Carbs; 2.4g Protein; 3.5g Sugars*

Ingredients

2 tablespoons olive oil
3/4 cup corn kernels
4 tablespoons butter
1-ounce packet ranch seasoning mix
Sea salt, to taste

Directions

- Press the "Sauté" button to preheat your Instant Pot.
- Now, heat the olive oil; add corn kernels. Sauté until corn kernels are well coated with oil.
- Secure the lid and choose the "Manual" function; cook for 5 minutes at High pressure. Once cooking is complete, use a quick release; carefully remove the lid.
- In a saucepan, melt the butter with ranch seasoning mix. Lastly, toss the ranch butter with popcorn; season with salt. Enjoy!

309. Cheesy Artichoke and Kale Dip
(Ready in about 15 minutes | Servings 8)

Make your party much better with this traditional version of cheese-artichoke dip. A quick and easy dipping sauce that is also freezer-friendly!

Per serving: *190 Calories; 13.2g Fat; 8.3g Carbs; 10.3g Protein; 1g Sugars*

Ingredients

12 ounces canned artichoke hearts, chopped
2 cups kale, chopped
1 cup Ricotta cheese
1 ¼ cups Romano cheese, grated
1/2 cup mayonnaise
1 teaspoon gourmet mustard
Salt and ground black pepper, to taste
1 teaspoon garlic powder
1/2 teaspoon shallot powder
1/2 teaspoon cumin powder

Directions

- Lightly grease a baking pan that fits inside your Instant Pot. Add all of the above ingredients and stir to combine well.
- Add a metal rack to the Instant Pot.
- Then, create a foil sling and place it on a rack; lower the baking pan onto the foil strip.
- Secure the lid and choose "Manual" function; cook for 9 minutes at High pressure. Once cooking is complete, use a quick release; remove the lid carefully.
- Serve with breadsticks on the side. Bon appétit!

310. Whiskey Glazed Ribs
(Ready in about 25 minutes | Servings 6)

Baby back ribs with a sweet and sticky sauce that is enriched with whiskey and ketchup. This recipe is so delicious because pork ribs can take on different flavors.

Per serving: *359 Calories; 17.9g Fat; 28g Carbs; 22.8g Protein; 25.1g Sugars*

Ingredients

1 ½ pounds baby back ribs
1 teaspoon salt
1/2 teaspoon ground black pepper
1 teaspoon smoked paprika
1/2 teaspoon ancho chili powder
1/2 teaspoon granulated garlic
1 teaspoon shallot powder
1/2 teaspoon mustard seeds
1 teaspoon celery seeds
1/2 cup whiskey
1 cup ketchup
1/3 cup dark brown sugar
1/4 cup rice vinegar
1 teaspoon fish sauce
1 teaspoon Worcestershire sauce

Directions

- Season the ribs with salt, black pepper, paprika, chili powder, garlic, shallot powder, mustard seeds, and celery seeds.
- Add the seasoned ribs to the Instant Pot.
- In a mixing bowl, thoroughly combine whiskey, ketchup, sugar, vinegar, fish sauce, and Worcestershire sauce.
- Then, pour the sauce into the Instant Pot.
- Secure the lid and choose the "Meat/Stew" function; cook for 20 minutes at High pressure. Once cooking is complete, use a natural release; carefully remove the lid. Reserve the ribs.
- Press the "Sauté" button to preheat your Instant Pot. Simmer the sauce until it has reduced to your desired thickness. Pour the glaze over the ribs and serve. Bon appétit!

311. Sticky Chinese-Style Cocktail Sausages
(Ready in about 15 minutes | Servings 8)

Cocktail sausages are a classic. We've just given them a new twist, adding Chinese seasonings, Dijon mustard, and ketchup.
Per serving: *270 Calories; 20g Fat; 5.4g Carbs; 16.4g Protein; 3.5g Sugars*

Ingredients

2 teaspoons toasted sesame oil
10 hot dogs, chopped into thirds
1/2 cup ketchup
1/3 cup chicken stock
2 tablespoons tamari sauce
1 tablespoon rice vinegar
1 teaspoon chili powder
Salt, to taste
1/2 teaspoon Szechuan pepper
1 teaspoon cayenne pepper
1 teaspoon Dijon mustard
1/2 teaspoon fresh ginger, peeled and grated

Directions

- Add all of the above ingredients to the Instant Pot.
- Secure the lid. Choose "Manual" mode and High pressure; cook for 5 minutes. Once cooking is complete, use a quick pressure release; carefully remove the lid.
- Serve with cocktail sticks; garnish with sesame seeds if desired. Enjoy!

312. Herby and Garlicky Fingerling Potatoes
(Ready in about 25 minutes | Servings 6)

Fingerling potatoes are a good source of vitamin C and vitamin B6. They can improve liver detoxification and protect our nervous system.
Per serving: *391 Calories; 35.1g Fat; 19.9g Carbs; 2.4g Protein; 0.8g Sugars*

Ingredients

4 tablespoons butter, melted
1 ½ pounds fingerling potatoes
2 sprigs thyme
2 sprigs rosemary
1 teaspoon garlic paste
3/4 cup vegetable broth

Sea salt, to taste
1/2 teaspoon ground black pepper
1/2 teaspoon cayenne pepper
1/2 teaspoon shallot powder
1/2 teaspoon porcini powder

Directions

- Press the "Sauté" button to preheat your Instant Pot; now, melt the butter.
- Sauté the potatoes, rolling them around for about 9 minutes. Now, pierce the middle of each potato with a knife.
- Secure the lid. Choose the "Manual" mode and High pressure; cook for 10 minutes. Once cooking is complete, use a quick pressure release; carefully remove the lid.
- Serve with toothpicks and enjoy!

313. Vegetable and Turkey Cocktail Meatballs
(Ready in about 15 minutes | Servings 8)

Entertaining your guests and family during the holiday season doesn't have to leave you stuck in the kitchen all day long. Simply drop meatballs into the inner pot, press the button and enjoy!
Per serving: *319 Calories; 21.9g Fat; 12.6g Carbs; 17.5g Protein; 3g Sugars*

Ingredients

2 shallots, peeled and finely chopped
2 garlic cloves, minced
1 parsnip, grated
2 carrots, grated
1 cup button mushrooms, chopped
1/2 cup all-purpose flour
Sea salt and ground black pepper, to taste
2 pounds turkey, ground

2 tablespoons olive oil
3 ripe tomatoes, pureed
1 teaspoon dried oregano
2 sprigs rosemary, leaves picked
2 sprigs thyme, leaves picked
3/4 cup broth, preferably homemade

Directions

- In a mixing bowl, combine the shallots, garlic, parsnip, carrots, mushrooms, flour, salt, pepper, and ground turkey.
- Shape the mixture into small cocktail meatballs.
- Press the "Sauté" button and heat the olive oil. Once hot, sear the meatballs on all sides until they are browned.
- Thoroughly combine pureed tomatoes, oregano, rosemary, and thyme. Pour in tomato mixture and broth. Secure the lid.
- Now, choose the "Manual" function; cook for 9 minutes at High pressure. Once cooking is complete, use a natural release; remove the lid carefully.
- Serve with cocktail sticks or toothpicks. Bon appétit!

---

314. Buttery Carrot Sticks
(Ready in about 10 minutes | Servings 4)

These buttery carrots cooked in white wine and seasonings might become your next favorite Instant Pot appetizer!
Per serving: *199 Calories; 14.9g Fat; 13.7g Carbs; 4.5g Protein; 6.2g Sugars*

Ingredients

1 pound carrots, cut into sticks
1/2 cup dry white wine
1/4 cup water
Sea salt and white pepper, to taste
1/2 stick butter, softened
2 tablespoons agave nectar
1 teaspoon ground allspice
1/2 teaspoon caraway seeds
1 tablespoon fresh lime juice

Directions

- Add all of the above ingredients to your Instant Pot.
- Secure the lid. Choose the "Manual" mode and High pressure; cook for 2 minutes. Once cooking is complete, use a quick pressure release; carefully remove the lid.
- Transfer to a nice serving bowl and enjoy!

315. Beet Appetizer Salad with Cherry Vinaigrette
(Ready in about 15 minutes + chilling time | Servings 4)

Forget about processed food for the next super bowl party! Simply grab a few bunches of fresh red beets and get ready for a party-perfect, make-ahead cold appetizer!
Per serving: *197 Calories; 14.6g Fat; 13.1g Carbs; 4.3g Protein; 9.3g Sugars*

Ingredients

1 pound red beets
1 cup baby spinach leaves
1/2 cup cream cheese
2 tablespoons dried cherries
1/2 teaspoon ground cumin
2 tablespoons sherry vinegar
1/4 cup extra-virgin olive oil
Sea salt and freshly cracked black pepper

Directions

- Add 1 ½ cups of water and steamer basket to your Instant Pot. Place whole and unpeeled beets in the steamer basket.
- Secure the lid. Choose the "Steam" mode and High pressure; cook for 10 minutes. Once cooking is complete, use a quick pressure release; carefully remove the lid.
- Allow red beets to cool completely. Then, rub the skin off the beets and cut them into very thin slices.
- Transfer the beets to a salad bowl; add baby spinach, and cream cheese.
- In a food processor, purée dried cherries, cumin, vinegar, olive oil, salt, and black pepper. Add this vinaigrette to the salad; toss to combine and serve.

316. Mini Pork Tacos
(Ready in about 1 hour | Servings 10)

Do you need a standout appetizer recipe for the next family gathering? With these colorful, flavor-packed mini tacos on the menu, you will be ready for it!
Per serving: *388 Calories; 25.9g Fat; 13.1g Carbs; 25.1g Protein; 9.4g Sugars*

Ingredients

2 tablespoons olive oil
2 pounds pork shoulder
2 tablespoons honey
Kosher salt, to taste
1/4 teaspoon freshly ground black pepper
1 teaspoon cayenne pepper
1/2 teaspoon celery seeds

1 teaspoon ground cumin
1/3 cup rice wine
1 tablespoon rice vinegar
1 cup beer
1/2 cup ketchup
2 cups coleslaw, for serving

Directions

- Press the "Sauté" button to preheat your Instant Pot. Then, heat the oil until sizzling.
- Once hot, cook the pork until well browned on all sides. Add honey, salt, black pepper, cayenne pepper, celery seeds, cumin, wine, vinegar, and beer to your Instant Pot.
- Secure the lid. Choose the "Manual" mode and High pressure; cook for 50 minutes. Once cooking is complete, use a natural pressure release; carefully remove the lid.
- Then, shred the meat with two forks. Return it to the Instant Pot. Add ketchup and seal the lid one more time.
- Press the "Sauté" button and let it simmer for 2 to 3 minutes more or until heated through. Serve in 6-inch corn tortillas, garnished with coleslaw.

317. Harissa Meat and Tomato Dip
(Ready in about 20 minutes | Servings 10)

With a high-quality ground meat, aromatic spices, and ripe tomatoes, this scrumptious dipping sauce is super addicting. Don't trust words and try it now!
Per serving: *226 Calories; 15.4g Fat; 2.2g Carbs; 18.6g Protein; 0.8g Sugars*

Ingredients

2 tablespoons canola oil
1 pound ground pork
1/2 pound ground beef
1/2 cup leeks, finely chopped
1 garlic clove, minced
1 ½ teaspoons Cajun seasonings
1 teaspoon harissa spice blend
1/2 teaspoon cayenne pepper
1 teaspoon sea salt
1/2 teaspoon ground black pepper, to taste
2 ripe tomatoes, chopped

Directions

- Press the "Sauté" button and heat the oil. Once hot, cook the ground meat, stirring with a Silicone spatula so that it gets broken up as it cooks.
- Stir in the leeks and garlic; cook until they are tender and fragrant. Stir in Cajun seasonings, harissa spice blend, cayenne pepper, sea salt, and ground black pepper.
- Add pureed tomatoes and secure the lid. Now, choose the "Manual" mode and cook for 13 minutes at High pressure.
- Once cooking is complete, use a natural release; remove the lid carefully. Serve with fresh veggie sticks. Bon appétit!

318. Cheese and Pepper Stuffed Mushrooms
(Ready in about 10 minutes | Servings 4)

Easy, cheesy and delicious, these stuffed mushrooms look spectacular on a serving platter. Consider preparing a double batch. Trust us!
Per serving: *304 Calories; 25.4g Fat; 10.9g Carbs; 10.7g Protein; 6.7g Sugars*

Ingredients

2 tablespoons butter, at room temperature
1/2 cup scallions, chopped
2 cloves garlic, minced
1 cup cream cheese, at room temperature
1 cup cheddar cheese, grated
1 bell pepper, seeded and chopped
1 chili pepper, seeded and minced

1 teaspoon dried oregano
1 teaspoon dried parsley flakes
1 teaspoon dried rosemary
16 medium-sized button mushrooms, stems removed

Directions

- Press the "Sauté" button to preheat your Instant Pot. Now, melt the butter and sauté the scallions until tender and fragrant.
- Stir in the garlic; continue to sauté an additional 30 seconds or until fragrant. Add cheese, peppers, oregano, parsley, and rosemary.
- After that, fill the mushroom caps with the pepper/cheese mixture.
- Place 1 cup of water and a steamer basket in the Instant Pot. Arrange the stuffed mushrooms in the steamer basket.
- Secure the lid. Choose the "Manual" mode and High pressure; cook for 5 minutes. Once cooking is complete, use a quick pressure release; carefully remove the lid. Bon appétit!

319. Pinto Bean Dip with Sour Cream
(Ready in about 30 minutes | Servings 12)

Serve with your favorite dippers such as bread sticks, tortilla chips, veggie sticks, or pita bread.
Per serving: *154 Calories; 2.6g Fat; 25.1g Carbs; 8.3g Protein; 3.1g Sugars*

Ingredients

2 cups dried pinto beans, soaked overnight
2 cloves garlic, minced
1/2 cup shallots, chopped
1 red chili pepper, minced
2 (14.5-ounce) cans tomatoes
1 cup beef bone broth
Sea salt and ground black pepper, to taste
1 teaspoon sweet paprika
1 teaspoon mustard powder
1 teaspoon marjoram, dried
1/4 teaspoon ground bay leaves
1 cup sour cream
2 heaping tablespoons fresh chives, roughly chopped

Directions

- Add beans, garlic, shallots, chili pepper, tomatoes, broth, salt, black pepper, paprika, mustard powder, marjoram, and ground bay leaves to your Instant Pot.
- Secure the lid. Choose "Bean/Chili" mode and High pressure; cook for 25 minutes. Once cooking is complete, use a natural pressure release; carefully remove the lid.
- Transfer the bean mixture to your food processor; mix until everything is creamy and smooth. Serve topped with sour cream and fresh chives. Enjoy!

320. Crispy Chicken Drumettes
(Ready in about 30 minutes | Servings 6)

If you love spicy and tangy chicken, you'll go crazy for these chicken drumettes. This just might be the best way to use chicken for a party.
Per serving: *212 Calories; 10.7g Fat; 4.6g Carbs; 23.6g Protein; 3.2g Sugars*

Ingredients

1 ½ pounds chicken drumettes
Kosher salt, to taste
1/2 teaspoon mixed peppercorns, crushed
1/2 teaspoon cayenne pepper
1 teaspoon shallot powder

1 teaspoon garlic powder
1/2 stick butter, melted
2 tablespoons hot sauce
1 tablespoon fish sauce
1/3 cup ketchup

Directions

- Prepare your Instant Pot by adding 1 cup of water and metal trivet to its bottom. Place chicken drumettes on the trivet.
- Secure the lid. Choose the "Manual" mode and High pressure; cook for 6 minutes. Once cooking is complete, use a natural pressure release; carefully remove the lid.
- Toss chicken wings with the remaining ingredients.
- Arrange chicken wings, top side down, on a broiler pan. Place rack on top. Broil for 10 minutes; flip over and broil for 10 minutes more.
- Top with remaining sauce and serve immediately.

321. Spicy Boiled Peanuts
(Ready in about 1 hour 25 minutes | Servings 8)

Are you thinking of a snack recipe for late night movie marathon? If you want something spicy and salty, here's the right recipe for you!
Per serving: *340 Calories; 28.1g Fat; 13.6g Carbs; 14.1g Protein; 3.6g Sugars*

Ingredients

1 ½ pounds raw peanuts in the shell, rinsed an cleaned
1/2 cup salt
Water
3 jalapenos, sliced
2 tablespoons red pepper flakes
2 tablespoons Creole seasoning
1 teaspoon garlic powder
1 teaspoon lemon pepper

Directions

- Place peanuts and salt in your Instant Pot; cover with water. Add all seasonings and stir to combine.
- Place a trivet on top to hold down the peanuts.
- Secure the lid and choose the "Manual" mode. Cook for 1 hour 20 minutes at High pressure.
- Once cooking is complete, use a natural release; remove the lid carefully. Enjoy!

---

322. Party Cauliflower Balls
(Ready in about 25 minutes | Servings 6)

Prepare these elegant cauliflower balls for the next potluck and delight your friends! They literally melt in your mouth!
Per serving: *194 Calories; 13.8g Fat; 6.5g Carbs; 11.6g Protein; 1.8g Sugars*

Ingredients

1 pound cauliflower, broken into small florets
2 tablespoons butter
2 cloves garlic, minced
1/2 cup Parmesan cheese, grated
2 eggs, beaten
1 cup Swiss cheese, shredded
2 tablespoons fresh parsley, minced
1 teaspoon cayenne pepper
Sea salt and ground black pepper, to taste

Directions

- Prepare your Instant Pot by adding 1 cup of water and a steamer basket to its bottom.
- Place the cauliflower florets in the steamer basket.
- Secure the lid. Choose the "Steam" mode and High pressure; cook for 3 minutes. Once cooking is complete, use a quick pressure release; carefully remove the lid.
- Transfer the cauliflower florets to your blender. Add the remaining ingredients; process until everything is well incorporated.
- Roll the cauliflower mixture into bite-sized balls. Bake in the preheated oven at 400 degrees F for 16 minutes. Bon appétit!

323. Double Cheese Burger Dip
(Ready in about 15 minutes | Servings 10)

You can bake this dip in a preheated oven at 350 degrees F about 20 minutes or until the top is golden brown. Otherwise, serve it directly from the Instant Pot.
Per serving: 253 Calories; 17.7g Fat; 4.2g Carbs; 19.3g Protein; 1.6g Sugars

Ingredients

1 tablespoon canola oil
1 pound ground turkey
1 onion, chopped
1 clove garlic, chopped
2 cups ripe tomato purée
1/4 cup vegetable broth
1 tablespoon Worcestershire sauce
10 ounces Ricotta cheese, crumbled
10 ounces Colby cheese, shredded

Directions

- Press the "Sauté" button to preheat your Instant Pot. Once hot, heat the oil.
- Then, cook ground turkey, onion and garlic for 2 to 3 minutes or until the meat is no longer pink. Add tomato purée, broth, and Worcestershire sauce.
- Secure the lid. Choose the "Manual" mode and High pressure; cook for 5 minutes. Once cooking is complete, use a quick pressure release; carefully remove the lid.
- Now, stir in cheese. Stir until everything is well incorporated; serve immediately.

---

324. Minty Party Meatballs
(Ready in about 15 minutes | Servings 8)

If you use a lean ground chuck, you can add fat cheese and eggs. It all boils down to the balance.
Per serving: 241 Calories; 10.9g Fat; 14.5g Carbs; 19.2g Protein; 6.5g Sugars

Ingredients

1 pound ground chuck
1/2 pound ground pork
1 cup scallions, chopped
1/2 cup tortilla chips, crushed
2/3 cup Parmesan cheese, grated
1 egg, beaten
3 tablespoons full-fat milk

1 teaspoon garlic, minced
Sea salt and ground black pepper, to taste
1 teaspoon dried oregano
1 teaspoon dried basil
2 cups tomato sauce
1/4 cup fresh mint, plus minced

Directions

- In a mixing bowl, thoroughly combine ground meat, scallions, tortilla chips, Parmesan cheese, egg, milk, garlic, salt, black pepper, oregano, and basil.
- Shape the mixture into balls using an ice cream scoop.
- Spritz the bottom and sides of the Instant Pot with a nonstick cooking spray; add meatballs; pour in the sauce.
- Secure the lid. Choose the "Manual" setting and cook for 9 minutes under High pressure. Once cooking is complete, use a quick pressure release; carefully remove the lid.
- Sprinkle minced mint leaves over the meatballs and serve. Bon appétit!

325. Party Deviled Eggs
(Ready in about 20 minutes | Servings 8)

Here's a party favorite! Chives and mustard add an extra zing!
Per serving: *138 Calories; 10.4g Fat; 1.2g Carbs; 9.1g Protein; 0.7g Sugars*

Ingredients

1 ½ cups water
8 eggs
3 teaspoons mayonnaise
1 tablespoon sour cream
1 teaspoon gourmet mustard
1/2 teaspoon hot sauce
1/3 teaspoon ground black pepper
Crunchy sea salt, to taste
3 tablespoons fresh chives, thinly sliced

Directions

- Pour the water into the base of your Instant Pot.
- Now, arrange eggs in the steaming basket. Transfer the steaming basket to the Instant Pot.
- Secure the lid and choose the "Manual" function; cook for 13 minutes at Low pressure. Once cooking is complete, use a quick release; remove the lid carefully.
- Peel the eggs under running water. Remove the yolks and smash them with a fork; reserve.
- Now, mix mayonnaise, sour cream, gourmet mustard, hot sauce, black pepper, and salt; add reserved yolks and mash everything.
- Fill whites with this mixture, heaping it lightly. Garnish with fresh chives and place in the refrigerator until ready to serve. Bon appétit!

---

326. Super Bowl Italian Dip
(Ready in about 10 minutes | Servings 10)

When you need to get fancy with a party sauce, this Italian-style recipe is here to help. You can use Provolone and Fontina d'Aosta as well.
Per serving: *209 Calories; 11.4g Fat; 5.3g Carbs; 21.1g Protein; 3.3g Sugars*

Ingredients

8 ounces Asiago cheese, grated
9 ounces Mozzarella cheese, crumbled
2 ripe Roma tomatoes, puréed
8 ounces pancetta, chopped
1/2 cup green olives, pitted and halved
1 bell pepper, chopped
1 teaspoon garlic powder
1 teaspoon shallot powder

1 teaspoon porcini powder
1 teaspoon dried oregano
1 teaspoon dried basil
1 teaspoon dried marjoram
2/3 cup beef bone broth
6 ounces Parmigiano-Reggiano cheese, grated

Directions

- Combine all ingredients, except for Parmigiano-Reggiano cheese, in your Instant Pot.
- Secure the lid. Choose the "Manual" mode and High pressure; cook for 5 minutes. Once cooking is complete, use a quick pressure release; carefully remove the lid.
- Top with Parmigiano-Reggiano cheese; cover and allow it to sit in the residual heat until cheese is melted. Bon appétit!

327. Bacon Wrapped Lil Smokies
(Ready in about 10 minutes | Servings 12)

Little smoked sausages cooked in chili sauce and grape jelly. Yummy! How could you go wrong preparing lil smokies for a party?
Per serving: *317 Calories; 21.5g Fat; 12.8g Carbs; 17.1g Protein; 8.2g Sugars*

Ingredients

2 pounds Little Smokies sausage
1 pound bacon slices
1 (12-ounce) bottle chili sauce
1 cup grape jelly

Instructions

- Wrap each sausage in a piece of bacon; secure with toothpicks; place in your Instant Pot.
- Add chili sauce and grape jelly.
- Secure the lid. Choose the "Manual" mode and High pressure; cook for 5 minutes. Once cooking is complete, use a quick pressure release; carefully remove the lid. Bon appétit!

328. Barbecue Chicken Dip
(Ready in about 10 minutes | Servings 12)

Here's your new go-to party appetizer! It is perfect for dipping crackers, chips, pretzel bun bites or veggie sticks in.
Per serving: *179 Calories; 7.5g Fat; 14.3g Carbs; 12.9g Protein; 10.3g Sugars*

Ingredients

1 pound chicken white meat, boneless
1 cup barbecue sauce
1/3 cup water
6 ounces Ricotta cheese
3 ounces blue cheese dressing
1 parsnip, chopped
1/2 teaspoon dried rosemary
1/2 teaspoon cayenne pepper
1/4 teaspoon ground black pepper, or more to taste
Sea salt, to taste

Directions

- Place all of the above ingredients in your Instant Pot.
- Secure the lid. Choose the "Manual" mode and High pressure; cook for 6 minutes. Once cooking is complete, use a natural pressure release; carefully remove the lid.
- Transfer to a nice serving bowl and serve warm or at room temperature. Bon appétit!

329. Aunt's Traditional Queso
(Ready in about 15 minutes | Servings 10)

Packed full of goodness, this dipping sauce features hot breakfast sausage, tomatoes, and green chiles. Processed cheese adds a completely new dimension to the dip. Enjoy!
Per serving: *295 Calories; 24.2g Fat; 10.1g Carbs; 13g Protein; 2.4g Sugars*

Ingredients

1 pound hot breakfast sausage, ground
2 shallots, chopped
2 cloves garlic, minced
2 cups tomatoes, pureed
2 cans green chiles, chopped
1 cup broth
1 pound block processed cheese

Directions

- Press the "Sauté" button to heat up your Instant Pot. Now, cook ground sausage with shallots.
- Stir in garlic and cook 30 seconds more, stirring frequently. Add the tomatoes, green chiles, and broth.
- Secure the lid and choose "Manual" function; cook for 6 minutes at Low pressure. Once cooking is complete, use a quick release; remove the lid carefully.
- Add block processed cheese and stir until it has melted. Bon appétit!

---

330. Creamy Ricotta Hummus
(Ready in about 45 minutes | Servings 10)

This delicious dip can be made one week ahead. To make it last longer, drizzle a tablespoon of two of olive oil over the top and place your hummus in the refrigerator.
Per serving: *153 Calories; 5.7g Fat; 19.8g Carbs; 6.7g Protein; 3.3g Sugars*

Ingredients

1 ½ cups dried garbanzo beans, soaked overnight
4 cups water
1/4 cup extra-virgin olive oil
2 tablespoons light tahini
2 tablespoons fresh lemon juice
1 teaspoon garlic, minced
1 teaspoon onion powder

1/2 teaspoon dried dill weed
1/2 teaspoon dried oregano
1/2 teaspoon cumin powder
1 teaspoon spicy brown mustard
1 teaspoon kosher salt
1/3 cup ricotta cheese
1/2 teaspoon red chili pepper

Directions

- Add soaked garbanzo beans with 4 cups of water to your Instant Pot.
- Secure the lid and choose the "Bean/Chili" function; cook for 40 minutes at High pressure. Once cooking is complete, use a natural release; carefully remove the lid.
- Drain garbanzo beans, reserving cooking liquid. Transfer chickpeas to your food processor. Add olive oil, tahini, lemon juice, garlic, onion powder, dill weed, oregano, cumin powder, mustard, and salt.
- Add ricotta cheese and about 1 cup of cooking liquid; process until everything is creamy and smooth. Sprinkle red chili pepper over the top. Bon appétit!

331. Crispy and Cheesy Broccoli Tots
(Ready in about 30 minutes | Servings 8)

Looking for more creative ways to eat broccoli? These bites are perfect for the best Saturday night ever.
Per serving: *142 Calories; 8.1g Fat; 9.6g Carbs; 9.5g Protein; 2.7g Sugars*

Ingredients

1 head of broccoli, broken into florets
1 ½ cups water
1 white onion, minced
1 garlic clove, minced
2 eggs, beaten
1 cup Colby cheese, grated
1 tablespoon fresh parsley, chopped
1 tablespoon fresh coriander, chopped
Sea salt and ground black pepper, to taste

Directions

- Add 1 cup of water and a steamer basket to the bottom of your Instant Pot. Place broccoli florets in the steamer basket.
- Secure the lid and choose the "Steam" mode; cook for 6 minutes under High pressure. Once cooking is complete, use a quick release; carefully remove the lid.
- Allow broccoli florets to cool completely; then, add the remaining ingredients.
- Mash the mixture and shape into tots with oiled hands.
- Place broccoli tots on a lightly greased baking sheet. Bake in the preheated oven at 390 degrees F approximately 18 to 20 minutes, flipping them once. Bon appétit!

---

332. Salad Snack on a Stick
(Ready in about 10 minutes | Servings 6)

Shrimp, onion, bell pepper, cherry tomatoes, and olives are piled onto skewers and sprinkled with spices. Your kids will be thrilled!
Per serving: *185 Calories; 7.3g Fat; 5.1g Carbs; 23.9g Protein; 2.3g Sugars*

Ingredients

1 ½ pounds shrimp, peeled and deveined
2 tablespoon apple cider vinegar
1 tablespoon lime juice
1 cup water
1 red onion, cut into wedges
1 red bell pepper, sliced
1 green bell pepper, sliced
1 orange bell pepper, sliced

1/2 cup black olives, pitted
1 ½ cups cherry tomatoes
2 tablespoons olive oil
1/2 cup ground black pepper
Sea salt, to taste
1 teaspoon paprika
1 teaspoon oregano

Directions

- Place the shrimp, vinegar, lime juice, and water in your Instant Pot.
- Secure the lid. Choose the "Manual" mode and High pressure; cook for 1 minute. Once cooking is complete, use a quick pressure release; carefully remove the lid.
- Thread the cooked shrimp, onion, peppers, olives and cherry tomatoes onto cocktail sticks.
- Drizzle olive oil over them; sprinkle with black pepper, salt, paprika, and oregano. Bon appétit!

333. Traditional Eggplant Dip
(Ready in about 10 minutes | Servings 10)

Three words – vegan, gluten-free and delicious! Serve with Indian naan and enjoy!
Per serving: *209 Calories; 18.9g Fat; 8.5g Carbs; 4.6g Protein; 1.5g Sugars*

Ingredients

1 cup water
3/4 pound eggplant
3 tablespoons olive oil
1/2 cup yellow onion, chopped
1 garlic cloves, roasted and 1 raw, crushed
Sea salt, to taste
1 teaspoon fresh oregano, chopped
1/3 teaspoon cayenne pepper
1/4 teaspoon ground black pepper, or more to taste
1 tablespoon fresh lime juice
¼ cup tahini, plus more as needed
¼ cup brine-cured black olives, brine-cured

Directions

- Add water to the base of your Instant Pot. Now, choose the "Manual" and cook eggplant in the steaming basket for 4 minutes at High Pressure.
- Once cooking is complete, use a quick release; remove the lid carefully.
- Drain excess water out of the eggplant. Then, peel and slice the eggplant.
- Press the "Sauté" button and add the oil. Once hot, cook the eggplant with onions and garlic until they have softened.
- Season with salt, oregano, cayenne pepper, and ground black pepper. Transfer the mixture to your blender or food processor.
- Add lime juice, tahini, and olives. Blend until everything is well incorporated. Serve well chilled and enjoy!

334. Lager and Cheese Dip
(Ready in about 10 minutes | Servings 12)

Sit back and dip into this beer inspired flavorful recipe. It is a must-have party food.
Per serving: *131 Calories; 10.2g Fat; 3.1g Carbs; 6.3g Protein; 1.4g Sugars*

Ingredients

1/2 cup sour cream
1/2 cup cheddar cheese, grated
12 ounces cream cheese, softened
1/2 teaspoon garlic powder
1 teaspoon shallot power
1 teaspoon porcini powder
1/4 teaspoon cumin powder

1/2 teaspoon dried basil
1/2 teaspoon dried oregano
1/2 cup lager
1/2 pound ham, cooked and chopped
2 heaping tablespoons fresh chives, chopped
2 heaping tablespoons fresh cilantro, chopped

Directions

- Spritz the bottom and sides of your Instant Pot with a nonstick cooking spray.
- Then, add sour cream, cheese, spices, lager, and ham.
- Secure the lid. Choose the "Manual" mode and High pressure; cook for 4 minutes. Once cooking is complete, use a quick pressure release; carefully remove the lid.
- Top with fresh chives and cilantro. Serve with your favorite dippers. Bon appétit!

335. Hearty Nacho Dip
(Ready in about 15 minutes | Servings 16)

This recipe combines chicken, tomatoes, cheese, and tortilla chips into a simple and quick Mexican-inspired dip. It only takes 15 minutes to whip up this party classic.
Per serving: *145 Calories; 6.5g Fat; 11.6g Carbs; 9.8g Protein; 1.9g Sugars*

Ingredients

1 pound chicken breasts, boneless and skinless
20 ounces tomato, puréed
2 bell peppers, chopped
1 tablespoon jalapeño, seeded and minced
1 cup beef stock
1 cup Mexican cheese blend, grated
1/2 cup avocado, chopped
10 ounces tortilla chips, baked

Directions

- Place chicken, tomato, peppers, and stock in your Instant Pot.
- Secure the lid. Choose the "Manual" mode and High pressure; cook for 7 minutes. Once cooking is complete, use a natural pressure release; carefully remove the lid.
- Add Mexican cheese blend to the Instant Pot. Seal the lid and let it sit until warmed through.
- Shred chicken with two forks; top with chopped avocado and serve with tortilla chips. Enjoy!

336. Classic Chicken Collard Wraps
(Ready in about 25 minutes | Servings 8)

We use collard in this recipe but you can use lettuce with sturdy, broad leaves like butter or Bibb lettuce. Swiss chard also works well.
Per serving: *179 Calories; 9.5g Fat; 6.4g Carbs; 16.1g Protein; 3.5g Sugars*

Ingredients

2 chicken breasts, boneless and skinless
1 yellow onion, chopped
2 cloves garlic, minced
1 ½ cups roasted vegetable broth
1 cup tomato, puréed
2 tablespoons hoisin sauce
1 head butter lettuce
2 carrots, grated

1 cucumber, grated
2 tablespoons mayonnaise
2 tablespoons olives, pitted and chopped
1 teaspoon Dijon mustard

Directions

- Place chicken, onion, garlic, broth, and puréed tomatoes in the Instant Pot.
- Secure the lid. Choose the "Poultry" mode and High pressure; cook for 15 minutes. Once cooking is complete, use a natural pressure release; carefully remove the lid.
- Remove the chicken from the Instant Pot; now, shred the chicken with two forks and return to the Instant Pot.
- Add hoisin sauce. Press the "Sauté" button and let it simmer until cooking liquid has reduced by half.
- To serve, place a generous spoonful of chicken mixture in the middle of a lettuce leaf; top with carrots, cucumber, mayo, olives, and mustard. Bon appétit!

337. Vegetable and Tahini Dipping Sauce
(Ready in about 10 minutes | Servings 8)

Gently cooked chunky vegetables and naturally tender, silky tahini are smartly paired in this amazing sauce for dipping.
Per serving: *77 Calories; 5.5g Fat; 5.9g Carbs; 2.9g Protein; 1.7g Sugars*

Ingredients

1 ½ cups water
1 head cauliflower, cut into florets
1 cup broccoli, cut into florets
1 celery, sliced
1 carrot, sliced
1/3 cup tahini
2 tomatoes, pureed
1 serrano pepper, chopped

2 bell pepper, chopped
2 garlic cloves, chopped
Salt and ground black pepper, to taste
1 teaspoon onion powder
1/2 teaspoon cayenne pepper
1/2 teaspoon cumin powder

Directions

- Add the water, cauliflower, broccoli, celery, and carrot to your Instant Pot.
- Choose the "Manual" function and cook at High pressure for 3 minutes. Once cooking is complete, use a quick release; carefully remove the lid.
- Then, drain excess water out of vegetables. Transfer to a food processor and add the other ingredients.
- Blend until everything is well incorporated. Serve with pita bread and enjoy!

---

338. Garlicky Petite Potatoes
(Ready in about 15 minutes | Servings 6)

This is a delicious appetizer loaded with herbs, butter, and garlic. Serve with Ginger Spritz or Beer Americano as an aperitif.
Per serving: *166 Calories; 4.6g Fat; 28.1g Carbs; 4.2g Protein; 1.6g Sugars*

Ingredients

1 tablespoon butter, melted
2 pounds baby potatoes
3 garlic cloves, with outer skin
Sea salt and ground black pepper, to taste
1/2 teaspoon cayenne pepper
1 sprig thyme, leaves only
1 sprig rosemary, leaves only
1 tablespoon olive oil
1 cup vegetable broth
1/4 cup fresh Italian parsley, chopped

Directions

- Press the "Sauté" button to preheat your Instant Pot. Once hot, warm the butter; now, cook potatoes with garlic for 5 to 6 minutes.
- Add the salt, black pepper, cayenne pepper, thyme, rosemary, olive oil, and broth.
- Secure the lid. Choose the "Manual" mode and High pressure; cook for 5 minutes. Once cooking is complete, use a quick pressure release; carefully remove the lid.
- Scatter chopped parsley over potatoes and serve warm.

339. Sesame Turnip Greens
(Ready in about 10 minutes | Servings 6)

A simple appetizer with so many health benefits! Turnip greens are loaded with valuable vitamins, minerals, and antioxidants; they can help to slow aging naturally. Sesame seeds can protect heart health, lower cholesterol levels, improve bone health, and manage diabetes. Impressive!

Per serving: *73 Calories; 4.3g Fat; 7.1g Carbs; 2.6g Protein; 1.2g Sugars*

Ingredients

1 tablespoon sesame oil
1 shallot, chopped
2 garlic cloves, minced
1 pound turnip greens, leaves separated
1 cup vegetable broth
Sea salt, to taste
1/2 teaspoon ground black pepper
1 teaspoon red pepper flakes
2 teaspoons Worcestershire sauce
2 tablespoons sesame seeds, toasted

Directions

- Place the "Sauté" button to preheat your Instant Pot. Once hot, heat the sesame oil.
- Then, cook the shallot and garlic until they are fragrant and tender. Add turnip greens, broth, salt, black pepper, red pepper flakes, and Worcestershire sauce.
- Secure the lid. Choose the "Manual" mode and High pressure; cook for 3 minutes. Once cooking is complete, use a quick pressure release; carefully remove the lid.
- Sprinkle sesame seeds over the top and serve right away!

340. Kalbi (Korean Short Ribs)
(Ready in about 1 hour 5 minutes | Servings 6)

Looking for the perfect appetizer for your next summer party? Try these fall-off-the-bone ribs with a Korean flair.

Per serving: *250 Calories; 13.1g Fat; 7.9g Carbs; 24.1g Protein; 6.2g Sugars*

Ingredients

2 pounds Korean-style beef short ribs
1 Asian pear, peeled and grated
2 tablespoons brown sugar
1/2 teaspoon salt
1/3 teaspoon ground black pepper

1 teaspoon granulated garlic
1/2 cup water
1/2 cup soy sauce
1/4 cup mirin
1 teaspoon liquid smoke

Directions

- Add all of the above ingredients to your Instant Pot.
- Secure the lid. Choose the "Manual" mode and High pressure; cook for 60 minutes. Once cooking is complete, use a natural pressure release; carefully remove the lid.
- Cut ribs, slicing between bones. Serve with a barbecue sauce, if desired. Enjoy!

341. Perfect Cocktail Wieners
(Ready in about 10 minutes | Servings 12)

Little wieners are cooked in a tangy barbeque sauce with jalapenos and yellow onion. Great snack for cocktail parties and entertaining!
Per serving: *333 Calories; 23.4g Fat; 19.6g Carbs; 10g Protein; 13.2g Sugars*

Ingredients

2 (16-ounce) packages little wieners
1/2 (18-ounce) bottle barbeque sauce
1/2 cup ketchup
3 tablespoons honey
1/2 yellow onion, chopped
2 jalapenos, sliced
1 teaspoon garlic powder
1 teaspoon cumin powder
1/2 teaspoon mustard powder

Directions

- Add little wieners, barbecue sauce, ketchup, honey, onion, jalapenos, garlic powder, cumin, and mustard powder to the Instant Pot. Stir to combine well.
- Choose "Manual" setting and cook at Low pressure for 2 minutes.
- Once cooking is complete, use a natural release; carefully remove the lid. You can thicken the sauce to your desired thickness on the "Sauté" function.
- Serve warm with toothpicks. Bon appétit!

342. Barbecue Corn with Potato Chips
(Ready in about 10 minutes | Servings 4)

You can use classic toppings such as butter, garlic, and coarse salt. On the other hand, you can use fresh and innovative toppings that will blow your mind.
Per serving: *260 Calories; 5.2g Fat; 52.5g Carbs; 5.7g Protein; 7.8g Sugars*

Ingredients

4 ears corn on the cob, husks removed
1/3 cup barbecue sauce
1/2 cup potato chips, crushed

Directions

- Add water and metal trivet to the base of your Instant Pot. Place ears corn on the cob on a metal trivet.
- Secure the lid. Choose the "Steam" mode and cook for 2 minutes under High pressure. Once cooking is complete, use a quick release; carefully remove the lid.
- Brush each corn on the cob with barbecue sauce; sprinkle with crushed chips. Bon appétit!

343. Fish and Cucumber Bites
(Ready in about 10 minutes + chilling time | Servings 5)

This is the cutest way to eat your favorite Mediterranean food. It's like a whole plate of fish with Greek salad in one convenient bite!
Per serving: *217 Calories; 14.3g Fat; 10g Carbs; 12.7g Protein; 6.1g Sugars*

Ingredients

1/2 pound fish fillets
4 medium-sized tomatoes, chopped
1/3 cup Kalamata olives, pitted and chopped
1/2 cup feta cheese, crumbled
1 tablespoon fresh lemon juice
2 cloves garlic, minced
2 tablespoons olive oil
1/2 teaspoon oregano
1/2 teaspoon dried rosemary
Sea salt and freshly ground black pepper, to taste
5 cucumbers

Directions

- Add 1 cup of water and steamer basket to your Instant Pot. Then, place fish fillets in the steamer basket.
- Secure the lid. Choose the "Steam" mode and cook for 3 minutes under Low pressure. Once cooking is complete, use a quick release; carefully remove the lid.
- Flake the fish with a fork. Now, add tomatoes, olives, cheese, lemon juice, garlic, olive oil, oregano, rosemary, salt, and black pepper; mix until everything is well combined.
- Cut cucumbers into pieces. Then, make a well in each cucumber using a spoon. Spoon the prepared fish mixture into cucumber pieces. Serve well-chilled and enjoy!

---

344. Mediterranean Calamari Bites
(Ready in about 15 minutes | Servings 6)

Calamari is always a good idea for any gathering! Serve with a garlic-mayo sauce on the side if desired.
Per serving: *155 Calories; 6.9g Fat; 5.7g Carbs; 17.1g Protein; 1.3g Sugars*

Ingredients

2 teaspoons olive oil
1 pound squid, cleaned and sliced into rings
4 garlic cloves, whole
1 cup dry white wine
1 teaspoon dried basil
1 teaspoon dried rosemary
1 teaspoon dried marjoram

1 cup tomatoes, puréed
1 cup chicken stock
Sea salt and ground black pepper, to taste
1/2 teaspoon red pepper flakes
1 heaping tablespoon fresh cilantro leaves, chopped
1 fresh lemon, cut into wedges

Directions

- Press the "Sauté" button to preheat your Instant Pot. Once hot, heat the olive oil. Then, sauté the squid with garlic for 3 to 4 minutes or so.
- Add a splash of wine to deglaze the bottom of the Instant Pot.
- Now, add basil, rosemary, marjoram, puréed tomatoes, chicken stock, salt, black pepper, and red pepper flakes.
- Secure the lid. Choose the "Manual" mode and cook for 4 minutes under High pressure. Once cooking is complete, use a natural release; carefully remove the lid.
- Serve garnished with fresh cilantro leaves and lemon wedges. Enjoy!

345. Movie Night Almond Popcorn
(Ready in about 10 minutes | Servings 4)

Spice up your next movie night with this nutty and salty popcorn. It also makes a great after-school snack for kids.
Per serving: *119 Calories; 9.5g Fat; 7.3g Carbs; 1.3g Protein; 0.1g Sugars*

Ingredients

3 tablespoons butter, at room temperature
1/4 cup popcorn kernels
A pinch of sugar
Sea salt, to taste
2 tablespoons Habanero BBQ almonds

Directions

- Press the "Sauté" button to heat up the Instant Pot. Melt the butter until sizzling.
- Stir in popcorn kernels; stir until they are covered with melted butter.
- Once popcorn starts popping, cover with the lid. Shake for a few seconds.
- Now, turn off the Instant Pot when 2/3 of kernels have popped. Allow all kernels to pop.
- Add salt and Habanero BBQ almonds; toss and serve immediately. Enjoy!

---

346. Sticky Chicken Nuggets
(Ready in about 20 minutes | Servings 6)

Finger licking good chicken nuggets that are sweet, spicy and crispy! How does it get any better than this?
Per serving: *313 Calories; 20.4g Fat; 6.1g Carbs; 25.3g Protein; 4.1g Sugars*

Ingredients

1 ½ pounds chicken breast, cut into 1-inch chunks
1/4 cup soy sauce
1/4 cup tomato, puréed
1/2 cup chicken stock
Sea salt and ground black pepper, to taste
1/2 stick butter
2 tablespoons hoisin sauce
1 teaspoon fresh ginger root, peeled and grated
1 tablespoon Sriracha
2 green onions, thinly sliced

Directions

- Add chicken, soy sauce, puréed tomatoes, stock, salt, pepper, butter, hoisin sauce, ginger, and Sriracha to the Instant Pot.
- Secure the lid. Choose the "Manual" mode and cook for 6 minutes under High pressure. Once cooking is complete, use a quick release; carefully remove the lid.
- Transfer the ingredients to a baking dish. Bake in the preheated oven at 390 degrees F for 10 minutes.
- Serve topped with green onions. Bon appétit!

347. Artichokes with Hollandaise Sauce
(Ready in about 15 minutes | Servings 3)

Here is the perfect idea for Sunday appetizer – artichokes! They go wonderfully with a lovely and smooth sauce such as Hollandaise.

Ingredients

3 small-sized artichokes
1 teaspoon lemon zest
The Sauce:
1/2 stick butter, at room temperature
2 egg yolks
1/2 tablespoon lemon juice
1/2 teaspoon salt
1/4 teaspoon ground black pepper
1/4 teaspoon cayenne

Directions

- Add 1 ½ cups of water and lemon zest to the Instant Pot. Now, place a metal rack on the top.
- Lower the artichokes onto the rack.
- Secure the lid. Choose the "Manual" mode and cook for 7 minutes under High pressure. Once cooking is complete, use a quick release; carefully remove the lid.
- To make the sauce, melt the butter in a pan. When the butter has melted, remove the pan from the heat.
- Then, in a blender, mix egg yolks with lemon juice, salt, black pepper, and cayenne pepper.
- Transfer the egg mixture to a heatproof bowl; place it over the pan of simmering water over a low heat.
- Then, keep whisking the mixture, adding the melted butter slowly and gradually; whisk until everything is well incorporated.
- Serve the prepared artichokes with Hollandaise on the side. Bon appétit!

348. The Best Party Mix Ever
(Ready in about 25 minutes | Servings 10)

Spicy and crunchy, this snack mix blends textures and flavors in a wonderful way. Serve with manchego and dry sherry. Enjoy!
Per serving: *208 Calories; 16.8g Fat; 16.9g Carbs; 6.5g Protein; 3.1g Sugars*

Ingredients

2 tablespoons butter
2 cups puffed-rice cereal
1 cup raw walnuts, halved
2 cups raw almonds
1/3 cup raw pumpkin seeds
1/3 cup raw sunflower seeds
1 cup roasted peas

2 tablespoons light brown sugar
1/2 teaspoon cayenne pepper
1/2 teaspoon garlic powder
1/2 teaspoon dried oregano
Salt and black pepper, to taste
1/2 teaspoon Tabasco sauce

Directions

- Press the "Sauté" button to heat up the Instant Pot. Now, melt the butter.
- Add the other ingredients and stir until they are coated with butter; add water as needed. Secure the lid.
- Select the "Manual" mode and cook for 11 minutes at High pressure. Once cooking is complete, use a natural release; carefully remove the lid.
- Transfer the mixture to a parchment-lined cookie sheet.
- Next, preheat your oven to 365 degrees F. Bake the party mix for 8 minutes, turning halfway through cooking time. Store in an airtight container. Bon appétit!

349. Chunky Cream Cheese and Sausage Dip
(Ready in about 20 minutes | Servings 12)

If you love cream cheese and sausage, you will love this easy, creamy and spicy dip. It will be a hit for a party!
Per serving: *157 Calories; 11.4g Fat; 6.3g Carbs; 8.1g Protein; 4.1g Sugars*

Ingredients

1 tablespoon canola oil
1 pound turkey smoked sausage
1 (28-ounce) can tomatoes, crushed
1/2 cup water
2 red chili peppers, minced
1 teaspoon yellow mustard
1 teaspoon basil
1 teaspoon oregano
1 (8-oz) package cream cheese, at room temperature
1/2 cup sour cream

Directions

- Press the "Sauté" button to preheat your Instant Pot. Once hot, heat the oil. Then, cook the sausage until it is delicately browned, crumbling it with a fork.
- Then, add canned tomatoes, water, peppers, mustard, basil, and oregano.
- Secure the lid. Choose the "Manual" mode and cook for 6 minutes under High pressure. Once cooking is complete, use a natural release; carefully remove the lid.
- Add cream cheese and sour cream; seal the lid. Allow it to sit for at least 5 minutes or until heated through. Serve with tortilla chips or pretzel bun bites. Enjoy!

---

350. Blue Cheese and Sweet Potato Balls
(Ready in about 1 hour 5 minutes | Servings 10)

Blue cheese and potato balls are a delicious and impressive appetizer for a fancy dinner party or a girls' night in. Sweet potatoes cook perfectly in the Instant Pot.
Per serving: *200 Calories; 10.6g Fat; 19.7g Carbs; 7.1g Protein; 1.8g Sugars*

Ingredients

2 pounds sweet potatoes, peeled and diced
1 onion, chopped
1 garlic clove, minced
Sea salt and ground black pepper, to taste
1 teaspoon dried marjoram
1 teaspoon basil

1/2 teaspoon ground allspice
1/2 stick butter, softened
1 cup blue cheese, crumbled
2 eggs, whisked
2/3 cup breadcrumbs

Directions

- Prepare your Instant Pot by adding 1 ½ cups of water and a metal trivet to its bottom. Lower sweet potatoes onto the trivet.
- Secure the lid. Choose the "Manual" mode and cook for 15 minutes under High pressure. Once cooking is complete, use a natural release; carefully remove the lid.
- Peel and mash the prepared sweet potatoes with the onion, garlic, and all of the seasonings. Now, stir in softened butter, cheese, and eggs.
- Place this mixture in your refrigerator for 30 minutes; then, shape into bite-sized balls.
- Coat each ball with breadcrumbs. Now, sprits the balls with a nonstick cooking spray. Bake the balls in the preheated oven at 425 degrees F approximately 15 minutes. Bon appétit!

VEGAN

351. Refreshing Bean Salad

(Ready in about 35 minutes + chilling time | Servings 4)

This salad is so easy to prepare in the Instant Pot. This is nutritious and budget-friendly as well.
Per serving: *207 Calories; 5.1g Fat; 31.2g Carbs; 10.6g Protein; 2.3g Sugars*

Ingredients

1 cup Great Northern beans
6 cups water
1 cucumber, peeled and sliced
1 red bell pepper, seeded and chopped
1 green bell pepper, seeded and chopped
1 teaspoon ground sumac
3 tablespoons extra-virgin olive oil
1 tablespoon fresh lime juice
1/4 cup fresh parsley leaves, roughly chopped
1/4 teaspoon freshly ground black pepper
1/2 teaspoon red pepper flakes
Salt, to taste

Directions

- Place beans and water in your Instant Pot.
- Secure the lid. Choose the "Bean/Chili" mode and cook for 30 minutes under High pressure. Once cooking is complete, use a natural release; carefully remove the lid.
- Allow the prepared beans to cool completely. Now, add the remaining ingredients to the Instant Pot.
- Toss to combine and serve well chilled. Enjoy!

352. Green Pea Medley

(Ready in about 25 minutes | Servings 6)

This vegan medley literally cooks itself. In addition, it only takes about 25 minutes to make!
Per serving: *173 Calories; 6.6g Fat; 22.7g Carbs; 7.7g Protein; 7.9g Sugars*

Ingredients

2 tablespoons canola oil
1 teaspoon cumin seeds
1 shallot, diced
2 cloves garlic, minced
2 carrots, chopped
2 parsnips, chopped
1 red bell pepper, seeded and chopped

2 bay leaves
Sea salt and ground black pepper, to taste
1 teaspoon cayenne pepper
1/2 teaspoon dried dill
2 ½ cups green peas, whole
2 ripe Roma tomatoes, seeded and crushed
3 cups roasted vegetable stock

Directions

- Press the "Sauté" button to preheat the Instant Pot. Once hot, add the oil. Then, sauté the cumin seeds for 30 seconds.
- Add shallot, garlic, carrots, parsnip and pepper; continue to sauté for 3 to 4 minutes more or until vegetables are tender.
- Now, stir in the remaining ingredients.
- Secure the lid. Choose the "Manual" mode and cook for 18 minutes under High pressure. Once cooking is complete, use a natural release; carefully remove the lid.
- Serve with cream cheese if desired. Bon appétit!

353. Spicy Veggie and Adzuki Bean Soup
(Ready in about 30 minutes | Servings 4)

Sriracha sauce is a Thai hot sauce made from chili peppers, garlic, distilled vinegar, sugar, and salt. Great alternatives for Sriracha include Louisiana hot sauces and harissa paste.
Per serving: *474 Calories; 7.6g Fat; 84g Carbs; 20.5g Protein; 7.8g Sugars*

Ingredients

2 tablespoons olive oil
2 onions, chopped
2 carrots chopped
2 parsnips, chopped
1 celery with leaves, chopped
2 Yukon gold potatoes, peeled and diced
2 ripe tomatoes, pureed
12 ounces Adzuki brans, soaked overnight

Kosher salt and ground black pepper, to taste
1 teaspoon cayenne pepper
1 teaspoon dried basil
1/2 teaspoon marjoram
1 teaspoon black garlic powder
1 teaspoon dried chive flakes
A few drops Sriracha
4 cups boiling water

Directions

- Press the "Sauté" button to heat up the Instant Pot. Now, heat the olive oil and sweat the onions until just tender.
- Add the other ingredients; stir to combine well. Secure the lid and choose the "Manual" mode. Cook for 10 minutes at High Pressure.
- Once cooking is complete, use a natural release for 15 minutes; remove the lid carefully.
- Ladle into individual serving bowls and eat warm. Bon appétit!

354. Italian-Style Asparagus Salad
(Ready in about 10 minutes | Servings 4)

Enjoy the best of Italian cuisine with this Instant Pot recipe! This decadent and healthy salad is sure to become your favorite.
Per serving: *230 Calories; 19.1g Fat; 10.1g Carbs; 7.9g Protein; 4.9g Sugars*

Ingredients

1 pound asparagus, trimmed
2 tomatoes, diced
4 tablespoons olive oil
1 shallot, chopped
1 teaspoon garlic, minced
Sea salt and ground black pepper, to taste
2 tablespoons lemon juice
1 tablespoon Dijon mustard
1/2 cup Romano cheese, grated
1 handful Italian parsley

Directions

- Add 1 cup of water and metal trivet to the Instant Pot. Place asparagus on the trivet.
- Secure the lid. Choose the "Manual" mode and cook for 1 minute under High pressure. Once cooking is complete, use a quick release; carefully remove the lid.
- Toss the prepared asparagus with remaining ingredients; toss to combine well. Place in your refrigerator until ready to serve. Enjoy!

355. Pumpkin Porridge with Dried Cherries
(Ready in about 25 minutes | Servings 4)

Learn to make a pumpkin purée from scratch. It is easier than you think. You can make a big batch and freeze leftovers in containers or ice cube trays.
Per serving: *201 Calories; 1.1g Fat; 51.8g Carbs; 5g Protein; 31.9g Sugars*

Ingredients

2 ½ pounds pumpkin, cleaned and seeds removed
1/2 cup rolled oats
4 tablespoons honey
1/2 teaspoon ground cinnamon
A pinch of salt
A pinch of grated nutmeg
4 tablespoons dried berries
1 cup water

Directions

- Add 1 ½ cups of water and a metal trivet to the Instant Pot. Now, place the pumpkin on the trivet.
- Secure the lid. Choose the "Manual" mode and cook for 12 minutes under High pressure. Once cooking is complete, use a natural release; carefully remove the lid.
- Then, purée the pumpkin in the food processor.
- Wipe down the Instant Pot with a damp cloth. Add the remaining ingredients to the Instant Pot, including pumpkin purée.
- Secure the lid. Choose the "Manual" mode and cook for 10 minutes under High pressure. Once cooking is complete, use a natural release; carefully remove the lid.

---

356. Easy Vegan Risotto
(Ready in about 15 minutes | Servings 2)

Try this combo of garlic, onion, Arborio rice and spices. A festival in your mouth!
Per serving: *291 Calories; 20g Fat; 35.4g Carbs; 11.3g Protein; 2.8g Sugars*

Ingredients

1 tablespoon olive oil
2 garlic cloves, minced
1 white onion, finely chopped
1 cup Arborio rice
1 cup water
1 cup vegetable stock
1/2 teaspoon dried basil
1/2 teaspoon dried oregano
Sea salt and ground black pepper, to taste
1 teaspoon smoked paprika

Directions

- Press the "Sauté" button to preheat your Instant Pot. Heat the oil and sauté the garlic and onion until tender and fragrant or about 3 minutes.
- Add the remaining ingredients; stir to combine well.
- Secure the lid. Choose the "Manual" mode and cook for 5 minutes under High pressure. Once cooking is complete, use a quick release; carefully remove the lid.
- Ladle into individual bowls and serve warm. Enjoy!

357. Root Vegetable and Noodle Soup
(Ready in about 20 minutes | Servings 6)

A homey, veggie soup with flavorful, golden noodles. A hearty, noodle soup always reminds us of grandma's kitchen, right?
Per serving: *194 Calories; 5.4g Fat; 29.9g Carbs; 8g Protein; 5.1g Sugars*

Ingredients

2 tablespoons olive oil
2 shallots, peeled and chopped
1 carrot, chopped
1 parsnip, chopped
1 turnip, chopped
3 garlic cloves, smashed
1 teaspoon cumin powder

1/2 teaspoon dried rosemary
1/2 teaspoon dried thyme
6 cups vegetable stock, preferably homemade
9 ounces vegan noodles
1 cup corn kernels
Salt and freshly ground black pepper, to taste

Directions

- Press the "Sauté" button to heat up your Instant Pot. Now, heat the oil and sauté the shallots with carrot, parsnip, and turnip until they have softened.
- Stir in the garlic and cook an additional 40 seconds. Add cumin powder, rosemary, thyme, stock, and noodles.
- Now, secure the lid and choose the "Soup" setting.
- Cook for 7 minutes at High pressure. Once cooking is complete, use a quick release; remove the lid carefully.
- Add corn kernels, cover with the lid, and cook in the residual heat for 5 to 6 minutes more. Season with salt and pepper. Taste adjust the seasoning and serve warm. Bon appétit!

358. Quinoa Pilaf with Cremini Mushrooms
(Ready in about 15 minutes | Servings 4)

Quinoa is a great source of protein; further, it also contains a significant amount of iron, magnesium and riboflavin. Quinoa is good for your skin, bones, and heart.
Per serving: *401 Calories; 12.1g Fat; 60.2g Carbs; 14.1g Protein; 2.7g Sugars*

Ingredients

2 cups dry quinoa
3 cups water
2 tablespoons olive oil
1 onion, chopped
1 bell pepper, chopped
2 garlic cloves, chopped

2 cups Cremini mushrooms, thinly sliced
1/2 teaspoon sea salt
1/3 teaspoon ground black pepper, or more to taste
1 teaspoon cayenne pepper
1/2 teaspoon dried dill
1/4 teaspoon ground bay leaf

Directions

- Add quinoa and water to your Instant Pot.
- Secure the lid. Choose the "Manual" mode and cook for 1 minute under High pressure. Once cooking is complete, use a natural release; carefully remove the lid.
- Drain quinoa and set it aside.
- Press the "Sauté" button to preheat your Instant Pot. Once hot, heat the oil. Then, sauté the onion until tender and translucent.
- Add bell pepper, garlic, and mushrooms and continue to sauté for 1 to 2 minutes more or until they are fragrant. Stir the remaining ingredients into your Instant Pot.
- Add the reserved quinoa and stir to combine well. Serve warm. Bon appétit!

359. Butternut Squash and Barley Bowl
(Ready in about 45 minutes | Servings 4)

These veggie barley bowls are sure to wow your family! Sprinkle with crunchy pepitas if desired.
Per serving: *360 Calories; 6.4g Fat; 70g Carbs; 8.7g Protein; 2.2g Sugars*

Ingredients

2 tablespoons olive oil divided
2 cloves garlic, minced
1/2 cup scallions, chopped
2 cups butternut squash, peeled and cubed
1/2 teaspoon turmeric powder
2 cups barley, whole
4 ½ cups water
Sea salt and ground black pepper, to taste

Directions

* Press the "Sauté" button to preheat your Instant Pot. Once hot, heat the oil. Now, cook the garlic and scallions until tender.
* Add the remaining ingredients and stir to combine.
* Secure the lid. Choose the "Multigrain" mode and cook for 40 minutes under High pressure. Once cooking is complete, use a natural release; carefully remove the lid.
* Ladle into individual bowls and serve warm.

---

360. Colorful Veggie and Coconut Soup
(Ready in about 25 minutes | Servings 5)

This classic vegan soup consists of vegetables, coconut cream, and fresh herbs. It is creamy, nourishing and delicious.
Per serving: *176 Calories; 13.1g Fat; 9.3g Carbs; 7.9g Protein; 3.4g Sugars*

Ingredients

1 tablespoon olive oil
1/2 cup white onions, chopped
1 teaspoon garlic, minced
2 carrots, chopped
1 parsnip, chopped
1 celery, chopped
1 head cauliflower, cut into small florets
1 zucchini, diced
5 cups vegetable stock
Sea salt and ground black pepper, to taste
1/2 cup coconut cream
2 tablespoons fresh cilantro, chopped

Directions

* Press the "Sauté" button to preheat your Instant Pot. Now, heat the oil until sizzling.
* Sauté the onion and garlic until tender. Add the carrots, parsnip, celery, cauliflower, zucchini, stock, salt, and black pepper, and stir to combine.
* Secure the lid. Choose the "Soup" mode and cook for 20 minutes under High pressure. Once cooking is complete, use a quick release; carefully remove the lid.
* Add coconut cream and seal the lid; let it sit until heated through. Ladle into soup bowls and serve garnished with fresh cilantro. Bon appétit!

361. Broccoli and Carrots with Peanut Sauce
(Ready in about 10 minutes | Servings 4)

Never underestimate a power of steamed vegetables. They are healthy, weight loss friendly, and extremely delicious.
Per serving: *90 Calories; 4.3g Fat; 9.3g Carbs; 5.2g Protein; 4.3g Sugars*

Ingredients

1 ¼ cups water
1 pound broccoli florets
1 carrot, diced
1/2 teaspoon sea salt
1/2 teaspoon cayenne pepper
1/4 teaspoon ground white pepper

For the Sauce:
4 tablespoons silky peanut butter
3 tablespoons water
1 tablespoon champagne vinegar
1 tablespoons poppy seeds

Directions

- Add 1 ¼ cups of water to the base of your Instant Pot. Arrange broccoli and carrots in a steaming basket and transfer them to the Instant Pot.
- Secure the lid, choose the "Manual" mode, and cook for 3 minutes at High pressure. Once cooking is complete, use a quick release; carefully remove the lid.
- Season your vegetables with salt, cayenne pepper, and ground white pepper.
- Meanwhile, in a mixing bowl, thoroughly combine peanut butter, water, vinegar, and poppy seeds.
- Serve steamed broccoli and carrots with the peanut sauce on the side. Bon appétit!

---

362. Delicious Old-Fashioned Chili
(Ready in about 15 minutes | Servings 6)

This chili is quick, endlessly crave-worthy, and surprisingly delicious. A healthy, protein dish where vegetables and beans make a great blend.
Per serving: *204 Calories; 6.5g Fat; 27.9g Carbs; 10.4g Protein; 6.9g Sugars*

Ingredients

2 tablespoons olive oil
1 red onion, chopped
3 cloves garlic minced or pressed
1 red bell pepper, diced
1 green bell pepper, diced
1 red chili pepper, minced
Sea salt and ground black pepper, to taste

1 teaspoon cayenne pepper
1/2 teaspoon ground cumin
2 cups vegetable stock
2 ripe tomatoes, chopped
2 (15-ounce) cans beans, drained and rinsed
1 handful fresh cilantro leaves, chopped
1/2 cup tortilla chips

Directions

- Press the "Sauté" button to preheat your Instant Pot. Now, heat the oil until sizzling.
- Sauté the onion tender and translucent. Add garlic, peppers, salt, and pepper; continue to sauté until they are tender.
- Now, stir in cayenne pepper, cumin, stock, tomatoes, and beans.
- Secure the lid. Choose the "Manual" mode and cook for 10 minutes under High pressure. Once cooking is complete, use a quick release; carefully remove the lid.
- Divide chili between six serving bowls; top with fresh cilantro and tortilla chips. Enjoy!

363. Traditional Russian Borscht
(Ready in about 15 minutes | Servings 4)

Bring some freshness to your everyday menu with this traditional soup that combines sweet red beets, vinegar, vegetables, and fresh dill.
Per serving: *183 Calories; 7.3g Fat; 22.5g Carbs; 8.4g Protein; 7.7g Sugars*

Ingredients

1 ½ tablespoons olive oil
1/2 cup onions, chopped
2 garlic cloves, pressed
Kosher salt and ground black pepper, to taste
1/2 pound potatoes, peeled and diced
2 carrots, chopped
1/2 pound beets, peeled and coarsely shredded
2 tablespoons red-wine vinegar
1 tomato, chopped
4 cups vegetable stock
1/2 teaspoon caraway seeds
1/4 cup fresh dill, roughly chopped

Directions

- Press the "Sauté" button to preheat your Instant Pot. Heat the oil and cook the onions and garlic until tender and fragrant.
- Add the remaining ingredients, except for fresh dill.
- Secure the lid. Choose the "Manual" mode and cook for 10 minutes under High pressure. Once cooking is complete, use a natural release; carefully remove the lid.
- Serve the soup with chopped fresh dill. Enjoy!

---

364. Winter Curry Cabbage
(Ready in about 20 minutes | Servings 4)

Here's an amazing cabbage recipe that you would never dream of making. This curry cabbage is delicious served with hot cooked rice and a pickled salad.
Per serving: *223 Calories; 8.2g Fat; 33.8g Carbs; 7.6g Protein; 15.1g Sugars*

Ingredients

2 tablespoons olive oil
1 medium-sized leek, chopped
2 cloves garlic, smashed
1 ½ pounds white cabbage, shredded
1 cup vegetable broth
1 cup tomatoes, puréed
1 parsnip, chopped
2 carrots, chopped
2 stalks celery, chopped

1 turnip, chopped
1/2 tablespoon fresh lime juice
1 teaspoon dried basil
1/2 teaspoon dried dill
1 teaspoon ground coriander
1 teaspoon ground turmeric
1 bay leaf
Kosher salt and ground black pepper, to taste
1 (14-ounce) can coconut milk

Directions

- Press the "Sauté" button to preheat your Instant Pot. Now, heat the oil and cook the leeks and garlic until tender and fragrant.
- After that, add the remaining ingredients; stir to combine well.
- Secure the lid. Choose the "Manual" mode and cook for 12 minutes under High pressure. Once cooking is complete, use a natural release; carefully remove the lid.
- Ladle into soup bowls and serve immediately.

365. The Easiest Hummus Ever
(Ready in about 35 minutes | Servings 8)

Each ingredient in this dip plays a part in its rich and incredible flavor. Serve with pita bread and veggie sticks.
Per serving: *186 Calories; 7.7g Fat; 22.8g Carbs; 7.6g Protein; 4g Sugars*

Ingredients

10 cups water
3/4 pound dried chickpeas, soaked
2 tablespoons tahini
1/2 lemon, juiced
1 teaspoon granulated garlic
Salt and black pepper, to taste
1/3 teaspoon ground cumin
1/2 teaspoon cayenne pepper
1/2 teaspoon dried basil
3 tablespoon olive oil

Directions

- Add water and chickpeas to the Instant Pot. Secure the lid.
- Choose the "Manual" mode and cook for 25 minutes under High pressure. Once cooking is complete, use a natural release; carefully remove the lid.
- Now, drain your chickpeas, reserving the liquid. Transfer chickpeas to a food processor. Add tahini, lemon juice, and seasonings.
- Puree until it is creamy; gradually pour in the reserved liquid and olive oil until the mixture is smooth and uniform. Serve with a few sprinkles of cayenne pepper. Bon appétit!

---

366. Green Beans with Shiitake Mushrooms
(Ready in about 25 minutes | Servings 4)

This vegan dish is easy to prepare and it is packed with flavor and nutrition. Cooked with shiitake mushrooms and spices, this hearty meal can be served on any occasion.
Per serving: *119 Calories; 7.6g Fat; 12.6g Carbs; 2.6g Protein; 2.6g Sugars*

Ingredients

2 cups water
6 dried shiitake mushrooms
2 tablespoons sesame oil
2 cloves garlic, minced
1/2 cup scallions, chopped
1 ½ pounds green beans, fresh or frozen (and thawed)

1/4 teaspoon ground black pepper
1/2 teaspoon red pepper flakes, crushed
1 bay leaf
Sea salt, to taste

Directions

- Press the "Sauté" button and bring the water to a rapid boil; remove from the heat; add the dried shiitake mushrooms.
- Allow the mushrooms to sit for 15 minutes to rehydrate. Then cut the mushrooms into slices; reserve the mushroom stock.
- Wipe down the Instant Pot with a kitchen cloth. Press the "Sauté" button to preheat your Instant Pot. Once hot, heat the sesame oil.
- Then, sauté the garlic and scallions until tender and aromatic. Add green beans, black pepper, red pepper, bay leaf, salt, reserved mushrooms and stock; stir to combine well.
- Secure the lid. Choose the "Manual" mode and cook for 4 minutes under High pressure. Once cooking is complete, use a quick release; carefully remove the lid. Serve warm.

367. Collard Greens with Vegan Sauce
(Ready in about 15 minutes | Servings 4)

This nutrient-packed vegan supper pairs greens with a silky vegan sauce that consists of tofu and spices. Serve with crunchy breadsticks.

Per serving: *199 Calories; 13.1g Fat; 11.1g Carbs; 13.7g Protein; 1.9g Sugars*

Ingredients

1 cup silken tofu, cut into cubes
Salt and black pepper, to taste
1/2 teaspoon mustard powder
1/2 teaspoon cumin powder
1/2 teaspoon red pepper flakes, crushed
1/4 teaspoon curry powder
1 tablespoon balsamic vinegar
2 tablespoons toasted sesame oil
1 teaspoon garlic, minced
1 cup button mushrooms, sliced
1 pound collard greens, torn into pieces

Directions

- In your food processor, blend tofu, salt, black pepper, mustard powder, cumin powder, red pepper, curry powder, and balsamic vinegar.
- Pour the sauce into a pan and cook over low heat for 2 to 3 minutes; reserve.
- Press the "Sauté" button to preheat your Instant Pot. Now, heat the sesame oil and cook the garlic and mushrooms until tender and fragrant.
- Add collard greens to the Instant Pot. Secure the lid. Choose the "Manual" mode and cook for 4 minutes under High pressure. Once cooking is complete, use a quick release; carefully remove the lid.
- Serve with a dollop of reserved vegan sauce. Enjoy!

---

368. Saucy Brussels Sprouts with Cashews
(Ready in about 15 minutes | Servings 4)

Brussels sprouts are so versatile. Bursting with flavor, this vegetable is great on its own or combined with nuts and other vegetables.

Per serving: *132 Calories; 5.7g Fat; 17.8g Carbs; 6.3g Protein; 5.9g Sugars*

Ingredients

1 pound Brussels sprouts, cut into halves
1/2 cup water
1/2 cup tomato purée
Salt and ground black pepper, to taste
1/2 teaspoon cayenne pepper or more to taste

2 tablespoons soy sauce
1 fresh lime juice
1/4 cup cashew nuts, chopped
1/4 cup fresh cilantro leaves, chopped

Directions

- Add the Brussels sprouts, water, tomato purée, salt, black pepper, and cayenne pepper to the Instant Pot.
- Secure the lid. Choose the "Manual" mode and cook for 4 minutes under High pressure. Once cooking is complete, use a quick release; carefully remove the lid.
- Drizzle soy sauce and lime juice over the top. Add cashew nuts and fresh cilantro leaves. Serve immediately.

369. Aromatic Risotto with Tomatoes
(Ready in about 25 minutes | Servings 4)

Try one of the favorite risotto recipes that reheats well. This risotto recipe is easy to follow and quick to prepare. It might become a staple in your summer kitchen.

Per serving: *251 Calories; 6.2g Fat; 44.1g Carbs; 4.2g Protein; 3g Sugars*

Ingredients

1 tablespoon sesame oil
1 yellow onion, peeled and chopped
2 cloves garlic, minced
1 cup tomatoes, pureed
1 carrot, chopped
1 tablespoon tomato powder
1 teaspoon curry powder
1 teaspoon citrus & ginger spice blend
1/2 teaspoon paprika
Sea salt and freshly ground black pepper, to taste
1 cup white rice, soaked for 30 minutes
2 ½ cups water

Directions

- Press the "Sauté" button to heat up the Instant Pot. Heat sesame oil until sizzling.
- Sweat the onion for 2 to 3 minutes. Add garlic and cook an additional 30 to 40 seconds.
- Add tomatoes and carrot; cook for a further 10 minutes, stirring periodically. Add seasonings, rice, and water to the Instant Pot. Secure the lid.
- Select the "Manual" mode and cook for 8 minutes at High pressure. Once cooking is complete, use a natural release; remove the lid carefully.
- Taste, adjust the seasonings and serve warm. Bon appétit!

---

370. Vegan Lentil and Tomato Bowl
(Ready in about 20 minutes | Servings 4)

Lentils are protein packed food that can be used in various recipes. They cook fast in the Instant Pot; they are easy to digest as well.

Per serving: *405 Calories; 5.9g Fat; 67.5g Carbs; 24.5g Protein; 3.8g Sugars*

Ingredients

1 tablespoon olive oil
2 cups red lentils
1/2 cup scallions, finely chopped
1 teaspoon garlic, minced
1 teaspoon turmeric powder
Sea salt and ground black pepper, to taste

1 teaspoon sweet paprika
1 (15-ounce) can tomatoes, crushed
1 bay leaf
1 handful fresh cilantro leaves, chopped

Directions

- Add olive oil, lentils, scallions, garlic, turmeric, salt, black pepper, paprika, tomatoes, and bay leaf to your Instant Pot.
- Secure the lid. Choose the "Manual" mode and cook for 12 minutes under High pressure. Once cooking is complete, use a natural release; carefully remove the lid.
- Discard bay leaf and spoon lentil into serving bowls. Serve topped with fresh cilantro. Enjoy!

371. Minty Split Pea Dip
(Ready in about 15 minutes | Servings 8)

Thanks to the Instant pot, you can have a hearty protein dip in less than 15 minutes. Add some extra herbs before serving, if desired.
Per serving: *79 Calories; 4.5g Fat; 4.4g Carbs; 5.6g Protein; 2.3g Sugars*

Ingredients

1 pound dried split peas, rinsed
6 cups vegetable stock
1 tablespoon fresh lemon juice
4 tablespoons extra-virgin olive oil
1 teaspoon fresh mint, chopped
1 tablespoon fresh parsley, chopped
1/2 teaspoon paprika
Sea salt and freshly ground black pepper, to taste

Directions

- Add split peas and vegetable stock to your Instant Pot.
- Secure the lid. Choose the "Manual" mode and cook for 5 minutes under High pressure. Once cooking is complete, use a natural release; carefully remove the lid.
- Transfer split peas to your food processor; add the remaining ingredients. Process until everything is creamy and well combined. Serve well chilled. Bon appétit!

---

372. Classic Tomato Soup with Pepitas
(Ready in about 15 minutes | Servings 4)

Pair cooked tomatoes with vegetables and pepitas and your taste buds will rejoice. This soup is perfect for a fancy Sunday lunch!
Per serving: *125 Calories; 9.4g Fat; 8.1g Carbs; 4.2g Protein; 1.8g Sugars*

Ingredients

2 tablespoons olive oil
1/2 cup green onions, chopped
2 cloves garlic, crushed
2 carrots, roughly chopped
1 red chili pepper, seeded and chopped
1 pound ripe tomatoes, puréed
1 zucchini, chopped
1 teaspoon dried rosemary
1/2 teaspoon dried basil
1/2 teaspoon dried marjoram
1 teaspoon sweet paprika
Sea salt and ground black pepper, to taste
1 cup vegetable stock
2 tablespoons fresh chives, chopped
2 tablespoons pepitas

Directions

- Press the "Sauté" button to preheat your Instant Pot. Then, heat the oil until sizzling.
- Now, cook green onions and garlic until tender and fragrant. Add carrots, chili pepper, tomatoes, zucchini, seasonings, and stock.
- Secure the lid. Choose the "Manual" mode and cook for 6 minutes under High pressure. Once cooking is complete, use a quick release; carefully remove the lid.
- Then, purée the mixture with an immersion blender until the desired thickness is reached.
- Ladle into soup bowls; serve garnished with fresh chives and pepitas. Enjoy!

373. Penne with Leek-Tomato Sauce
(Ready in about 15 minutes | Servings 4)

You can't go wrong with an Instant Pot pasta. Make an extraordinary pasta in 15 minutes and amaze your family!
Per serving: *281 Calories; 5g Fat; 54g Carbs; 7.6g Protein; 8.8g Sugars*

Ingredients

1 tablespoon canola oil
1 small-sized leek, chopped
1 teaspoon garlic, smashed
1 ¼ pounds penne pasta
4 ripe tomatoes, pureed
2 cups roasted vegetable stock, preferably homemade
1 teaspoon dried rosemary
1/2 teaspoon dried oregano
1/2 teaspoon daikon radish seeds
A pinch of sugar
Sea salt and freshly ground black pepper, to your liking
1 teaspoon cayenne pepper
1/3 cup dry sherry

Directions

- Press the "Sauté" button to heat up your Instant Pot. When hot, add canola oil and sauté the leeks and garlic until aromatic.
- Stir in penne, tomatoes, and roasted vegetable stock. Now, add the other ingredients and secure the lid. Choose the "Manual" function and cook for 6 minutes under High pressure.
- Once cooking is complete, use a natural release; remove the lid carefully.
- Divide among four serving bowls and serve garnished with vegan parmesan. Bon appétit!

---

374. Red Kidney Bean Delight
(Ready in about 30 minutes | Servings 4)

all red kidney beans, vegetables and seasonings in your Instant Pot. Pour in a vegan broth and press the right button. It couldn't be easier to make!
Per serving: *418 Calories; 2.1g Fat; 72.9g Carbs; 30.1g Protein; 4.5g Sugars*

Ingredients

1 pound dried red kidney beans
1/2 cup shallots, chopped
2 cloves garlic, chopped
2 roasted peppers, cut into strips
1 teaspoon ground cumin
1/2 teaspoon mustard powder
1 teaspoon celery seeds
Sea salt and ground black pepper, to taste
2 cups roasted vegetable broth

Directions

- Add all of the above ingredients to your Instant Pot.
- Secure the lid. Choose the "Bean/Chili" mode and cook for 25 minutes under High pressure. Once cooking is complete, use a natural release; carefully remove the lid.
- You can thicken the cooking liquid on "Sauté" function if desired. Serve warm.

375. Chinese Soup with Zha Cai
(Ready in about 35 minutes | Servings 4)

Whether you're a vegan or not, you'll love this hearty vegetable soup. Serve with zha cai (pickled vegetables).
Per serving: *177 Calories; 8.8g Fat; 18.5g Carbs; 7.8g Protein; 7.1g Sugars*

Ingredients

1 tablespoon toasted sesame oil
1 yellow onion, peeled and chopped
2 garlic cloves, minced
1 teaspoon fresh ginger, peeled and grated
1 jalapeño pepper, minced
1 celery stalk, chopped
2 carrots, chopped
1 teaspoon Five-spice powder
Sea salt, to taste

1/2 teaspoon ground black pepper, to taste
1/2 teaspoon red pepper flakes
1 teaspoon dried parsley flakes
4 cups vegetable broth
2 ripe tomatoes, finely chopped
1 tablespoon soy sauce
1 cup sweet corn kernels, frozen and thawed
1 cup zha cai

Directions

- Press the "Sauté" button to preheat your Instant Pot. Once hot, add the oil. Sauté the onion, garlic, ginger and jalapeño pepper for 2 to 3 minutes, stirring occasionally.
- Add the remaining ingredients, except for corn and zha cai; stir to combine well.
- Secure the lid. Choose the "Bean/Chili" mode and cook for 25 minutes under High pressure. Once cooking is complete, use a natural release; carefully remove the lid.
- After that, add corn and seal the lid again. Let it sit until heated through. Serve in individual bowls with zha cai on the side. Enjoy!

---

376. Mushroom Soup with Rice Noodles
(Ready in about 25 minutes | Servings 6)

You can easily customize this soup recipe to suit your preferences; you can use fresh or frozen vegetables, it's up to you.
Per serving: *292 Calories; 13.7g Fat; 37.7g Carbs; 5.5g Protein; 3.1g Sugars*

Ingredients

6 cups vegan cream of mushroom soup
1/2 teaspoon dried basil
1 teaspoon dried oregano
1 teaspoon dried parsley flakes
1 teaspoon fennel seeds
2 carrots, thinly sliced
1 celery stalk, chopped
1 parsnip, chopped
1 red onion, chopped

2 cloves garlic, minced
1 cup brown mushrooms, chopped
2 cups rice noodles
1/2 tablespoon miso paste
1/2 teaspoon freshly ground black pepper
1/4 teaspoon red pepper flakes, crushed
Salt, to taste

Directions

- Place the cream of mushroom soup, basil, oregano, parsley, fennel seeds, carrots, celery, parsnip, onion, garlic, mushrooms in your Instant Pot.
- Secure the lid. Choose the "Soup" mode and cook for 8 minutes under High pressure. Once cooking is complete, use a natural release; carefully remove the lid.
- Add rice noodles, miso paste, black pepper, red pepper, and salt to the Instant Pot.
- Press the "Sauté" button and cook an additional 7 to 10 minutes. Ladle into individual bowls and serve right away!

377. Purple Cabbage with Basmati Rice
(Ready in about 25 minutes | Servings 4)

Purple cabbage, also known as red cabbage, is a powerhouse of precious nutrients. It boosts the immune system, promotes healthy bones, and fights chronic disease.
Per serving: *242 Calories; 13.3g Fat; 35.2g Carbs; 7.8g Protein; 10g Sugars*

Ingredients

2 tablespoons olive oil
2 shallots, diced
1 garlic clove, minced
1 head purple cabbage, cut into wedges
2 ripe tomatoes, pureed
2 tablespoons tomato ketchup
1 cup basmati rice
1 ½ cups water
1 bay leaf
1/4 teaspoon marjoram
1/2 teaspoon cayenne pepper
Salt and freshly ground black pepper, to taste
1/4 cup fresh chives, chopped

Directions

- Press the "Sauté" button to preheat the Instant Pot. Heat olive oil and sauté the shallots until they are just tender.
- Now, stir in minced garlic and cook until it is lightly browned and aromatic.
- Stir in cabbage, tomatoes, ketchup, rice, water, bay leaf, marjoram, cayenne pepper, salt, and black pepper.
- Secure the lid. Select the "Manual" mode and cook for 6 minutes under High pressure. Once cooking is complete, use a natural release for 15 minutes; remove the lid carefully. Serve warm garnished with fresh chopped chives. Bon appétit!

378. Summer Zucchini Bowl
(Ready in about 15 minutes | Servings 4)

Zucchini is having a renaissance! They also cook wonderfully under high pressure.
Per serving: *143 Calories; 9.4g Fat; 12.7g Carbs; 5.6g Protein; 4.4g Sugars*

Ingredients

2 tablespoons garlic-infused olive oil
1 garlic clove, minced
1/2 cup scallions, chopped
1 pound zucchinis, sliced
1/2 cup tomato paste
1/2 cup vegetable broth
Salt, to taste

1/2 teaspoon ground black pepper
1/2 teaspoon dried oregano
1/2 teaspoon dried basil
1 teaspoon paprika
1/2 cup Kalamata olives, pitted and sliced

Directions

- Press the "Sauté" button to preheat the Instant Pot. Now, heat the oil; sauté the garlic and scallions for 2 minutes or until they are tender and fragrant.
- Add zucchinis, tomato paste, broth, salt, black pepper, oregano, basil, and paprika.
- Secure the lid. Choose the "Manual" mode and Low pressure; cook for 4 minutes. Once cooking is complete, use a quick pressure release; carefully remove the lid.
- Serve garnished with Kalamata olives. Bon appétit!

379. Jasmine Rice with Curried Sauce

(Ready in about 20 minutes | Servings 3)

Are you looking for a quick recipe to have on hand during your busy week? We've got a great recipe for you! You can double or triple the recipe, if desired.

Per serving: *353 Calories; 9.6g Fat; 56.8g Carbs; 8g Protein; 1.7g Sugars*

Ingredients

1/4 cup water
2 cups vegetable broth
1 tablespoon olive oil
1 cup jasmine rice
1 tablespoon vegan margarine
1 yellow onion, chopped
1 teaspoon curry powder
Fresh juice of 1/2 lemon
Zest of 1/2 lemon
Sea salt and ground black pepper, to taste

Directions

- Place the water, 1 cup of vegetable broth, olive oil, and rice in your Instant Pot.
- Secure the lid. Choose the "Manual" mode and High pressure; cook for 2 minutes. Once cooking is complete, use a natural pressure release for 10 minutes; carefully remove the lid.
- Fluff the rice with a fork and reserve.
- Wipe down the Instant Pot with a kitchen cloth. Press the "Sauté" button and melt margarine. Then, sauté the onion until tender and translucent.
- Add the remaining cup of vegetable broth, curry powder, lemon, salt, and black pepper. Press the "Sauté" button and stir until everything is incorporated.
- Spoon the sauce over hot rice. Bon appétit!

---

380. Quinoa and Chickpea Bowl

(Ready in about 10 minutes | Servings 4)

If you've never had quinoa with chickpeas, then you've been missing out. Here is a great opportunity to prepare this insanely yummy combo of grains, beans, and veggies.

Per serving: *392 Calories; 8.1g Fat; 66.9g Carbs; 15.5g Protein; 7.9g Sugars*

Ingredients

2 teaspoons sesame oil
1 shallot, thinly sliced
2 bell peppers, thinly sliced
1 jalapeño pepper, seeded and sliced
1 teaspoon garlic, minced
Sea salt and ground black pepper, to taste
1/2 teaspoon mustard powder

1 teaspoon fennel seeds
1/2 teaspoon ground cumin
1 ½ cups quinoa, rinsed
1 ½ cups water
1 cup tomato purée
1 (15-ounce) can chickpeas, drained and rinsed
1 lime, cut into wedges

Directions

- Press the "Sauté" button to preheat your Instant Pot. Heat the sesame oil. Then, sweat the shallot and peppers until they are tender and fragrant.
- Now, add the garlic, salt, black pepper, mustard powder, fennel seeds, cumin, quinoa, water, tomato purée, and chickpeas.
- Secure the lid. Choose the "Manual" mode and High pressure; cook for 1 minute. Once cooking is complete, use a natural pressure release; carefully remove the lid.
- Serve with fresh lime wedges. Bon appétit!

381. Spaghetti Squash with Pesto Sauce
(Ready in about 15 minutes | Servings 4)

Have you ever tried vegetable spaghetti? This healthy, comfort food is extremely easy to prepare in the Instant Pot.
Per serving: *218 Calories; 16.9g Fat; 15.6g Carbs; 4.4g Protein; 0.5g Sugars*

Ingredients

1 cup water
1 pound spaghetti squash, cut into halves
For the Pesto:
1/2 cup raw walnut halves
1 ½ tablespoons nutritional yeast
Salt, to taste

1/4 teaspoon ground black
1/4 teaspoon cayenne pepper
1 ½ cups fresh basil
1 tablespoon fresh lemon juice
2 cloves garlic, minced
3 tablespoons olive oil

Directions

- Grab your spaghetti squash and scoop out the seeds and most of the stringy parts with an ice cream.
- Pour water into the base of your Instant Pot. Add squash to your Instant Pot and secure the lid.
- Select the "Manual" mode and cook for 7 minutes under High pressure. Once cooking is complete, use a quick release; remove the lid carefully.
- Next, place walnuts, nutritional yeast, salt, black pepper, and cayenne pepper in your food processor; pulse until it is the consistency of fine meal.
- Add the remaining ingredients for the pesto and pulse again until evenly combined. Serve the spaghetti squash with pesto sauce. Bon appétit!

---

382. Beluga Lentil Stew with Kale
(Ready in about 15 minutes | Servings 4)

This delicious and nutritious lentil stew is easy to make in the Instant Pot. Black beluga lentils are protein-packed food with lots of health benefits.
Per serving: *311 Calories; 22.9g Fat; 21.8g Carbs; 9.9g Protein; 6.7g Sugars*

Ingredients

2 teaspoons toasted sesame oil
1 yellow onion, chopped
2 cloves garlic, pressed
1 teaspoon fresh ginger, grated
1 bell pepper, chopped
1 serrano pepper, chopped
1/2 teaspoon ground allspice
1/2 teaspoon ground cumin
1/2 teaspoon dried basil
1 teaspoon dried parsley flakes

Sea salt and black pepper, to taste
1 ½ cups tomato purée
2 cups vegetable stock
1 cup beluga lentils
2 cups kale leaves, torn into pieces
1 teaspoon fresh lemon juice
1/2 cup cashew cream

Directions

- Press the "Sauté" button to preheat your Instant Pot. Now, heat the oil; sauté the onion until tender and translucent.
- Then, add the garlic, ginger, and peppers; continue to sauté until they have softened.
- Add seasonings, tomato purée, stock and lentils.
- Secure the lid. Choose the "Manual" mode and High pressure; cook for 8 minutes. Once cooking is complete, use a natural pressure release; carefully remove the lid.
- Add kale and lemon juice; seal the lid again and let it sit until thoroughly warmed. Serve dolloped with cashew cream. Enjoy!

383. Jamaican-Style Chili
(Ready in about 25 minutes | Servings 4)

This is a complete family lunch that everyone will love. It requires only the Instate Pot so the clean up is minimal.
Per serving: *300 Calories; 11.4g Fat; 36.1g Carbs; 8.3g Protein; 7.9g Sugars*

Ingredients

2 tablespoons sesame oil
1/2 cup red onion, sliced
2 cloves garlic crushed
1 roasted bell pepper, cut into strips
1 teaspoon habanero pepper, minced
1 pound sweet potatoes, peeled and cut into bite-sized chunks
1 cup vegetable broth
1 cup water
Sea salt, to taste
1 teaspoon black peppercorns, crushed

1/4 teaspoon allspice
1/8 teaspoon ground clove
1 teaspoon sweet paprika
1/2 teaspoon smoked paprika
1 pound red kidney beans, soaked overnight and well-rinsed
1/2 (15-ounce) can tomatoes, diced
1/4 cup rum
1 (7-ounce) can salsa verde

Directions

- Press the "Sauté" button to preheat your Instant Pot. Now, heat the oil; sauté the onion until tender and translucent or about 2 minutes.
- Then, stir in the garlic and peppers; continue to sauté for a further 2 minutes. Now, add sweet potatoes, broth, water, spices, beans, and tomatoes.
- Secure the lid. Choose the "Bean/Chili" mode and High pressure; cook for 15 minutes. Once cooking is complete, use a natural pressure release; carefully remove the lid.
- Add rum and salsa verde. Press the "Sauté" button and continue to cook until everything is thoroughly heated. Enjoy!

---

384. Thai Rice with Green Peas
(Ready in about 20 minutes | Servings 3)

This recipe doesn't require some special ingredients. You can come up with a great meal using ingredients you already have in your kitchen.
Per serving: *306 Calories; 16.7g Fat; 42.7g Carbs; 9.1g Protein; 18.2g Sugars*

Ingredients

1 cup basmati rice, rinsed
1 ¼ cups water
Kosher salt and white pepper, to taste
2 tablespoons fresh coriander
4 ounces fresh green peas
2 fresh green chilies, chopped
1 garlic clove, pressed
1/2 cup candy onions, chopped
4 whole cloves
1/2 cup creamed coconut
1 tablespoon fresh lime juice

Directions

- Combine all of the above ingredients, except for lime juice, in your Instant Pot.
- Secure the lid. Choose the "Manual" mode and High pressure; cook for 2 minutes. Once cooking is complete, use a natural pressure release for 10 minutes; carefully remove the lid.
- Serve in individual bowls, drizzled with fresh lime juice. Bon appétit!

385. Mom's Peppery Beans

(Ready in about 50 minutes | Servings 6)

Refried beans are always welcomed. You can buy cannellini beans in a can, but every now and then, it is a good idea to make an old-fashion version with dried and soaked beans.

Per serving: *159 Calories; 10.1g Fat; 13.5g Carbs; 8.4g Protein; 3.2g Sugars*

Ingredients

2 tablespoons olive oil
1 yellow onion, chopped
2 garlic cloves, roughly chopped
2 medium-sized bell peppers, deveined and thinly sliced
1 teaspoon habanero pepper, minced
1 teaspoon dried rosemary
1/2 teaspoon ground cumin
Salt and ground black pepper, to taste
1 ½ pounds dried Cannellini beans
2 bay leaves
6 cups water

Directions

- Press the "Sauté" button. Heat olive oil and cook the onion until tender and fragrant.
- Now, add garlic and peppers; cook until they have softened, about 4 minutes. Add the remaining ingredients.
- Secure the lid. Select the "Bean/Chili" mode and cook for 25 minutes under High pressure.
- Once cooking is complete, use a natural release for 20 minutes; remove the lid carefully. Serve warm and enjoy!

---

386. Italian Lasagna Bowl

(Ready in about 25 minutes | Servings 4)

Comforting and delicious, this Italian-inspired recipe is sure to please. This is a true vegan decadence.

Per serving: *269 Calories; 3.9g Fat; 49.2g Carbs; 11.8g Protein; 6.4g Sugars*

Ingredients

2 teaspoons canola oil
1 red onion, chopped
2 cloves garlic, minced
2 carrots chopped
2 bell peppers, chopped
1/2 cup French green lentils, well-rinsed
2 ripe tomatoes, puréed
1 tablespoon Italian seasoning

Sea salt and ground black pepper, to taste
1 teaspoon red pepper flakes, crushed
1 cup water
1 cup vegetable stock
6 ounces lasagna sheets, broken into small pieces
1/2 cup vegan mozzarella, to serve

Directions

- Press the "Sauté" button to preheat your Instant Pot. Now, heat the oil and cook the onion until tender and translucent.
- Now, add the garlic and continue to sauté it for 30 seconds more.
- Add carrots, peppers, lentils, tomatoes, seasonings, water vegetable stock, and lasagna sheets.
- Secure the lid. Choose the "Manual" mode and High pressure; cook for 10 minutes. Once cooking is complete, use a natural pressure release for 10 minutes; carefully remove the lid.
- Serve with vegan mozzarella. Bon appétit!

387. Curried Cumin Baby Potatoes
(Ready in about 15 minutes | Servings 6)

Opt for a cruelty-free comfort food today! Prepare these delicious curried potatoes in no time and serve them as a vegan main course.
Per serving: *246 Calories; 12.4g Fat; 31.1g Carbs; 5.3g Protein; 3.1g Sugars*

Ingredients

1 tablespoon canola oil
1/2 cup scallions, chopped
2 cloves garlic, minced
1 teaspoon red chili pepper, minced
2 pounds baby potatoes, diced
1 tablespoon curry paste
1 cup water

1 cup vegetable broth
1 cup full-fat coconut milk
Salt, to taste
1/2 teaspoon ground black pepper
1 teaspoon cayenne pepper
1 teaspoon cumin

Directions

- Press the "Sauté" button to preheat your Instant Pot. Now, heat the canola oil until sizzling; sauté the scallions until just tender.
- Add garlic and chili pepper; allow it to cook an additional 30 seconds, stirring continuously. Add the remaining ingredients.
- Secure the lid. Choose the "Manual" mode and High pressure; cook for 5 minutes. Once cooking is complete, use a quick pressure release; carefully remove the lid. Serve hot.

---

388. Russet Potato and Chanterelle Stew
(Ready in about 25 minutes | Servings 4)

Rich, flavorful and rustic, this stew will warm you up on windy winter nights. Russet potatoes and wild chanterelle mushrooms combine very well and cook perfectly in a pressure cooker.
Per serving: *456 Calories; 5.7g Fat; 99g Carbs; 15.4g Protein; 7.9g Sugars*

Ingredients

1 pound russet potatoes, peeled and diced
3/4 pound chanterelle mushrooms, sliced
1 tablespoon olive oil
1 carrot, chopped
1 parsnip, chopped
1 yellow onion, chopped
2 cloves garlic, peeled and minced
2 sprigs fresh rosemary
2 sprigs fresh thyme

1 teaspoon red chili flakes
2 tablespoons fresh parsley, chopped
2 cups vegetable stock
1/3 cup port wine
1 ripe Roma tomato, chopped
Sea salt and ground black pepper, to taste
1 tablespoon paprika
1 tablespoon flax seeds meal

Directions

- Throw all ingredients, except for flax seeds meal, in your Instant Pot.
- Secure the lid. Choose the "Soup" mode and High pressure; cook for 20 minutes. Once cooking is complete, use a natural pressure release; carefully remove the lid.
- Stir the flax seeds into your Instant Pot. Press the "Sauté" button and let it simmer until cooking liquid has thickened and reduced. Serve hot. Bon appétit!

389. Easy Breakfast Coconut Oatmeal
(Ready in about 15 minutes | Servings 2)

Want a quick, easy, and nutritious breakfast? A fine, old-fashioned coconut oatmeal is just the thing for you!
Per serving: *243 Calories; 11.8g Fat; 48g Carbs; 12.6g Protein; 2.5g Sugars*

Ingredients

4 cups water
1 ½ cups steel cut oats
1 tablespoon coconut oil
1/2 teaspoon cardamom
1/4 teaspoon grated nutmeg
1/2 teaspoon ground cinnamon
1/2 teaspoon vanilla essence
1/2 teaspoon ground star anise
1/2 cup coconut, flaked

Directions

- Add water and oats to your Instant Pot.
- Secure the lid and choose the "Manual" mode. Cook for 10 minutes at High pressure.
- Once cooking is complete, use a quick release; remove the lid carefully. Add coconut oil and seasonings to the warm oatmeal and stir to combine well.
- Divide among individual bowls and serve topped with flaked coconut. Bon appétit!

390. The Best Mac and Cheese Ever
(Ready in about 15 minutes | Servings 4)

A tasty side dish or complete lunch, it's up to you! Delight your vegan friends with this unique combination of pasta and creamy sauce.
Per serving: *415 Calories; 11.5g Fat; 66g Carbs; 14.4g Protein; 6.7g Sugars*

Ingredients

1 (8-ounce) box elbow macaroni
3 Yukon gold potatoes, peeled and diced
1 yellow onion, chopped
1 garlic clove, minced
2 cups water
3 tablespoons nutritional yeast flakes
Seasoned salt and ground black pepper, to taste
1/2 teaspoon red pepper flakes
1/2 cup cashews
1/3 cup almond milk

Directions

- Place macaroni, potatoes, onion, garlic, and water in your Instant Pot.
- Secure the lid. Choose the "Soup" mode and High pressure; cook for 4 minutes. Once cooking is complete, use a quick pressure release; carefully remove the lid.
- Then, remove potatoes from cooking liquid using a slotted spoon; transfer them to your blender. Add nutritional yeast flakes, salt, black pepper, red pepper, cashews, and almond milk; blend until everything is creamy, uniform and smooth.
- Add "cheese" mixture to the Instant Pot; stir with warm pasta and serve immediately.

391. Old-Time Mashed Potatoes
(Ready in about 15 minutes | Servings 6)

Airy light, garlicky and luxurious, these old-fashioned mashed potatoes are so good! To serve, you can drizzle aromatized oil over the top to add some extra flavor.
Per serving: *196 Calories; 8.3g Fat; 27.2g Carbs; 4.2g Protein; 1.4g Sugars*

Ingredients

2 pounds potatoes, peeled and diced
3 garlic cloves, peeled
1 cup vegetable stock
Salt, to taste
1/3 teaspoon ground black pepper
A pinch of grated nutmeg
4 tablespoons vegan butter, softened
2 tablespoons soy milk
1 teaspoon paprika powder

Directions

- Add the potatoes, garlic, stock, salt, pepper, nutmeg and butter to your Instant Pot.
- Secure the lid. Choose the "Manual" mode and High pressure; cook for 5 minutes. Once cooking is complete, use a quick pressure release; carefully remove the lid.
- Then, purée the mixture with a potato masher; add soy milk and continue to mash until your desired texture is reached.
- Sprinkle paprika over the top and serve warm. Bon appétit!

---

392. Garden Vegetable and Wild Rice Soup
(Ready in about 35 minutes | Servings 4)

Get ready for a little piece of heaven. A gorgeous combo of fresh garden vegetables, wild rice, and spices.
Per serving: *235 Calories; 8.1g Fat; 34.2g Carbs; 8.6g Protein; 6.3g Sugars*

Ingredients

2 tablespoons olive oil
1/2 cup leeks, roughly chopped
2 garlic cloves, minced
1 bell pepper, chopped
1 serrano pepper, chopped
2 carrots, chopped
1 fennel, diced
3/4 cup wild rice

1 cup tomato purée
2 cups water
2 cups vegetable broth
2 tablespoons fresh coriander, chopped
1 teaspoon fresh or dried rosemary
Salt, to taste
1/2 teaspoon ground black pepper

Directions

- Press the "Sauté" button to preheat your Instant Pot. Once hot, heat the oil.
- Then, sauté the leeks, garlic, and pepper for 2 to 4 minutes, stirring periodically; add a splash of broth if needed.
- Stir the remaining ingredients into your Instant Pot; stir to combine well.
- Secure the lid. Choose the "Soup" mode and High pressure; cook for 30 minutes. Once cooking is complete, use a natural pressure release; carefully remove the lid.
- Taste and adjust the seasonings; ladle into soup bowls and serve hot. Enjoy!

393. Hearty Mushroom Goulash with Chickpeas

(Ready in about 15 minutes | Servings 4)

Here's a protein-packed vegan dish that can be served for lunch or dinner. Cremini mushrooms contain about 3.1 grams of protein per 100 grams. Chickpeas contain 19 grams of protein per 100 grams.
Per serving: *198 Calories; 9.1g Fat; 22.9g Carbs; 10.5g Protein; 6.7g Sugars*

Ingredients

2 tablespoons peanut oil
1 cup scallions, chopped
1 ½ pounds Cremini mushrooms, thinly sliced
2 garlic cloves, smashed
1/4 cup white wine
Sea salt and freshly ground black pepper, to taste
1/2 teaspoon cayenne pepper
1/4 teaspoon dried dill weed
1/2 teaspoon dried rosemary
1 can chickpeas, drained well
1/4 cup fresh parsley, roughly chopped

Directions

- Press the "Sauté" button and heat peanut oil. Now, cook scallions until they are tender.
- Add the mushrooms and garlic; cook for 3 to 4 minutes, stirring periodically. Add a splash of white wine to deglaze the pot.
- Season with salt, black pepper, cayenne pepper, dill, and rosemary.
- Secure the lid. Choose the "Manual" mode and High pressure; cook for 10 minutes. Once cooking is complete, use a quick pressure release; carefully remove the lid.
- Add chickpeas and stir. Divide among serving plates and serve garnished with fresh chopped parsley. Bon appétit!

394. Great Northern Beans on Toast

(Ready in about 35 minutes | Servings 6)

Eating beans is the best way to maintain the ideal body weight and fuel your energy level through a busy day. You can serve your beans on toast as well.
Per serving: *393 Calories; 6.5g Fat; 67.4g Carbs; 18.4g Protein; 16.8g Sugars*

Ingredients

2 cups Great Northern beans
1 red onion, peeled and chopped
1 cup water
2 cups vegetable broth
1/2 cup ketchup
Garlic salt, to taste
1 teaspoon chili powder
1/2 teaspoon mixed peppercorns, crushed

1/4 cup dark brown sugar
2 cloves garlic, minced
2 sprigs fresh sage, roughly chopped
2 tablespoons canola oil
6 slices sourdough bread, toasted

Directions

- Add beans, onion, water, and broth to the Instant Pot.
- Secure the lid. Choose the "Soup" mode and High pressure; cook for 25 minutes. Once cooking is complete, use a natural pressure release; carefully remove the lid.
- Add ketchup, salt, chili powder, mixed peppercorns, sugar, garlic, sage, and oil. Press the "Sauté" button.
- Let it simmer an additional 5 to 7 minutes or until everything is heated through. Spoon the hot beans over toast and serve immediately.

395. Classic Lentil Gumbo
(Ready in about 15 minutes | Servings 4)

This gumbo brings the flavors of New Orleans' cuisine into your kitchen! It is packed with nutrition and tastes so good.
Per serving: *196 Calories; 8.8g Fat; 22.7g Carbs; 9.6g Protein; 7.7g Sugars*

Ingredients

2 tablespoons sesame oil
1 shallot, chopped
3 cloves garlic, minced
1 teaspoon jalapeño pepper, minced
1 celery stalk, chopped
1 carrot, chopped
1 parsnip, chopped
1/2 teaspoon dried basil
1 teaspoon dried parsley flakes

1 teaspoon red pepper flakes, crushed
1 1/3 cups lentils, regular
4 cups vegetable broth
1 ½ cups fresh or frozen chopped okra
2 ripe tomatoes, chopped
Salt, to taste
1/2 teaspoon ground black pepper
1 teaspoon light brown sugar

Directions

- Press the "Sauté" button to preheat the Instant Pot. Heat the oil andnow, sauté the shallot until tender and fragrant.
- After that, stir in garlic; cook an additional 30 seconds or until aromatic. Then, stir in the remaining ingredients.
- Secure the lid. Choose the "Manual" mode and High pressure; cook for 12 minutes. Once cooking is complete, use a natural pressure release; carefully remove the lid.
- Taste, adjust the seasonings and serve warm. Bon appétit!

---

396. Mediterranean-Style Wheat Berry Salad
(Ready in about 45 minutes + chilling time | Servings 6)

Include this salad into your weekly dinner rotation and you will be delighted! This is incredibly easy to make in the Instant Pot.
Per serving: *207 Calories; 7.1g Fat; 32.2g Carbs; 6.2g Protein; 1.5g Sugars*

Ingredients

2 cups wheat berries, soaked overnight and rinsed well
6 cups water
Salt and pepper, to taste
1 cup baby tomatoes, halved
1 red onion, thinly sliced
1/3 cup Kalamata olives, halved
1/4 cup extra-virgin olive oil
1/4 cup red wine vinegar
1 tablespoon tahini
1 teaspoon yellow mustard
3 cloves garlic, minced

Directions

- Add the soaked wheat berries and water to the Instant Pot.
- Secure the lid. Choose the "Multigrain" mode and High pressure; cook for 40 minutes. Once cooking is complete, use a natural pressure release; carefully remove the lid.
- Place in a salad bowl. Add salt, pepper, tomatoes, onion and Kalamata olives.
- In a small-sized mixing bowl, whisk the remaining ingredients for the dressing. Dress your salad and serve well-chilled.

397. Creamy Chowder with Peppers
(Ready in about 15 minutes | Servings 4)

This delicious chowder highlights the amazing taste of two types of peppers – bell pepper and serrano peppers. Prepare extremely creative and imaginative chowders in your Instant Pot!
Per serving: *282 Calories; 22.2g Fat; 18.4g Carbs; 6.1g Protein; 7.9g Sugars*

Ingredients

3 teaspoons sesame oil
1/2 cup leeks, chopped
1 garlic clove, minced
1 celery with leaves, chopped
1 carrot, trimmed and chopped
1 red bell pepper, thinly sliced
1 green bell pepper, thinly sliced
1 serrano pepper, deveined and thinly sliced

4 ½ cups water
Salt and ground black pepper, to taste
1 tablespoon soy sauce
1/2 cup raw cashews, soaked for 3 hours
1/2 cup almond milk, unsweetened

Directions

- Press the "Sauté" button on your Instant Pot. Heat sesame oil and sauté the leeks until they are just tender.
- Add garlic, celery, carrot, and peppers; continue sautéing until they have softened, about 3 minutes.
- Add water, salt, and pepper. Choose the "Manual" mode and cook for 4 minutes at High pressure.
- Once cooking is complete, use a quick release; remove the lid carefully.
- Next, puree soy sauce, raw cashews, and almond milk in your food processor or blender; process until creamy and uniform.
- Stir this cream base into the soup; cook in the residual heat until everything is well incorporated.
- Divide warm chowder among individual serving bowls. Side with crackers and enjoy!

---

398. Lentil Gazpacho Salad
(Ready in about 15 minutes + chilling time | Servings 4)

This plant-based salad is packed with protein, fiber, and iron. Serve with a country-style white bread.
Per serving: *375 Calories; 9.4g Fat; 55.7g Carbs; 20.3g Protein; 5.9g Sugars*

Ingredients

1 ½ cups yellow lentils
3 cups water
2 bay leaves, dry or fresh
1 sprig thyme
1 sprig rosemary
2 garlic cloves, halved
1 red bell pepper, sliced
1 green bell pepper, sliced
1 cucumber, sliced
2 cups baby spinach leaves

1/2 cup red onion, thinly sliced
1/2 cup black olives, pitted and sliced
1 jalapeño, minced
A large handful fresh parsley, finely chopped
2 ripe tomatoes, chopped
1/4 cup extra-virgin olive oil
1 tablespoon peanut butter
1 tablespoon lime juice

Directions

- Add lentils, water, bay leaves, thyme, rosemary, and garlic to your Instant Pot.
- Secure the lid. Choose the "Manual" mode and High pressure; cook for 2 minutes. Once cooking is complete, use a natural pressure release; carefully remove the lid.
- Allow lentils to cool to room temperature. Then, add the remaining ingredients; toss to combine well.
- Serve well chilled and enjoy!

399. Tempeh and Sweet Potato Curry
(Ready in about 15 minutes | Servings 4)

An exotic family dinner is read! This vegan dish is a low-calorie and delicious meal for the whole family.
Per serving: *272 Calories; 11.1g Fat; 31.2g Carbs; 15.6g Protein; 3.8g Sugars*

Ingredients

1 tablespoon toasted sesame oil
1 onion, thinly sliced
2 garlic cloves, minced
1 red chili pepper, chopped
1/2 pound tempeh, steamed
1 cup vegetable broth
1 teaspoon curry paste

1/2 teaspoon cumin
Sea salt and ground black pepper, to taste
1 pound sweet potatoes, peeled and diced
1 tablespoon peanut butter
4 ounces coconut milk
2 cups spinach leaves

Directions

- Press the "Sauté" button to preheat your Instant Pot. Now, heat the oil; sauté the onion until tender and translucent.
- Add garlic and chili pepper; continue to sauté an additional 40 seconds.
- Add tempeh, broth, curry paste, cumin, salt, black pepper, sweet potatoes, peanut butter and coconut milk.
- Secure the lid. Choose the "Manual" mode and High pressure; cook for 8 minutes. Once cooking is complete, use a natural pressure release; carefully remove the lid.
- Add spinach leaves; seal the lid again and let it sit until wilted completely. Serve in individual bowls and enjoy!

---

400. Spring Green Lentil Salad
(Ready in about 25 minutes | Servings 4)

There are many reasons to include lentils in your dietary regimen. Lentils are among the healthiest foods on the planet Earth. They can improve functions of the digestive system and cardiovascular system. They can also lower cholesterol levels and promote weight loss.
Per serving: *183 Calories; 13.8g Fat; 13.7g Carbs; 3.5g Protein; 4g Sugars*

Ingredients

3 cups water
1 ½ cups dried French green lentils, rinsed
2 bay leaves
A bunch of spring onions, roughly chopped
2 garlic cloves, minced
2 carrots, shredded
1 green bell pepper, thinly sliced
1 red bell pepper, thinly sliced

1/2 cup radishes, thinly sliced
1 cucumber, thinly sliced
1/4 cup extra-virgin olive oil
2 tablespoons balsamic vinegar
1/4 cup fresh basil, snipped
1 teaspoon mixed peppercorns, freshly cracked
Sea salt, to taste

Directions

- Place water, lentils, and bay leaves in your Instant Pot. Secure the lid.
- Choose "Soup" function and cook for 20 minutes under High pressure. Once cooking is complete, use a quick release; carefully remove the lid.
- Drain green lentils and discard bay leaves; transfer to a large salad bowl.
- Add spring onions, garlic, carrots, bell peppers, radishes, cucumber, olive oil, vinegar, and basil. Season with crushed peppercorns and sea salt.
- Toss to combine and place in your refrigerator until ready to serve. Bon appétit!

DESSERTS

401. Cherry and Almond Crisp Pie
(Ready in about 15 minutes | Servings 4)

This cherry crisp is perfect for any occasion. You can use fresh or frozen cherries but make sure to use those that are sweet.
Per serving: *335 Calories; 13.4g Fat; 60.5g Carbs; 5.9g Protein; 38.1g Sugars*

Ingredients

1 pound sweet cherries, pitted
1 teaspoon ground cinnamon
1/3 teaspoon ground cardamom
1 teaspoon pure vanilla extract
1/3 cup water
1/3 cup honey
1/2 stick butter, at room temperature
1 cup rolled oats
2 tablespoons all-purpose flour
1/4 cup almonds, slivered
A pinch of salt
A pinch of grated nutmeg

Directions

- Arrange cherries on the bottom of the Instant Pot. Sprinkle cinnamon, cardamom, and vanilla over the top. Add water and honey.
- In a separate mixing bowl, thoroughly combine the butter, oats, and flour. Spread topping mixture evenly over cherry mixture.
- Secure the lid. Choose the "Manual" mode and High pressure; cook for 10 minutes. Once cooking is complete, use a natural pressure release; carefully remove the lid.
- Serve at room temperature. Bon appétit!

---

402. Chocolate and Mango Mug Cakes
(Ready in about 15 minutes | Servings 2)

With its luscious flavor and gooey texture, chocolate mug cakes will blow your mind! They are easy to whip up in the Instant Pot.
Per serving: *268 Calories; 10.5g Fat; 34.8g Carbs; 10.6g Protein; 31.1g Sugars*

Ingredients

1/2 cup coconut flour
2 eggs
2 tablespoons honey
1 teaspoon vanilla
1/4 teaspoon grated nutmeg
1 tablespoon cocoa powder
1 medium-sized mango, peeled and diced

Directions

- Combine the coconut flour, eggs, honey, vanilla, nutmeg and cocoa powder in two lightly greased mugs.
- Then, add 1 cup of water and a metal trivet to the Instant Pot. Lower the uncovered mugs onto the trivet.
- Secure the lid. Choose the "Manual" mode and High pressure; cook for 10 minutes. Once cooking is complete, use a quick pressure release; carefully remove the lid.
- Top with diced mango and serve chilled. Enjoy!

403. Carrot Pudding with Almonds and Figs
(Ready in about 30 minutes | Servings 4)

Delicate jasmine rice, flavorful fresh carrots, nuts, and sweet dried figs. You just can't get enough of this pudding recipe. Serve cold or hot.
Per serving: *331 Calories; 17.2g Fat; 44.5g Carbs; 13.9g Protein; 19.5g Sugars*

Ingredients

1 ½ cups jasmine rice
1 ½ cups milk
1/2 cup water
2 large-sized carrots, shredded
1/4 teaspoon kosher salt
1/3 cup granulated sugar
2 eggs, beaten
1/3 cup almonds, ground
1/4 cup dried figs, chopped
1/2 teaspoon pure almond extract
1/2 teaspoon vanilla extract
1/3 teaspoon ground cardamom
1/2 teaspoon ground star anise

Directions

- Place jasmine rice, milk, water, carrots, and salt in your Instant Pot.
- Stir to combine and secure the lid. Choose "Manual" and cook at High pressure for 10 minutes. Once cooking is complete, use a natural release for 15 minutes; carefully remove the lid.
- Now, press the "Sauté" button and add the sugar, eggs, and almonds; stir to combine well. Bring to a boil; press the "Keep Warm/Cancel" button.
- Add the remaining ingredients and stir; the pudding will thicken as it sits. Bon appétit!

---

404. Italian Bread Pudding with Dried Apricots
(Ready in about 20 minutes | Servings 6)

Instant Pot desserts mean less fuss and more spare time! It will be hard to say No to this bread pudding with succulent dried apricots, fresh milk and flavorful cream.
Per serving: *410 Calories; 24.3g Fat; 37.4g Carbs; 11.5g Protein; 25.6g Sugars*

Ingredients

4 cups Italian bread, cubed
1/2 cup granulated sugar
2 tablespoons molasses
1/2 cup dried apricots, soaked and chopped
2 tablespoons coconut oil
1 teaspoon vanilla paste
A pinch of grated nutmeg

A pinch of salt
1 teaspoon cinnamon, ground
1/2 teaspoon star anise, ground
2 cups milk
4 eggs, whisked
1 1/3 cups heavy cream

Directions

- Add 1 ½ cups of water and a metal rack to the Instant Pot.
- Grease a baking dish with a nonstick cooking spray. Throw bread cubes into the prepared baking dish.
- In a mixing bowl, thoroughly combine the remaining ingredients. Pour the mixture over the bread cubes. Cover with a piece of foil, making a foil sling.
- Secure the lid. Choose the "Porridge" mode and High pressure; cook for 15 minutes. Once cooking is complete, use a quick pressure release; carefully remove the lid. Enjoy!

405. Chocolate and Cranberry Oatmeal Bars
(Ready in about 20 minutes | Servings 8)

Oats are not just breakfast cereals; they also make a great, luscious dessert. These bars are great to serve at gatherings
Per serving: *201 Calories; 7.3g Fat; 27.2g Carbs; 6.9g Protein; 11.8g Sugars*

Ingredients

3 eggs, whisked
1/2 cup sour cream
1/4 cup honey
2 teaspoons coconut oil, melted
1/2 teaspoon rum extract
1/2 teaspoon vanilla extract
3/4 cup quick oats, pudding-y
1/3 cup all-purpose flour

1 teaspoon baking soda
1 teaspoon baking powder
1/2 teaspoon cardamom
1/2 teaspoon cinnamon
1 cup dark chocolate chips
A pinch of kosher salt
3/4 cup cranberries

Directions

- Add 1 cup of water and a metal trivet to the Instant Pot. Now, spritz a baking pan with a nonstick cooking spray.
- In a mixing bowl, whisk the eggs, sour cream, honey, coconut oil, rum extract, and vanilla extract.
- Add oats, flour, baking soda, baking powder, cardamom, cinnamon, salt, and chocolate chips; stir until everything is well incorporated. After that, fold in cranberries.
- Scrape the batter into the baking pan.
- Secure the lid. Choose the "Manual" mode and High pressure; cook for 12 minutes. Once cooking is complete, use a natural pressure release; carefully remove the lid.
- Serve chilled and enjoy!

---

406. Coconut and Avocado Delight
(Ready in about 20 minutes | Servings 8)

It is such a delicious treat for you and your family! Before serving, you can add colored sanding sugars to the top.
Per serving: *144 Calories; 5.1g Fat; 27.3g Carbs; 1.3g Protein; 16.9g Sugars*

Ingredients

1/3 cup avocado, mashed
2 plantains
1 ½ tablespoons butter, softened
1/4 cup agave syrup
4 tablespoons cocoa powder
1/2 cup coconut flakes
1 teaspoon baking soda
1/2 teaspoon vanilla paste
1 teaspoon star anise, ground
1/8 teaspoon cream of tartar

Directions

- Prepare your Instant Pot by adding 1 cup of water and a metal rack to its bottom. Grease the sides and bottom of a baking pan with melted butter.
- Then, mix all of the above ingredients in your blender or food processor. Next, pour the batter into the prepared baking pan.
- Secure the lid. Choose the "Porridge" mode and High pressure; cook for 15 minutes. Once cooking is complete, use a quick pressure release; carefully remove the lid.
- Garnish with some fresh or dried fruit if desired. Bon appétit!

407. Coconut and Chocolate Cheesecake
(Ready in about 1 hour + freezing time | Servings 10)

The Instant Pot makes fantastic cheesecake, cooking it equally all the way through! The steam will make it extra fluffy and flavorful.
Per serving: *487 Calories; 33.5g Fat; 39.1g Carbs; 8.7g Protein; 28.2g Sugars*

Ingredients

1 ½ cups vanilla sugar cookies, crumbled
1/2 stick butter, melted
For the Filling:
22 ounces cream cheese, room temperature
3/4 cup granulated sugar
1 ½ tablespoons cornstarch
2 eggs, room temperature

1/3 cup sour cream
1/2 teaspoon coconut extract
1/2 teaspoon pure anise extract
1/4 teaspoon freshly grated nutmeg
6 ounces semisweet chocolate chips
3 ounces sweetened shredded coconut

Directions

- Lightly oil a baking pan that fits in your Instant Pot. Cover the bottom with a baking paper.
- Thoroughly combine crumbled cookies with melted butter; now, press the crust into the baking pan and transfer to your freezer.
- Next, beat the cream cheese with a mixer on low speed. Stir in the sugar and cornstarch and continue mixing on low speed until everything is uniform and smooth.
- Fold in the eggs, one at a time, and continue to beat with the mixer. Now, stir in sour cream, coconut extract, anise extract, and nutmeg; mix again.
- Then, microwave the chocolate chips about 1 minute, stirring once or twice. Add the melted chocolate to the cheesecake batter; add shredded coconut and stir to combine.
- Pour the chocolate mixture into the baking pan on top of the crust.
- Add 1 cup of water and trivet to the Instant Pot. Lower the prepared pan onto the trivet and secure the lid. Select the "Manual" mode. Bake at High pressure for 40 minutes.
- Once cooking is complete, use a natural release for 15 minutes; remove the lid carefully.
- Allow your cheesecake to cool completely before slicing and serving. Enjoy!

---

408. Double-Chocolate and Peanut Fudge
(Ready in about 15 minutes | Servings 6)

Here's a delicious way to end a party dinner! Make a fudge pudding in your Instant pot and see the difference.
Per serving: *347 Calories; 22.3g Fat; 30.7g Carbs; 5.6g Protein; 21.4g Sugars*

Ingredients

8 ounces semisweet chocolate, chopped
2 ounces milk chocolate, chopped
1/3 cup applesauce
1 egg, beaten
1/2 teaspoon vanilla extract

1/2 teaspoon almond extract
1/4 teaspoon ground cinnamon
1/3 cup peanut butter
A pinch of coarse salt
1/4 cup arrowroot powder

Directions

- Add 1 ½ cups of water and a metal trivet to the Instant Pot. Press the "Sauté" button and add the chocolate to a heatproof bowl; melt the chocolate over the simmering water. Press the "Cancel" button.
- In a mixing dish, thoroughly combine the applesauce, egg, and vanilla, almond extract, cinnamon, peanut butter and salt.
- Then, add arrowroot powder and mix well to combine. Afterwards, fold in the melted chocolate; mix again.
- Spritz six heat-safe ramekins with a nonstick cooking spray. Pour in the batter and cover with foil.
- Secure the lid. Choose the "Manual" mode and High pressure; cook for 5 minutes. Once cooking is complete, use a quick pressure release; carefully remove the lid.
- Let your dessert cool on a wire rack before serving. Bon appétit!

409. Festive Rum Cheesecake
(Ready in about 25 minutes + chilling time | Servings 6)

This silky and delicious cheesecake is so cute and so easy to prepare in the Instant Pot. For the best results, use any type of full-fat cream cheese like Philadelphia.
Per serving: *399 Calories; 23.7g Fat; 36.7g Carbs; 9.9g Protein; 34.6g Sugars*

Ingredients

14 ounces full-fat cream cheese
3 eggs, whisked
1/2 teaspoon vanilla extract
1 teaspoon rum extract
1/2 cup agave syrup
1/4 teaspoon cardamom
1/4 teaspoon ground cinnamon
Butter-Rum Sauce:

1/2 cup granulated sugar
1/2 stick butter
1/2 cup whipping cream
1 tablespoon dark rum
1/3 teaspoon nutmeg

Directions

- Add cream cheese, eggs, vanilla, rum extract, agave syrup, cardamom, and cinnamon to your blender or food processor; blend until everything is well combined.
- Transfer the batter to a baking pan; cover with a sheet of foil.
- Add 1 ½ cups of water and a metal trivet to the Instant Pot. Lower the pan onto the trivet.
- Secure the lid. Choose the "Soup" mode and High pressure; cook for 20 minutes. Once cooking is complete, use a natural pressure release; carefully remove the lid.
- In a sauté pan, melt the sugar with butter over a moderate heat. Add whipping cream, rum, and nutmeg.
- Drizzle warm sauce over cooled cheesecake. Serve and enjoy!

---

410. Indian Rice Pudding (Kheer)
(Ready in about 10 minutes | Servings 4)

Jaggery is made from unrefined sugar, which makes it a healthier than white sugar. This dessert looks impressive in elegant serving bowls.
Per serving: *408 Calories; 18.7g Fat; 62.4g Carbs; 13.8g Protein; 35.6g Sugars*

Ingredients

1 ½ cups basmati rice
3 cups coconut milk
1 teaspoon rosewater
A pinch of coarse salt
1⁄4 teaspoon saffron, crushed
4 tablespoons unsalted pistachios, minced
1/2 cup jaggery
1/2 cup raisins

Directions

- Add all of the above ingredients, except for raisins, to your Instant Pot; stir to combine well.
- Secure the lid. Choose the "Soup" mode and High pressure; cook for 3 minutes. Once cooking is complete, use a natural pressure release; carefully remove the lid.
- Serve topped with raisins and enjoy!

411. Chocolate-Glazed Little Pumpkin Puddings
(Ready in about 30 minutes + chilling time | Servings 4)

Mini pumpkin puddings are an easy but impressive dessert that you can prepare up to two days ahead of time. A silky chocolate ganache will add a touch of glamour and sophistication to your dessert.

Per serving: *366 Calories; 19.3g Fat; 40.1g Carbs; 11.4g Protein; 29g Sugars*

Ingredients

1/2 cup half-and-half
1 cup pumpkin puree
1/3 cup Turbinado sugar
1 egg plus 1 egg yolk, beaten
1/3 teaspoon crystallized ginger
1/2 teaspoon ground cinnamon
1/4 teaspoon ground nutmeg

A pinch of table salt

For the Chocolate Ganache:
1/2 cup chocolate chips
1/4 cup double cream

Directions

- Prepare your Instant Pot by adding the water and a steam rack to the pot. Butter four ramekins and set them aside.
- In a mixing bowl, thoroughly combine half-and-half with pumpkin puree, and sugar; now, gently fold in the eggs and mix to combine well.
- Then, scrape the mixture into the prepared ramekins, dividing evenly, and place side by side on the steam rack.
- Secure the lid. Choose the "Manual" setting and cook at High pressure for 25 minutes. Once cooking is complete, use a quick release; carefully remove the lid.
- Let the pudding cool about 2 hours before serving.
- Meanwhile, make the chocolate ganache by melting the chocolate in the microwave for 30 seconds; stir and microwave for a further 15 seconds.
- Add double cream and stir to combine well.
- Lastly, pour this chocolate ganache over pumpkin puddings, letting it run over sides; spread gently with a table knife. Let them set in your refrigerator. Enjoy!

412. Country Berry Compote
(Ready in about 10 minutes | Servings 4)

Use your favorite combination of berries in this recipe. You can eat this compote with pancakes, French toast, or Greek yogurt.

Per serving: *236 Calories; 0.8g Fat; 61.3g Carbs; 1.1g Protein; 50.2g Sugars*

Ingredients

1 pound mixed berries, fresh
1 cup mixed berries, dried
3/4 cup sugar
1/2 cup rose wine
2 tablespoons fresh orange juice
1 teaspoon cloves
1 vanilla bean, split in half
1 cinnamon stick

Directions

- Simply throw all of the above ingredients into your Instant Pot.
- Secure the lid. Choose the "Manual" and cook at High pressure for 6 minutes. Once cooking is complete, use a natural release; carefully remove the lid.
- Serve over vanilla ice cream if desired and enjoy!

413. Mini Molten Butterscotch Cakes
(Ready in about 20 minutes | Servings 6)

These mini molten lava cakes are awesome! Dipping into that ooey-gooey middle is really great feeling!
Per serving: *393 Calories; 21.1g Fat; 45.6g Carbs; 5.6g Protein; 35.4g Sugars*

Ingredients

1 stick butter
6 ounces butterscotch morsels
3/4 cup powdered sugar
3 eggs, whisked
1/2 teaspoon vanilla extract
7 tablespoons all-purpose flour
A pinch of coarse salt

Directions

- Add 1 ½ cups of water and a metal rack to the Instant Pot. Line a standard-size muffin tin with muffin papers.
- In a microwave-safe bowl, microwave butter and butterscotch morsels for about 40 seconds. Stir in powdered sugar.
- Add the remaining ingredients. Spoon the batter into the prepared muffin tin.
- Secure the lid. Choose the "Manual" and cook at High pressure for 10 minutes. Once cooking is complete, use a quick release; carefully remove the lid.
- To remove, let it cool for 5 to 6 minutes. Run a small knife around the sides of each cake and serve. Enjoy!

---

414. Mini Coconut Cream Cakes
(Ready in about 15 minutes | Servings 4)

If you have a sweet tooth, this is a must-try dessert recipe for Instant Pot. You can serve it with fresh or frozen berries, pineapple od banana.
Per serving: *425 Calories; 33.6g Fat; 20.2g Carbs; 11.4g Protein; 16.7g Sugars*

Ingredients

12 ounces cream cheese
2 ounces sour cream
1/3 cup coconut sugar
1/2 teaspoon vanilla extract
1/2 teaspoon coconut extract
1 teaspoon orange zest
1/2 cup coconut flakes
2 eggs
4 tablespoons orange curd

Directions

- Start by adding 1 ½ cups of water and a metal trivet to the bottom of the Instant Pot.
- In a mixing bowl, combine cream cheese, sour cream, coconut sugar, vanilla, coconut extract, and orange zest.
- Now, add coconut flakes and eggs; whisk until everything is well combined.
- Divide the batter between four jars. Top with orange curd. Lower the jars onto the trivet. Now, cover your jars with foil.
- Secure the lid. Choose the "Manual" and cook at High pressure for 9 minutes. Once cooking is complete, use a natural pressure release; carefully remove the lid.
- Garnish with fruits if desired. Bon appétit!

415. Vanilla and Wine Poached Peaches
(Ready in about 15 minutes | Servings 4)

For this recipe, use a lighter and fruity white wine. Serve with a dollop of vanilla ice cream if desired.
Per serving: *405 Calories; 0.8g Fat; 75.1g Carbs; 3g Protein; 67.8g Sugars*

Ingredients

8 firm peaches, cut into halves
1/2 orange, cut into rounds
1/2 lemon, cut into rounds
1/2 cup water
1/2 cup apple juice
1 bottle white wine
1 ½ cups sugar
2 cinnamon sticks
2 whole cloves
1 large vanilla bean pod, split open lengthwise
1 tablespoon crystallized ginger

Directions

- Arrange peaches in the bottom of your Instant Pot.
- Mix the remaining ingredients until they are thoroughly combined. Add this poaching liquid to the Instant Pot.
- Secure the lid. Choose the "Manual" mode and cook at Low pressure for 3 minutes. Once cooking is complete, use a quick pressure release; carefully remove the lid.
- Remove the peaches from the Instant pot and set them aside. Press the "Sauté" button and simmer the poaching liquid until reduced by half, about 10 minutes.
- Serve the peaches in individual bowls drizzled with the sauce. Bon appétit!

416. Mom's Orange Flan
(Ready in about 25 minutes | Servings 4)

There are so many recipes for a homemade flan out there, but you only need this old-fashioned recipe from a family cookbook.
Per serving: *343 Calories; 17.8g Fat; 28.2g Carbs; 16.9g Protein; 27.4g Sugars*

Ingredients

2/3 cup muscovado sugar
3 tablespoons water
5 eggs, whisked
15 ounces condensed milk, sweetened
10 ounces evaporated milk
1/4 cup orange juice
1/2 teaspoon pure vanilla extract

Directions

- Place sugar and water in a microwave-safe dish; microwave approximately 3 minutes.
- Now, pour the caramel into four ramekins.
- Then, whisk the eggs with milk, orange juice, and vanilla. Pour the egg mixture into ramekins.
- Add 1 ½ cups of water and a metal rack to the Instant Pot. Now, lover your ramekins onto the rack.
- Secure the lid. Choose the "Manual" and cook at High pressure for 9 minutes. Once cooking is complete, use a natural pressure release for 10 minutes; carefully remove the lid.
- Refrigerate overnight and enjoy!

417. Bundt Cake with Sour Cream Glaze
(Ready in about 35 minutes | Servings 10)

You can store leftover cake at room temperature for several days. It also freezes well.
Per serving: *200 Calories; 10.9g Fat; 18.7g Carbs; 6.9g Protein; 9.2g Sugars*

Ingredients

Nonstick cooking spray
4 eggs, beaten
1/3 cup sugar
1 tablespoon coconut oil, softened
1/2 cup full-fat cream cheese
1 cup sour cream
1 teaspoon vanilla extract
1/2 teaspoon cardamom

3/4 cup whole wheat flour
A pinch of coarse salt
1 teaspoon baking soda
1 teaspoon baking powder
Sour Cream Glaze:
1/2 cup sour cream
1/2 cup powdered sugar
1 teaspoon vanilla extract

Directions

- Prepare your Instant Pot by adding 1 cup of water and a metal rack to its bottom. Spritz a bundt pan with a nonstick cooking spray.
- Then, whisk the eggs and sugar until creamy and pale. Add the coconut oil, cheese, sour cream, vanilla, and cardamom; beat until everything is well incorporated.
- In another mixing bowl, thoroughly combine the flour with salt, baking soda, and baking powder. Add the flour mixture to the egg mixture. Spoon the batter into the prepared pan. Lower the pan onto the rack.
- Secure the lid. Choose the "Bean/Chili" and cook at High pressure for 25 minutes. Once cooking is complete, use a natural pressure release; carefully remove the lid.
- Meanwhile, make the glaze by whisking sour cream, powdered sugar, and vanilla. Brush the cake with glaze and place in your refrigerator until ready to serve.

418. Chocolate Pots de Crème
(Ready in about 15 minutes | Servings 4)

A perfect dessert for any occasion, festive or not. Add cocoa powder, cream and nutmeg to get a classic mousse flavor.
Per serving: *299 Calories; 17.2g Fat; 24.8g Carbs; 14.8g Protein; 18.6g Sugars*

Ingredients

1/2 cup granulated sugar
1/3 cup cocoa powder
2 tablespoons carob powder
2/3 cup whipping cream
1 cup coconut milk
1 teaspoon vanilla
1/2 teaspoon hazelnut extract
5 eggs, well-beaten
1/4 teaspoon nutmeg, preferably freshly grated
A pinch of coarse salt

Directions

- In a sauté pan, melt the sugar, cocoa powder, carob powder, cream, milk, vanilla, and hazelnut extract over medium-low heat; whisk until everything is well incorporated and melted.
- Fold in the eggs; whisk to combine well. Add nutmeg and salt. Divide the mixture among jars.
- Place 1 cup of water and a metal trivet in the Instant Pot.
- Secure the lid. Choose the "Manual" and cook at High pressure for 7 minutes. Once cooking is complete, use a quick pressure release; carefully remove the lid.
- Place in your refrigerate for about 4 hours and serve chilled. Enjoy!

419. Blood Orange Upside-Down Cake
(Ready in about 45 minutes | Servings 8)

This totally yummy cake is loaded with blood oranges, butter, and spices. It will definitely impress your guests.
Per serving: *354 Calories; 13.1g Fat; 55.4g Carbs; 4.3g Protein; 37.1g Sugars*

Ingredients

Nonstick cooking spray
3 teaspoons granulated sugar
3 blood oranges, peeled and cut into slices
1 egg plus 1 egg yolk, beaten
1 cup sugar
1 stick butter, at room temperature
1/3 cup plain 2% yogurt

1/2 teaspoon ground cloves
1/4 teaspoon ground cardamom
1/4 teaspoon ginger flavoring
2 tablespoons fresh orange juice
1 1/3 cups cake flour
1 ½ teaspoons baking powder
A pinch of table salt

Directions

- Spritz a baking pan with a nonstick cooking spray. Now, arrange the orange slices in the bottom your pan.
- In a mixing bowl, whisk the eggs until they are frothy. Now, add the sugar and mix well. Stir in the butter and mix again.
- After that, add yogurt, cloves, cardamom, ginger flavoring, and fresh orange juice. In another mixing bowl, thoroughly combine the flour with baking powder and salt.
- Slowly and gradually, stir the flour mixture into the wet egg mixture; pour the batter on top of the orange slices.
- Add 1 cup of water and a metal trivet to the bottom of your Instant Pot. Lower the baking pan onto the trivet.
- Secure the lid. Choose the "Soup" mode and cook for 40 minutes at High pressure. Once cooking is complete, use a quick release; remove the lid carefully.
- Place a platter on the cake and invert the baking pan, lifting it to reveal the oranges on top. Bon appétit!

---

420. Decadent Bourbon Bread Pudding
(Ready in about 2 hours 45 minutes | Servings 8)

A simple bread pudding is arguably the most convenient choice when it comes to the Instant Pot deserts. This recipe calls for Brioche but feel free to use Challah or Pullman loaf.
Per serving: *352 Calories; 13.2g Fat; 43.9g Carbs; 14.2g Protein; 10.1g Sugars*

Ingredients

1 loaf Brioche bread, cubed
2 ½ cups milk
4 eggs, beaten
1 teaspoon vanilla extract
1/2 teaspoon coconut extract
1/4 cup coconut oil, melted
4 tablespoons agave syrup
1/4 cup bourbon whiskey

Directions

- Place the bread in a baking dish that is previously greased with a nonstick cooking spray.
- Then, in another bowl, thoroughly combine the milk, eggs, vanilla, coconut extract, coconut oil, agave syrup, and bourbon whiskey.
- Pour the milk/bourbon mixture over the bread; press with a wide spatula to soak and place in the refrigerator for 1 to 2 hours.
- Add 1 ½ cups of water and a metal trivet to your Instant Pot. Lower the baking dish onto the trivet.
- Secure the lid. Choose the "Soup" mode and cook for 40 minutes at High pressure. Once cooking is complete, use a quick release; remove the lid carefully. Serve warm or at room temperature.

421. Country-Style Fruit Compote
(Ready in about 15 minutes | Servings 5)

Using fresh fruits and freshly squeezed fruit juices as the base, this old-fashioned yet elegant fruit compote is easy to pull off in your Instant Pot.
Per serving: *164 Calories; 0.3g Fat; 42.9g Carbs; 1.4g Protein; 16.9g Sugars*

Ingredients

1/2 pound peaches, pitted and halved
1/2 pound pears, cored and quartered
1 cup prunes, pitted
1/4 cup granulated sugar
1 tablespoon fresh apple juice
1 tablespoon fresh lemon juice
1/2 teaspoon apple pie spice mix
1 cinnamon stick
1 teaspoon whole cloves
1 large vanilla bean pod, split open lengthwise

Directions

- Add all of the above ingredients to your Instant Pot. Secure the lid.
- Choose the "Manual" mode and cook under High Pressure for 3 minutes. Once cooking is complete, use a natural release for 10 minutes; remove the lid carefully.
- Serve warm or at room temperature. Enjoy!

---

422. Peanut Butter and Cheese Fudge
(Ready in about 10 minutes + chilling time | Servings 8)

A giant pan of a sweet, gooey goodness! Cocoa butter, cream cheese, and coconut oil is a winning combination.
Per serving: *415 Calories; 36.3g Fat; 21.9g Carbs; 3.4g Protein; 20.8g Sugars*

Ingredients

8 ounces cream cheese, at room temperature
4 ounces coconut cream, at room temperature
1/2 cup coconut oil
1/2 cup cocoa butter
1/2 cup peanut butter
1 teaspoon pure vanilla extract
1 teaspoon pure almond extract
2/3 cup almond flour
1/2 cup agave syrup

Directions

- Press the "Sauté" button to preheat your Instant Pot. Add the cheese, sour cream, coconut oil, cocoa butter, and peanut butter to your Instant Pot.
- Let it simmer until it is melted and warmed through.
- Add vanilla, almond extract, almond flour, and agave syrup; continue to stir until everything is well combined.
- Then, spoon the mixture into a cookie sheet lined with a piece of foil. Place in your refrigerator; refrigerate at least for 2 hours.
- Cut into squares and serve.

423. Hazelnut Millet Pudding
(Ready in about 15 minutes | Servings 4)

A creamy and yummy millet pudding is way easier to prepare in a pressure cooker than you might imagine.
Per serving: *320 Calories; 3.3g Fat; 63.1g Carbs; 9.3g Protein; 6.7g Sugars*

Ingredients

1 ½ cups millet
1 ½ cups water
1 (14-ounce) can coconut milk
1/2 cup Medjool dates, finely chopped
1/2 teaspoon ground cardamom
1/2 teaspoon ground cinnamon

Directions

- Add all of the above ingredients to your Instant Pot; stir to combine well.
- Secure the lid. Choose the "Manual" mode and cook for 1 minute at High pressure. Once cooking is complete, use a natural pressure release for 10 minutes; carefully remove the lid.
- Serve warm or at room temperature.

---

424. Apples with Wine-Cranberry Sauce
(Ready in about 20 minutes | Servings 4)

This Instant Pot dessert makes itself! Add a mint, coconut extract or any other type of berries to customize the flavor.
Per serving: *184 Calories; 0.2g Fat; 47.5g Carbs; 0.6g Protein; 42.2g Sugars*

Ingredients

1 pound Bramley apples cored
1/3 cup cranberries, dried
1/2 cup red wine
1/2 cup orange juice
1 teaspoon grated orange peel
1/2 cup granulated sugar
1/3 teaspoon ground star anise
1/3 teaspoon cinnamon

Directions

- Place the cored apples in your Instant Pot. Now, add the remaining ingredients.
- Secure the lid. Choose the "Manual" mode and cook for 3 minutes under High pressure. Once cooking is complete, use a natural pressure release for 10 minutes; carefully remove the lid.
- Serve with whipped cream if desired. Bon appétit!

425. Blackberry Pudding Cake
(Ready in about 45 minutes | Servings 8)

You no longer need to preheat an entire oven to bake a pudding cake – you just need an Instant Pot! Enjoy this easy and delicious ooey gooey pudding cake.

Per serving: *164 Calories; 0.3g Fat; 42.9g Carbs; 1.4g Protein; 16.9g Sugars*

Ingredients

Nonstick cooking spray
3/4 cup all-purpose flour
1/2 teaspoon baking soda
1 teaspoon baking powder
A pinch of grated nutmeg
A pinch of salt
1 stick butter, cold

1/4 cup vanilla cookies, crumbled
1/3 cup brown sugar
2 eggs, whisked
1/2 cup almond milk
2 cups blackberries
4 dollops of vanilla ice cream, to serve

Directions

- Spritz a baking pan with a nonstick cooking spray.
- In a mixing bowl, thoroughly combine the flour, baking soda, baking powder, nutmeg, and salt.
- Cut in the butter using two knives; now, add crumbled cookies and sugar; mix until everything is combined well. Add the eggs and almond milk; fold in the blackberries.
- Finally, scrape the mixture into the prepared baking pan. Cover with a sheet of foil; make sure that foil fits tightly around sides and under the bottom of your baking pan.
- Add water and a metal trivet to the Instant Pot. Lower the baking pan onto the trivet and secure the lid.
- Select the "Manual" mode. Bake for 30 minutes at High pressure.
- Once cooking is complete, use a quick release; remove the lid carefully. Remove the baking pan from the Instant Pot using rack handles. Remove foil and allow the cake to cool approximately 10 minutes.
- Serve on individual plates, garnished with a dollop of vanilla ice cream.

426. Irish Crème Brûlée
(Ready in about 15 minutes + chilling time | Servings 4)

This classy dessert takes only 10 to 15 minutes to prepare in the Instant Pot. Take your dinner parties to the next level!

Per serving: *334 Calories; 25.7g Fat; 20.7g Carbs; 5.6g Protein; 19.9g Sugars*

Ingredients

1 ½ cups double cream
4 egg yolks
1/3 cup Irish cream liqueur
1 teaspoon pure vanilla extract
8 tablespoons golden caster sugar
1/8 teaspoon kosher salt
1/8 teaspoon grated nutmeg

Directions

- Start by adding 1 cup of water and a metal rack to your Instant Pot.
- Then, microwave double cream until thoroughly warmed.
- In a mixing bowl, whisk egg yolks, Irish cream liqueur, vanilla extract, 4 tablespoons caster sugar, salt, and nutmeg.
- Gradually add warm cream, stirring continuously. Spoon the mixture into four ramekins; cover with foil; lower onto the rack.
- Secure the lid. Choose the "Manual" mode and cook for 6 minutes under High pressure. Once cooking is complete, use a natural pressure release; carefully remove the lid.
- Place in your refrigerator for 4 to 5 hours to set. To serve, top each cup with a tablespoon of sugar; use a kitchen torch to melt the sugar and form a caramelized topping. Serve right away.

427. Delicious Stewed Fruit
(Ready in about 15 minutes | Servings 6)

Looking for a light dessert to kick off your party dinner? We've got an amazing recipe that you will make in minutes. Place in your refrigerator until ready to serve and keep for up to 2 days.

Per serving: *193 Calories; 0.4g Fat; 48.8g Carbs; 1.1g Protein; 44.5g Sugars*

Ingredients

1/2 pound blueberries
1/2 pound blackberries
1/2 pound mango, pitted and diced
1 cup Muscovado sugar
1 cinnamon stick
1 vanilla pod
1 teaspoon whole cloves
2 tablespoons orange juice
1 teaspoon orange zest

Directions

- Add all of the above ingredients to your Instant Pot.
- Secure the lid. Choose the "Manual" mode and cook for 7 minutes under High pressure. Once cooking is complete, use a natural pressure release; carefully remove the lid.
- Transfer to a nice serving bowl; serve with frozen yogurt or shortcake. Bon appétit!

428. Pumpkin Cake with Cream Cheese Frosting
(Ready in about 25 minutes + chilling time | Servings 10)

Inspired by pumpkin purée, you can come up with a dessert that literally melts in your mouth! When you are just not in the mood to cook, it's good to have a can of pumpkin purée on hand.

Per serving: *357 Calories; 15.2g Fat; 52.6g Carbs; 4.1g Protein; 34.9g Sugars*

Ingredients

Batter:
2 cups pumpkin purée
3/4 cup applesauce
1 cup granulated sugar
1 tablespoon molasses
1/2 teaspoon crystallized ginger
1/8 teaspoon salt
1/8 teaspoon grated nutmeg
1/4 teaspoon cardamom, ground

1/2 teaspoon cinnamon, ground
1 teaspoon vanilla extract
1 ½ cups all-purpose flour
1 teaspoon baking powder
Cream Cheese Frosting:
7 ounces cream cheese, at room temperature
1 stick butter, at room temperature
2 cups powdered sugar

Directions

- In a mixing bowl, combine all dry ingredients for the batter. Then, in a separate mixing bowl, thoroughly combine all wet ingredients.
- Then, add wet mixture to the dry mixture; pour the batter into a cake pan that is previously greased with melted butter.
- Add 1 ½ cups of water and metal trivet to the Instant Pot. Lower the cake pan onto the trivet.
- Secure the lid. Choose the "Porridge" mode and cook for 20 minutes under High pressure. Once cooking is complete, use a natural pressure release; carefully remove the lid.
- Meanwhile, make the frosting. Beat the cream cheese and butter with an electric mixer on high speed. Add powdered sugar.
- Continue to beat until the frosting has thickened. Spread the frosting on the cooled cake. Refrigerate until ready to serve. Bon appétit!

429. Pear and Plum Crumble Delight
(Ready in about 25 minutes | Servings 6)

This fruity dessert is perfect for fall and winter, but you can also make it with peaches in the summer. To serve, drizzle caramel syrup over each serving.
Per serving: *227 Calories; 8.1g Fat; 42.8g Carbs; 3.4g Protein; 28.1g Sugars*

Ingredients

2 pears, cored, peeled and sliced
10 plums, pitted and halved
3/4 cup rolled oats
3 tablespoons flour
1/4 cup sugar
2 tablespoons maple syrup
2 tablespoons caramel syrup, plus more for topping
2 tablespoons fresh orange juice
1 teaspoon ground cinnamon
A pinch of salt
3 tablespoons coconut oil

Directions

- Arrange pears and plums in the bottom of a lightly buttered baking pan.
- In a mixing bowl, thoroughly combine rolled oats, flour, sugar, maple syrup, caramel syrup, orange juice, cinnamon, salt and coconut oil.
- Top the prepared pears and plums with the oat layer. Now, distribute the oat layer evenly using a spatula.
- Add 1 cup of water and a metal trivet to your Instant Pot. Lower the baking pan onto the trivet. Cover with a sheet of foil.
- Secure the lid. Select the "Manual" mode and cook at High pressure for 10 minutes. Once cooking is complete, use a natural release for 10 minutes; carefully remove the lid.
- Remove the foil and let your crumble cool to room temperature before serving. Bon appétit!

---

430. Banana Bread in a Jar
(Ready in about 1 hour 5 minutes| Servings 8)

An easy to follow banana bread recipe! You have almost zero chance of overcooking or creating a dry banana bread in the Instant Pot.
Per serving: *453 Calories; 17.1g Fat; 69.4g Carbs; 7.9g Protein; 26.3g Sugars*

Ingredients

1 stick butter, at room temperature
3/4 cup granulated sugar
3 eggs, whisked
1/2 pound overripe bananas, mashed
1/4 cup sour cream
2 ½ cups all-purpose flour

1 teaspoon baking soda
A pinch of salt
A pinch of nutmeg, preferably freshly grated
1/2 teaspoon pumpkin pie spice
1/2 cup semi-sweet chocolate chips

Directions

- Start by adding 1 ½ cups of water and a metal trivet to the base of your Instant Pot.
- In a mixing bowl, thoroughly combine butter, sugar, eggs, banana, and sour cream. Then, in another mixing bowl, combine the flour, baking soda, salt, nutmeg, and pumpkin pie spice.
- Then, add butter mixture to the flour mixture; mix to combine well. Fold in the chocolate chips. Divide the batter between mason jars. Lower the jars onto the trivet.
- Secure the lid. Choose the "Multigrain" mode and cook for 55 minutes under High pressure. Once cooking is complete, use a natural pressure release; carefully remove the lid.
- Let it sit for 5 to 10 minutes before serving. Bon appétit!

431. Easy Cherry Cobbler
(Ready in about 20 minutes | Servings 6)

This cherry cobbler can be made quite easily in the Instant Pot. You can use a store-bought cake mix or make your own. It's up to you.
Per serving: *499 Calories; 16.2g Fat; 82g Carbs; 4.5g Protein; 24.3g Sugars*

Ingredients

30 ounces cherry pie filling
1 box yellow cake mix
1/2 cup coconut butter, melted
1/2 teaspoon ground cinnamon
1/2 teaspoon ground cardamom
1/4 teaspoon grated nutmeg

Directions

- Add 1 cup of water and metal rack to the Instant Pot. Place cherry pie filling in a pan.
- Mix the remaining ingredients; spread the batter over the cherry pie filling evenly.
- Secure the lid. Choose the "Manual" mode and cook for 10 minutes under High pressure. Once cooking is complete, use a natural pressure release; carefully remove the lid.
- Serve with whipped topping. Enjoy!

432. Summer Pineapple Cake
(Ready in about 30 minutes | Servings 8)

Make this decadent fruit cake and delight your senses! Besides being incredibly moist and tasty, it turns great every time.
Per serving: *258 Calories; 14.4g Fat; 33.2g Carbs; 1.8g Protein; 26.5g Sugars*

Ingredients

1 pound pineapple, sliced
1 tablespoon orange juice
1/2 cup cassava flour
1/2 cup almond flour
1 teaspoon baking powder
1/2 teaspoon baking soda
1/4 teaspoon salt
1/2 cup margarine, melted
1/2 cup honey
1/2 teaspoon vanilla extract
1/2 teaspoon coconut extract
1 tablespoon gelatin powder

Directions

- Add 1 ½ cups of water and a metal rack to the Instant Pot. Cover the bottom of your cake pan with a parchment paper.
- Then, spread pineapple slices evenly in the bottom of the cake pan; drizzle with orange juice.
- In a mixing bowl, thoroughly combine the flour, baking powder, baking soda, and salt.
- In another bowl, combine the margarine, honey, vanilla, and coconut extract; add gelatin powder and whisk until well mixed.
- Add the honey mixture to the flour mixture; mix until you've formed a ball of dough. Flatten your dough; place on the pineapple layer.
- Cover the pan with foil, creating a foil sling.
- Secure the lid. Choose the "Bean/Chili" mode and cook for 25 minutes under High pressure. Once cooking is complete, use a natural pressure release; carefully remove the lid.
- Lastly, turn the pan upside down and unmold it on a serving platter. Enjoy!

433. Favorite Almond Cheesecake
(Ready in about 45 minutes | Servings 8)

Classic desserts deserve a comeback in every kitchen. This stunning cheesecake recipe features creamy and silky Neufchâtel cheese, super-healthy almonds and versatile graham cracker crumbs.

Per serving: *445 Calories; 33.2g Fat; 15.3g Carbs; 21.2g Protein; 7.4g Sugars*

Ingredients

24 ounces Neufchâtel cheese
1 cup sour cream
5 eggs
1/4 cup flour
1/2 teaspoon pure vanilla extract
1/2 teaspoon pure almond extract
1 ½ cups graham cracker crumbs
1/2 cup almonds, roughly chopped
1/2 stick butter, melted

Directions

- In a mixing bowl, beat Neufchâtel cheese with sour cream. Now, fold in eggs, one at a time.
- Stir in the flour, vanilla extract, and almond extract; mix to combine well.
- In a separate mixing bowl, thoroughly combine graham cracker crumbs, almonds, and butter. Press this crust mixture into a baking pan.
- Pour the egg/cheese mixture into the pan. Cover with a sheet of foil; make sure that foil fits tightly around sides and under the bottom of your baking pan.
- Add 1 cup of water and a metal trivet to your Instant Pot. Secure the lid. Choose the "Bean/Chili" mode and bake for 40 minutes at High pressure.
- Once cooking is complete, use a quick release; carefully remove the lid. Allow your cheesecake to cool completely before serving. Bon appétit!

---

434. Fancy Buckwheat Pudding with Figs
(Ready in about 15 minutes | Servings 4)

A creamy buckwheat pudding is combined with milk, honey, and dried figs; then, it is pressure cooked and served with a splash of milk. Lovely!

Per serving: *320 Calories; 7.5g Fat; 57.7g Carbs; 9.5g Protein; 43.2g Sugars*

Ingredients

1 ½ cups buckwheat
3 ½ cups milk
1/2 cup dried figs, chopped
1/3 cup honey
1/2 teaspoon ground cinnamon
1 teaspoon pure vanilla extract
1/2 teaspoon pure almond extract

Directions

- Add all of the above ingredients to your Instant Pot.
- Secure the lid. Choose the "Multigrain" mode and cook for 10 minutes under High pressure. Once cooking is complete, use a natural pressure release; carefully remove the lid.
- Serve topped with fresh fruits, nuts or whipped topping. Bon appétit!

435. Cardamom and Banana Tapioca Pudding
(Ready in about 20 minutes | Servings 4)

No more excuses for not making desserts! This dessert is light, creamy and irresistible and it is a cinch to make in the Instant Pot.
Per serving: *449 Calories; 8.5g Fat; 86.1g Carbs; 9.8g Protein; 45.7g Sugars*

Ingredients

1 cup small pearl tapioca, soaked and well-rinsed
1 teaspoon cardamom
4 cups coconut milk
1 teaspoon vanilla extract
1/2 cup coconut sugar
2 bananas, peeled and sliced
4 peaches, diced

Directions

- Start by adding 1½ cups of water and a metal trivet to the base of your Instant Pot.
- Mix tapioca, cardamom, coconut milk, vanilla, and sugar in a baking dish. Lower the dish onto the trivet.
- Secure the lid. Choose the "Multigrain" mode and cook for 10 minutes under High pressure. Once cooking is complete, use a quick pressure release; carefully remove the lid.
- Add banana and peaches; gently stir to combine and serve.

---

436. Chocolate, Raisin and Coconut Cake
(Ready in about 45 minutes | Servings 8)

With an amazing combo of raisins, chocolate, and coconut milk, this creamy cheesecake might become your favorite dessert. To make a homemade and inexpensive coconut milk, just mix shredded coconut and hot water in a blender; squeeze out the coconut milk.
Per serving: *575 Calories; 35.6g Fat; 54.1g Carbs; 11.1g Protein; 33.1g Sugars*

Ingredients

10 ounces cream cheese
7 ounces sour cheese
1 cup granulated sugar
3 eggs
2 tablespoons cornstarch
1 teaspoon vanilla extract
14 ounces chocolate cookies, crumbled

1/3 cup raisins, soaked for 15 minutes
3 teaspoons coconut oil
Topping:
4 ounces dark chocolate, melted
1 cup sweetened coconut milk
1/2 cup coconut, shredded

Directions

- In a mixing bowl, thoroughly combine cream cheese, sour cream, and sugar. Add eggs and mix again; add cornstarch and vanilla.
- In another bowl, thoroughly combine cookies, raisins, and coconut oil. Press the crust into the bottom of a cake pan.
- Spread the cheesecake mixture over the crust.
- Add 1 ½ cups of water and metal trivet to the Instant Pot. Lower the pan onto the trivet. Cover with a foil, making a foil sling.
- Secure the lid. Choose "Multigrain" mode and cook for 40 minutes under High pressure. Once cooking is complete, use a quick pressure release; carefully remove the lid.
- Meanwhile, make the topping by vigorously whisking all ingredients. Spread the topping over the cake.
- Place in your refrigerator to cool completely. Enjoy!

437. Tropical Bread Pudding
(Ready in about 25 minutes | Servings 8)

This dessert will bring the tropical flavors into your kitchen! Serve in individual bowls, drizzled with some extra honey.
Per serving: *333 Calories; 7.2g Fat; 53.7g Carbs; 13.4g Protein; 16.5g Sugars*

Ingredients

Nonstick cooking spray
3 eggs, beaten
3/4 cup almond milk
1/4 cup honey
1 teaspoon pure vanilla extract
1/2 teaspoon pure coconut extract
1/2 teaspoon ground cinnamon
1/4 teaspoon grated nutmeg
1/2 teaspoon ground cardamom
1 tablespoon finely grated orange zest
A pinch of salt
1 loaf day-old challah bread, cubed into 1-inch pieces
1/2 cup sweetened shredded coconut
4 tablespoons crushed pineapple, drained

Directions

- Spritz the sides and bottom of a baking pan with a nonstick cooking spray.
- In a mixing bowl, whisk eggs with almond milk, honey, vanilla, coconut extract, cinnamon, cardamom, orange zest, and salt.
- Stir in bread pieces along with shredded coconut and crushed pineapple; press down into pan slightly.
- Cover the baking pan with a sheet of foil and make a foil sling. Add 1 cup of water and the metal trivet to the Instant Pot.
- Lower the baking pan onto the trivet. Secure the lid. Choose the "Manual" mode, High pressure, and 20 minutes. Once cooking is complete, use a quick release; carefully remove the lid.
- Serve at room temperature. Bon appétit!

---

438. Almond Chocolate Brownie
(Ready in about 25 minutes | Servings 8)

Conquer your next family gathering with this lavish dessert. Besides being super yummy, it is also easy to make in the Instant Pot.
Per serving: *265 Calories; 16.4g Fat; 24.9g Carbs; 6.5g Protein; 12.4g Sugars*

Ingredients

3 ounces chocolate, chopped into small chunks
1/3 cup coconut oil
1/2 cup brown sugar
3 eggs, well beaten
1/2 teaspoon almond extract
1 teaspoon vanilla extract

2/3 cup all-purpose flour
1 teaspoon baking powder
A pinch of salt
3 tablespoons cocoa powder
1 tablespoon carob powder
1/2 cup almonds, chopped

Directions

- Microwave the chocolate and coconut oil for until melted.
- In a bowl, thoroughly combine sugar, eggs, almond, vanilla extract, and melted chocolate mixture.
- Add flour, baking powder, salt, cocoa powder, and carob powder; mix well to combine. Afterwards, fold in the almonds. Transfer the mixture to a lightly greased baking pan.
- Add 1 cup of water and a metal rack to the Instant Pot. Lower the baking pan onto the rack.
- Secure the lid. Choose the "Manual" mode and cook for 18 minutes under High pressure. Once cooking is complete, use a quick pressure release; carefully remove the lid. Serve well chilled and enjoy!

439. Lava Dulce de Leche Cake
(Ready in about 20 minutes | Servings 6)

Lava molten cake is one of the most popular desserts in the world. Now, you can make it in your Instant Pot. Awesome!
Per serving: *301 Calories; 15.4g Fat; 32.5g Carbs; 7.7g Protein; 26.1g Sugars*

Ingredients

A nonstick cooking spray
1 tablespoon granulated sugar
1/4 cup butter, melted
3 eggs, beaten
1 teaspoon vanilla extract
1/2 teaspoon pure almond extract
1/4 teaspoon star anise, ground
1/4 teaspoon ground cinnamon
1/3 cup powdered sugar
3/4 cup canned dulce de leche
4 tablespoons all-purpose flour
1/8 teaspoon kosher salt

Directions

- Spritz a cake pan with a nonstick cooking spray. Then, sprinkle the bottom of your pan with granulated sugar.
- Beat the butter with eggs, vanilla, almond extract, star anise, and ground cinnamon. Add powdered sugar, canned dulce de leche, flour, and salt. Mix until a thick batter is achieved.
- Scrape the batter into the prepared cake pan.
- Place 1 cup of water and metal trivet in the Instant Pot. Place the cake pan on the trivet.
- Secure the lid. Choose the "Manual" mode and cook for 10 minutes under High pressure. Once cooking is complete, use a quick pressure release; carefully remove the lid. Serve hot with ice cream.

---

440. Crumble-Stuffed Nectarines
(Ready in about 15 minutes | Servings 4)

Here is a new twist to an old classic – bright and sweet nectarine with crisp and aromatic filling, topped with chilled vanilla yogurt. Use firm-ripe nectarines for this recipe.
Per serving: *463 Calories; 12.8g Fat; 87.1g Carbs; 4.3g Protein; 40.6g Sugars*

Ingredients

1/4 cup tapioca starch
5 tablespoons honey
3 tablespoons coconut oil
1 teaspoon ground cinnamon
1/2 teaspoon ground cardamom
1/8 teaspoon nutmeg, preferably freshly grated
1/8 teaspoon salt
2 gingersnaps, crushed
1/2 teaspoon pure vanilla extract
1/2 teaspoon pure coconut extract
4 large-sized nectarines, halved and pitted
1/2 cup low-fat vanilla yogurt

Directions

- Start by adding 1 cup of water and a metal trivet to the bottom of your Instant Pot.
- Mix tapioca, honey, coconut oil, cinnamon, cardamom, nutmeg, salt, gingersnaps, vanilla, and coconut extract in a bowl.
- Divide this mixture among nectarine halves. Place the nectarines on the metal trivet.
- Secure the lid. Choose the "Manual" mode and cook for 4 minutes under High pressure. Once cooking is complete, use a natural pressure release; carefully remove the lid.
- Serve topped with vanilla yogurt. Enjoy!

441. Lemon Curd Mousse
(Ready in about 35 minutes | Servings 4)

You will love the combination of lemon and blueberries. Anyway, the curd is one of the most popular dessert recipes for the Instant Pot.
Per serving: *445 Calories; 30.1g Fat; 40.6g Carbs; 5.4g Protein; 36.7g Sugars*

Ingredients

1 stick butter, softened
1 ¼ cups sugar
3 eggs
1 large egg yolks
1/2 cup fresh lemon juice
1 tablespoon lemon zest, finely grated
A pinch of salt
2 teaspoons cornstarch
1/4 cup heavy whipping cream
6 tablespoons blueberries
Mint leaves, for garnish

Directions

- Beat the butter and sugar with an electric mixer. Gradually, add the eggs and yolks; mix until pale and smooth.
- Add the lemon juice and lemon zest; add salt and cornstarch; mix to combine well. Pour the mixture into four jars; cover your jars with the lids.
- Add 1 cup of water and a trivet to the Instant Pot. Lower the jars onto the trivet; secure the lid. Select "Manual" mode, High pressure and 15 minutes.
- Once cooking is complete, use a natural release for 15 minutes; carefully remove the lid. Serve well-chilled, garnished with heavy whipping cream, blueberries, and mint leaves. Bon appétit!

442. Apricot and Almond Cupcakes
(Ready in about 30 minutes | Servings 6)

These are the best apricot cupcakes you've ever had! With a gorgeous almond butter frosting, they are perfect for any occasion!
Per serving: *311 Calories; 13.9g Fat; 46.5g Carbs; 4.3g Protein; 44.2g Sugars*

Ingredients

Cupcakes:
1 cup apricots, pitted and chopped
3/4 cup almond flour
1 teaspoon baking powder
A pinch of coarse salt
2 eggs, beaten
1/2 teaspoon vanilla paste

1/2 cup honey
1/4 almond milk
Frosting:
1/3 cup almond butter
1 teaspoon cocoa powder
3 tablespoons honey

Directions

- Thoroughly combine all ingredients for the cupcakes. Spoon the batter into cupcake liners; cover with foil.
- Add 1 cup of water and a metal trivet to the bottom of your Instant Pot. Now, place the cupcake liners on the trivet.
- Secure the lid. Choose the "Bean/Chili" mode and cook for 25 minutes under High pressure. Once cooking is complete, use a natural pressure release; carefully remove the lid.
- Meanwhile, prepare the frosting by mixing all ingredients. Transfer to a plastic bag for piping the frosting on your cupcakes. Bon appétit!

443. Key Lime Mini Cakes
(Ready in about 35 minutes | Servings 6)

Key lime brings amazing citrus flavor to these mini cakes. To serve, top with a grated lime peel. Enjoy!
Per serving: *320 Calories; 20.7g Fat; 29.6g Carbs; 5.9g Protein; 29.2g Sugars*

Ingredients

Cakes:
3 eggs, beaten
3 tablespoons butter, melted
3 tablespoons coconut milk
1 teaspoon vanilla extract
1/2 cup coconut flour
1 teaspoon baking powder

1/2 cup agave syrup
1/4 cup fresh key lime juice
Frosting:
3 ounces cream cheese
3 tablespoons butter, softened
2 tablespoons agave syrup

Directions

- Spritz the bottom and sides of four ramekins with a nonstick cooking spray.
- In a mixing bowl, whisk the eggs with melted butter, coconut milk, vanilla, coconut flour, baking powder, agave syrup, and key lime juice.
- Spoon the batter into greased ramekins and cover them loosely with foil.
- Add 1 cup of water and a metal rack to the bottom of your Instant Pot. Now, lower the ramekins onto the rack.
- Secure the lid. Choose the "Bean/Chili" mode and cook for 25 minutes under High pressure. Once cooking is complete, use a natural pressure release; carefully remove the lid.
- Meanwhile, prepare the frosting by mixing cream cheese and butter with an electric mixer. Add agave syrup and continue mixing until everything is well incorporated.
- Transfer the mixture to a plastic bag for piping the frosting on your cupcakes. Bon appétit!

444. Rum and Raisin Custard
(Ready in about 15 minutes | Servings 4)

Prepare this make-ahead recipe in the Instant Pot and free up some time for the weekend. You can caramelize the top of the custard with sugar and blowtorch if desired.

Ingredients

2 cups milk
3 eggs, beaten
1/2 cup superfine sugar
2 tablespoons molasses
1/2 teaspoon vanilla paste
1/4 cup dark rum
1/4 cup raisins

Directions

- Add milk to a sauté pan that is preheated over a moderate flame; bring to a boil.
- Let it cool to room temperature.
- In a mixing bowl, whisk the eggs, sugar, molasses, and vanilla paste until sugar dissolves.
- Then, slowly and gradually pour milk into the egg mixture, stirring continuously. Mix until smooth and uniform. Finally, add the rum and raisins.
- Spoon the mixture into four ramekins. Cover with a foil.
- Add 1 ½ cups of water and metal trivet to your Instant Pot. Then, lower the ramekins onto the trivet.
- Secure the lid. Choose the "Manual" mode and cook for 9 minutes under High pressure. Once cooking is complete, use a quick pressure release; carefully remove the lid.
- The custard will still wobble slightly but will firm up as it cools. Bon appétit!

445. Almond and Chocolate Delight
(Ready in about 15 minutes | Servings 3)

This is a great base recipe for mini cakes so that you can make it with different spices and flavors.
Per serving: 304 Calories; 18.9g Fat; 23.8g Carbs; 10g Protein; 21.1g Sugars

Ingredients

3 eggs
2 tablespoons butter
3 tablespoons whole milk
3 tablespoons honey
1 teaspoon pure vanilla extract
1/4 teaspoon freshly grated nutmeg
1/4 teaspoon ground cardamom
A pinch of salt
1 cup almond flour
3 chocolate cookies, chunks

Directions

- In a mixing bowl, beat the eggs with butter. Now, add milk and continue mixing until well combined.
- Add the remaining ingredients in the order listed above. Divide the batter among 3 ramekins.
- Add 1 cup of water and a metal trivet to the Instant Pot. Cover ramekins with foil and lower them onto the trivet.
- Secure the lid and select "Manual" mode. Cook at High pressure for 12 minutes. Once cooking is complete, use a quick release; carefully remove the lid.
- Transfer the ramekins to a wire rack and allow them to cool slightly before serving. Enjoy!

---

446. Rich Brownie Fudge
(Ready in about 25 minutes | Servings 6)

It doesn't get more fudgy than these Instant Pot brownies! They have just become even better with an addition of eggs and Greek yogurt. Did you know that chocolate is a powerhouse of antioxidants?
Per serving: 270 Calories; 12.5g Fat; 41.1g Carbs; 6g Protein; 14.2g Sugars

Ingredients

1/2 stick butter, at room temperature
1 egg, beaten
2 tablespoons Greek yogurt
1/2 cup cake flour
1/2 teaspoon baking soda
1/4 cup cocoa powder
1/8 teaspoon salt

1/8 teaspoon nutmeg, freshly grated
1/2 teaspoon ground cinnamon
1 teaspoon vanilla extract
1/4 cup honey
1/4 cup chocolate, cut into chunks

Directions

- Begin by adding 1 ½ cups of water and a metal trivet to the bottom of your Instant Pot.
- Thoroughly combine the butter, egg, Greek yogurt, flour, baking soda, cocoa powder, salt, nutmeg, cinnamon, vanilla, and honey.
- Fold in the chocolate chunks; stir to combine well.
- Scrape the batter into a cake pan and cover with a piece of foil. Place the pan on top of the trivet.
- Secure the lid. Choose "Porridge" mode and cook for 20 minutes under High pressure. Once cooking is complete, use a quick pressure release; carefully remove the lid. Enjoy!

447. Winter Date Pudding
(Ready in about 15 minutes | Servings 3)

This pudding is a must-eat food during the winter season. To make it even fancier, stir some dark chocolate chips through the batter just before cooking.
Per serving: *270 Calories; 12.5g Fat; 41.1g Carbs; 6g Protein; 14.2g Sugars*

Ingredients

2 teaspoons coconut oil, softened
1 ½ cups jasmine rice, rinsed
1 ½ cups water
10 dates, pitted, soaked and chopped
2 eggs, beaten
1 teaspoon pure vanilla extract
1/8 teaspoon pumpkin pie spice

Directions

- Press the "Sauté" button to preheat your Instant Pot. Now, add coconut oil and rice; stir until it is well coated.
- Add the remaining ingredients and stir again.
- Secure the lid. Choose the "Manual" mode and cook for 2 minutes under High pressure. Once cooking is complete, use a natural pressure release for 10 minutes; carefully remove the lid.
- Divide between three dessert bowls and serve with double cream. Enjoy!

---

448. Luscious Butterscotch Pudding
(Ready in about 20 minutes | Servings 4)

Everything gets better with a sweet, bountiful pudding! Just before serving, add a generous amount of cinnamon if desired.
Per serving: *565 Calories; 25.9g Fat; 79.6g Carbs; 6.4g Protein; 51.5g Sugars*

Ingredients

1 stick butter, melted
1/4 cup milk
2 eggs, well-beaten
1/2 teaspoon vanilla essence
1/3 cup sugar
1 cup cake flour
1/2 teaspoon baking powder

1/4 cup freshly squeezed orange juice
4 caramels
Sauce:
1 cup boiling water
2 teaspoons corn flour
1/2 cup golden syrup

Directions

- Melt butter and milk in the microwave. Whisk in the eggs, vanilla, and sugar. After that, stir in the flour, baking powder, and orange juice.
- Lastly, add caramels and stir until everything is well combined and melted.
- Divide between the four jars. Add 1 ½ cups of water and a metal trivet to the bottom of the Instant Pot. Lower the jars onto the trivet.
- To make the sauce, whisk boiling water, corn flour, and golden syrup until everything is well combined. Pour the sauce into each jar.
- Secure the lid. Choose the "Steam" mode and cook for 15 minutes under High pressure. Once cooking is complete, use a natural pressure release; carefully remove the lid. Enjoy!

449. Grandma's Walnut Cake
(Ready in about 55 minutes | Servings 6)

Here is an easy and stress-free way to make a family dessert. The simplest things are often the best! Grandma knows that!
Per serving: *244 Calories; 17.3g Fat; 21.3g Carbs; 2.7g Protein; 18.8g Sugars*

Ingredients

1 ¼ cups coconut flour
1/4 cup walnuts, ground
1 ½ teaspoons baking powder
1 cup sugar
1 teaspoon ground cinnamon
1/2 teaspoon grated nutmeg

1 teaspoon orange zest, finely grated
1/4 teaspoon ground star anise
2 eggs plus 1 egg yolk, whisked
1/2 stick butter, at room temperature
3/4 cup double cream

Directions

- Add 1 ½ cups of water and a steamer rack to your Instant Pot. Spritz the inside of a baking pan with a nonstick cooking spray.
- Thoroughly combine dry ingredients. Then, mix the wet ingredients. Add the wet mixture to the dry flour mixture and mix until everything is well incorporated.
- Scrape the batter mixture into the prepared baking pan. Now, cover the baking pan with a piece of foil, making a foil sling.
- Place the baking pan on the steamer rack and secure the lid.
- Select "Manual" mode. Bake for 35 minutes at High pressure. Once cooking is complete, use a natural release for 15 minutes; carefully remove the lid.
- Just before serving, dust the top of the cake with icing sugar. Lastly cut the cake into wedges and serve. Bon appétit!

---

450. Old-Fashioned Sponge Pudding
(Ready in about 25 minutes | Servings 6)

This old-fashioned pudding cake turns out great every time! What is the best part? Thanks to the Instant Pot, it will be ready in less than 25 minutes!
Per serving: *426 Calories; 26.4g Fat; 39.9g Carbs; 7.3g Protein; 17.3g Sugars*

Ingredients

Nonstick cooking spray
3 tablespoons crumbled butter cookies
1 stick butter, at room temperature
1 cup sugar
1/2 teaspoon pure vanilla extract
1/2 teaspoon pure coconut extract
3 eggs, beaten
1 ¼ cups cake flour
1/4 cup coconut milk

Directions

- Spritz the bottom and sides of a steam bowl with a nonstick cooking spray. Add crumbled butter cookies to the bottom.
- Then, beat the butter, sugar, vanilla, and coconut extract until very creamy; now, add the eggs, one at a time and continue to mix.
- Stir in the flour and milk; mix to combine well. Scrape the batter into the prepared steam bowl.
- Secure the lid. Choose the "Steam" mode and cook for 20 minutes under High pressure. Once cooking is complete, use a natural pressure release; carefully remove the lid. Bon appétit!

OTHER INSTANT POT FAVORITES

451. Lazy Sunday Banana Bread
(Ready in about 1 hour 15 minutes | Servings 8)

You can always swap out pecans for almonds and walnuts, or toss in chocolate chips. Start by making the recipe as written; the next time you can adjust it according to your taste.
Per serving: 485 Calories; 13.3g Fat; 89.3g Carbs; 6.3g Protein; 42.7g Sugars

Ingredients

2 ½ cups cake flour
1 teaspoon baking soda
1/2 teaspoon baking powder
1/8 teaspoon kosher salt
1/4 teaspoon grated nutmeg
1/2 teaspoon ground cinnamon
1 pound ripe bananas, mashed
1 tablespoon fresh lemon juice

1 stick butter, at room temperature
1 cup sugar
1/2 cup maple syrup
2 eggs plus 1 egg yolk, beaten
1/2 teaspoon vanilla paste
1 teaspoon rum extract
1 1/3 cups soy milk
2 tablespoons pecans, ground

Directions

- Add water and a metal trivet to the Instant Pot. Spritz a bread loaf pan with a nonstick cooking spray.
- In a mixing bowl, thoroughly combine cake flour, baking soda, baking powder, salt, nutmeg, and cinnamon.
- In another mixing bowl, mix mashed bananas with fresh lemon juice; reserve.
- Now, cream the butter with sugar and maple syrup using an electric mixer. Fold in the eggs and mix again until smooth and uniform.
- Stir in vanilla, rum extract, soy milk, and ground pecans.
- Then, stir in the dry flour mixture, and combine well. Afterwards, stir in the banana/lemon mixture and mix again.
- Scrape the batter into the prepared pan. Lower the pan onto the trivet and secure the lid.
- Choose the "Manual" mode; bake for 1 hour at High pressure. Once cooking is complete, use a natural release for 15 minutes; carefully remove the lid.
- Transfer the pan to a wire rack to cool before serving and enjoy!

---

452. Caramel Monkey Bread
(Ready in about 25 minutes | Servings 8)

A finger-licking-good sweet bread that is ready in just about 25 minutes! It's hard to believe that a store-bought biscuit dough can make such a flavorful meal.
Per serving: *283 Calories; 9.1g Fat; 49.2g Carbs; 2.5g Protein; 28.9g Sugars*

Ingredients

1 (12-ounce) package biscuit dough, cut in quarters
2/3 cup white sugar
1 teaspoon apple pie spice
1/4 cup coconut oil
1/3 cup brown sugar
A pinch of coarse salt

Directions

- Prepare your Instant Pot by adding 1 cup of water and a metal trivet to its bottom.
- Coat biscuit dough with white sugar evenly. Arrange the biscuit pieces in a fluted tube pan that is previously greased with a nonstick cooking spray.
- In a mixing bowl, thoroughly combine apple pie spice, coconut oil, brown sugar, and salt; microwave for 40 to 50 seconds or until butter is melted.
- Spread this butter sauce over the biscuit pieces. Place the fluted tube pan onto the trivet; cover the top with a foil.
- Secure the lid. Choose the "Manual" mode and cook for 22 minutes under High pressure. Once cooking is complete, use a natural pressure release; carefully remove the lid. Bon appétit!

453. Bacon, Cheese and Veggie Frittata
(Ready in about 25 minutes | Servings 4)

A no-fuss homemade meal for the whole family! Transform a standard frittata into a real masterpiece using your Instant Pot.
Per serving: *429 Calories; 30.5g Fat; 11.3g Carbs; 28.1g Protein; 5.6g Sugars*

Ingredients

6 ounces Canadian bacon, chopped
2 bell peppers, chopped
1 red chili pepper, seeded and chopped
1 carrot, trimmed and chopped
1 yellow onion, peeled and chopped
1/2 cup Kalamata olives, pitted and sliced
5 eggs

1/2 cup double cream
Sea salt and ground pepper, to taste
1/2 teaspoon cayenne pepper
1 teaspoon dried parsley flakes
1/2 teaspoon dried oregano
1 1/3 cup Colby cheese, grated

Directions

- Prepare your Instant Pot by adding 1 ½ cups of water and a metal rack to its bottom.
- Then, add bacon and vegetables to a lightly greased baking pan.
- In a mixing bowl, whisk the eggs with double cream, salt, black pepper, cayenne pepper, parsley, and oregano.
- Pour the egg/cheese mixture over your vegetables in the Instant Pot. Top with grated cheese.
- Secure the lid. Choose the "Manual" mode and cook for 21 minutes under High pressure. Once cooking is complete, use a natural pressure release; carefully remove the lid. Serve warm.

---

454. Classic Capellini with Chicken
(Ready in about 15 minutes | Servings 4)

Here's a great recipe for cozy weeknights. You can cook almost everything in your Instant Pot, even the best pasta dishes.
Per serving: *537 Calories; 33.3g Fat; 26.9g Carbs; 33.3g Protein; 5.3g Sugars*

Ingredients

2 tablespoons olive oil
1 pound chicken breasts, chopped
2 garlic cloves, minced
Seasoned salt and freshly ground black pepper, to taste
1 cup double cream
1/3 cup milk
2 ½ cups vegetable broth
10 ounces capellini
1/2 cup Parmigiano-Reggiano cheese, grated
1 lemon, cut into wedges

Directions

- Press the "Sauté" button to preheat your Instant Pot. Heat the oil until sizzling. Now, sear the chicken until it is delicately browned; reserve.
- Then, add garlic and continue to sauté an additional 30 seconds or until it is fragrant. Add salt, black pepper, cream and milk.
- Bring to a simmer and press the "Cancel" button. Add the broth and pasta.
- Secure the lid. Choose the "Manual" mode and cook for 8 minutes under High pressure. Once cooking is complete, use a natural pressure release; carefully remove the lid.
- Top with Parmigiano-Reggiano cheese and serve immediately with fresh lemon wedges. Enjoy!

455. Two-Cheese and Cauliflower Frittata
(Ready in about 30 minutes | Servings 4)

Two types of cheese, cauliflower and eggs are all cooked together in this amazingly delicious frittata for a savory breakfast.
Per serving: *489 Calories; 41.2g Fat; 10.2g Carbs; 21g Protein; 4.6g Sugars*

Ingredients

1 cup cream cheese, room temperature
5 eggs, beaten
2 tablespoons olive oil
1/2 cup scallions, chopped
1 teaspoon garlic, minced
Sea salt and ground black pepper, to your liking
1/2 teaspoon cayenne pepper
1/4 teaspoon dried dill weed
1 cup Swiss cheese, shredded
1 head cauliflower, cut into florets

Directions

- Add 1 cup of water and the metal trivet to your Instant Pot Spritz a baking pan with a nonstick cooking spray.
- Thoroughly combine cream cheese with eggs and olive oil. Now, add scallions, garlic, salt, black pepper, cayenne pepper, and dill; mix to combine well.
- After that, stir in Swiss cheese and cauliflower. Mix to combine and spoon the mixture into the prepared baking pan.
- Lower the baking pan onto the trivet and secure the lid. Choose "Manual" function, High pressure and 10 minutes.
- Once cooking is complete, use a natural release for 15 minutes; remove the lid carefully. Serve warm and enjoy!

---

456. Cottage Cheese and Crab Dip
(Ready in about 10 minutes | Servings 12)

This Instant Pot recipe is faster than take-out! Who said dinner parties had to be stressful?
Per serving: *128 Calories; 8.3g Fat; 3.7g Carbs; 9.5g Protein; 1.8g Sugars*

Ingredients

1 tablespoon butter, softened
1/2 cup shallots, chopped
2 garlic cloves, minced
2 cups lump crabmeat
1/3 cup tomato paste
Sea salt, to taste
1 teaspoon paprika

1/3 teaspoon freshly ground black pepper
12 ounces cottage cheese, at room temperature
1/2 cup mayonnaise
1/2 cup sour cream
1 handful fresh cilantro, chopped

Directions

- Press the "Sauté" button to preheat your Instant Pot. Melt the butter; once hot, cook the shallots and garlic until they are tender and fragrant.
- Then, stir in the remaining ingredients, except for fresh cilantro.
- Secure the lid. Choose the "Manual" mode and cook for 3 minutes under High pressure. Once cooking is complete, use a quick pressure release; carefully remove the lid.
- Top with fresh cilantro. Serve at room temperature with your favorite dippers. Bon appétit!

457. Italian Pan di Spagna
(Ready in about 55 minutes | Servings 4)

A great way to make pancakes for the whole family! You don't have to slave over a hot stove, just turn the instant Pot on, sit back, and relax.
Per serving: *434 Calories; 9.8g Fat; 74.2g Carbs; 13.6g Protein; 37.9g Sugars*

Ingredients

3 eggs
1 cup milk
1/2 cup water
1 ½ cups white flour
1 teaspoon baking powder
1/2 teaspoon kosher salt
1 teaspoon brown sugar
1 teaspoon grated lemon zest
1/2 cup golden syrup
1/2 cup strawberries, hulled and sliced

Directions

- Whisk the eggs until frothy. Add milk and water; whisk again.
- Then, add flour, baking powder, salt, brown sugar, and lemon zest. Mix until everything is well combined.
- Spritz the bottom and sides of your Instant Pot with a nonstick cooking spray. Scrape the batter into the Instant Pot.
- Secure the lid. Choose the "Multigrain" mode and cook for 50 minutes under High pressure. Once cooking is complete, use a quick pressure release; carefully remove the lid.
- Serve topped with golden syrup and strawberries. Enjoy!

458. "Hot Chocolate" Banana Oatmeal
(Ready in about 15 minutes | Servings 4)

A chocolate dessert for breakfast?! Yes, please! Top your oatmeal with banana and start your day off right!
Per serving: *193 Calories; 6.6g Fat; 37.2g Carbs; 10.3g Protein; 10.8g Sugars*

Ingredients

1 ½ cups steel-cut oats
2 cups chocolate milk
2 cups water
1/3 cup dark chocolate chips
1/2 teaspoon ground cinnamon
1/8 teaspoon salt
1/4 teaspoon crystallized ginger
1/8 teaspoon grated nutmeg
1 large banana, thinly sliced

Directions

- Throw all of the above ingredients, except banana, in your Instant Pot.
- Secure the lid. Choose the "Manual" mode and cook for 5 minutes under High pressure. Once cooking is complete, use a natural pressure release; carefully remove the lid.
- Taste and adjust the sweetness. Serve in individual bowls topped with sliced banana. Bon appétit!

459. Polish Chocolate Nalesniki with Coconut
(Ready in about 50 minutes | Servings 4)

Nalesniki are Polish crepes. Serve with jam, fresh or dried fruits, and other toppings.
Per serving: *302 Calories; 7.4g Fat; 46.5g Carbs; 11.5g Protein; 10g Sugars*

Ingredients

1 ½ cups flour
1 teaspoon baking powder
1 teaspoon baking powder
1 cup coconut milk
2 eggs, whisked
1/4 cup granulated sugar
2 teaspoons cocoa powder
1/4 cup coconut, shredded
A pinch of salt
A pinch of grated nutmeg

Directions

- Mix the ingredients until everything is well incorporated.
- Spritz the inside of your Instant Pot with a nonstick cooking spray.
- Choose the "Meat/Stew" function, High pressure and 45 minutes. Once cooking is complete, use a quick release; carefully remove the lid. Serve warm. Bon appétit!

---

460. Scrambled Eggs with Ricotta and Parsley
(Ready in about 10 minutes | Servings 4)

It's hard to beat scrambled eggs for a fast and easy nutrition-packed breakfast. We added fresh ricotta cheese to make it even better.
Per serving: *205 Calories; 16.1g Fat; 2.7g Carbs; 12.1g Protein; 0.9g Sugars*

Ingredients

2 tablespoons butter, at room temperature
6 whole eggs
Sat and ground black pepper, to taste
1/2 teaspoon paprika
1/2 cup ricotta cheese, crumbled
2 tablespoons fresh parsley leaves, roughly chopped

Directions

- Press the "Sauté" button to preheat the Instant Pot. Melt the butter and add beaten eggs.
- Add the salt, black pepper and paprika; stir to combine well. Scramble the eggs in the Instant Pot using a wide spatula.
- Secure the lid. Choose the "Manual" mode and cook for 5 minutes under High pressure. Once cooking is complete, use a quick pressure release; carefully remove the lid.
- Divide between serving plates; top with fresh chopped parsley and serve warm. Bon appétit!

461. Italian Breakfast Casserole
(Ready in about 30 minutes | Servings 5)

Keep this recipe in your back pocket! For an extra indulgence, serve with a slice of a homemade crusty bread.
Per serving: *549 Calories; 39.9g Fat; 25.8g Carbs; 23.4g Protein; 3.5g Sugars*

Ingredients

1 tablespoon olive oil
4 ounces Italian salami, chopped
1 red bell pepper, seeded and chopped
1 green bell pepper, seeded and chopped
1 Peperoncino, seeded and chopped
2 ½ cups hash browns, frozen
5 eggs

1/3 cup milk
3/4 cup cream cheese, at room temperature
Sea salt and ground black pepper, to taste
1/2 teaspoon dried basil
1/2 teaspoon dried oregano
1/2 teaspoon paprika

Directions

- Press the "Sauté" button to preheat the Instant Pot. Now, heat the oil until sizzling. Cook salami for 2 minutes or until crispy.
- Add peppers and hash browns; stir and continue to cook for a further 3 minutes.
- Spritz the bottom and sides of a casserole dish with a nonstick cooking spray. Scrape the hash brown mixture into the dish.
- In a mixing bowl, thoroughly combine the eggs, milk, cheese, salt, black pepper, basil, oregano, and paprika. Pour the mixture into the casserole dish.
- Add 1 ½ cups of water and a metal rack to the Instant Pot. Lower the casserole dish onto the rack.
- Secure the lid. Choose the "Meat/Stew" mode and cook for 20 minutes under High pressure. Once cooking is complete, use a quick pressure release; carefully remove the lid. Serve warm.

---

462. Turkey, Cheese and Rice Bake
(Ready in about 20 minutes | Servings 5)

A creamy Italian rice is cooked with browned turkey breast and peppers; then, it is topped with mellow Colby cheese. Awesome!
Per serving: *552 Calories; 24.1g Fat; 46.3g Carbs; 36.1g Protein; 1.7g Sugars*

Ingredients

3 teaspoons olive oil
1 pound turkey breast, cut into strips
1/2 cup shallots, thinly sliced
1 teaspoon garlic, minced
Sea salt and freshly ground black pepper, to taste
1/2 teaspoon cayenne pepper
1/2 teaspoon dried oregano
1/2 teaspoon dried basil
1 ½ cups Arborio rice, well-rinsed
2 cups vegetable broth
1 red bell pepper, seeded and sliced
1 green bell pepper, seeded and sliced
1 ½ cups Colby cheese, grated

Directions

- Press the "Sauté" button to preheat your Instant Pot. Heat the oil until sizzling. Now, cook the turkey with shallot and garlic.
- Add seasonings, rice, broth, and peppers. Stir to combine well.
- Secure the lid. Choose the "Manual" mode and cook for 10 minutes under High pressure. Once cooking is complete, use a quick pressure release; carefully remove the lid.
- Top with cheese and seal the lid again; let it sit in the residual heat until everything is heated through. Serve warm and enjoy!

463. Buttery Steamed Sweet Potatoes
(Ready in about 35 minutes | Servings 4)

Sweet potatoes are an excellent source of vitamin B6, vitamin C, vitamin D, potassium, carotenoids, and so on. They can improve bone health and nerve function as well as boost your immune system.
Per serving: *154 Calories; 5.9g Fat; 23.5g Carbs; 2.3g Protein; 7.3g Sugars*

Ingredients

1 pound whole small sweet potatoes, cleaned
1/4 teaspoon salt
1/4 teaspoon freshly grated nutmeg
2 tablespoons light butter

Directions

- Add 1 cup of water and a steamer basket to the Instant Pot. Arrange sweet potatoes in the steamer basket.
- Secure the lid and choose the "Steam" mode. Cook for 10 minutes at High pressure. Once cooking is complete, use a natural release for 20 minutes; remove the lid carefully.
- Toss steamed sweet potatoes with salt, nutmeg, and butter. Eat warm. Bon appétit!

464. Three-Seed Breakfast Porridge
(Ready in about 15 minutes | Servings 4)

Rich and satisfying, this pressure cooked porridge is dairy free, vegan, and extremely healthy, which makes it a great idea for a family breakfast.
Per serving: *379 Calories; 23.7g Fat; 50.6g Carbs; 9.4g Protein; 23.6g Sugars*

Ingredients

1 ½ cups rolled oats
1 ½ cups coconut milk
2 cups water
1/2 teaspoon pure vanilla extract
1/2 teaspoon ground cinnamon
1/4 teaspoon grated nutmeg
1/8 teaspoon kosher salt
1/3 cup agave nectar
1 tablespoon flaxseeds
1 tablespoon sunflower seeds
1 tablespoon pumpkin seeds

Directions

- Add all of the above ingredients to your Instant Pot.
- Secure the lid. Choose the "Manual" mode. Cook for 10 minutes at High pressure. Once cooking is complete, use a natural release; carefully remove the lid.
- Divide between four serving bowls and serve topped with some extra fresh or dried fruits, if desired. Bon appétit!

465. Hard-Boiled Eggs with Toasted Bread
(Ready in about 15 minutes | Servings 6)

It may sound like a cliché but breakfast is really the most important meal of the day. Enjoy your mornings!
Per serving: *227 Calories; 13.5g Fat; 12.3g Carbs; 13.2g Protein; 2.9g Sugars*

Ingredients

6 eggs
6 tablespoons Feta cheese
6 slices toasted bread
Salt, to taste
1/2 teaspoon paprika

Directions

- Place 1 ½ cups of water and a steamer basket in the bottom of the Instant Pot. Add eggs to the steamer basket.
- Secure the lid. Choose the "Manual" mode. Cook for 7 minutes at High pressure. Once cooking is complete, use a quick release; carefully remove the lid.
- Season your eggs with salt and paprika. Spread feta cheese on toasted bread. Serve with eggs and enjoy!

466. Refreshing Breakfast Fruit Salad
(Ready in about 15 minutes | Servings 8)

Save this recipe as a lovely addition to your special brunch. Feel free to experiment with this recipe and add your favorite combo of fruits.
Per serving: *276 Calories; 11.6g Fat; 45g Carbs; 1.2g Protein; 42.2g Sugars*

Ingredients

1/2 cup granulated sugar
1 stick butter, at room temperature
1/4 teaspoon ground nutmeg
1/2 teaspoon ground cinnamon
20 ounces peaches, pitted and sliced
10 ounces canned pineapple
2 cups water
1 cup pineapple juice
1/3 cup dried raisins, chopped
1/3 cup dried figs, chopped

Directions

- Add all of the above ingredients to your Instant Pot.
- Secure the lid. Choose the "Manual" mode. Cook for 8 minutes at High pressure. Once cooking is complete, use a natural release; carefully remove the lid.
- Ladle into individual bowls and serve with yogurt. Bon appétit!

467. Quinoa and Black Bean Salad
(Ready in about 15 minutes | Servings 6)

All-in-one – this salad combines quinoa, black beans, vegetables and condiment into one simple but tasty dish.
Per serving: *191 Calories; 4.4g Fat; 31.4g Carbs; 7.2g Protein; 1.3g Sugars*

Ingredients

1 ½ cups quick cooking quinoa, rinsed
3 cups water
A pinch of grated nutmeg
A pinch of salt
1/2 teaspoon paprika
1 (15-ounce) can black beans, drained
2 bell peppers, deveined and thinly sliced
2 tablespoons scallions, finely chopped
1 teaspoon Dijon mustard
2 tablespoons mayonnaise
1 tablespoon fresh lemon juice
2 tablespoons fresh cilantro, finely chopped

Directions

- Place quinoa, water, nutmeg, salt, and paprika in your Instant Pot.
- Secure the lid and choose the "Manual" mode. Cook for 8 minutes at High pressure. Once cooking is complete, use a quick release; carefully remove the lid.
- Allow your quinoa to cool completely and transfer it to a salad bowl. Then, toss quinoa with black beans, bell peppers, scallions, mustard, mayo, and lemon juice.
- Serve well-chilled and garnished with fresh cilantro. Bon appétit!

---

468. French Toast with Neufchâtel and Blackberries
(Ready in about 25 minutes | Servings 6)

Need more breakfast ideas? This breakfast staple has all the flavors of traditional French toast with none of the hassle.
Per serving: *435 Calories; 28.4g Fat; 35.6g Carbs; 12.2g Protein; 30.9g Sugars*

Ingredients

1 loaf Brioche bread, cubed
3/4 cup fresh blackberries
10 ounces Neufchâtel cheese, at room temperature
1/2 cup honey
3 eggs, beaten

1/2 teaspoon ground cinnamon
1/4 teaspoon grated nutmeg
1/2 cup milk
1/2 cup applesauce
1 stick butter, cold

Directions

- Start by adding 1 cup of water and a metal rack to the bottom of your Instant Pot. Now, spritz the bottom and sides of a baking pan with a nonstick cooking spray.
- Add bread to the prepared pan. Top with fresh blackberries.
- In a mixing bowl, thoroughly combine the cheese, honey, eggs, cinnamon, nutmeg, milk, and applesauce.
- Pour this mixture into the pan, pressing the bread down with a wide spatula. Cut in cold butter. Now, cover the pan with a few paper towels.
- Secure the lid. Choose the "Manual" mode. Cook for 20 minutes at High pressure. Once cooking is complete, use a natural release; carefully remove the lid. Bon appétit!

469. Fancy Twisted Applesauce
(Ready in about 15 minutes | Servings 6)

Forget a store-bought applesauce! This homemade applesauce is so easy to make in the Instant Pot and you won't be able to resist that flavor.
Per serving: *101 Calories; 0.2g Fat; 26.1g Carbs; 0.4g Protein; 20.4g Sugars*

Ingredients

2 pounds cooking apples, peeled, cored and diced
1 ¼ cups water
1/4 cup orange juice
1 vanilla bean, split lengthwise
1 cinnamon stick
3 tablespoons date sugar

Directions

- Add all ingredients to your Instant Pot.
- Secure the lid. Choose the "Manual" mode. Cook for 8 minutes at High pressure. Once cooking is complete, use a quick release; carefully remove the lid
- Next, allow the applesauce to cool completely. Afterwards, transfer it to jars and refrigerate for up to 9 days. Bon appétit!

470. Sweet Risotto with Berry Jam
(Ready in about 35 minutes | Servings 5)

This risotto is cooked to fluffy and creamy perfection in your Instant Pot. You can substitute your favorite jam in place of berry jam.
Per serving: *403 Calories; 10.2g Fat; 74.2g Carbs; 5.2g Protein; 36.4g Sugars*

Ingredients

1 cup white long-grain rice, well-rinsed
1 cup coconut milk
1/2 cup water
1/2 cup coconut cream
1/3 cup honey
A pinch of salt
A pinch of grated nutmeg
1/2 teaspoon pure vanilla essence
1/2 teaspoon cardamom, ground
1/4 teaspoon star anise, ground
1/2 cup berry jam

Directions

- Add rice, milk, water, coconut cream, honey, salt, nutmeg, vanilla, cardamom, and anise to the Instant Pot.
- Secure the lid. Choose the "Porridge" mode. Cook for 20 minutes at High pressure. Once cooking is complete, use a natural release for 10 minutes; carefully remove the lid
- Ladle into individual bowls; top with berry jam and serve immediately.

471. Moong Dal and Green Bean Soup

(Ready in about 45 minutes | Servings 6)

Moong dal, also known as yellow lentils are high in nutrition. They can lower cholesterol levels, improve cardiovascular system and increase your energy. Consequently, if you are looking for a way to balance your diet, consider eating yellow lentils at least once a week.
Per serving: *221 Calories; 4.3g Fat; 34.7g Carbs; 12.8g Protein; 2.1g Sugars*

Ingredients

1 ½ tablespoons olive oil
2 shallots, chopped
2 garlic cloves, minced
1 teaspoon cilantro, ground
1/2 teaspoon ground allspice
1/2 teaspoon smoked paprika
1 teaspoon celery seeds

1/2 teaspoon fennel seeds
1/2 teaspoon ground cumin
1 ½ cups moong dal
7 cups water
Sea salt and ground black pepper, to your liking
2 cups green beans, fresh

Directions

- Press the "Sauté" button to heat up your Instant Pot. Then, heat olive oil and cook the shallots until just tender.
- Now, add garlic and cook 30 to 40 seconds more or until it is aromatic and slightly browned. Stir in all seasonings; cook until aromatic or 2 minutes more, stirring continuously.
- Add the moong dal and water. Secure the lid. Select the "Manual" mode and cook for 17 minutes under High pressure.
- Once cooking is complete, use a natural release for 20 minutes; remove the lid carefully.
- Season with sea salt and black pepper; and green beans and secure the lid again. Select "Manual" mode one more time and cook for 2 minutes under High pressure.
- Once cooking is complete, use a quick release and remove the lid carefully. Serve immediately with garlic croutons. Bon appétit!

---

472. Easy Chocolate Porridge

(Ready in about 15 minutes | Servings 4)

Here's a nutritious and delicious breakfast on the fly! Garnish with some extra dried fruits, nuts or seeds, if desired.
Per serving: *247 Calories; 11.6g Fat; 39.8g Carbs; 10.9g Protein; 14.3g Sugars*

Ingredients

1 ½ cups rolled oats
2 cups water
2 cups almond milk
1 teaspoon carob powder
3 teaspoons cocoa powder
1/2 teaspoon cinnamon, ground
1/4 teaspoon star anise, ground
1/2 teaspoon pure vanilla extract
1/2 cup dark chocolate chips

Directions

- Simply throw all of the above ingredients, except for chocolate chips, into your Instant Pot; stir to combine well.
- Secure the lid. Choose the "Manual" mode. Cook for 10 minutes at High pressure. Once cooking is complete, use a natural release; carefully remove the lid.
- Divide between four serving bowls; serve garnished with dark chocolate chips and enjoy!

473. Breakfast Quinoa with Pears
(Ready in about 20 minutes | Servings 5)

Here's an extravagant and easy breakfast for the whole family! Make sure to use a natural release to prevent the porridge from splattering.
Per serving: *440 Calories; 12.1g Fat; 70.7g Carbs; 13.7g Protein; 21.2g Sugars*

Ingredients

2 cups quinoa
3 cups water
2 cups milk
1/4 cup Turbinado sugar
1 teaspoon vanilla paste
1/2 teaspoon cinnamon, ground
3 pears, cored and sliced
1/2 cup whipped cream

Directions

- Add all ingredients, except for whipped cream, to your Instant Pot.
- Secure the lid. Choose the "Manual" mode. Cook for 10 minutes at High pressure. Once cooking is complete, use a natural release; carefully remove the lid.
- Divide between five serving bowls. Just before serving, top each bowl with whipped cream. Enjoy!

474. Caramelized Onion Quiche with Bacon
(Ready in about 40 minutes | Servings 4)

This quiche cooks to perfection every time in the Instant Pot. It is a great brunch recipe to enjoy on a special day off.
Per serving: *485 Calories; 43.5g Fat; 5.7g Carbs; 18.3g Protein; 4.5g Sugars*

Ingredients

1 tablespoon butter
1 onion, thinly sliced
4 slices bacon, chopped
1 teaspoon garlic, minced
5 eggs
Sea salt and ground black pepper, to taste
1 teaspoon cayenne pepper
1 cup double cream
1/2 cup cream cheese
1/2 cup Monterey-Jack cheese, shredded

Directions

- Press the "Sauté" button to preheat your Instant Pot. Then, melt the butter and cook the onions for 15 minutes or until they are golden brown; reserve.
- Add bacon and garlic and cook an additional 2 to 3 minutes. Transfer the onion and bacon to the baking pan.
- In a mixing bowl, thoroughly combine the eggs, salt, black pepper, cayenne pepper, double cream, cream cheese. Pour this mixture into the pan.
- Secure the lid. Choose the "Porridge" mode. Cook for 20 minutes at High pressure. Once cooking is complete, use a quick release; carefully remove the lid.
- Top with shredded Monterey-Jack cheese; seal the lid and let it sit in the residual heat until thoroughly warmed. Carefully flip onto a serving plate. Bon appétit!

475. Quick and Easy Cashew Porridge
(Ready in about 10 minutes | Servings 4)

A warm and satisfying porridge is a perfect start to your day. Use fresh or dried fruits according to your taste. If you are going vegan, use a coconut oil and maple syrup.
Per serving: *468 Calories; 31.7g Fat; 43.6g Carbs; 9.5g Protein; 26.8g Sugars*

Ingredients

1 cup raw cashews
1 ½ tablespoons raw sunflower seeds
2 tablespoons raw pumpkin seeds
1 cup almonds
1/2 teaspoon ground cinnamon
1/2 teaspoon ground cloves

2 cups water
1/2 stick butter
4 tablespoons honey
2 bananas, peeled and sliced
A few drizzles of lemon juice

Directions

- Pulse cashews, sunflower seeds, pumpkin seeds, and almonds in your food processor until the mixture resembles a coarse meal.
- Transfer the mixture to the Instant Pot. Add cinnamon, cloves, water, butter, and honey. Secure the lid.
- Choose "Manual" mode, High pressure and 5 minutes. Once cooking is complete, use a quick release; carefully remove the lid.
- Divide your porridge among 4 serving bowls and serve topped with bananas. Drizzle banana slices with fresh lemon juice to prevent them from browning. Enjoy!

---

476. Scotch Eggs with a Twist
(Ready in about 20 minutes | Servings 5)

This recipe uses cooked ham, apple & onion stuffing mix, and ground sausage for a surprisingly delicious egg appetizer.
Per serving: *307 Calories; 21.2g Fat; 1.9g Carbs; 26.3g Protein; 0.6g Sugars*

Ingredients

5 eggs
3/4 pound ground sausage
1/4 pound ham, cooked and shredded
1 tablespoon apple & onion stuffing mix
1/2 teaspoon thyme, chopped
1/2 teaspoon rosemary, chopped
1/3 teaspoon sea salt
1 teaspoon black peppercorn, crushed
2 tablespoons canola oil

Directions

- Add 1 cup of water and a steamer basket to your Instant Pot. Place the eggs in the steamer basket.
- Secure the lid. Choose the "Manual" mode. Cook for 6 minutes at High pressure. Once cooking is complete, use a natural release; carefully remove the lid.
- Transfer the eggs to an ice-cold water in order to cool; peel them and set aside.
- In a mixing bowl, thoroughly combine ground sausage, ham, apple & onion stuffing mix, thyme, rosemary, salt, and crushed peppercorns.
- Divide the mixture into five balls; flatten each ball. Place the hard-boiled egg in the center of each ball; now, wrap the sausage mixture around the egg.
- Press the "Sauté" button to preheat your Instant Pot. Heat the oil and cook the Scotch eggs on all sides.
- Wipe down the Instant Pot with a damp cloth. Add 1 cup of water and a metal trivet to the bottom of your Instant Pot. Now, place the Scotch eggs on the trivet.
- Secure the lid. Choose the "Manual" mode. Cook for 5 minutes at High pressure. Once cooking is complete, use a quick release; carefully remove the lid. Bon appétit!

477. Easy Cornmeal Mash
(Ready in about 15 minutes | Servings 3)

Make an ordinary cornmeal mush a little more excessive by adding raisins and chopped walnuts.
Per serving: *341 Calories; 10.6g Fat; 50.9g Carbs; 9.9g Protein; 9.3g Sugars*

Ingredients

1 cup cornmeal
2 cups water
2 cups milk
1/2 teaspoon ground cinnamon
1/2 teaspoon ground cardamom
1/2 teaspoon vanilla essence
1/4 cup raisins
1/4 cup walnuts, finely chopped

Directions

- Add cornmeal, water, milk, cinnamon, cardamom, and vanilla to the Instant Pot.
- Secure the lid. Choose the "Manual" mode. Cook for 8 minutes at High pressure. Once cooking is complete, use a natural pressure release; carefully remove the lid.
- Divide between three serving bowls; serve topped with raisins and walnuts. Enjoy!

478. Bourbon Chicken Liver Pâté
(Ready in about 10 minutes | Servings 8)

Quick cook time and convenience are just a few of the things that make cooking of a classic chicken liver pâté in the Instant Pot so easy!
Per serving: *180 Calories; 7.9g Fat; 1.2g Carbs; 23.6g Protein; 0.5g Sugars*

Ingredients

3/4 pound chicken livers, trimmed
1/2 cup onions, chopped
1 teaspoon ginger-garlic paste
2/3 cup chicken stock
3 tablespoons bourbon
2 teaspoons butter, melted
1/2 cup heavy cream
1 teaspoon dried oregano
1/8 teaspoon ground allspice
Salt and ground black pepper, to taste
1/2 teaspoon marjoram
2 sage sprigs

Directions

- Add chicken livers, onions, ginger-garlic paste, chicken stock, bourbon, butter, heavy cream, oregano, allspice, salt, black pepper, and marjoram to your Instant Pot
- Secure the lid. Choose the "Manual" mode and High pressure; cook for 3 minutes. Once cooking is complete, use a quick pressure release; carefully remove the lid.
- Purée the mixture in a food processor until smooth. Transfer to a serving bowl and garnish with sage sprigs. Bon appétit!

479. Traditional Brown Rice Congee with Mushrooms
(Ready in about 55 minutes | Servings 3)

Are you craving a bowl of warm and nourishing brown rice? Try this recipe tonight!
Per serving: *360 Calories; 11.2g Fat; 57.7g Carbs; 8.6g Protein; 5.2g Sugars*

Ingredients

1 tablespoon sesame oil
A bunch of scallions, chopped
1/2 pound white mushrooms, chopped
1 cup brown rice, rinsed
2 cups water
1 teaspoon Chinese Five-spice powder
Salt and ground white pepper, to taste
1/2 teaspoon cayenne pepper
2 tablespoons soy sauce
2 tablespoons toasted sesame seeds

Directions

- Press the "Sauté" button to preheat your Instant Pot. Now, heat sesame oil. Once hot, sauté the scallions and mushrooms for 3 to 4 minutes.
- Add rinsed rice, water, spices, and soy sauce. Now, choose the "Porridge" setting and cook for 28 minutes under High pressure.
- Once cooking is complete, use a natural release for 20 minutes; carefully remove the lid. Taste, adjust the seasonings, and divide between three serving bowls.
- Garnish with toasted sesame seeds and serve.

480. Cheese, Pancetta and Beef Casserole
(Ready in about 45 minutes | Servings 5)

This rich, meaty casserole will become a hit with your family! You can add another combo of seasonings.
Per serving: *395 Calories; 28.7g Fat; 3.4g Carbs; 29.6g Protein; 2.1g Sugars*

Ingredients

5 eggs, beaten
1/4 cup full-fat milk
1/4 cup double cream
Sea salt and freshly ground black pepper, to taste
1/4 teaspoon cayenne pepper
1/2 teaspoon dried basil
1/2 teaspoon dried marjoram

1/2 teaspoon dried parsley flakes
1/2 cup scallions, chopped
1/2 pound pancetta, chopped
1/2 cup ground chuck, cooked
1 ½ cups Cheddar cheese, shredded

Directions

- Prepare your Instant Pot by adding 1 cup of water and a metal trivet to its bottom.
- In a mixing bowl, thoroughly combine the eggs, milk, cream, and seasonings.
- Add the remaining ingredients to the baking dish. Pour egg mixture into the baking dish.
- Secure the lid. Choose the "Bean/Chili" mode and High pressure; cook for 30 minutes. Once cooking is complete, use a quick pressure release; carefully remove the lid.
- Let it sit for 5 to 10 minutes before slicing and serving. Bon appétit!

481. Classic Sausage Gravy
(Ready in about 10 minutes | Servings 6)

Make your Christmas dinner party memorable with this easy and delicious gravy. Such a great idea to have something warm for cold nights!
Per serving: *181 Calories; 9.8g Fat; 14.8g Carbs; 9.5g Protein; 0.5g Sugars*

Ingredients

1 tablespoon olive oil
1/2 pound breakfast sausage, ground
1/2 cup onions, chopped
1/2 cup cornstarch
1/2 cup cold water
3 cups of pan juices from cooked beef
Sea salt and ground black pepper, to taste

Directions

- Press the "Sauté" button to preheat your Instant Pot. Now, heat the oil. Cook sausage and onions for 3 to 4 minutes.
- Add pan juices and continue to simmer until heated through. Make a slurry by mixing the cornstarch and water. Slowly mix in the cornstarch slurry.
- Make sure to stir continuously until the liquid has reduced, about 4 minutes. Press the "Cancel" button.
- Season with salt and black pepper. Bon appétit!

482. Perfect French Toast with Figs
(Ready in about 20 minutes | Servings 4)

Try a delicious breakfast recipe made with French bread, eggs, almond milk, and dried figs. You can use Brioche or Fougasse for this recipe.
Per serving: *392 Calories; 15.9g Fat; 52.8g Carbs; 12.4g Protein; 29.7g Sugars*

Ingredients

8 slices of French bread, cut into pieces
3 eggs, beaten
3/4 cup almond milk
1/4 cup honey
1/4 cup lemon marmalade
1/2 teaspoon ground cinnamon
1/2 teaspoon ground cardamom
1/2 teaspoon pure coconut extract
1/2 cup dried figs, chopped
2 tablespoons butter, melted

Directions

- Spritz a baking pan with a nonstick cooking spray. Add bread cubes to the pan.
- In a mixing bowl, thoroughly combine eggs, milk, honey, lemon marmalade, cinnamon, cardamom, and coconut extract.
- Pour the egg mixture into the baking pan. Top with dried figs and drizzle with melted butter.
- Secure the lid. Choose the "Manual" mode and High pressure; cook for 15 minutes. Once cooking is complete, use a quick pressure release; carefully remove the lid. Serve at room temperature.

483. Grandma's Blackberry Jam
(Ready in about 1 hour 15 minutes | Servings 12)

Here is a perfect breakfast or snack! Just toast a slice of crusty homemade bread and top with peanut butter and a dollop of grandma's blackberry jam. Yummy!
Per serving: *122 Calories; 0.1g Fat; 30.7g Carbs; 1.5g Protein; 26.5g Sugars*

Ingredients

3 pounds blackberries, washed and cleaned
1/4 cup lemon juice
1/2 cup granulated sugar

Directions

- Arrange blackberries in the Instant Pot. Pour the lemon juice and sugar over the blackberries. Allow them to rest about 1 hour.
- Secure the lid and choose "Manual" mode. Cook for 5 minutes at High pressure. Once cooking is complete, use a natural pressure release for 10 minutes; carefully remove the lid.
- Divide your jam among sterilized jars, cover with lids, and place in your refrigerator. Bon appétit!

---

484. Vegetarian Spicy Yellow Lentils
(Ready in about 15 minutes | Servings 5)

For a change of pace, serve lentils with pasta instead of rice. It is a good idea to serve with a dollop of a chilled sour cream.
Per serving: *243 Calories; 4.8g Fat; 37.3g Carbs; 14.3g Protein; 2.3g Sugars*

Ingredients

1 tablespoon sesame oil
1/2 cup green onions, chopped
2 garlic cloves, minced
1 tablespoon fresh ginger, minced
1 bell pepper, chopped
1 habanero pepper, chopped
1 medium-sized carrot, chopped
1 1/3 cups yellow lentils, rinsed
1 teaspoon turmeric powder
Salt and ground black pepper, to taste
1/2 teaspoon red pepper flakes
1/2 teaspoon fennel seeds
2 cups vegetable broth

Directions

- Press the "Sauté" button to preheat your Instant Pot. Now, heat the oil and cook green onions, garlic, ginger, peppers, and carrot until they are softened.
- Secure the lid. Choose the "Manual" mode and High pressure; cook for 2 minutes. Once cooking is complete, use a natural pressure release; carefully remove the lid.
- You can thicken the cooking liquid on "Sauté" function if desired. Bon appétit!

485. Ful Mudammas (Fava Beans)
(Ready in about 20 minutes | Servings 4)

This fava bean dish is a staple food in Egyptian cuisine. In Egyptian restaurant, it is served with hard-boiled egg, a tahina cream sauce, or garlic tomato sauce.
Per serving: *210 Calories; 5.4g Fat; 34.4g Carbs; 14.1g Protein; 17.8g Sugars*

Ingredients

1 tablespoon canola oil
1/2 cup shallots, chopped
2 garlic cloves, minced
1 red bell pepper, chopped
1 green bell pepper, chopped
1 pound dried fava beans, soaked overnight
1 cup water
2 cups vegetable broth
1/2 teaspoon ground cumin
2 bay leaves
Seasoned salt and freshly ground black pepper, to taste

Directions

- Press the "Sauté" button to preheat your Instant Pot. Now, heat the oil and cook the shallots, garlic, and peppers until they are softened; reserve.
- Add the remaining ingredients; stir to combine.
- Secure the lid. Choose the "Manual" mode and High pressure; cook for 12 minutes. Once cooking is complete, use a natural pressure release; carefully remove the lid.
- Divide cooked fava beans between four serving bowl; top with sautéed shallot/pepper mixture. Serve immediately.

---

486. One-Step Pumpkin Apple Butter
(Ready in about 15 minutes | Servings 8)

Here is a simple and easy way to make pumpkin apple butter. Serve on freshly baked waffles, muffins or butter cookies.
Per serving: *159 Calories; 3.1g Fat; 32.3g Carbs; 2.8g Protein; 22.7g Sugars*

Ingredients

1 can (15-ounce) can pumpkin puree
2 cups apple, cored and chopped
1 cup 100% apple juice
1 tablespoon apple pie spice
1/2 cup brown sugar
1/3 cup golden syrup
1/4 teaspoon ground allspice
1/8 teaspoon kosher salt

Directions

- Place all of the above ingredients in your Instant Pot.
- Secure the lid. Choose the "Manual" mode and High pressure; cook for 11 minutes. Once cooking is complete, use a natural pressure release; carefully remove the lid.
- Store in airtight container in the refrigerator for up to 2 months.

487. Cabernet Sauvignon Poached Apricots
(Ready in about 15 minutes | Servings 6)

Treat yourself to this beautiful dessert bursting with fresh apricots and a surprising dose of refreshment from Greek yoghurt.
Per serving: *257 Calories; 0.3g Fat; 48.3g Carbs; 7.4g Protein; 44.4g Sugars*

Ingredients

1 ½ cups Cabernet Sauvignon wine
1 ½ pounds apricots, pitted and halved
1/2 cup sugar
1/4 cup honey
1 teaspoon ground cloves
1/2 teaspoon ground cinnamon
14 ounces Greek yogurt

Directions

- Pour the wine into your Instant Pot. Add apricots and secure the lid.
- Choose the "Manual" mode and cook for 3 minutes under Low pressure.
- Once cooking is complete, use a natural release for 10 minutes; remove the lid carefully. Transfer the apricots to a nice serving bowl.
- Press the "Sauté" button and add sugar, honey, cloves, and cinnamon. Cook until the sauce has been concentrated and reduced by about half.
- Spoon the sauce over reserved apricots; garnish each serving with a dollop of Greek yogurt and serve at room temperature. Bon appétit!

---

488. Stuffed Zucchini with a Lebanese Twist
(Ready in about 1 hour | Servings 4)

Lebanese zucchini is slightly bulbous, perfect for stuffing. This is a unique way to make stuffed zucchinis. Cook your zucchini on the "Steam" mode in the Instant Pot; then, stuff them with the sautéed filling.
Per serving: *360 Calories; 21.6g Fat; 32.4g Carbs; 10.8g Protein; 6.6g Sugars*

Ingredients

1/3 cup brown rice, well-rinsed
Sea salt and ground black pepper, to taste
1/2 teaspoon cayenne pepper
4 Lebanese zucchinis, trimmed, seeded, cored out
2 tablespoons olive oil
1 yellow onion, chopped
2 cloves garlic, minced
1 large-sized carrot, grated

1 (15-ounce) can garbanzo beans, rinsed and drained
1/4 cup flat-leaf parsley, chopped
1/4 cup mint, chopped
1/4 cup coriander, chopped
1/2 teaspoon chili powder
1 teaspoon baharat
1/2 cup natural yogurt, to serve

Directions

- Cook the rice in a pan according to package directions; drain, season with salt, black pepper, and cayenne pepper; reserve.
- Add 1 cup of water and a steamer basket to the Instant Pot. Now, place zucchini in the steamer basket.
- Secure the lid. Choose the "Steam" mode and High pressure; cook for 3 minutes. Once cooking is complete, use a natural pressure release; carefully remove the lid.
- Wipe down the Instant Pot with a damp cloth. Press the "Sauté" button and heat the oil until sizzling.
- Once hot, cook the onion, garlic, and carrot until they are tender. Add the garbanzo beans, parsley, mint, coriander, chili powder, and baharat; continue to sauté an additional 2 to 3 minutes; add the reserved rice.
- Fill each zucchini with the stuffing; serve immediately with natural yogurt. Bon appétit!

489. Tucson Lentil Tacos
(Ready in about 30 minutes | Servings 6)

These tacos are budget-friendly, easy to make, and fun to eat! Here are some garnishing ideas: guacamole, jicama, lettuce, and salsa.
Per serving: *520 Calories; 42.1g Fat; 29.9g Carbs; 10.8g Protein; 0.7g Sugars*

Ingredients

2 tablespoons olive oil
1/2 cup leeks, chopped
2 garlic cloves, minced
Sea salt and ground pepper, to taste
1 (1.25-ounce) package taco seasoning
1/2 teaspoon ground cumin
1 cup vegetable broth

1 cup water
2 overripe Roma tomatoes, chopped
1 ¼ cups green lentils, dried
12 corn tortillas
1 tablespoon yellow mustard
1 cup baby spinach

Directions

- Press the "Sauté" button to preheat the Instant Pot. Once hot, add olive oil; now, sauté the leeks and garlic until they are tender and fragrant.
- Add the seasonings, broth, water, tomatoes, and lentils.
- Secure the lid. Choose the "Soup" mode and High pressure; cook for 20 minutes. Once cooking is complete, use a natural pressure release; carefully remove the lid.
- Spoon the lentil mixture on tortillas. Serve with mustard and baby spinach. Enjoy!

490. Mushroom and Sausage Stuffed Peppers
(Ready in about 25 minutes | Servings 4)

These stuffed peppers will look so yummy on your dining table. Pick the peppers of different colors for even better presentation.
Per serving: *478 Calories; 19.7g Fat; 65.6g Carbs; 19.6g Protein; 11.4g Sugars*

Ingredients

1 onion, chopped
2 cloves garlic, minced
1/2 pound Italian sausage, ground
1/2 pound button mushrooms, roughly chopped
3/4 cup buckwheat, soaked overnight
1 ½ cups chicken broth
Salt and ground black pepper, to taste

1/2 teaspoon red pepper flakes, crushed
1 teaspoon dried basil
1/2 teaspoon dried oregano
4 medium-sized bell peppers, cored
2 (15-ounce) cans tomatoes
1/2 teaspoon mustard seeds

Directions

- Press the "Sauté" button to preheat the Instant Pot. Once hot, add olive oil; now, sauté the onion and garlic until tender and aromatic.
- Add Italian sausage and mushrooms; continue to cook an additional 2 minutes; reserve the sausage/mushroom mixture.
- Now, add soaked buckwheat and chicken broth.
- Secure the lid. Choose the "Manual" mode and High pressure; cook for 3 minutes. Once cooking is complete, use a natural pressure release; carefully remove the lid.
- Add the reserved sausage/mushroom mixture and seasonings; stir to combine well. Stuff the peppers. Wipe down the Instant Pot with a damp cloth.
- Add 1 ½ cups of water and metal rack to the Instant Pot. Place stuffed peppers in a casserole dish; add tomatoes, mustard seeds, and bay leaf. Lower the dish onto the rack.
- Secure the lid. Choose the "Manual" mode and High pressure; cook for 10 minutes. Once cooking is complete, use a natural pressure release; carefully remove the lid. Serve warm and enjoy!

491. Stuffed Apples with Port-Caramel Sauce

(Ready in about 25 minutes | Servings 3)

There is something so comforting about stuffed apples. Serve drizzled with a delicate and silky caramel sauce that features brown sugar, ruby port, and coconut oil. So glam!

Per serving: *381 Calories; 25.5g Fat; 42.1g Carbs; 1.4g Protein; 33.4g Sugars*

Ingredients

4 tablespoons pecans, roughly chopped
1/2 teaspoon ground cardamom
1 teaspoon cinnamon
1/2 teaspoon pure vanilla essence
1/2 teaspoon pure almond extract
1/3 cup dried cranberries

3 apples, cored and cut into halves
1/3 cup brown sugar
1/2 cup water
1/4 cup ruby port
4 tablespoons coconut oil

Directions

- Add the pecans, cardamom, cinnamon, vanilla essence, and almond extract to your blender or food processor; blitz until the mixture resembles a coarse meal.
- Fold in dried cranberries and stir to combine well. Spoon the cranberry/pecan mixture into the apple halves.
- Press the "Sauté" button to heat up your Instant Pot. Now, add sugar and 3 tablespoons of water to make the caramel sauce; stir until the sugar has been dissolved or approximately 8 minutes.
- Add the remaining water along with ruby port, and whisk to combine well.
- Then, carefully lower the apple halves onto the caramel sauce and secure the lid. Choose "Manual" mode, Low pressure and 10 minutes.
- Once cooking is complete, use a quick release; remove the lid carefully. Transfer the stuffed apples to the serving plates.
- Press the "Sauté" button again and cook the sauce until it has slightly thickened. Afterwards, whisk in coconut oil.
- Drizzle your apples with the prepared caramel sauce and serve. Bon appétit!

---

492. Japanese-Style Congee with Chickpeas

(Ready in about 35 minutes | Servings 4)

This ultra-simple Asian dish is healthy, nutritious and delicious. You should cook rice until it turns into a pudding-like consistency.

Per serving: *366 Calories; 4.3g Fat; 70.5g Carbs; 11.7g Protein; 4.3g Sugars*

Ingredients

1 ½ cups brown rice
2 cups water
1 cup dashi stock
1/2 teaspoon garlic powder
Sea salt and ground black pepper, to taste
1/2 teaspoon cayenne pepper
1 (19-ounce) can chickpeas, drained
3 tablespoons shallots, chopped

Directions

- Place brown rice, water, dashi stock, garlic powder, salt, black pepper, and cayenne pepper in the Instant Pot; stir to combine well.
- Secure the lid. Choose the "Manual" mode and High pressure; cook for 30 minutes. Once cooking is complete, use a natural pressure release; carefully remove the lid.
- Add canned chickpeas and stir to combine; seal the lid and let it sit until thoroughly warmed.
- Serve topped with fresh shallots. Enjoy!

493. Basic Chickpea Salad
(Ready in about 45 minutes + chilling time | Servings 6)

This is a pressure cooking time for dry chickpeas. If you want to shorten the cooking time, you should soak chickpeas overnight.
Per serving: *266 Calories; 10.1g Fat; 35.1g Carbs; 10.9g Protein; 7.1g Sugars*

Ingredients

1 ½ cups dry chickpeas, well-rinsed
5 cups water
1 bay leaf
2 cloves garlic, peeled, whole
1 red onion, thinly sliced
1 green bell pepper, thinly sliced
2 red bell peppers, thinly sliced
2 tablespoons fresh lemon juice
3 tablespoons extra-virgin olive oil
Sea salt and ground black pepper, to taste
1/4 cup fresh basil, roughly chopped

Directions

- Add chickpeas, water, bay leaf and garlic to the Instant Pot.
- Secure the lid. Choose the "Bean/Chili" mode and High pressure; cook for 40 minutes. Once cooking is complete, use a natural pressure release; carefully remove the lid.
- Allow chickpeas to cool completely; then; transfer to a salad bowl. Add the remaining ingredients and stir to combine well. Serve well-chilled and enjoy!

494. Greek-Style Bread
(Ready in about 4 hours 30 minutes | Servings 8)

This bread is a perfect accompaniment to any Greek meal. Serve with feta cheese, Kalamata olives, or grilled eggplant. On the next day, you can reheat this bread approximately 10 minutes at 350 degrees F in the preheated oven.
Per serving: *205 Calories; 0.6g Fat; 40.9g Carbs; 7.7g Protein; 1.1g Sugars*

Ingredients

3 1/3 cups all-purpose flour
1 teaspoon kosher salt
1 teaspoon white sugar
1 teaspoon instant yeast
1 cup water
1 cup Greek-style yogurt
1 teaspoon dried oregano

Directions

- Thoroughly combine the flour, salt, sugar, and yeast.
- Pour in the water and yogurt; add dried oregano; knead the mixture by hand until a ball of dough is formed.
- Line the inside of the Instant Pot with a piece of parchment paper; place the dough in your Instant Pot.
- Secure the lid. Choose the "Yogurt" mode and High pressure; cook for 4 hours. Once cooking is complete, use a natural pressure release; carefully remove the lid.
- Bake your bread in the preheated oven at 450 degrees F for 25 minutes. Transfer to a cooling rack before slicing and serving. Bon appétit!

495. Pineapple Cobbler with Double Cream
(Ready in about 25 minutes | Servings 8)

A tropical fruit cobbler couldn't be easier. This pineapple recipe is perfect for a cool-down in the late afternoon.
Per serving: *477 Calories; 16.6g Fat; 80.1g Carbs; 4.1g Protein; 31.1g Sugars*

Ingredients

2 (20-ounce) cans pineapple chunks in juice, drained
1 box cake mix
1/3 cup coconut butter, melted
1/2 teaspoon ground cardamom
1/4 teaspoon grated nutmeg
1 teaspoon ground cinnamon
1 cup double cream

Directions

- Place pineapple chunks in the Instant Pot.
- Thoroughly combine cake mix with melted coconut butter, cardamom, nutmeg, and cinnamon. Spread the mixture over the pineapple chunks in the Instant Pot.
- Secure the lid. Press the "Manual" mode and cook for 12 minutes under high pressure. Once cooking is complete, use a natural release for 10 minutes; carefully remove the lid.
- Serve with a dollop of double cream and enjoy!

---

496. Festive Sweet Cornbread
(Ready in about 35 minutes | Servings 8)

This sweet cornbread is the perfect festive food! Loaded with eggs, canned corn and golden syrup, it will give you more than you could expect from a cornbread recipe.
Per serving: *191 Calories; 5.9g Fat; 29.2g Carbs; 5.1g Protein; 5.5g Sugars*

Ingredients

1/2 cup cornmeal
2/3 cup all-purpose flour
2 teaspoons baking powder
1/2 teaspoon salt
2 tablespoons sugar
3 teaspoons margarine, melted
1/4 cup heavy cream
2 eggs, beaten
2 tablespoons golden syrup
1/2 cup canned corn

Directions

- Combine dry ingredients in a bowl. In another bowl, thoroughly combine wet ingredients. Mix the dry mixture with wet mixture.
- Spritz a round baking pan with a nonstick cooking spray. Scrape the batter into the prepared pan. Cover with aluminum foil, making a foil sling.
- Add 1 cup of water and a metal trivet to the Instant Pot.
- Secure the lid. Choose the "Multigrain" mode and High pressure; cook for 20 minutes. Once cooking is complete, use a quick pressure release; carefully remove the lid.
- Transfer to a wire rack to sit for 5 to 10 minutes. Serve warm with butter, applesauce, or homemade jam. Bon appétit!

497. Southern Black-Eyed Peas
(Ready in about 15 minutes | Servings 3)

This is probably only black-eyed pea recipe you'll ever need for the Instant Pot! You can experiment with different flavors and use pancetta or ham in this versatile recipe.
Per serving: *266 Calories; 18.8g Fat; 10.2g Carbs; 13.3g Protein; 4.9g Sugars*

Ingredients

4 slices bacon
1 yellow onion, chopped
2 garlic cloves, minced
1/2 pound dried black-eyed peas, well-rinsed
4 cups vegetable broth
Salt and ground black pepper, to taste

Directions

- Press the "Sauté" button to preheat your Instant Pot. Once hot, cook the bacon until crisp; set aside to drain on paper towels.
- Add onion and garlic and continue to sauté in pan drippings. Cook until they are tender and aromatic.
- Add black-eyed peas, broth, salt, and black pepper to your Instant Pot.
- Secure the lid. Choose the "Manual" mode and High pressure; cook for 10 minutes. Once cooking is complete, use a natural pressure release; carefully remove the lid.
- Serve topped with reserved bacon. Bon appétit!

---

498. Sausage and Cheese Mini Frittatas
(Ready in about 40 minutes | Servings 4)

Are you excited to discover more Instant Pot recipes? These mini frittatas are easy to make and fun to eat.
Per serving: *490 Calories; 38.6g Fat; 9.1g Carbs; 26.4g Protein; 1.4g Sugars*

Ingredients

6 eggs, beaten
2 chorizo sausages, chopped
3/4 cup sour cream
1 cup scallions, chopped
Sea salt, to taste
1 teaspoon garlic powder
1 teaspoon fennel seeds
1/2 teaspoon lemon pepper
2 tablespoons fresh basil, snipped
1 ¼ cups Colby cheese, shredded
4 tablespoons fresh parsley leaves, roughly chopped

Directions

- Thoroughly combine the eggs, sausages, sour cream, scallions, salt, garlic powder, fennel seeds, lemon pepper, and fresh basil in a mixing bowl.
- Pour the mixture into individual baking molds. Add 1 ½ cups of water and a metal trivet to the Instant Pot.
- Place baking molds on the trivet. Secure the lid and choose "Manual" mode.
- Cook at High pressure for 18 minutes. Once cooking is complete, use a natural release for 15 minutes; remove the lid carefully.
- Scatter shredded Colby cheese on top of each mold; place under a preheated broiler for 6 minutes or until cheese is lightly browned. Garnish with fresh parsley leaves and eat warm. Bon appétit!

499. Italian-Style Breakfast Muffins
(Ready in about 15 minutes | Servings 6)

Insured by Italian flavors, you can come out with these great crustless muffins. It's easy to customize this recipe!
Per serving: *305 Calories; 26.1g Fat; 8.9g Carbs; 10.2g Protein; 5.8g Sugars*

Ingredients

6 bacon slices
3/4 cup tomato paste
1 cup cream cheese
1/2 cup cheddar cheese, grated
1 tablespoon Italian seasoning
8 olives, pitted and sliced

Directions

- Add 1 cup of water and a trivet to the bottom of your Instant Pot.
- Add 1 slice of bacon to each silicone mold. Divide the remaining ingredients among silicone molds.
- Lower the silicone molds onto the trivet.
- Secure the lid. Choose "Manual" mode and High pressure; cook for 8 minutes. Once cooking is complete, use a quick pressure release; carefully remove the lid. Bon appétit!

---

500. Cheesy Cornbread Cups with Coleslaw
(Ready in about 25 minutes | Servings 6)

Combine your favorites into one great bite! Cheese, butter and eggs combine well in these cornbread muffins that are served with famous coleslaw.
Per serving: *410 Calories; 20.7g Fat; 43.2g Carbs; 12.1g Protein; 7.5g Sugars*

Ingredients

1/2 cup all-purpose flour
1 1/3 cups yellow cornmeal
1 teaspoon baking powder
1 teaspoon baking soda
1 teaspoon sugar
1 teaspoon salt
1 cup milk
1/2 stick butter, melted
1 egg
1 cup Monterey-Jack cheese, shredded
1 cup prepared coleslaw

Directions

- Mix the flour, baking powder, baking soda, sugar, and salt in a bowl. In a separate bowl, whisk the milk, butter, and eggs.
- Add the wet mixture to the dry mixture. Fold in shredded cheese; mix again. Scrape the batter into a baking pan.
- Add 1 cup of water and a metal trivet to the bottom of your Instant Pot. Then, lower the baking pan onto the trivet.
- Secure the lid. Choose "Multigrain" mode and High pressure; cook for 20 minutes. Once cooking is complete, use a natural pressure release; carefully remove the lid.
- Transfer to a cooling rack before unmolding and serving. Serve with prepared coleslaw. Bon appétit!

Made in the USA
Columbia, SC
11 December 2018